Life Skill Development

Life Skill Development

Annjaan Daash

B L O O M S B U R Y
NEW DELHI • LONDON • OXFORD • NEW YORK • SYDNEY

BLOOMSBURY INDIA
Bloomsbury Publishing India Pvt. Ltd
Second Floor, LSC Building No. 4, DDA Complex,
Pocket C – 6 & 7, Vasant Kunj,
New Delhi 110070

BLOOMSBURY, BLOOMSBURY PRIME and the Diana logo are trademarks of Bloomsbury Publishing Plc

First published in India 2022
This edition published 2022

ISBN: 978-93-54351-18-1
2 4 6 8 10 9 7 5 3 1

Typeset by Fortune Graphics, Naraina, New Delhi
Printed and bound in India by Replika Press Pvt. Ltd

To find out more about our authors and books, visit www.bloomsbury.com and sign up for our newsletters

Contents

Preface vii

Life Skill Development Classes: Roadmap ix

Chapter 1: Reading Comprehension 1

Chapter 2: Vocabulary 2

Chapter 3: Grammar 7

Chapter 4: Jumbled Sentences 16

Chapter 5: Error Detection 18

Chapter 6: Group Discussion 20

Solved Practice Sets Type I 22

Practice Sets Type – II 110

Group Discussion 184

Personal Interview 194

Sample Interview Questions 201

Group Discussion Topics 218

Quantitative Aptitude and Reasoning 283

References 346

Some More Tips 347

Preface

Life Skill Development is an integral part of the syllabi of various competitive examinations like banking, insurance, management entrance, NDA, SSC (CGL, LDC), Bank PO, MBA, MCA, UPSC, etc. This new book is more relevant and useful for pre placement training aspirants of Engineering and MBA appearing for campus drives. It is basically a compilation work referring to various reputed authors and original inputs which would present the aspirant everything in a nutshell. Special gratitude to Mr. Jasobant Singhal of Identity Group for imparting Campus 2 Corporate training.

Life Skill Development has been divided into two main sections. Section A is a Foundation Module that apprises one about Verbal ability, Mock Group Discussion, Personal Interview and sample interview questions. Section B comprises of Quantitative Aptitude and numerical ability. It is a step by step guidance to tackle quantitative aptitude of various types and also includes theory, formulae, fully solved examples and practice sets.

This book provides an overall preparation of English and Quantitative Aptitude, Group Discussion, Personal Interview tricks and techniques in brief.

The book covers all important topics and every chapter also has self-explanatory examples and practice sets which are company specific near pattern questions. The book is written in a lucid style which is easy to use and understand. The author has also included practice papers which are fully solved, revision exercises and a workbook for making a self-assessment as one moves from topic to topic.

The **Life Skill Development Verbal Ability** is divided in 5 sections covering important topics:

- Comprehension Ability.
- Vocabulary Usage and Grammar.
- Jumbled Sentence.
- Selecting Phrases/Words.
- Error Detection.

The **Life Skill Development Group Discussion and PI** covers important topics:

- Types of Group Discussion
- Group Discussion tips
- Assessment Parameters
- Group Discussion Template
- Verbal and Non verbal communication

- Do's and Don'ts in Group Discussion
- Rules for writing resumes
- Preparing for the interview
- Sample Interview Questions and model answers.

The **Life Skill Development Quantitative Aptitude** covers the following important topics:

- Theory and formulae of important topics
- Fully solved examples and practice papers

Life Skill Development Classes: Roadmap

As a part of Life Skills Development, the students are trained in various fields of personality development and communicational skills. The students are given training in a spell of four/six semester's right from the first year onwards. The trainings are given in Quantitative Aptitude, Verbal Ability, Group Discussion and Mock PI.

All students are encouraged to attend the training programs for an enhanced performance in the campus interviews. We hand hold our students through career guidance; through motivational activities and counseling, through knowledge sharing activities and through various capacity building measures. The trainees are closely monitored for improvements and gauged through several practice sets.

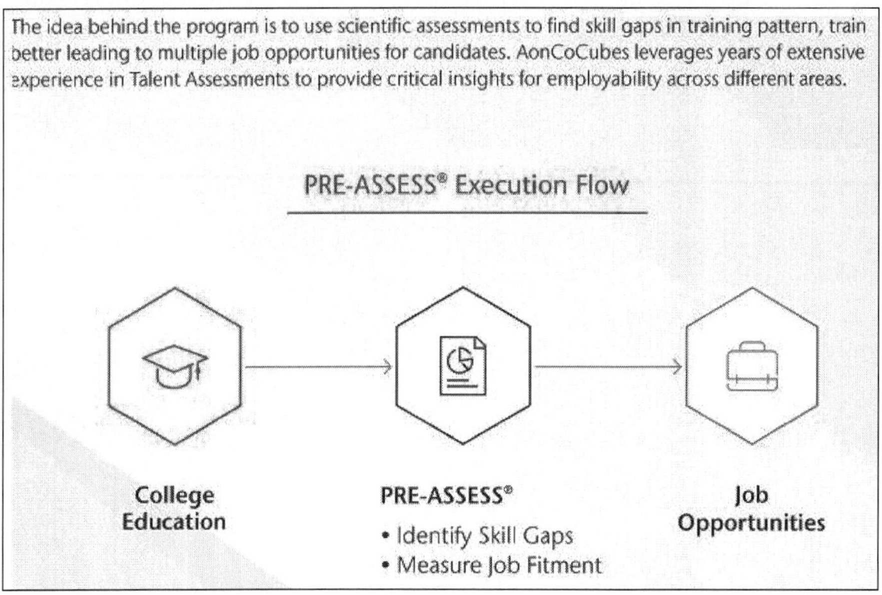

Source: www. cocubes.com

Importance of life skill development is generation of job opportunities, its relation.

Chapter 1

Reading Comprehension

DEFINITION

Reading comprehension is the textual understanding of a passage.

CONCEPT

To comprehend means to 'understand'. Read a passage, grasp it's gist, and then answer the passage-based questions.

INFORMATION-ELIMINATION-INFERENCE (IEI)

Formula

Passages offer information. So, there are questions that are straight forward and can be answered on the basis of the passage.

Elimination

The process of 'elimination' helps in saying 'no' to alternatives. It is used in solving true-false questions

Inference

Inference involves arriving at a logical conclusion.
Questions that cannot be solved through information and elimination can be solved by inference.

STEPS IN SOLVING READING COMPREHENSION

Numerous steps are involved in resolving reading comprehension. These are as follows:

STEP 1

↓

Read the question.

↓

Retain true-false and data-based questions.

↓

Underline the answers to the questions retained.

↓

Solve other questions by IEI.

Chapter 2

Vocabulary

VOCABULARY → ANTONYM → SYNONYM AND FIB

- Read a sentence twice to understand the meaning of a word. Read the earlier and latter sentences to get a better understanding of the word.
- In a sentence, see if there is a noun, adjective, or adverb. It makes the sentence technically and logically correct.
- If there is a sentence, try to find the keyword or the correct option, and then eliminate the incorrect option.

WORD PROFILE

- P: **Positive word** = A word that is used in a good sense is a 'P' word.
  Eg: Benign = Gentle and kind, appreciative, energetic, confident
- N: **Negative word** = A word that is used in a negative sense is an 'N' word.
  Eg: Cheating, furious, angry, and insulting
- NT: **Neutral word** = A word used in both positive and negative senses according to the need.
  Eg: Candid = Outspoken and frank
- C: **Concrete** = There are words that have definite shape and size; a physical entity, is a 'C' word.
  (Tangible, solid material)
  Eg: Lamp, house, door
- A: **Abstract** = There are words that have abstract form, i.e. it is usually the name of a quality, action, or state.
  Eg: Kindness, wisdom, action = denial, refusal state = independence.
- O: **Open** = Words that can be used in both concrete and abstract forms.
  Eg: Fan = Physical device and gives air.

SYNONYM

- It is a word that has the same or nearly the same meaning as the given word.
- When there is a sentence, find the keyword or the correct option and eliminate the incorrect options.
  Eg: He had the *nerve* to suggest that I was cheating.
  (a) Strength (b) Capacity (c) **Audacity** (d) Courage
  Audacity (daring boldness)

- The keyword here is 'cheating' = Negative word.
  Strength, capacity, and courage are positive words but audacity is a negative word.
- When there is only one word, then also use the elimination technique.
  Interest in the issue has continued to wane.
  Eg: Wane: To decrease in size; to diminish.
  (a) **Decline** (b) Tired (c) Dead (d) Shine
  Wane is a verb so 'dead' and 'tired' are eliminated.
  Answer: Decline
- In cases antonyms are put in the options, one needs to eliminate them.

Vocabulary Test – Special Type 1

- Stage 1: A – B; A – C; A – D
- Stage 2: B – C; B – D
- Stage 3: C – D

ANTONYM

- It is a word which has the opposite or nearly the opposite meaning of the given word.
- Given word and answer should belong to the same 'parts of speech'.
- The eight parts of speech are noun, pronoun, verb, adverb, adjective, preposition, conjunction, and interjection.
  Eg: Pragmatic: Dealing with things realistically/sensibly.
  (a) Angry (b) **Quixotic** (c) Colourful (d) Pungent
  Answer: Quixotic = Unrealistic; Pungent = Strong smell.
  His pragmatic view of public education comes from years of working in the city school.
  Options (d) and (a) are eliminated.
- Here, colourful is a noun and pragmatic is an adjective, so Option (c) is eliminated.
- The given word and answer should be of the same tense form.
  Eg: Perceived: Become aware, recognise.
  (a) **Ignored** (b) Created (c) Apprehend (d) Conceive
  Here, apprehend and conceive are in the present tense; so, they are rejected.
  Ignored gives the opposite meaning of perceived (past tense).
- Synonyms are mixed in the alternatives to confuse.

Tone Vocabulary List

Tone vocabulary are applied to communicate 'positive', 'negative', and 'humour/irony/sarcasm', 'sorrow-fear-worry', 'neutral' feelings. Presented next are some examples of tone vocabulary.

Positive Tone/Attitude Words			
Amiable	Consoling	Friendly	Playful
Amused	Content	Happy	Pleasant
Appreciative	Dreamy	Hopeful	Proud
Authoritative	Ecstatic	Impassioned	Relaxed
Benevolent	Elated	Jovial	Reverent
Brave	Elevated	Joyful	Romantic
Calm	Encouraging	Jubilant	Soothing
Cheerful	Energetic	Light-hearted	Surprised
Cheery	Enthusiastic	Loving	Sweet
Compassionate	Excited	Optimistic	Sympathetic
Complimentary	Exuberant	Passionate	Vibrant
Confident	Fanciful	Peaceful	Whimsical

Negative Tone/Attitude Words			
Accusing	Choleric	Furious	Quarrelsome
Aggravated	Course	Harsh	Shameful
Agitated	Cold	Haughty	Smooth
Angry	Condemnatory	Hateful	Snooty
Apathetic	Condescending	Hurtful	Superficial
Arrogant	Contradictory	Indignant	Surly
Artificial	Critical	Inflammatory	Testy
Audacious	Desperate	Insulting	Threatening
Belligerent	Disappointed	Irritated	Tired
Bitter	Disgruntled	Manipulative	Uninterested
Boring	Disgusted	Obnoxious	Wrathful
Brash	Disinterested	Outraged	
Childish	Facetious	Passive	

Humour-Irony-Sarcasm Tone/Attitude Words			
Amused	Droll	Mock-heroic	Sardonic
Bantering	Facetious	Mocking	Satiric
Bitter	Flippant	Mock-serious	Scornful
Caustic	Giddy	Patronizing	Sharp
Comical	Humorous	Pompous	Silly
Condescending	Insolent	Quizzical	Taunting
Contemptuous	Ironic	Ribald	Teasing

Critical	Irreverent	Ridiculing	Whimsical
Cynical	Joking	Sad	Wry
Disdainful	Malicious	Sarcastic	

Sorrow-Fear-Worry Tone/Attitude Words			
Aggravated	Embarrassed	Morose	Resigned
Agitated	Fearful	Mournful	Sad
Anxious	Foreboding	Nervous	Serious
Apologetic	Gloomy	Numb	Sober
Apprehensive	Grave	Ominous	Solemn
Concerned	Hollow	Paranoid	Somber
Confused	Hopeless	Pessimistic	Staid
Dejected	Horrific	Pitiful	Upset
Depressed	Horror	Poignant	
Despairing	Melancholy	Regretful	
Disturbed	Miserable	Remorseful	

Neutral Tone/Attitude Words			
Admonitory	Dramatic	Intimate	Questioning
Allusive (not illusive)	Earnest	Judgemental	Reflective
Apathetic	Expectant	Learned	Reminiscent
Authoritative	Factual	Loud	Resigned
Baffled	Fervent	Lyrical	Restrained
Callous	Formal	Matter-of-fact	Seductive
Candid	Forthright	Meditative	Sentimental
Ceremonial	Frivolous	Nostalgic	Serious
Clinical	Haughty	Objective	Shocking
Consoling	Histrionic	Obsequious	Sincere
Contemplative	Humble	Patriotic	Unemotional
Conventional	Incredulous	Persuasive	Urgent
Detached	Informative	Pleading	Vexed
Didactic	Inquisitive	Pretentious	Wistful
Disbelieving	Instructive	Provocative	Zealous

Concrete Words

Concrete words recognize things and events that can be viewed, tasted, heard, smelled, touched, and assessed. Eg: Apple, Arrow, House, Pencil, Ocean.

Abstract Words

Abstract words characterise things and concepts that are abstract (intellectual and untouchable). Eg: Anger, Knowledge, Mood, Effort, Happiness.

Try combining words to get a more precise description of tone as in these examples:

Cautious speculation	Dramatic revelation	Philosophical resignation
Weary resignation	Unqualified endorsement	Apologetic approval
Analytic objectivity	Tolerant acceptance	Grudging admiration
Unalloyed suspicion	Gentle mockery	Lofty indifference
Excited enthusiasm	Indulgent tolerance	Fascinated curiosity
Cautious skepticism	Disapproving dismissal	Politically offensive
Delightfully sentimental	Morally admirable	Carelessly irrelevant
Deep despair	Pretended indifference	Casual indifference
Calm assurance	Apprehensive resolve	Excited expectation
Unqualified appreciation	Fundamental dissatisfaction	Apathetic acceptance
Violent indignation	Apologetic regret	Self-righteous pomposity
Awe-struck fascination	Affectionate delight	Momentary doubt
Solemn apprehension	Flippant sarcasm	Sceptical suspicion
Aloof disinterest	Sentimental regret	Disguised irony

Chapter 3
Grammar

- A group of words that makes complete sense is called a **sentence**.
- A sentence contains a subject and a predicate.
- A **subject** is a word or a group of words that tell what the speaker is talking about.
- The **predicate** is a part of the sentence that makes a statement about the subject.
  Eg: The earth revolves around the sun.
  (The earth = Subject; revolves around the sun. = Predicate)
  Predicate = What the subject does.
- There are eight parts of speech, namely,

1. Noun	2. Pronoun	3. Adjective	4. Verb
5. Adverb	6. Preposition	7. Conjunction	8. Interjection

PARTS OF SPEECH

1. Noun

Definition: A noun is a name of a person, place, animal, thing, etc.
Name: Mohan, Indian
Place: House, Mumbai, Apartment
Animal: Tiger, Dog
Thing: Chair, Computer

2. Pronoun

- A pronoun is a word used in place of a noun.
- Eg: Mahesh went to Mahesh's cupboard and took out Mahesh's new suit.
- Here, the word Mahesh is repeated, so we can use 'his' and 'he', which are known as pronouns.

3. Verb

Definition: A verb is a word that tells what the person/thing is doing/being or being acted. It is used to express action/state.

- Eg: The teacher **teaches** English.
  teaches: verb
- Eg: The patient **has been advised** to stay in bed.
  has been advised – more than one word

- Eg: Kolkata **is** a big city.
  is: verb

4. Adjective

Definition: A word that describes a noun or a pronoun is called an 'adjective'.

- Eg: Mumbai is a **crowded** city.
  crowded: adjective
- Eg: **Most** boys like to play cricket .
  Most: adjective

5. Adverb

Definition: A word that modifies an adjective, verb, or another adverb is called an adverb.

- Eg: She speaks **softly**.
  softly: adverb
- She ran **fast.**
- Eg: He drank **very hot** tea.
  very: adverb
  hot: adjective

6. Preposition

Definition: A preposition is a word placed before a noun or a pronoun.

- Eg: The accident occurred **on** the bridge.
  on: relation between the bridge and occurred (preposition)
  bridge: object
- Prepositions show relationships between words.
- Movement, position

7. Conjunction

Definition: A conjunction is a word that joins words, phrases, or sentences.

A conjunction connects words.

- Eg: Ram **and** Shyam are friends.
  and: conjunction
- Eg: Either you **or** Rakesh will have to do it.
  or: conjunction

8. Interjection

Definition: A word that expresses a strong or sudden feeling such as surprise, joy, or sorrow.

Eg: Wow, oh, hurrah! we won the match.

ACTIVE/PASSIVE VOICE

Active Voice

In most English sentences with an action verb, the subject performs the action denoted by the verb.

These examples show that the subject is doing the verb's action.

The man must have eaten five hamburgers. The **man** (subject) is doing the **eating** (verb).
Marilyn mailed the letter. **Marilyn** (subject) is doing the **mailing** (verb).
Colourful parrots live in the rainforests. **Parrots** (subject) are doing the **living** (verb).

As the subject does or 'acts upon' the verb in such sentences, the sentences are said to be in the **active voice.** (What the subject does.)

The first sentence is in the past perfect tense, and the second sentence is in simple past.

Passive Voice

One can change the normal word order of many active sentences (those with a direct object) so that the subject is no longer active, but is, instead, being acted upon by the verb or is passive.

Note in these examples how the subject-verb relationship has changed.

Five hamburgers must have been eaten by the man. **Hamburgers** (subject) are being **eaten** (verb).
The letter was mailed by Marilyn. The **letter** (subject) was being **mailed** (verb).

Because the subject is being 'acted upon' (or is *passive*), such sentences are said to be in the **passive voice.**

Note: *Colourful parrots live in the rainforests* cannot be changed to passive voice because the sentence does not have a direct object.

To change a sentence from active to passive voice, the following is needed:

1. Move the active sentence's direct object into the sentence's subject slot.

ACTIVE VOICE	⟶	PASSIVE VOICE
Marilyn mailed the letter.	⟶	The letter...
↑ **direct object** (the letter)		↑ **subject** (The letter)

2. Place the active sentence's subject into a phrase beginning with the preposition *by*.

ACTIVE VOICE	⟶	PASSIVE VOICE
Marilyn mailed the letter.	⟶	The letter... by Marilyn.
↑		↖ ↗
subject		**prepositional phrase**

3. Add a form of the auxiliary verb (supporting verb) *be* to the main verb and change the main verb's form.

ACTIVE VOICE	⟶	PASSIVE VOICE
Marilyn **mailed** the letter.	⟶	The letter **was mailed** by Marilyn.
↑		↖ ↗
verb		**verb + *be* auxiliary**

Because passive voice sentences necessarily add words and change the normal *doer of action – receiver of action* direction, they may make the reader work harder to understand the intended meaning.

As the examples below illustrate, a sentence in active voice flows more smoothly and is easier to understand than the same sentence in passive voice.

ACTIVE VOICE

At each concert, the soprano sang at least one tune from a well-known opera.

doer of action (soprano) **action** (sang) **receiver of action** (tune)

PASSIVE VOICE

At each concert, at least one tune from a well-known opera was sung by the soprano.

doer of action (soprano) **receiver of action** (tune) **action** (sung)

ACTIVE VOICE

Asbestos abatement teams will remove large chunks of asbestos-laden material from the hallways on the second and third floors.

doer of action (teams) **action** (remove) **receiver of action** (material)

PASSIVE VOICE

Large chunks of asbestos-laden material will be removed from the hallways on the second and third floors by asbestos abatement teams.

receiver of action (chunks) **action** (removed) **doer of action** (teams)

It is generally preferable to use the ACTIVE voice.

To change a passive voice sentence into an active voice sentence, simply reverse the steps shown earlier.

1. Move the passive sentence's subject into the active sentence's direct object slot.

PASSIVE VOICE →	ACTIVE VOICE
The letter was mailed by Marilyn. →	... (mailed) the letter.
↑ **subject**	↑ **direct object**

2. Remove the auxiliary verb *be* from the main verb and change the main verb's form if needed.

PASSIVE VOICE →	ACTIVE VOICE
The letter was mailed ... →	... mailed the letter.
↑ **be auxiliary**	

3. Place the passive sentence's object of the preposition *by* into the subject slot.

PASSIVE VOICE →	ACTIVE VOICE
... by Marilyn. →	Marilyn mailed...
↑ **object of preposition by**	↑ **subject**

Because it is more direct, most writers prefer to use the active voice whenever possible.

The passive voice may be a better choice, however, when

- The doer of the action is unknown, unwanted, or unneeded in the sentence.

  Examples

The ballots have been counted.
Sometimes our efforts are not fully appreciated.

- The writer wishes to emphasise the action of the sentence rather than the doer of the action.

  Examples

The high-jump record was finally broken last Saturday.
A suspect was questioned for sixteen hours by the police.

- The writer wishes to use a passive voice for sentence variety.

RULES FOR ACTIVE-PASSIVE VOICE FOR ALL TENSES

There are two basic rules for converting sentences from active voice into passive voice, which are common for all tenses. These are as follows:

1. The place of the subject and the object will be interchanged in the sentence.

2. Only the third form of the word or past participle (e.g. written) will be used as a main verb in passive voice.

The rules or using an 'auxiliary verb' in a sentence are different for each tense. These are as follows:

Present Simple Tense Auxiliary verb used in passive voice: **is/are/am**	
Active voices	*Passive voices*
He writes a letter.	A letter **is** written by him.
They sell books.	Books **are** sold by them.
She helps me.	I am helped by her.

Present Progressive Tense Auxiliary verb used in passive voice: **is being/are being/am being**	
Active voices	*Passive voices*
She is singing a song.	A song **is being** sung by her.
They are eating apples.	Apples **are being** eaten by them.
You are disturbing me.	I **am being** disturbed by you.

Present Perfect Tense Auxiliary verb used in passive voice: **has been/have been**	
Active voices	*Passive voices*
He has completed the work.	The work **has been** completed by him.
Has he completed the work?	Has the work been completed by him?
I have made some cakes.	Some cakes **have been** made by me.

Simple Past Tense Auxiliary verb used in passive voice: **was/were**	
Active voices	*Passive voices*
He bought a car.	A car **was** bought by him.
Did he buy a car?	**Was** a car bought by him?
I helped them.	They **were** helped by me.

Past Progressive Tense Auxiliary verb used in passive voice: **was being/were being**	
Active voices	*Passive voices*
She was washing a shirt.	A shirt **was being** washed by her.
Was she washing a shirt?	**Was** a shirt **being** washed by her?
Boys were singing songs.	Songs **were being** sung by boys.

Past Perfect Tense Auxiliary verb used in passive voice: **had been**	
Active voices	*Passive voices*
They had won the game.	The game **had been** won by them.
Had they won the game?	**Had** the game **been** won by them?
He had collected coins.	Coins **had been** collected by him.

Simple Future Tense Auxiliary verb used in passive voice: **will be**	
Active voices	*Passive voices*
She will write a poem.	A poem **will be** written by her.
Will she write a poem?	**Will** a poem **be** written by her?
They will arrange the money.	The money **will be** arranged by them.

Future Perfect Tense Auxiliary verb used in passive voice: **will have been**	
Active voice	*Passive voice*
He will have received the letter.	The letter **will have been** received by him.
Will he have received the letter?	**Will** the letter **have been** received by him

DIRECT AND INDIRECT SPEECH

Spoken and written communication is like one big game of telephone. Sometimes we hear the original tale, and other times we hear a retelling of the story. In this lesson, we're going to explore what that means by studying the difference between direct and indirect speech and learning proper grammar techniques for both.

Direct Speech

Direct speech, also known as quoted speech, consists of words or phrases that are taken directly from the source. These words are quoted or written exactly as the words were originally spoken.

With regards to direct speech, there is no interpretation or annotation; the words are taken directly from one source and repeated to another. In other words, we take the words directly from the speaker and repeat them exactly as they were originally stated.

Here are some examples of direct speech:

- Jonah said, 'I don't like your hat'.
- Jonah said, 'Please take off that Yankees hat'.

- Jane said, 'It's not my fault that you are a Red Sox fan'.

In both examples, the direct speech is shown in quotations, which signifies that the speech is taken directly from the source with no alterations.

Indirect Speech

Indirect speech, also known as reported speech, is when words or phrases are reported in our words. The original words are modified and/or interpreted as opposed to being quoted.

When talking about indirect speech, we use words that refer to something that has already happened. To do so, we are speaking in the past tense and summarizing, modifying, or synthesizing what has already been said.

Here are some examples of indirect speech.

- Amy said it was cold.
- He said he had been on Facebook since 2010.
- She said she had been teaching college classes for 2 years.

Converting Direct Speech into Indirect Speech

When we use direct speech, we are repeating what was said. When we use indirect speech, we report what was said. Look at the examples mentioned next to learn how to change speech from direct to indirect. These examples will also reinforce the difference between direct and indirect speech.

Changing From Present Tense to Past Tense

When converting speech from direct to indirect, you must change the present tense verbs to the past tense and remove any quotation marks or commas.

Direct Speech (Present Tense)	*Indirect Speech (Past Tense)*
Jenn says, 'I love watching TV.'	Jenn said she loved watching TV.

Changing From Simple Past Tense to Past Perfect Tense

What if the direct speech is already written in the past tense? If the sentence is written in the simple past tense, you just remove the punctuation and change the verb to past perfect form to make it indirect speech.

Direct Speech (Simple Past Tense)	*Indirect Speech (Past Perfect Tense)*
Lana said, 'I saw him at the mall.'	Lana said she had seen him at the mall.

Changing Speech in the Form of a Question

What if direct speech is in the form of a question?

Eg: 'Do you want to go on a trip to Europe?'

To make a direct question indirect, follow the same tense change rules as before, add 'asked me' to signify reporting a question, and keep the question word.

Direct Speech	*Indirect Speech*
'Do you want to go on a trip to Europe?'	She asked me if I wanted to go on a trip to Europe.

Chapter 4

Jumbled Sentences

TIME-SAVER: CLUE QUALIFIER ELIMINATION (CQE TECHNIQUE)

- If there are five to six sentences that are in a disorderly sequence, then in most of the cases, the first and last statements are specified followed by alternatives.
- First, find the qualifier. The qualifier is a sentence that tells us something about the following sentence (main subject). The qualifier will be placed at the side of the qualified sentence.
- Find the clues (options).
- Find out the main subject of a sentence and follow the process of elimination.
- Start from the options and then for elimination, choose the main subject.

Example

Duryodhana was a wicked person/prince.

P: One day Bhima made Duryodhana fall from a tree from which Duryodhana was stealing fruits.

Q: He did not like that the Pandavas were loved and respected by the people of Hastinapur.

R: Duryodhana specially hated Bhima.

S: Among the Pandavas, Bhima was extraordinarily strong and powerful.

1: This enraged Duryodhana so much that he began to think of removing Bhima from his way.

(a) PSQR (b) QPRS (c) QSRP (d) PSRQ

- Here Q is the qualifier of a sentence (1) because he is the pronoun used for Duryodhana.
- So, the answer would start with Q.
- (c) is the right answer.

FLOW CHART

STEP 1
Find clues to locate the qualifier.
↓
STEP 2
Locate a qualifier.
↓
STEP 3
Eliminate alternatives with the qualifier.
↓
STEP 4
Read and catch sequence.
(Read the entire sequence.)

Chapter 5

Error Detection

1. Articles
   - The words **a**, **an**, and **the** are called **articles.**
   - **A** and **an** are **indefinite articles** because they talk about indefinite persons or things spoken of.

   Eg: A doctor, a boy
   - '**The**' is a **definite article** because it points out a definite person or thing.

   Eg: Let's go to the park
2. We use '**An**' before words beginning in vowels **a, e, i, o, u.**

   Eg: An apple, an umbrella
   - Before words beginning with '**H**' (**silent**).
     Eg: An hour, an honourable man, an honest man
   - **F, H, L, M, N, R, S, X** beginning with vowel sounds.
     Eg: An MLA, an X-ray
3. We use '**A**' before words beginning with **consonants.**

   Eg: A boy, a box
   - We can use '**A**' before the **consonant value.**
     Eg: A university (**yu**)
     A unit (**yu**)
   - We use '**The**' when we talk about a particular person or thing.
     Eg: The book you want is out of print
     (Which book? The one you want.)
   - Rivers, oceans, mountains
     Eg: The Himalayas, The Puranas, The Bible
   - Before the name of **empires/events.**
     Eg: The Gupta dynasty, the first World War
4. Prepositions
   - It is a word that is used with a noun or pronoun to show its relationship between words.
   - '**At**' is used with a definite point (exact point) of time.
     Eg: I usually get up at 6.00 AM.
     Eg: He studied at Oxford.
   - '**In**' is used to refer to a day, month, season, large areas, etc.
     Eg: He takes a walk in the morning.
     Eg: He lives in BBRS.
   - '**On**' is used with days and dates.

Eg: My brother will arrive on Monday.

- **'By'** refers to the latest time when the action is completed.
  Eg: The exam will be over by 5.00 PM.
- **'For'** is used for perfect continuous tense.
  Eg: I have been here for 3 years.
- **'Since'** is used to show the point of time when the action begins and continues.
  Eg: He has been ill since the last week.
- **'From'** is the starting point of action.
  Eg: She is from Mumbai.
- **'Between'** denotes a person or things.
  Eg: It is a secret between you and me.
- **'Among'** is used where there are more than two persons or things.
  Eg: Divided the sweets among/amongst us.

Chapter 6
Group Discussion

TYPES OF GROUP DISCUSSIONS

There are numerous kinds of group discussions. These are as follows:

Topic-based Discussion

- **Controversy**
  Eg: China is the biggest threat to India.
  Caste-based reservation.
  You are required to take a stand and support the statement with suitable examples.
  Balanced approach.
- **Descriptive**
  Eg: Indo-US relations
  Poverty in India.
  You need to know the subject.
- **Abstract topics**
  Sky
  Gold
  Black
  Your creativity plays an important role.
- **A case study**
  You would be given a real-life experience or situation or an imaginary case. You have to present your opinion on the given situation.
- A group discussion is an interactive oral-communication situation.
- It is a selection tool as the candidates are tested very precisely on a specific skill set that is required by the company.
- It is a process in which participants sit together, discuss a topic, and try to reach a consensus.

GROUP DISCUSSION TIPS

1. Be as natural as possible, i.e. be yourself.
2. Sit with a confident and straight posture.
3. Testing Officer:
   Good morning to you all. Today, there will be a group discussion from where you have to select one topic.

Five minutes would be given to you to select a particular topic.

4. You will not be asked to speak. You have to take your opportunity to do so. Always be confident.
5. Grab the opportunity to speak first, make the move only if you have complete knowledge of the subject.
6. Do not change your stand and give logical justification in support of your view point.
7. Facilitate contribution from others. Be active and dynamic.
8. Make eye contact with all the participants.
9. After discussion, give a conclusion to the topic.
10. Why companies conduct group discussions?
    - Organisations want to ensure that the candidate is suitable for a particular job.

    Characteristics:
    - There needs to be a right mix of assertiveness (make your point strongly) and the willingness to secure customers.
    - Display confidence.
    - Be aloud and speak more.
    - Maintain eye contact.
    - Check body language, communication skills, fluency, pronunciation, and content.
    - Use easy words.
11. Read newspapers (current affairs).
12. For controversial topics, use a balanced approach.

JAM

1. Speak on Bhubaneswar city.
2. A memorable day in my life.
3. Your college life.
4. Favourite movie.
5. Flood scene.
6. Pet animal.
7. Your hobby.
8. Accident scene.

Solved Practice Sets Type I

PRACTICE SET 1

Directions: *Read the following passage and answer the questions based on it.*

Work expands to fill the time available for its completion. The general recognition of this fact is shown in the proverbial phrase, 'It is the busiest man who has time to spare.' An elderly lady at leisure can spend the entire day writing a postcard to her niece. An hour will be spent in finding the postcard, hunting for spectacles, half an hour to search for the address, an hour and a quarter in composition, and 20 minutes in deciding whether or not to take an umbrella when going to the pillar-box in the street. The total effort that would occupy a busy man for 3 minutes, all told, may in this fashion leave another person completely exhausted after a day of doubt, anxiety, and toil.

1. What happens when the time to be spent on some work increases?
   (a) The work is done smoothly.
   (b) The work is done leisurely.
   (c) The work consumes all the time.
   (d) The work needs additional time.
2. Explain the sentence: 'Work expands so as to fill the time available for its completion.'
   (a) The more work there is to be done, the more time is needed.
   (b) Whatever time is available for a given amount of work, all of it will be used.
   (c) If you have more time, you can do more work.
   (d) If you have some important work to do, you should always have some additional time.
3. Who is the person likely to take more time to do work?
   (a) A busy man of leisure (b) A man of leisure
   (c) An elderly person (d) An exhausted person
4. What is the total time spent by the elderly lady in writing a postcard?
   (a) 3 minutes (b) 4 hours and 5 minutes
   (c) Half an hour (d) A full day
5. What does the expression 'pillar box' stand for?
   (a) A box attached to the pillar (b) A box in the pillar
   (c) Box office (d) A pillar-type post box

Directions: *Choose the word or phrase which is nearest in meaning to the keyword.*

6. Prognosis
   (a) Scheme (b) Forecast (c) Preface (d) Identification

7. Docile
   (a) Vague (b) Gentle (c) Stupid (d) Stubborn
8. Aromatic
   (a) Crippled (b) Fragrant (c) Sentimental (d) Stinking
9. Reading poetry is not *congenial* to his taste.
   (a) Suited (b) Beneficial (c) Helpful (d) Preferable
10. A bone got stuck in my *gullet.*
   (a) Stomach (b) Molars (c) Chest (d) Throat

Directions: *Choose the word or phrase which is nearest in opposite meaning to the keyword.*

11. Virtue
   (a) Vice (b) Fraud (c) Wickedness (d) Crime
12. Erudite
   (a) Professional (b) Immature (c) Unimaginative (d) Ignorant
13. Acquitted
   (a) Entrusted (b) Convicted (c) Burdened (d) Freed
14. We should not *belittle* others' achievements.
   (a) Recommend (b) Praise (c) Encourage (d) Inspire
15. There has always been a feeling of *rancour* between the two families.
   (a) Rivalry (b) Competition (c) Friendliness (d) Suspicion

Directions: *The following questions comprise two words each having a certain relationship between them followed by four alternatives. Select the pair that has the same relationship as the original pair of words.*

16. Education: Development
   (a) Man: Speech (b) Nutrition: Health
   (c) Game: Play (d) Child: Growth
17. House: Room
   (a) Struggle: Fight (b) Transport: Car
   (c) School: College (d) Boy: Girl
18. Gill: Fin
   (a) Salad: Rice (b) Sea: Fish
   (c) Kill: Bomb (d) Question: Team
19. Glove: Ball
   (a) Summer: Winter (b) Game: Study
   (c) Stadium: Seats (d) Hook: Fish
20. Sculptor: Chisel
   (a) Pathology: Disease (b) Tailor: Needle
   (c) Engineer: Sit

SOLUTIONS WITH EXPLANATIONS

1. (c) Lady who has enough leisure time takes entire day in writing postcard.
2. (b) Entire time allotted to a work is used up.
3. (b) The more time you have, the more time you need.
4. (d) Information is available in the passage.
5. (d) The lady has to go to the pillar box to drop the letter.
6. (d) **Prognosis:** An opinion based on medical experience of how someone will recover from illness; judgement about what is going to happen in the future.
    - Scheme – systematic plan.
    - Forecast – to predict
    - Preface – introduction to a book
    - **Answer:** Identification – identify illness
7. (b) **Docile:** Easily led/managed; ready to accept control/submissive.
    - Vague – not clear in meaning.
    - **Answer:** Gentle – mild, soft, delicate, easy
    - Stupid – brainless
    - Stubborn – refusing to change ideas.
8. (b) **Aromatic:** Pleasant smell; fragrant
    - Crippled – unable to walk
    - **Answer:** Fragrant – perfumed, scented
    - Sentimental – emotional, tender
    - Stinking – fool smell
9. (a) **Congenial:** Suitable, appropriate; pleasant
    - **Answer:** Suited
    - Beneficial: advantageous
    - Helpful: useful
    - Preferable: more desirable
10. (d) **Gullet:** Passage of food from the throat to the stomach (oesophagus)
    - **Answer:** Throat
11. (c) **Virtue:** A quality considered to be morally good
    - Vice: immoral conduct.
    - Fraud: dishonest method to acquire something.
    - **Answer:** Wickedness: morally wrong, reckless behaviour to cause serious harm.
    - Crime: offense.
12. (d) **Erudite:** Having/showing great knowledge
    Answer: Ignorant: Lack of knowledge.
13. (b) **Acquitted:** Free someone from a criminal charge.
    - Entrusted: assign responsibility.
    - **Answer:** Convicted: to find someone guilty.

- Burdened: load, responsibility.
- Freed: released, liberated.

14. (b) **Belittle:** Unimportant/dismiss/underestimate
    - Recommend: put forward for approval.
    - **Answer:** Praise: Glorify, laud, applaud.
    - Encourage: give support, hope to some one.
    - Inspire: motivate, encourage.
15. (c) **Rancour:** Bitterness/resentful/hatredness
    Answer: Friendliness
16. (b) **Education: Development:** Cause and effect relation. Here education is the cause for development.
    Nutrition: Health: Nutrition is a cause of good health.
17. (b) **House: Room:** Part and whole relationship. Room is a part of the house.
    Struggle: fight: to try hard: use physical force.
    Answer: Transport: Car: Car is a part of the transport.
18. (a) **Gill: Fin:** Part relationship: Gill and fin are two parts of fish.
    Answer: Salad: Rice: Parts of food.
19. (d) **Glove: Ball:** Purpose relationship: Glove helps to catch a ball.
    Answer: Hook: Fish: Hook helps in catching a fish.
20. (b) **Sculptor: Chisel:** Work and tool relationship: Sculpter works on the chisel.
    Answer: Tailor: Needle: Tailor works on needle.

PRACTICE SET 2

Directions: *Read the following passage carefully and answer the following questions.*

By the time a child is six or seven, she has all the essential avoidances well enough by heart to be trusted with the care of a younger child. And she also develops a number of simple techniques. She learns to weave firm square balls from palm leaves, to make pinwheels of palm leaves or frangipani blossoms, climb a coconut tree by walking up the trunk on flexible little feet, break open a coconut with one firm well-directed blow of a knife as long as she is tall, and play a number of group games and sing the songs which go with them, tidy the house by picking up the litter on the stony floor, bring water from the sea, spread out the copra to dry and help gather it in when rain threatens, go to a neighbouring house and bring back a lighted faggot for the chief's pipe or the cook-house fire. But in the case of the little girls, all these tasks are merely supplementary to the main business of baby-tending. Very small boys also have some care of the younger children, but at 8 or 9 years of age, they are usually relieved of it. Whatever rough edges have not been smoothed off by this responsibility for younger children are worn off by their contact with older boys. For little boys are admitted to interesting and important activities only so long as their behaviour is circumspect and helpful. Where small girls are brusquely pushed aside, small boys will be patiently tolerated and they become adept at making themselves useful. The four or five little boys who wish to assist at the important business of helping a grown youth lasso reef eels, organise themselves into a highly efficient working team; one boy holds the bait, another holds an extra lasso, others poke eagerly about in holes in the reef looking for prey, while still another tucks the captured eels into his lavalava. The small girls, burdened with heavy babies or the care of little staggerers who are too small to adventure on the reef, discouraged by the hostility of the small boys and the scorn of the older ones, have little opportunity for learning the more adventurous forms of work and play. So, while the little boys first undergo the chastening effects of baby-tending and then have many opportunities to learn effective cooperation under the supervision of older boys, the girls' education is less comprehensive. They have a **high standard of individual responsibility**, but the community provides them with no lessons in cooperation with one another. This is particularly apparent in the activities of young people: the boys organise quickly; the girls waste hours in bickering, **innocent of** any technique for quick and efficient cooperation.

1. The primary purpose of the passage with reference to the society under discussion is to:
   (a) explain some differences in the upbringing of girls and boys.
   (b) criticise the deficiencies in the education of girls.
   (c) give a comprehensive account of a day in the life of an average young girl.
   (d) delineate the role of young girls.
   (e) show that young girls are trained to be useful to adults.
2. It can be inferred that the 'high standard of individual responsibility' is:
   (a) developed mainly through child-care duties.
   (b) only present in girls.
   (c) taught to a girl before she is entrusted with babies.
   (d) actually counterproductive.
   (e) weakened as the girl grows older.
3. It can be inferred that in the community under discussion all of the following are important except:
   (a) domestic handicrafts (b) well-defined social structure
   (c) fishing skills (d) formal education
   (e) division of labour
4. The list of techniques in the earlier paragraph could best be described as:
   (a) household duties (b) rudimentary physical skills
   (c) important responsibilities (d) useful social skills
   (e) monotonous tasks

5. The expression 'innocent of' is best taken to mean:
   (a) not guilty of
   (b) unskilled in
   (c) unsuited for
   (d) uninvolved in
   (e) uninterested in

Directions: *In the following passage there are blanks, each of which has been numbered. These numbers are printed below the passage and against each, five words are suggested, one of which fits the blank appropriately. Select the appropriate word.*

Our company has set up a foundation which is ___(6)___ to spreading literacy. To further this cause, the foundation has a project called 'A Library for Every School' through ___(7)___ the foundation donates books mainly to government school libraries so that children have easy access to books on a variety of subjects. In my ___(8)___ as Chairperson of the foundation, I travel extensively in rural areas. All this travelling has ___(9)___ me to understand what children want to read in different parts of the country. During my travels, I frequently stay in the houses of people. I meet as ___(10)___ there are no hotels in small towns and villages that I visit. In India, a guest is always treated well; an old Sanskrit saying is *Atithi Devo Bhava*, meaning that God comes in the form of a guest.

6.	(a) dedicated	(b) responsible	(c) trying	(d) catered	(e) involved
7.	(a) those	(b) which	(c) whom	(d) where	(e) these
8.	(a) feeling	(b) decision	(c) role	(d) knowledge	(e) order
9.	(a) Ensured	(b) provided	(c) enabled	(d) deprived	(e) made
10.	(a) while	(b) usual	(c) neither	(d) often	(e) either

Directions: *Choose from the five alternatives the one having the correct order of the sentences.*

11. A. I wish I had more time so that I could visit the odd nooks and corners of India.
    B. And yet I have not seen many parts of the country we love so much and seek to serve.
    C. Our country is a little world by itself with an infinite variety and places for us to discover.
    D. I had travelled a great deal in this country and I have grown in years.
    (a) DCBA (b) DBAC (c) ADBC (d) CDBA (e) CBAD
12. A. By increasing these connections, intelligence is also increased.
    B. Classical music has been proved to be very helpful in child development.
    C. Many doctors now-a-days use it for therapeutic purposes, which are based on the findings of the research.
    D. The research has demonstrated that listening to classical music increases the rate of nervous connections in the brain.
    (a) BDCA (b) DBAC (c) ACBD (d) BDAC (e) BCAD

13. A. This right, however, comes along with the responsibility which the press is forced to work with.
    B. It means that the pressmen have every right to expose matters related to public and national interest.
    C. Such responsibilities include not broadcasting matters related to national security and other sensitive issues.
    D. Freedom of the press is symbolic of democracy.
    (a) DBCA (b) DBAC (c) ABCD (d) BDAC (e) BCDA

Directions: *Pick the most effective word from the given words to fill the blanks to make the sentence meaningfully complete.*

14. The sword of Chhatrapati Shivaji was ____________ to England by the British rulers and has been recovered after our independence.
    (a) handed over (b) taken place (c) caught cold
    (d) looked down upon (e) taken away
15. Had you visited Hyderabad, you __________ seen the Martyrs memorial in front of the Andhra Assembly building.
    (a) might have (b) will have (c) had
    (d) would have (e) have had
16. __________ of youths and students were beaten and caned mercilessly by policemen in and around Hyderabad.
    (a) Thousand (b) Thousands (c) Two-thirds
    (d) Billion (e) Innumerable

Directions: *In the following questions choose the word which best expresses the meaning of the given word.*

17. Decimate
    (a) Disseminate (b) Dissipate (c) Disfigure (d) Destroy
18. Audacious
    (a) Obvious (b) Daring (c) Manifest (d) Venture

Directions: *In the following the questions choose the word which is closest to the opposite in meaning of the given word.*

19. Hoard
    (a) Deposit (b) Supply (c) Satisfy (d) Accumulate
20. Acumen
    (a) Intelligence (b) Imbecility (c) Potentiality (d) Unfamiliarity

SOLUTIONS WITH EXPLANATIONS

1. (a) explain some differences in the upbringing of girls and boys
2. (a) developed mainly through child-care duties
3. (d) formal education

- Domestic handicrafts – third line weaving
- Well – defined social structure – continuous interaction between young and older boys
- Fishing skills – game boys play
- **Answer:** Formal education – not given

4. (d) useful social skills
5. (b) unskilled in: no idea of any technique
6. (a) **dedicated:** used for particular purpose
   - **Answer:** Responsible: involving important duties
   - Trying: Difficult, hard, taxing
   - Catered: to serve food.
   - Involved: challenging, intricate
7. (b) which
8. (c) role: responsibility
9. (c) Ensured: sure, certain
   - enabled: to make possible
   - Deprived: not having something (food)
   - Made: formed, produced
   - Provided: supplied
10. (d) often: most of the time
11. (d) CDBA: Start from the option, go for elimination, and choose the main subject. Option (c) is the qualifier (main idea).
12. (d) BDAC: Option (b) is the main subject = qualifier. Option (d) talks about the benefit of classical music, (d) and (a) nervous connection is common.
13. (b) DBAC: D becomes the qualifier because we are talking about freedom of pressmen, every right is common between options (b) and (a).
14. (e) Handed over – India giving it
   - taken by British rulers
15. (d) if you had gone to Hyderabad you would have seen the martyrs memorial
16. (b) plural (youths)
17. (d) Decimate: destroy/drastically reduce the strength or effectiveness.
   - Disseminate: to spread/dispense
   - Dissipate: disappear
   - **Answer:** destroy
   - Disfigure: deface, damage
18. (b) Audacious: willingness to take risk; very confident and daring
   - **Answer:** daring
   - manifest: able to be seen; visible
   - Venture: to start something new/different involving risk unknown
   - Obvious: apparent, evident
19. (b) Hoard: large amount of valuable kept hidden (accumulation)
   - Answer: supply: to give, donate

- Accumulate: to gather
- Satisfy: meet the expectations
- Deposit: Store

20. (b) Acumen: judgement in practical matters/ability to think clearly/make good decision
    - Answer: foolishness/stupid.

Keywords

- Pinwheels: Fire work device that spins like a wheel
- Frangipani: Perfume derived from the odour of the flower
- Litter: Things thrown on the ground
- Copra: Dried coconut from where one derives coconut oil
- Faggot: Seasoned chopped liver baked/fried
- Baby tending: Taking care of an infant
- Brusquely: Blunt/unfriendly way
- Adept: Expert/trained
- Lasso reef eels: Rope, reduce the area by folding, long fish
- Bait: Food
- Lava lave: Rectangular cloth
- Hostility: Unfriendliness
- Scorn: Harsh criticism is cold
- Chastening: To cause someone to feel sad about what happened

PRACTICE SET 3

Directions: *Read the following passage carefully and answer the questions that follow:*

A book is written, not to multiply the voice or carry it merely, but to perpetuate it. The author has something to say which he perceives to be true and useful or helpfully beautiful so far he knows no one has said it, so far as he knows no one else can say it. He is bound to say it clearly and melodiously if he may; clearly at all events. In the sum of his life, he finds this to be the thing or group of things, manifests him; this, the piece of true knowledge, or sight, which his share of sunshine and earth has permitted him to seize. That is a book.

1. The opening sentence of the passage implies that the aim of writing a book is to:
   (a) repeat the message it contains.
   (b) enable the author to express his ideas in writing.
   (c) preserve from extinction the message it contains.
   (d) propagate the ideology of the author.
2. Which of the following is the most suitable title for this passage?
   (a) Contribution of an author

(b) Aim of writing a book
(c) Book: The source of true knowledge
(d) Writers and their books

3. According to the writer, a person is impelled to write a book because:
   (a) he wishes to satisfy his ego.
   (b) he has something nice and pleasing to say.
   (c) he is capable of expressing whatever he wants to say.
   (d) he had discovered something unique, true, and good which he must convey distinctly and musically.
4. Which of the following is not implied in the passage?
   (a) A writer is motivated to write a book if he discerns a great truth.
   (b) An author of a book generally gathers some common truths and gives them a popular and pleasing expression.
   (c) A great writer is convinced that whatever he says is not an echo, or imitation of what others have said.
   (d) An eminent writer's message is conveyed through plain unambiguous language.
5. Which of the following is opposite in meaning to the word 'manifest' given in the passage?
   (a) unclear (b) dark (c) pure (d) hard

Directions: *Against each key word are given some suggested meanings. Choose the word or phrase which is the nearest in opposite meaning to the keyword.*

6. His interpretation of the poem is *superficial.*
   (a) mystical (b) profound (c) difficult (d) mysterious
7. This is only the most *tenuous* evidence for it.
   (a) abundant (b) enough (c) reasonable (d) less
8. The principal hardly managed to give the papers a *cursory* glance.
   (a) superficial (b) through (c) thorough (d) curious
9. Mohini was often teased as *corpulent* by her friends.
   (a) belligerent (b) gaunt (c) garrulous (d) fat
10. People who are actually running the system often take a *myopic* view of the situation.
    (a) blind (b) visionary (c) glassy (d) farsighted

Directions: *In the following questions, choose the word which best expresses the meaning of the given word.*

11. **Truncate**
    (a) cancel (b) act cruelly (c) cut off (d) end swiftly
12. **Jovial**
    (a) merry (b) funny (c) smart (d) triumphant

13. **Avaricious**
    (a) abundant (b) envious (c) greedy (d) unwilling
14. **Risque**
    (a) slightly humorous (b) slightly improper
    (c) slightly risky (d) very risky
15. **Voracious**
    (a) quick (b) angry (c) hungry (d) wild

Directions: *In the following passage there are blanks, each of which has been numbered. These numbers are printed below the passage, and against each, five words are suggested, one of which fits the blank appropriately.*

India's ____(16)____ over the past half-century since independence has been unique and commendable in many ways. Yet the record is ____(17)____ in relation to what the country set out to achieve and could certainly have been accomplished. It is ____(18)____ to look at both sides; the alternative is to be weighed down by unrelieved gloom or unwarranted ____(19)____. the fact is that after eight Five-Year Plans about 40 per cent of the population is still below the poverty line. The human development indices are ____(20)____ low, placing India at the 126th position at the world table, far below many countries that came into being much later than it did.

16. (a) development (b) domination (c) predicament
    (d) history (e) excellence
17. (a) outshining (b) broken (c) disappointing
    (d) brighter (e) played
18. (a) proposed (b) futile (c) impracticable
    (d) necessary (e) suggested
19. (a) progress (b) debating (c) meticulous
    (d) haste (e) complacency
20. (a) deplorably (b) admirably (c) surprisingly
    (d) not (e) amusingly

SOLUTIONS WITH EXPLANATIONS

1. (d) Propagate the ideology of the author: to make an idea to many people
    - Ideology – set of ideas
2. (c) Book – The source of true knowledge: book provides knowledge
3. (d) Impelled: strong desire to do something.
    - He had discovered something unique, true and good which he must convey distinctly ad musically.
4. (b) Not implied: false statement
    - An author of a book generally gathers some common truths and gives them a popular and pleasing expression: author has something unique to say through a book.

5. (a) Manifest: clear
    - **Answer:** Unclear
6. (b) Superficial: on the surface, outward.
    - Mystical: having spiritual meaning
    - **Answer:** Profound: showing good knowledge
    - Mysterious: strange
    - Difficult: tough
7. (c) Tenuous: weak, not definite, negligible
    - reasonable: minimum evidence
8. (c) Cursory: rapidly, superficial
    - thorough: in-depth
9. (b) Corpulent: fat, obese
    - Belligerent: angry, aggressive
    - **Answer:** Gaunt: very thin
    - Garrulous: talkative
    - Fat: fat, obese
10. (d) Myopic: short sighted
    - Visionary: strong imagination things to be done in future
    - **Answer:** Farsighted
    - Blind: Person who cannot see
    - Glassy: Using spectacles
11. (c) Truncate: to make less in duration, cut down.
    - Cut off
12. (a) Jovial: cheerful, friendly, full of happiness.
    - Merry : cheerful
13. (c) Avaricious: extreme greed for wealth
    - Abundant: Plentiful
    - envious: a feeling of discontented (dissatisfied)
    - **Answer:** greedy
    - Unwilling: against one's wish, reluctant
14. (b) Risqué: indecency
    - slightly improper
15. (c) Voracious: huge appetite; wanting great quality of food
    - Hungry: having a strong desire for food, craving
16. (d) excellence
17. (c) disappointing
18. (d) necessary: required
19. (d) haste
20. (a) Deplorably: causes shock/fear

PRACTICE SET 4

Directions: *Read the following passage carefully and answer the questions that follow:*

Gandhiji had to travel by train from Durban to Pretoria in connection with his job. Once while travelling by train, he was asked by the white passengers to leave the first-class compartment and shift to the van compartment. He refused to do so. Thereafter, he was pushed forcibly out of the compartment and his luggage was thrown on the platform. It was winter and he kept shivering all night. He did not go to the waiting room because the white men sleeping there might insult him further. This event was a turning point in the life of Gandhiji and he decided to stay back in South Africa and fight against this blatant injustice.

1. The white people asked Gandhiji to abandon the first-class compartment because:
   (a) they wanted to annoy him.
   (b) they wanted to avenge themselves on Gandhi.
   (c) they treated Indians as inferior to them.
   (d) they were looking for a chance to talk to him.
2. Why was he thrown out of the compartment?
   (a) He misbehaved with the whites.
   (b) They wanted him to spend the night in the waiting room.
   (c) They wanted to insult him.
   (d) He refused to shift to the van compartment.
3. Why did he not go to the waiting room to spend the night?
   (a) The room was unclean.
   (b) He wanted to sleep in the open.
   (c) He was badly hurt and so could not move to the room.
   (d) He feared that the white men there might insult him further.
4. This event was a turning point in the life of Gandhiji. The event being talked about here is:
   (a) Gandhiji being ill-treated by the whites.
   (b) Gandhiji's spending the night on the platform.
   (c) Gandhiji's travel by train.
   (d) Gandhiji's staying back in South Africa.
5. Gandhiji stayed back in South Africa:
   (a) to avenge himself on the whites who had insulted him.
   (b) because his work was still not complete.
   (c) to fight against racial discrimination in Africa.
   (d) to build up an army and fight against the white people.

Directions: *In each of the following questions, four words are given of which two are most nearly the same or opposite in meaning. Find two words that are most nearly the same or opposite in meaning.*

6. A. expanded B. proclaimed C. shrunk D. facilitated
   (a) A-D (b) B-D (c) C-D
   (d) B-C (e) A-C
7. A. inedible B. erasable C. insignificant D. temporary
   (a) A-C (b) C-B (c) A-B
   (d) B-D (e) C-D
8. A. intangible B. restless C. vast D. meagre
   (a) C-A (b) C-D (c) C-B
   (d) B-A (e) B-D
9. A. cutting B. establishing C. transferring D. pruning
   (a) A-B (b) C-D (c) B-C
   (d) A-C (e) A-D
10. A. fixed B. indelible C. soapy D. stiff
    (a) A-D (b) A-B (c) A-C
    (d) B-C (e) C-D

Directions: *Pick out the most effective words to fill the blanks to make the sentences meaningfully complete.*

11. They wasted all the money on the purchase of some _________ items.
    (a) excellent (b) important (c) significant
    (d) quality (e) trivial
12. When he found the wallet his face glowed, but soon it faded as the wallet was __________.
    (a) empty (b) vacant (c) recovered
    (d) stolen (e) expensive
13. I will ________ them for saving me from the agonies of old age.
    (a) fire (b) beat (c) thank
    (d) admonish (e) shout
14. I have not done things that anyone else makes me feel are ______ recording.
    (a) useless (b) worth (c) good
    (d) history (e) bad
15. I was handed ________ to Harish Singh.
    (a) back (b) over (c) through
    (d) upon (e) again
16. We were __________ with the names of notorious criminals.
    (a) constantly (b) convenient (c) familiar
    (d) obvious (e) ignorant
17. I do not know what ________ my father choose that particular school.
    (a) happened (b) control (c) made

(d) asked (e) thrilled

18. He knelt at his side and comforted him with ___________ words.
    (a) harsh (b) silent (c) kind
    (d) cruel (e) flowers
19. We cannot __________ of life without a suitable environment.
    (a) live (b) by (c) extract
    (d) dreams (e) think
20. He thought the boy ___________ to benefit the blacksmith.
    (a) wants (b) wanting (c) desire
    (d) have (e) loose

SOLUTIONS WITH EXPLANATIONS

1. (c) They treated Indians as inferior to them
    - Avenge: retaliate, harm someone who harmed you
2. (d) he refused to shift to the van compartment
3. (d) He feared that the White men there might insult him further
4. (a) Gandhiji' being ill-treated by the whites (inference)
5. (c) To fight against racial discrimination in Africa
6. (e) Expanded: Become large
    - Proclaimed: To say in public, to declare
    - Shrunk: become smaller in size
    - Facilitated: to help something run smoothly and effectively
7. (c) Inedible: not suitable to eat, that cannot be removed
    - Erasable: removable, delete
    - Insignificant: not important
8. (b) Restless: not relaxed, nervous.
    - Vast: large extent
    - Meagre: very small
9. (e) Pruning: cutting away, trimming, shaping of trees or bush.
10. (a) Fixed: Inflexible, rigid.
    - Indelible: marks that can't be removed, permanent marker.
    - Soapy: lathered
    - Stiff: rigid
11. (c) Trivial: little importance.
12. (a)
13. (c) Fire: blaze
    - Beat: hit
    - Thank: acknowledge, credit
    - Admonish: reprimand; to speak in a way that expresses criticism.
    - Shout: howl, yell

14. (b) worth: value
15. (b) over: to give something to someone.
16. (c) familiar: closely acquainted
17. (c) made: produce, create, form
    - Thrilled: very excited
18. (c) kind: soothing, feeling of comfort
19. (e) think: imagine, believe
20. (a) wants: earnest wish (plural)

Keyword

- Blatant: very obvious, offensive.

PRACTICE SET 5

Directions: *Read the following passage carefully and answer the questions that follow:*

An independent, able, and upright judiciary is the hallmark of a free democratic country. Therefore, the process of judicial appointments is of vital importance. At present, on account of the Supreme Court's last advisory opinion, the role of the executive and its interference in the appointment of judges is minimal, which, in light of our previous experience, is most welcome. However, there is a strong demand for a National Judicial Commission on the ground of wider participation in the appointment process and greater transparency. The composition, the role, and the procedures of the proposed National Judicial Commission must be spelled out. Lest it be a case of jumping **from the frying-pan into the fire**.

Recently, there has been a lively debate in England on the subject. A judicial commission has been proposed but there are not many takers for that proposal. In the paper issued this month by the Lord Chancellor's Department on judicial appointments, the Lord Chancellor has said, 'I want every vacancy on the Bench to be filled by the best person available. Appointments must and will be made on merit, irrespective of ethnic origin, gender, marital status, political affiliation, religion, or disability. These are not mere words. They are firm principles. I will not tolerate any form of discrimination.'

At present, there are hardly any persons from the ethnic minorities manning the higher judiciary and so far not a single woman has made it to the House of Lords. The most significant part of Lord Chancellor's paper is the requirement that 'allegations of professional misconduct made in the course of consultations about a candidate for judicial office must be specific and subject to disclosure to the candidate.' This should go a long way in ensuring that principles of natural justice and fair play are not on phenomenon.

1. What according to the passage should go a long way in judicial appointments?
   (a) Decisions that all sections of the society are represented.
   (b) Candidate's qualifications and seniority are considered.
   (c) Candidate must know the charge of professional misconduct levelled against them.
   (d) There should be a strong reason for discrimination.
   (e) None of these.
2. According to the passage, there has been a demand for National Judicial Commission to:
   (a) clear the backing of court cases.
   (b) make judiciary see eye-to-eye with the executive.
   (c) wipe out corruption at higher places.
   (d) make the appointment process of judges more broad-based and clear.
   (e) safeguard the interest of natural justice and fair play in judicial pronouncement.
3. What has been the subject of lively debate in England?
   (a) Role of judiciary in free and democratic nations.
   (b) Appointment of the judicial commission.
   (c) Seniority is the basis of the appointment of judges.
   (d) Appointment of judicial post.
   (e) None of these.
4. Which of the following words is similar in meaning to the word **jettison** as used in the passage?
   (a) Sacrifice (b) Accept (c) Modify (d) Destroy (e) Advocate
5. What does the expression 'from the frying-pan into the fire' mean?
   (a) Seeing one dream after another.
   (b) Making plan after plan.
   (c) Crossing one hurdle after another.
   (d) Jumping from one high place to another.
   (e) None of these.

Directions: *In the following questions four words are given of which two are most nearly the same or opposite in meaning. Find out two words which are most nearly the same or opposite in meaning.*

6. A. Enthralling B. Respecting C. Projecting D. Alluring
   (a) A-B (b) B-C (c) C-D
   (d) A-D (e) B-D
7. A. Swoop B. Perturb C. Plump D. Boil
   (a) A-D (b) B-C (c) A-C
   (d) B-D (e) C-D
8. A. Concise B. Elegant C. Indifferent D. Indecorous
   (a) B-C (b) A-C (c) A-B

(d) C-D (e) B-D

9. A. Acquit B. Defend C. Forbid D. Condemn
(a) B-C (b) A-C (c) C-D
(d) B-D (e) A-D

10. A. Fallacy B. Adage C. Dictum D. Endorse
(a) B-D (b) C-D (c) B-C
(d) A-D (e) A-B

Directions: *Pick the most effective word from the given words to fill the blanks to make the sentence meaningfully complete.*

11. After careful thought, I bought for my daughter a combination _______ with little shiny stones that could even be mistaken for diamonds.
(a) presented (b) looked (c) hid
(d) decorated (e) put

12. One of the issues which were _______ in the meeting was raised by Sainky.
(a) raised (b) discussed (c) staged
(d) developed (e) settled

13. Great __________ depth is required to be a teacher of philosophy.
(a) intelligent (b) intellectuals (c) intellectual
(d) instructive (e) insufferable

14. ____________ is a previous case taken as an authoritative example for subsequent procedures.
(a) Precedent (b) President (c) Precedence
(d) Practical (e) Emolument

15. Alok informed me about the accident which had _______ 4 days before.
(a) took place (b) had taken (c) occurred
(d) had happened (e) passed

16. Mulk Raj Anand is one of the most _________ Indo-Anglian novelist and story writers of today.
(a) an eminent (b) a famous (c) notorious
(d) eminent (e) best

17. Mrs Laljee in her modest way __________ a little and slipped the chain inside her dress.
(a) broken (b) pushed (c) pressed
(d) flushed (e) slipped

Directions: *Choose from the five alternatives the one having the correct order of sentences.*

18. A. It was with the invincible spirit that Netaji opposed the wavers offer.
B. Japan's surrender is not India's surrender, he said.
C. The revolutionary spirit of Netaji was never dampened, even after the surrender of Japan.

D. He knew that a war of liberation demanded great spirit, great sacrifice, courage, and patience.

(a) BCDA (b) BCAD (c) CBAD (d) DCBA (e) CBDA

19. A. But all work is not education.

B. In India, a majority of our people do hard work, strenuous physical work, but all are not educated.

C. It aims at concrete and objective realisation of the ideas and is of great educative value.

D. 'Work' is that activity of man which has a definite objective.

(a) DCAB (b) BCDA (c) BACD (d) DBCA (e) CBAD

20. A. Hari Prasad Nanda is one such person who worked his way to the top from scratch.

B. A few of them had a spark of proved adventure and their initiative, dedication, and sincerity brought them spectacular success.

C. The partition of India into India and Pakistan made a number of migrants to India penniless.

D. He rose to become a first-generation entrepreneur with the second-largest complex to his credit.

(a) ADBC (b) ADCB (c) CBAD (d) CBDA (e) BCDA

SOLUTIONS WITH EXPLANATIONS

1. (c) Candidate must know the charge of professional misconduct levelled against them.
   - Allegation must be specific and should be disclosed.
2. (d) Make the appointment process of judges more broad-based and clear
   - Been a demand: main object/purpose.
   - **Answer:** To bring clarity: transparency.
3. (b) Appointment of judicial commission
4. (a) Jettison: voluntary sacrifice, disposal, dumping, scrapping.
5. (e) From the frying-pan into the fire: recruitment process should be transparent, fair play, best person available.
   - **Answer:** None of these
6. (d) A-D (same meaning)
   - Enthralling: attractive, to capture someone's attention
   - Respecting: due regard.
   - Projecting: forecast, estimate, pointing
   - Alluring: quality of being attractive
7. (c) A-C (same meaning)
   - Swoop: move rapidly downwards through air
   - Perturb: to make someone very worried anxious
   - Plump: to fall heavily.

- Boil: heat, simmer

8. (e) B-D (opposite meaning)
   - Concise: brief
   - Elegant: graceful
   - Indifferent: having no interest
   - Indecorous: showing lack of dignity, manners and taste
9. (d) B-D (opposite meaning)
   - Acquit: to declare not guilty of crime
   - Defend: to action support
   - Forbid: shot well known statement (opposite)
   - Condemn: express complete disapproval (idea)
10. (c) B-C (same meaning)
    - Fallacy: mistaken belief
    - Adage: proverb: short statement expressing general truth.
    - Dictum: short well known statement
    - Endorse: declare one's public approval, support of

13. (c) intellectual : learned, knowledgeable

14. (c) Precedence

14. (c) occurred

16. (d) eminent: stand out, notable, successful
    - A famous: popular
17. (d) flushed: glowing red (cheek)
18. (e) start from the option and go for elimination by choosing the main subject.
    - This passage is talking about revolutionary spirit of Netaji, so this(c) become the qualifier.
    - Option B pronoun follows option C. it is talking about surrender of Japan.
    - Option D is a pronoun which is continuation to option B.
19. (a) DCAB
    - It is talking about work which is in option D (qualifier). Option C is the continuation of option D.
    - Option A comes after option C.
20. (c) CBAD
    - Option C is the qualifier because it is talking about partition of migrants between India and Pakistan.
    - Option B is continuation of C because it is talking about migrants had a spark.
    - Option A comes after option B because it gives an example of one such migrants.

PRACTICE SET 6

Directions: *Read the following passage and answer the questions that follow.*

India is a country of villages. The rural population still dominates the urban population as far as the numbers are concerned. This is despite the fact that there is rampant migration of rural families to urban centres. Generally, the gains of being a unit of the urban population are less than the disadvantages and risks that are in-built in urban life. Crimes, riots, etc., are some of the examples of such urban life risks. The forces that generate conditions conducive to crimes and riots are stronger in urban communities than in rural areas. Urban living is more anonymous. It often releases the individual from the community restraints more common in tradition-oriented societies, but more freedom from constraints and controls also provides greater freedom to deviate. Living in the more impersonalised, formally-controlled urban society means that regulatory orders of conduct are often directed by distant bureaucrats. The police are strangers executing the prescriptions on an anonymous set of subjects.

Minor offences in small towns or villages are often handled without resorting to the police station. As disputable as such an action may seem, it results in fewer recorded violations of law compared to those in cities. Although, perhaps causing some decision difficulties for the police in small towns, formal and objective law enforcement is not always acceptable to villagers. Urban areas with mass population, greater wealth, more commercial establishments, and more products of technology also provide more frequent opportunities for theft. Victims are impersonalised, property is insured, and consumer goods in abundance are vividly displayed and are more portable. The crime rate increases despite formal moral education given in schools.

1. The word 'conducive' in the passage means ______________.
   (a) prohibitive against (b) prone to minimise
   (c) helping to reduce (d) tending to promote
2. The passage mainly emphasises the ______________.
   (a) comparative account of wealth in rural and urban areas
   (b) increasing crime rate in rural areas
   (c) need for formal moral education in in schools
   (d) reasons for the growing crime rate in urban areas as compared to that in rural areas
3. Which of the following is a characteristic of an urban setting?
   (a) Unreported minor crimes (b) Deviation from freedom
   (c) Less forceful social control (d) Fewer recorded law violations
4. According to the passage, all of the following contribute to higher crime rates in urban areas, except ______________.
   (a) vivid display of consumer goods
   (b) urban impersonalised living

(c) higher standard of living
(d) inadequate police force

5. Which of the following inference(s) can be drawn from the passage?
   A. Migration of people from rural to urban areas is almost negligible.
   B. Strangers can enforce laws in a more impartial manner than known people can.
   C. Wealth has concentrated more in urban centres than in rural centres.
   (a) A and B only (b) B and C only
   (c) A and C only (d) All three

Directions: *Find the synonyms of the following words.*

6. Benevolent
   (a) Charitable (b) Sympathetic (c) Liberal (d) Beneficial
7. Ironic
   (a) Good-natured (b) Inflexible (c) Disguisedly sarcastic
   (d) Bitter
8. Colossus
   (a) Towering (b) Tall (c) Lofty (d) Huge

Directions: *Find the antonyms of the following words.*

9. Smooth
   (a) Ugly (b) Awkward (c) Hard (d) Rough
10. Comic
   (a) Painful (b) Fearful (c) Tragic (d) Emotional
11. Evacuate
   (a) Admit (b) Emerge (c) Abandon (d) Division

Directions: *Which of the phrases—(a), (b), (c), or (d)—in options should replace the bold phrase in the questions?*

12. He is working hard **to success for** the examination.
   (a) for succeeding (c) to succeed in
   (b) for success off (d) for success into
13. The police are **tried hard for tracking up** the robbers.
   (a) trying hard to track down (c) tried hard to track in
   (b) trying hard to track up (d) tried hard for tracking down
14. Newspapers have great power **because** their enormous circulation.
   (a) on account (c) as a result
   (b) because of (d) owing
15. The bridge **in connection with** the two cities will remain closed for security reasons
   (a) connects between (c) being connected from
   (b) in connection to (d) connecting

Directions: *In the passage, there are numbered blanks. Against each number in the questions are five options. Choose which one fits the blank appropriately.*

Economic backwardness of a region is characterised by the co-existence of unutilised or underutilised manpower on the one hand, and ____(16)____ natural resources on the other. Economic development essentially means a process of ____(17)____ change, whereby the real per-capita income of an economy ____(18)____ over a period of time. Then, a simple but meaningful question arises: 'What causes economic development or what makes a country developed?' The question has absorbed the attention of scholars of socio-economic change for decades. Going through the ____(19)____ history of developed countries like America, Russia, and Japan, man is essentially found as pivotal in the process of economic development. Japan, whose economy was badly damaged from the ravages of the Second World War, is the clearest example of our time to ____(20)____ kingpin role in economic development.

16. (a) exhaustive (b) unexploited (c) abundant
    (d) indefinite (e) unreliable
17. (a) upward (b) drastic (c) negligible
    (d) incredible (e) sudden
18. (a) diminishes (b) degenerates (c) increases
    (d) succumbs (e) stabilises
19. (a) existing (b) glorious (c) ancient
    (d) economic (e) discouraging
20. (a) enlighten (b) validate (c) negate
    (d) underestimate (e) belittle

SOLUTIONS WITH EXPLANATIONS

1. (d) Conductive: make it easily, possible, tending to promote/assist
2. (d) Increasing crime rate in rural areas
3. (c) less forceful social control
4. (d) Urban impersonalizes living: thief shows no interest in individual people, shows no feeling towards individual.
5. (b) Inference: conclusion : 2 and 3 only
6. (a)
    - Benevolent: kind, generous
    - Charitable: help people who are poor
    - Liberal: willing to respect/accept behaviour or opinions different from one's own
    - Sympathetic: showing concern
    - Beneficial: producing good result
7. (c)
    - Ironic: using language that normally signifies opposite meaning / sarcasm
    - Inflexible: unwilling to change

- Disguisedly sarcastic: use of words, i.e. opposite of what we want to say
- Bitter: not sweet, pungent taste (strong)
- Good natured: amiable, agreeable

8. (a)
   - Colossus: something that is much bigger than life size (very large gigantic size)
   - Towering: very tall
   - Lofty: great height
   - Huge: very large
   - Tall: of suitable height
9. (d) rough: uneven
10. (b)
    - Comic: relating to comedy, causing laughter, amusement
    - Fearful: extreme fear
    - Tragic: strong feeling of sadness
    - Emotional: a state of feeling
    - Painful: aching, hurting
11. (a)
    - Evacuate: to leave/to remove someone from a place
    - Admit: allow someone to enter a place
    - Emerge: move out and become visible
    - Abandon: to leave and never return
    - Division: partition, separation
12. (c) to succeed in
13. (a) Trying hard to track down
14. (b) Because of: Due to
15. (d) connecting
16. (b) unexploited
17. (b) drastic: dramatic
18. (c) Increases
19. (d) economic
20. (b)
    - Enlighten: impark knowledge.
    - Validate: confirm, make legally valid, recognize

Keywords

- Rampant: Spreading/uncontrollable.
- Conductive: Making it easy possible.
- Restraints: Way of limiting.
- Freedom from constraints: Restriction.
- Impersonalised: Showing no interest in individual.

PRACTICE SET 7

Directions: *In each of the following questions, out of the given alternatives, choose the one which best expresses the meaning of the given word.*

1. Admonish
   (a) Threaten (b) Praise (c) Appeal (d) Support
2. Lethal
   (a) Dreary (b) Dreadful (c) Deadly (d) Strange
3. Aberration
   (a) Deviation (b) Steadfastness (c) Privilege (d) Procrastination
4. Tedious
   (a) Easy (b) Difficult (c) Tiring (d) Troublesome

Directions: *In each of the following sentences, choose the word opposite in meaning to the given word.*

5. Factitious
   (a) Ridiculous (b) Genuine (c) Engineered (d) Magnificent
6. Magnanimous
   (a) *Naïve* (b) Small (c) Generous (d) Selfish
7. Cordial
   (a) Official (b) Cold (c) Distrustful (d) Indifferent
8. Sceptical
   (a) Sanguine (b) Hopeful (c) Certain (d) Doubtful

Directions: *In each of the following questions, out of the four alternatives, choose the one which can be substituted for the given phrases.*

9. To examine one's own thoughts and feelings.
   (a) Meditation (b) Retrospection
   (c) Reflection (d) Introspection
10. List of headings of the businesses to be transacted at a meeting.
    (a) Schedule (b) Proceedings
    (c) Agenda (d) Excerpts
11. These essays are intellectually ___________ and represent various levels of complexity.
    (a) revealing (b) modern (c) superior
    (d) demanding (e) persistent
12. Since one cannot read every book, one should be content with making a ________ selection.
    (a) normal (b) standard (c) sample
    (d) moderate (e) judicious
13. The soldiers were instructed to ________ restraint and handle the situation peacefully.

(a) exercise (b) control (c) prevent
(d) enforce (e) remain

14. Baggage can be covered __________ loss or accident during travel.
    (a) against (b) for
    (c) along (d) with
15. The more we looked at the piece of the modern art, ______________.
    (a) it looked better (b) the more we like it
    (c) the less me liked it (d) better we liked it

Directions: *Read the following passage and answer the questions.*

Nature is like business. Business sense dictates that we guard our capital and live off the interest. Nature's capital is the enormous diversity of living things. Without it, we cannot feed ourselves, cure ourselves of illness, or provide the industry with raw materials of wealth creation. Professor Edward Wilson of Harvard University says, 'The folly our descendants are least likely to forgive us is the ongoing loss of genetic and species diversity. This will take millions of years to correct'.

Only 150 plant species have ever been widely cultivated. Yet, over 75,000 edible plants are known in the wild. In a hungry world, with a population growing by 90 million each year, so much wasted potential is tragic. Medicines from the wild are worth around 40 billion dollars a year. Over 5,000 species are known to yield chemicals with cancer fighting potential. Scientist currently estimate that that the total number of species in the world is between 10 and 30 million with only around 1.4 million identified.

The web of life is torn when mankind exploits natural resources in short-sighted ways. The trade in tropical hardwoods can destroy whole forests to extract just a few commercially attractive specimens. Bad agricultural practices trigger 24 billion tonnes of top soil erosion a year, losing the equivalent of 9 million tonnes of grain output. Cutting this type of suitable exploitation and instituting 'sustainable utilisation' will help turn the environmental crisis around.

16. Why does the author compare nature to business?
    (a) Because of the capital depletion in nature and business
    (b) Because of the similarity with which one should use both
    (c) Because of the same interest level yield
    (d) Because of the diversity of various capital inputs
17. 'The folly our descendants are least likely to forgive us'. What is the business equivalent of the folly that the author is referring to?
    (a) Reducing the profit margins
    (b) Not pumping some money out of profits into the business
    (c) Eroding the capital lease of the business
    (d) Putting interest on capital back into the business

18. Which of the following statements is false in the context of the given passage?
    (a) The diversity of plant life is essential for human existence
    (b) Scientists know the usefulness of most of the plant species
    (c) Chemicals for cancer treatment are available from plants
    (d) There are around 10 times more undiscovered plant species as compared to the discovered ones
19. Which of the following correctly reflects the opinion of the author to take care of hunger in the world?
    (a) Increase the number of edible plants being cultivated
    (b) Increase cultivation of the 150 species presently under cultivation
    (c) Increase the scale of cultivation of medical plants
    (d) Increase the potential of the uncultivated edible plants
20. Which of the following is mentioned as the immediate cause of the destruction of plant species?
    (a) Soil erosion
    (b) Destruction of habitat
    (c) Cultivation
    (d) Agricultural practice

SOLUTIONS WITH EXPLANATIONS

1. (a)
    - Admonish: reprimand firmly, scold
    - Threaten: intention to harm
    - Praise: applaud, admiration
    - Appeal: heartfelt, request
    - Support: help provide basic necessities
2. (c)
    - Lethal: able to cause death
    - Dreary: dull, depressing
    - Dreadful: causing great suffering
    - Deadly: able to cause death
    - Strange: unusual, difficult to explain
3. (a)
    - Aberration: deviation from normal; divergence
    - Steadfastness: firm
    - Privilege: special right, entitlement
    - Procrastination: postponing, delaying something
    - Deviation: divergence, deflection
4. (c)
    - Tedious: tiresome, too long
    - Easy: effortless , without effort
    - Difficult: needs much effort
    - Tiring: causing one to need rest
    - Troublesome: causing difficulty
5. (b)
    - Factitious: artificially created of developed
    - Ridiculous: very silly, absurd, unreasonable
    - Genuine: authentic, original.
    - Engineered: design, build, machine, structure.

- Magnificent: impressive, attractive.

6. (d)
   - Magnanimous: forgiving, generous
   - Naïve: lacking experience, judgement
   - Small: less than normal size
   - Generous: giving readiness to give
   - Selfish: lacking consideration.
7. (b)
   - Cordial: warm and friendly
   - Official: relating to authority
   - Distrustful: a feeling that someone cannot be relied upon.
   - Indifferent: unconcerned having no particular interest.
   - Cold : not warm
8. (b)
   - Sceptical: having doubt, not easily convinced
   - Sanguine: optimistic
   - Hopeful: feeling of expectation
   - Certain: surety, definite
   - Doubtful: feeling of uncertainly
9. (d)
   - Retrospection: reviewing past events
   - Reflection: sending back light without absorbing
   - Introspection: examination of one's own mental and emotional processes
   - Meditation: deep thinking
10. (c)
    - Schedule: plan, program
    - Proceeding: set of activities involving a set procedure. Action taken by court to settle disputes.
    - Agenda: a list of meeting activities to be discussed in a meeting.
    - Excerpts: a short extract from a film, piece of meeting.
11. (d) Demanding: taxing, challenging, laborious
12. (e) Judicious: sensible judgement.
13. (a) Enforce: ensure law is obeyed, compel observance of law
14. (a) Against
15. (a) better we liked it
16. (b) Because of the similarity with which one should use both
17. (c) Eroding the capital lease of the business
    - Eroding: corrosion, wear and tear. Money is used up
18. (b) Scientists know the usefulness of the most plant species: option B is false others are true.
19. (d) Increase the potential of the uncultivated edible plants.
20. (b) Destruction of habitat

Keywords

- Capital: Money, wealth
- Diversity: Variety

- Folly: Foolishness
- Descendants: Coming generation
- Edible: Suited to eat, consumable
- The trade in tropical hardwoods: Timbers, woods

PRACTICE SET 8

Directions: *Read the following passage carefully and answer the questions that follow.*

Religion is the greatest instrument in raising us. It is amazing that a person not intellectually bright, perhaps not even educated, is capable of grasping and living by something so advanced as the principles of Christianity. Yet, this is a common phenomenon. It is not, however, in my province to talk about religion, but rather to stress the power which great literature and the great personalities whom we meet in it and in history have to open and enlarge over minds, and to show us what first rate in human personality and human character is by showing us goodness and greatness.

1. In the passage, the author's ultimate intention is to talk about ________.
   (a) religion (b) history (c) education (d) character
2. The phrase 'so raising us' means ________.
   (a) giving us a sense of spiritual superiority
   (b) making us feel that we are more important than we really are
   (c) improving our mental abilities
   (d) making us realise that we all are children of God
3. What surprises the author is that ________.
   (a) even uneducated people are attracted towards Christianity
   (b) Christianity is practiced by a large number of people
   (c) despite being difficult and complex, the principles of Christianity are practiced by so many people
   (d) even very intelligent people cannot understand the principles of Christianity
4. The author hesitates to talk about religion because ________.
   (a) he does not feel himself competent to talk about it
   (b) nobody around him likes to talk about it
   (c) he does not believe in any religion
   (d) he does not fully understand its importance.
5. According to the author, we come across examples of greatness and nobility in ________.
   (a) great works of literature
   (b) literary and historical works
   (c) historical records
   (d) books on Christianity

Directions: *In the following questions, choose the word which best expresses the meaning of the given word.*

6. Extinct
   (a) Feeble (b) Aggressive (c) Scattered (d) Non-existent
7. Propitiate
   (a) Evict (b) Incite (c) Praise (d) Conciliate
8. Propensity
   (a) Characteristic (b) Quality (c) Natural tendency
   (d) Aptitude
9. Antidote
   (a) Remedy for (b) Consequence of
   (c) Cause for (d) Result of
10. Sensuous
    (a) Sensible (b) Sensual (c) Sentimental (d) Sensitive

Directions: *Pick out the most effective word from the given words to make the sentence meaningfully complete.*

11. Boistersous
    (a) Calm (b) Comfortable (c) Rude (d) Happy
12. Defiance
    (a) Dismay (b) Suspicion (c) Obedience (d) Anxiety
13. Presumption
    (a) Resumption (b) Proposition (c) Humility (d) Assumption
14. Callous
    (a) Confident (b) Sentimental (c) Sensitive (d) Capable
15. Concealment
    (a) Identification (b) Broadness (c) Evidence (d) Indication

Directions: *Pick out the most effective word from the given words to fill in the blanks to make the sentence meaningfully complete.*

16. All the Board members were present with the __________ of the treasurer.
    (a) exception (b) absence (c) delay
    (d) omission (e) refusal
17. People have become ___________ under the burden of heavy taxes.
    (a) reckless (b) isolated (c) punished
    (d) fatigue (e) impatient
18. His _______ background has made him so docile.
    (a) famous (b) lucrative (c) rich
    (d) advanced (e) humble
19. _________ he is a hard worker; his quality of work is not of a desirable level.
    (a) Despite (b) Because (c) Although
    (d) Somehow (e) However

20. Onions grow in _______ in this part and hence, they are always cheap here.
    (a) demand (b) abundance (c) peak
    (d) excessive (e) dearth

SOLUTIONS WITH EXPLANATIONS

1. (c) Education: Education helps in broadening mind which in turn helps in broader way what is religion. If a person knows morality truthfulness can understands religion.
2. (d) Making us realize that we all are children of GOD.
    - God created us, we have different names of god but god is one.
3. (c) Despite being difficult and complex, the principles of Christianity are practiced by so many people.
    - Information in the passage
4. (a) He does not feel himself competent to talk about it
    - Religion is vast and complicated. The author is not the right person to explain about it
5. (b) Literary and historical works
    - Information is available in the passage
6. (d) Feeble: weak
7. (d)
    - Propitiate: to make someone pleased, saying something desired
    - Evict: force someone to leave a place
    - Incite: to cause someone to act in angry, violent way
    - Praise: express warm approval
    - Conciliate: to gain goodwill by to make someone less angry
8. (c)
    - Propensity: natural tendency to behave in a particular way
    - Aptitude: natural ability to do something, to learn something
    - Characteristics: attribute, feature
    - Quality: standard
9. (a) Antidote: cure, neutralizer
10. (d)
    - Sensuous: appealing, pleasant, affecting the senses in pleasant way.
    - Sensible: showing good sense, able to make good judgement.
    - Sensual: pleasurable.
    - Sentimental: emotional
11. (a) Boisterous: very noisy and active.
12. (c)
    - Defiance: refusal to obey
    - Dismay: shock, surprise
    - Obedience: compliance
    - Anxiety: feeling nervous
    - Suspicion: doubt
13. (d)
    - Presumption: an idea, i.e. taken to be tree on the basic of probability.
    - Humility: quality of having modest.

- Assumption: thing, i.e. accepted to be true without proof.
- Resumption: renewal, restart
- Proposition: hypothesis, supposition

14. (c)
- Callous: having no emotion, heartless.
- Sentimental: emotional
- Sensitive: sensitive persons are sentimental.
- Confident: assured, secured
- Capable: competent

15. (a) Concealment: action of hiding something.
16. (a)
- Exception: person who is excluded
- Absence: failure to be present
- Omission: action of leaving something out.
- Delay: hold back, wait
- Refusal: denial

17. (e) Impatient: tiredness, weariness
18. (e) Docile: easy to control
19. (c) although
20. (b) dearth: lack of, scarcity

PRACTICE SET 9

Directions: *Read the following passage carefully and answer the following questions.*

Primitive man was probably more concerned with fire as a source of warmth and as a means of cooking food than as a source of light. Before he discovered less laborious ways of making fire, he had to preserve it, and whenever he went on a journey, he carried a firebrand with him. His discovery that the firebrand—from which the torch may very well have developed—could be used for illumination, was probably incidental to the primary purpose of preserving a flame.

Lamps, too, were probably developed by accident. Early man may have had his first conception of a lamp while watching a twig or a fibre burning in the molten fat dropped from a roasting carcass. All he had to do was fashion a vessel to contain fat and float a lighted reed in it. Such lamps, which were made of hallowed stones or sea shells, have persisted in identical form up to quite recent times.

1. Primitive man's most important use for fire was ________.
   (a) to provide warmth (b) to cook food
   (c) to provide light (d) both (a) and (b)
2. The firebrand was used to ________.
   (a) prevent accidents (b) provide light
   (c) scare animals (d) save labour
3. By 'primary' the author means ________.
   (a) primitive (b) fundamental (c) elemental (d) essential.

4. Lamps probably developed through mere __________.
   (a) hazard (b) fate (c) chance (d) planning.
5. Early lamps were made by __________.
   (a) using a reed as a wick in the fat
   (b) letting reed soak the fat
   (c) putting the fat in a shell and lighting it
   (d) floating a reed in a sea-shell

Directions: *Select a word out of the following words which has the OPPOSITE meaning to the following words in question.*

6. Languid
   (a) Smart (b) Energetic (c) Fast (d) Ferocious
7. Stringent
   (a) Magnanimous (b) Lenient (c) Vehement (d) General
8. Alienate
   (a) Gather (b) Identify (c) Assemble (d) Unite
9. Malicious
   (a) Boastful (b) Indifferent (c) Kind (d) Generous
10. Exodus
   (a) Restoration (b) Return (c) Homecoming (d) Influx

Directions: *In the following questions, choose the word which best expresses the meaning of the given word.*

11. Surreptitious
   (a) Mysterious (b) Abstract (c) Secretive (d) Secret
12. Feign
   (a) Elaborate (b) Pretend (c) Drag (d) Deliberate
13. Colossus
   (a) Towering (b) Tall (c) Lofty (d) Huge
14. Sordid
   (a) Harmful (b) Dirty (c) Splendid (d) Dangerous
15. Deft
   (a) Skilful (b) Vigorous (c) Swift (d) Deceitful

Directions: *In each of the following questions, choose the one word which can be substituted for the given phrases.*

16. A person who lives at the same time as another.
   (a) Bellicose (b) Orator (c) Philanthropist
   (d) Cosmopolitan (e) Pacifist
17. A person who regards the whole world as his country.
   (a) Bellicose (b) Orator (c) Philanthropist
   (d) Cosmopolitan (e) Pacifist

18. One who makes an eloquent public speech.
    (a) Bellicose (b) Orator (c) Philanthropist
    (d) Cosmopolitan (e) Pacifist
19. A person who believes in total abolition of war.
    (a) Bellicose (b) Orator (c) Philanthropist
    (d) Cosmopolitan (e) Pacifist
20. A person who is fond of fighting.
    (a) Bellicose (b) Orator (c) Philanthropist
    (d) Cosmopolitan (e) Pacifist

SOLUTIONS WITH EXPLANATIONS

1. (d) both (a) and (b)
2. (b) provide light
    - Fire board can be used as a torch.
3. (d) essential
    - The most important, essential.
4. (c) Chance
    - Lamps were developed by accident.
5. (a) Using a reed as a wick in the fat.
6. (b)
    - Languid: lacking energy, weak.
    - Ferocious: violent.
    - Smart: showing intelligence, good judgement
    - Energetic: Active, Lively
7. (b)
    - Stringent: strict
    - Magnanimous: generous, forgiving
    - Lenient: mild
    - Vehement: showing strong feeling.
    - General: involving many people
8. (b)
    - Alienate: to make someone isolated, estranged, unfriend someone. Conciliate reconcile.
    - Gather: come together
    - Assemble: come together
    - Unite: come together
    - Identify: pin point, single out
9. (d)
    - Malicious: intended to harm somebody.
    - Boastful: showing too much pride in oneself.
    - Indifferent: having no interest
    - Generous: unselfish, liberal, compassionate
    - Kind: sympathetic, helpful
10. (d)
    - Exodus: mass departure of people
    - Homecoming: return to home

- Influx: sudden arrival of large number of people.
- Return: come back
- Restoration: repairing

11. (d)
- Surreptitious: done in secret way, kept secret, clandestine
- Secretive: not disclosing information
- Secret: not known
- Abstract: theoretical, conceptual
- Mysterious: puzzling, strange

12. (b)
- Feign: pretend to feel or be affected by; give false appearance.
- Elaborate: is to describe lengthy
- Drag: pull forcefully
- Deliberate: done intentionally
- Pretend: deceptive appearance

13. (b)
- Colossus: enormous size, gigantic
- Towering: extremely tall
- Lofty: tall
- Tall: more than average height
- Huge: extremely large

14. (b)
- Sordid: dirty; unpleasant, immoral actions.
- Splendid: magnificent.
- Harmful: likely to cause harm
- Dangerous : hazardous

15. (a)
- Deft: skilful and quick in one's movement
- Vigorous: strong, full of energy
- Deceitful: who deceives people, dishonest
- Skilful: artful, deft
- Swift: brisk

16. (c) Wealthy person who gives money and time to make life better.
17. (d) Person who lives and knows different parts of world.
18. (b) Person who makes speeches and is good at it.
19. (e) The belief that it is wrong to use war and settles disputes.
20. (a) Tendency to agree and fight.

Keywords

- Twig: Small branchlet.
- Carcass: Dead body, corpse of animal.
- Fashion a vessel to contain fat and float a lighted reed: Tall thin grass grows on wet areas.

PRACTICE SET 10

Direction: *Read the following passage carefully and answer the questions that follow.*

The public distribution system (PDS), which provides food at low prices, is a subject of vital concern. There is a growing realisation that though India has enough food to feed its masses two square meals a day, the monsters of starvation and food insecurity continue to haunt the poor in our country. Increasing the purchasing power of the poor by providing them with productive employment leading to rising income, and thus good standard of living, is the ultimate objective of the public policy. However, till then, there is a need to provide assured supply of food through a restructured, more efficient, and decentralised PDS. Although the PDS is extensive—it is one of the largest such systems in the world—it has yet to reach the rural poor and the far-off places. It remains an urban phenomenon, with the majority of the rural poor still out of its reach due to lack of economic and physical access. The poorest in the cities and the migrants are left out, for they generally do not possess ration cards. The allocation of PDS supplies in big cities is larger than that in rural areas. In view of such deficiencies in the system, the PDS urgently needs to be streamlined. Also, considering the large food grains production combined with food subsidy on one hand, and the continuing slow starvation and dismal poverty of the rural population on the other, there is a strong case for making PDS target-group-oriented.

The growing salaried class is provided job security, regular income, and social security. It enjoys almost hundred per cent insulation against inflation. These gains of development have not percolated down to the vast majority of our working population. If one compares only the dearness allowance to the employees in the public and private sectors and looks at its growth in the past few years, the rising food subsidy is insignificant to the point of inequity. The food subsidy is a kind of D.A. to the poor, the self-employed, and those in the unorganised sector of the economy. However, what is most unfortunate is that out of the large budget of the so-called food subsidy, the major part of it is administrative cost and wastages. A small portion of the above budget goes to the real consumer and an even lesser portion to the poor who are in real need.

It is true that subsidies should not become a permanent feature, except for the destitute, disabled widows, and the old. It is also true that subsidies often create a psychology of dependence and hence is habit-forming, killing the general initiative of the people. By making PDS target-group-oriented, not only would the poorest and neediest be reached without additional cost, but it will actually cut overall costs incurred on large cities and for better-off localities. When food and food subsidy are limited, the rural and urban poor should have priority in the PDS supplies. The PDS should be closely linked with programmes of employment generation and nutrition improvement.

1. The word 'square' as used in the passage means ________.
   (a) rich (b) sumptuous (c) sufficient
   (d) quality (e) None of these
2. Which of the following words is the same in meaning as 'power' as used in the passage?
   (a) Vigour (b) Energy (c) Influence (d) Capacity
3. What, according to the passage, is the main concern about the PDS?
   (a) It has not been able to develop confidence in people at large.
   (b) It has not been able to utilise the entire food grains stock available
   (c) It has effectively channelised the food grains to all sectors
   (d) It has not been able to provide sufficient food to the poorer section of the society
   (e) None of these
4. What should be an appropriate step to make the PDS effective?
   (a) To make it target-group-oriented
   (b) To increase the amount of good grains per ration card
   (c) To decrease the allotment of food grains to the urban sector
   (d) To reduce administrative cost
   (e) To increase the amount of food grains available for distribution
5. Which of the following, according to the passage, is compared with dearness allowance?
   (a) Food for Work Programme (b) Unemployment allowance
   (c) Food subsidy (d) Procurement price of food grains
   (e) Poverty Alleviation Programme
6. Food subsidy leads to which of the following?
   (a) Sense of insecurity (b) Increased dependence
   (c) Shortage of food grains (d) Decrease in food grains production
   (e) None of these
7. What, according to the passage, would be the outcome of making the PDS target-group-oriented?
   (a) It will abolish the imbalance of urban and rural sectors
   (b) It will remove poverty
   (c) It will give food to the poorest without additional cost
   (d) It will motivate the target group population to work more
8. Which word the same in meaning as 'system' as used in the passage?
   (a) Routine (b) Mechanism (c) Machine
   (d) Procedure (e) Collection
9. Which, according to the passage, consumes the major part of the allocated food subsidy?
   A. Urban population B. High administrative cost C. Wastage
   (a) A only (b) A and B (c) B and C
   (d) B or C (e) A and C

10. What does 'cut', as used in the passage, mean?
    (a) Damage (b) Cease (c) Destroy
    (d) Reduce (e) None of these
11. Which word is the same in meaning as the word 'point'?
    (a) Extent (b) Direct (c) Tip
    (d) Position (e) None of these
12. The author's writing style is __________.
    (a) Simplistic (b) Argumentative (c) Verbose
    (d) Descriptive (e) Analytic

Directions: *Read the following passage carefully and answer the questions given below it.*

The crowd surged forward through the narrow streets of Paris. There was a clatter of shutters being closed hastily by trembling hands—the citizens of Paris knew that once the fury of the people was excited, there was no telling what they might do. They came to an old house which had a workshop on the ground floor. A head popped out of the door to see what it was all about. 'Get him! Get Thimonier! Smash his devilish machines!', yelled the crowd.

They found the workshop without its owner. M.Thimonier had escaped through the back door. Now, the fury of the demonstrators turned against the machines that were standing in the shop, ready to be delivered to buyers. They were systematically broken up and destroyed—dozens of them. Only when the last wheel and spindle had been trampled underfoot did the infuriated crowd recover their senses.

'That is the end of Monsieur Thornier and his sewing machines,' they said to one another, and went home satisfied. Perhaps now they would find work, for they were all unemployed tailors and seamstresses who believed that their livelihood was threatened by that new invention.

13. The passage throws light on __________.
    (a) why inventions should be avoided altogether
    (b) how a well-meant invention can be misunderstood
    (c) what mischief an inventor can do to ordinary people
    (d) how dangerous an invention can prove to be
14. The crowd was protesting against __________.
    (a) the closing of workshops (b) the misdoings of Thimonier
    (c) the newly-invented sewing machine
    (d) Thimonier keeping the invention a secret
15. The aim of the crowd was to __________.
    (a) kill Thimonier (b) drive Thimonier away
    (c) bring discredit to Thimonier (d) destroy the sewing machines
16. The people thought that __________.
    (a) their lives were in danger (b) Thimonier was mad

(c) the sewing machine was dangerous
(d) Thimonier was depriving them of their livelihood

17. Shutters were being closed hastily because the shopkeepers ________.
(a) wanted to attack the crowd (b) wanted to protect Thimonier
(c) feared their shops would be invaded
(d) wanted to show their solidarity with the crowd

Directions: *Pick out the most appropriate word from the given words to fill in the blank to make the sentence meaningfully complete.*

18. The improvement made by the changes in the system was ________ and did not warrant the large expenses.
(a) large (b) small (c) minute
(d) marginal (e) uncertain
19. The man who is ________ hesitating which of the two things he will do first, will do neither.
(a) persistently (b) constantly (c) insistently
(d) consistently (e) perpetually
20. He is too ________ to be deceived easily.
(a) strong (b) modern (c) kind
(d) honest (e) intelligent
21. In ________ of the recommendation's the Board had established a counter to entertain the complaints from consumers.
(a) adherence (b) relation (c) pursuance
(d) accordance (e) relevance

Directions: *In each of the following passages, there are blanks, each of which has been numbered. These numbers are printed below the passage and against each, some words are suggested, one of which fits the blank appropriately. Find out the appropriate words.*

Many parents greet their children's teenage years with needless dread. While teens ___(22)___ assault us with heavy-metal music, ___(23)___ outlandish clothes, and spend all ___(24)___ time with friends, such behaviour ___(25)___ adds up to full-scale revolt. Teenage ___(26)___, according to psychologist Laurence Steinberg, has been ___(27)___ exaggerated. 'The ___(28)___ that teenagers inevitably rebel is a ___(29)___ that has the potential for great family ___(30)___', says Sociologist Sanford Dornbusch. He believes the notion can ___(31)___ communication during this critical time for parents to influence youngsters.

22. (a) can (b) must (c) may (d) should
23. (a) show (b) dress (c) put (d) flaunt
24. (a) her (b) his (c) their (d) our
25. (a) sporadically (b) always (c) infrequently (d) scarcely

26. (a) rebellion	(b) subversion	(c) mania	(d) revolution
27. (a) always	(b) never	(c) greatly	(d) hardly
28. (a) complaint	(b) surmise	(c) accusation	(d) idea
29. (a) myth	(b) story	(c) fact	(d) reality
30. (a) ruin	(b) downfall	(c) harm	(d) defeat
31. (a) destroy	(b) suffocate	(c) damage	(d) injure

Directions: *In each of the following questions, find out which part of the sentence has an error: If there is no mistake, the answer is 'No error'.*

32. The famous Dr. Chandra (a)/is only dentist (b)/in our village. (c)/No error (d)
33. This candidate lacks (a)/an experience (b)/otherwise he is well qualified. (c)/ No error (d)
34. A person I met (a)/in the theatre (b)/was the playwright himself. (c)/No error (d)
35. The war of Mahabharata (a)/is the full-length illustration (b)/of a righteous war. (c)/No error (d)

SOLUTIONS WITH EXPLANATIONS

1. (c) Sufficient: enough to meet needs of situation; providing as much as needed, i.e. two meals a day.
2. (d) Purchasing power: capacity
3. (b) It has not been able to utilize the entire food grains stack available.
4. (d) To reduce administrative cost.
5. (c) Food subsidy.
6. (b) Increased dependence.
7. (c) • It will give food to the poorest without additional cost.
   • Food subsidy: money paid by government to keep the price low.
8. (d) procedure.
9. (c) B and C
10. (d) reduce
11. (a) Extent
12. (b) argumentative
13. (b) How a well-meant invention can be misunderstood.
14. (c) the newly invented sewing machine
15. (a) Kill Thimonier, i.e. they were looking for Thimonier did not get so destroyed swing machine.
16. (d) Thimonier was depriving them of their livelihood.
17. (c) Feared their shops would be invaded
18. (d) • Minute: small
    • Marginal: not very important, small.

19. (a) • Persistently: existing for longer than usual time.
 • Constantly: happening all the time.
 • Insistently: persistent.
 • Perpetually: continuing for ever lasting.
20. (e) • Deceived: to make someone believe something that is not true.
21. (c) • Adherence: to act as per rule.
 • Pursuance: try to get, do something over a period of time, involved in activity.
 • Accordance: agreement, congruence
 • Relevance: in relation to the matter in hand.
22. (c) May: possibility
23. (d) • Show: allow to be seen.
 • Flaunt: show in such a way that people notice.
24. (c) their
25. (b) • Sporadically: not regularly, infrequent.
 • Always: constantly
 • Infrequently: rarely
 • Scarcely: barely
26. (a) • Rebellion: open opposition
 • Subversion: systematic attempt
 • Mania: mental illness where person is over excited or emotional.
 • Revolution: violent attempt to end a rule government.
27. (c)
28. (d) • Complaint: objection
 • Surmise: supposition, idea based on scantly evidence
 • Accusation: a claim that someone has done
 • Idea: illegal wrong thing
29. (d) • Myth: story believed by many people but not true
 • Fact: someone had done
 • Reality: truth
 • Fact: actuality
30. (a) • Ruin: destroy
 • Downfall: decline
 • Harm: hurt
 • Defeat: loss
31. (b) • Destroy: state of complete destruction.
 • Injure: harm, damage something.
 • Suffocate: stifle, choke
32. (b) 'The only' is right in this sentence.
33. (b) Remove 'an' (wrong)
34. (a) 'The person' is right
35. (a) 'Of the Mahabharata' is wright.

PRACTICE SET 11

Directions: *Read the following passage carefully and answer the questions that follow.*

Democratic societies from the earliest times have expected their governments to protect the weak against the strong. No '*era of good feeling*' can justify discharging of police force or giving up the idea of public control over concentrated private wealth. On the other hand, it is obvious that a spirit of self-denial and moderation on the part of those who hold economic power will greatly soften the demand for absolute equality. Men are more interested in freedom and security than in an equal distribution of wealth. The extent to which the government must interfere with business, therefore, it is not exactly measured by which economic power is concentrated into a few hands. The required degree of government interference depends mainly on whether economic powers are oppressively used and on the necessity of keeping economic factors in a '*tolerable state of balance*'.

With the necessity of meeting all these dangers and threats to liberty the powers of the government are unavoidably increased, whichever political party may be in office. The growth of the government is a necessary result of the growth of technology and of the problems that go with the use of machines and science. Since the government in our nation must take on more power to meet its problems, there is no way to preserve freedom except by making democracy more powerful.

1. The advent of science and technology has increased the ________.
   (a) freedom of people (b) tyranny of the political parties
   (c) powers of the government (d) chances of economic inequality
2. A spirit of moderation on the economically sound people would make them less privileged ________.
   (a) unhappy with the rich people
   (b) more interested in freedom and security
   (c) unhappy with their lot
   (d) clamour less for absolute equality
3. The growth of the government is necessitated to ________.
   (a) make the rich and poor unhappy
   (b) curb the accumulation of wealth in a few hands
   (c) monitor science and technology
   (d) deploy the police force wisely
4. 'Era of good feeling' in sentence 2 refers to ________.
   (a) time of prosperity (b) time of adversity
   (c) time without government (d) time of police atrocities
5. 'Tolerable state of balance' in the last sentence of the first paragraph may mean ________.
   (a) an inadequate level of police force
   (b) a reasonable level of economic inequality

(c) a reasonable amount of government interference
(d) a reasonable check on economic power

Directions: *In the following the questions, choose the word which best expresses the meaning of the underlined word.*

6. The old man was fond of giving homilies whenever we went to him with a problem.
   (a) Alternatives (b) Advice (c) Suggestions (d) Sermon
7. If you want the quality of your writing to improve, then avoid redundant words.
   (a) Unwilling (b) Mistaken (c) Wrong (d) Unnecessary
8. The accident occurred due to his lapse.
   (a) Haste (b) Error (c) Ignorance (d) Carelessness
9. He tried to cajole her, but it was in vain.
   (a) Enjoin (b) Coax (c) Rejoice (d) Inspire
10. He gave such a vivid description of the house we wanted to rent that we did not have to look at it.
   (a) Simple (b) Detailed (c) Clear (d) Confused

Directions: *In the following the questions, choose the word which is closest to the opposite in meaning to the underlined word.*

11. He is a very timid person.
   (a) Dashing (b) Outgoing (c) Bold (d) Chivalrous
12. The treaty was ratified by the heads of states.
   (a) Set aside (b) Unsettled (c) Destroyed (d) Annulled
13. They had an insipid conversation.
   (a) Curious (b) Loud (c) Argumentative (b) Lively
14. Her impetuous behaviour was attributed to her upbringing.
   (a) Poised (b) rash (c) Quiet and gentle (d) Sluggish
15. Silence in this place is mandatory.
   (a) Optional (b) Compulsory (c) Imperative (d) Irritating

Directions: *In each of the following questions, choose the one word which can be substituted for the given phrases.*

16. A person who does not believe in any religion.
   (a) Philatelist (d) Rationalist (c) Atheist (d) Pagan
17. To cause troops to spread out in readiness for battle.
   (a) Align (b) Collocate (c) Deploy (d) Disperse
18. The policy of extending a country's empire and influence.
   (a) Imperialism (b) Capitalism
   (c) Internationalism (d) Communism
19. A post without remuneration.
   (a) Voluntary (b) Sinecure (c) Honorary (d) Involuntary

20. Opposed to great or sudden change.
    (a) Static (b) Revolutionary
    (c) Conservative (d) Evolutionary

SOLUTIONS WITH EXPLANATIONS

1. (c) Powers of the government
2. (d) • Clamour less for absolute equality
   • Clamour: Shout loudly.
3. (c) Monitor science and technology
4. (a) Time of prosperity
5. (c) A reasonable amount of government interference
6. (d) • Homilies: religious discourse for spiritual edification, intellectual improvement
   • Advice: guidance
   • Suggestions: plan, idea
   • Sermon: talk on religious, moral subjects
   • Alternatives: choices
7. (d) • Redundant: no longer needed, superficies
   • Unwilling: not ready
   • Unnecessary: not required
   • Mistaken: incorrect
   • Wrong: mistaken
8. (c) • Lapse: temporarily failure of concentration, memory judgement.
   • Ignorance: lack of knowledge and judgement, small interval, could not know what to do.
   • Carelessness: who is not careful?
   • Haste: hurry
   • Error: mistake
9. (b) • Cajole: persuade someone by loaning
   • Enjoin: instruct to do something
   • Coax: persuade gently
   • Rejoice: show great joy
   • Inspire: motivate others to do something.
10. (c) • Vivid: clear images in mind producing powerful feelings, lifelike
   • Simple: uncomplicated
   • Detailed: complete
   • Clear: lucid, see through
   • Confused: unable to think clearly
11. (c) • Timid: showing lack of courage
   • Bold: not afraid of danger
   • Chivalrous: courteous

- Dashing: confident, stylish, debonair
- Outgoing: extrovert

12. (d)
- Ratified: to sign; give formal consent
- Unsettled: lack stability
- Annulled: declare invalid, nullify
- Destroyed: demolish
- Set aside: put aside

13. (d)
- Insipid: lacking flavour, lacking interest, dull, boring
- Curious: eager to know
- Lively: very active, energetic
- Loud: noisy
- Argumentative: quarrelsome

14. (c)
- Impetuous: the way the child is raised, rash, hasty.
- Poised: composed
- Quiet and gentle: silent
- Rash: hasty, reckless
- Sluggish : slow moving

15. (a)
- Mandatory: compulsory
- Imperative: important crucial
- Optional: non compulsory
- Compulsory: forced
- Irritating: annoying

16. (c)
- Philatelist: stamp collector
- Rationalist: someone who believes action are based on practical reasons and knowledge.
- Pagan: person holding religious belief
- Atheist: a person who does not believe in God

17. (c)
- Align: arrange in a straight line
- Collocate: arrange in a place
- Deploy: move troops into position
- Disperse: scatter

18. (a)
- Imperialism: policy of extending country's empire and influence
- Capitalism: economic and political system where country's trade are controlled by private, where for profit
- Communism: state ownership
- Internationalism: neutralist

19. (c)
- Voluntary: undertaken one owns free will
- Sinecure: office providing little work with salary
- Honorary: holding a person without payment
- Involuntary: done without will

20. (c)
- Conservative: traditional values
- Evolutionary: gradual process of change

- Revolutionary: extremist
- Static: not moving

PRACTICE SET 12

Directions: *Read the following passage carefully and answer the questions that follow.*

The strength of the electronics industry in Japan is the Japanese ability to organise production and marketing rather than their achievements in original research. The British are generally recognised as a far more inventive collection of individuals, but never seem able to exploit what they invent. There are many examples, from the TSR Z Hovercraft, high-speed train, and Sinclair Scooter to the Triumph, BSA and Norton Motorcycle, which all prove this sad rule. The Japanese were able to exploit their strengths in marketing and development many years ago, and their success was at first either not understood in the West or was dismissed as something which could have been produced only at their low price. They were sold because they were cheap copies of other people's ideas churned out of a workhouse which was dedicated to hard grind above all else. (Genpact, 2014)

1. It is evident from the passage that the strength of a country's industry depends upon ______________.
   (a) original research (b) international cooperation
   (c) dedicated workforce (d) electronic development
2. The sad rule mentioned in this passage refers to ______________.
   (a) the inability of the Japanese to be inventive like the British
   (b) the inability of the British to be industrious like the Japanese
   (c) the lack of variety in Japanese inventions
   (d) the poor marketing ability of the British
3. The TSR Z Hovercraft, high speed train, Sinclair scooter, etc., are the symbols of ______________.
   (a) Japanese success (b) British failure
   (c) British success (d) Japanese failure
4. According to the passage, prosperity in industry depends upon ________.
   (a) productivity (b) inventiveness
   (c) marketing ability (d) official patronage
5. The main theme of this passage is ______________.
   (a) electronic industry in Japan
   (b) industrial comparison between Japan and the Britain
   (c) the role of marketing efficiency in industrial prosperity
   (d) the importance of original research in industry

Directions: *Fill in the blanks with the correct option.* (HCL 2012)

6. We are not in a position to do __________ we promised to do.

(a) all thing (b) the whole (c) all (d) it all

7. She will no doubt feed the cat when she _________.
   (a) will come (b) would come (c) will have come (d) comes
8. She bakes her own bread so they all eat ______ bread at lunch
   (a) homemade (b) house making
   (c) making at home (d) made home
9. It is raining ______ she wants to go out.
   (a) although (b) unless (c) and yet (d) since
10. _________ what he said was ironical.
   (a) Most (b) The most (c) Almost (d) Most of

Directions: *One sentence has been divided into four parts. One part has an error. Identify the part that contains the error.* (Genpact, 2013)

11. (a) As he is (b) very short-tempered
   (c) his colleagues (d) dislike to speak to him.
12. (a) The rain was (b) so continual
   (c) that people were forced (d) to stay indoors.
13. (a) Unless you do not collect (b) the quota of your ration today
   (c) you will forfeit your claim (d) at least for this week.
   (e) No error
14. (a) He made me to repeat his instructions
   (b) to make sure that I understand (c) what I was supposed to do
   (d) after he had gone. (e) No error
15. (a) Meerabai was sent away from her home
   (b) because she spend most of the time
   (c) in the company of holy men. (d) No error

Directions: *In each of the following questions, a sentence has been given in active (or passive) voice. Out of the four alternatives suggested, select the one which best expresses the same sentence in passive (or active) voice.*

16. Mona was writing a letter to her father.
   (a) A letter was written to her father by Mona.
   (b) A letter has been written to her father by Mona.
   (c) A letter was being written by Mona to her father.
   (d) A letter was written by Mona to her father.
17. He teaches us grammar.
   (a) Grammar is taught to us by him.
   (b) We are being taught Grammar by him.
   (c) Grammar is being taught us by him.
   (d) We are taught Grammar by him.
18. After driving professor Kumar to the museum, she dropped him at his hotel.

(a) After being driven to the museum, Professor Kumar was dropped at his hotel.
(b) Professor Kumar was being driven dropped at his hotel.
(c) After she had driven Professor Kumar to the museum, she had dropped him at his hotel.
(d) After she was driven Professor Kumar to the museum, she had dropped him at his hotel.

19. I remember my sister taking me to the museum.
    (a) I remember I was taken to the museum by my sister.
    (b) I remember being taken to the museum by my sister.
    (c) I remember myself being taken to the museum by my sister.
    (d) I remember taken to the museum by my sister.
20. They greet me cheerfully every morning.
    (a) Every morning I was greeted cheerfully
    (b) I am greeted cheerfully by them every morning.
    (c) I am being greeted cheerfully by them every morning.
    (d) Cheerful greeting is done by them every morning to me.

SOLUTIONS WITH EXPLANATIONS

1. (c) Japan were able to use their marketing and development skill as they had dedicated (devoted, committed) workforce which us didn't have.
2. (d) British ere were innovative but did not exploit their innovativeness through their marketing starting.
3. (b) • TSR Z hovercraft: vehicle that moves above the surface.
   • All these are products of British ere and they invented it but could not market it.
4. (c) Apart from production you need to have marketing ability.
5. (c) Importance of marketing ability.
6. (c) We can't do all things that we had promised before.
7. (d) Future tense: she is not present now, after she comes she will feed the cat.
8. (a) • Bakes: cook in oven
   • Baking takes place at home
9. (c) She wants to go out even though it is raining
10. (c) • Ironical: using words that is opposite of what you really think.
    • Almost: very nearly to all
    • Most of: all part
11. (d) dislike to speak to him: disliked
12. (b) • so continual: continuous, continuing indefinitely
    • Continual: recurring in steady usually rapid succession
13. (a) • Unless: if condition (until, unless)

- Forfeit: something that is lost/given up

14. (b) Understood: (agreed upon) to know the meaning, i.e. you agree on the instruction.
15. (b)
    - spend: (future)
    - Spent: (past tense) already spent
16. (c)
    - Doer: action – receiver of action
    - When the subject 'does' or acts upon the verb, the sentence is in active voice
    - The subject in 'acted upon' what happens to subject is called passive voice
17. (d)
    - Active – passive convert
    - Active subject verb object
18. (a)
    - Something happens to the subject
    - Present continuous
    - Museum not mentioned in option B
19. (b) Change passive subject to active direct object
20. (b) Active Voice to Passive Voice

PRACTICE SET 13

Directions: *In the following the questions choose the word which best expresses the meaning of the given word.*

1. Corpulent (IBPS, 2011)
   (a) Lean (b) Gaunt (c) Emaciated (d) Obese
2. Brief (IBPS, 2011)
   (a) Limited (b) Small (c) Little (d) Short
3. Embezzle (Mindtree, 2012)
   (a) Misappropriate (b) Balance (c) Remunerate (d) Clear
4. Vent (Mindtree, 2012)
   (a) Opening (b) Stodge (c) End (d) Past tense of go
5. August (Vedanta)
   (a) Common (b) Ridiculous (c) Dignified (d) Petty

Directions: *Choose the correct answer for each question.*

6. He made his escape by jumping ______ a window and jumping ______ a waiting car.
   (a) over/into (b) between/into (c) out of/between (d) out of/into
7. To get to the marketing department, you have to go ______ those stairs and then ______ the corridor to the end. (L&T, 2012)
   (a) up/along (b) over/into (c) between/into (d) out of/into
8. I saw something about it ______ television.
   (a) in (b) on (c) at (d) through (e) with

9. I could not get in ______ the door so I had to climb ______ a window.
   (a) through/in (b) between/into (c) out of/between (d) out of/into
10. She took the key _____ her pocket and put it _____ the lock. (IBPS, 2012)
    (a) over/into (b) between/into (c) out of/in (d) by/on

Directions: *In the following questions, choose the word which is the exact opposite meaning of the given word.*

11. Enormous (Genpact, 2011)
    (a) Soft (b) Average (c) Tiny (d) Weak
12. Commissioned (Infosys, 2011)
    (a) Started (b) Closed (c) Finished (d) Terminated
13. Artificial (IBPS, 2012)
    (a) Red (b) Natural (c) Truthful (d) Solid
14. Exodus (Infosys, 2012)
    (a) Influx (b) Home-coming (c) Return (d) Restoration

Directions: *In each of the following questions, a sentence has been given in active (or passive) voice. Out of the four alternatives suggested, select the one which best expresses the same sentence in passive (or active) voice.*

15. After driving professor Kumar to the museum she dropped him at his hotel. (IBPS, 2012)
    (a) After being driven to the museum, Professor Kumar was dropped at his hotel.
    (b) Professor Kumar was being driven dropped at his hotel.
    (c) After she had driven Professor Kumar to the museum she had dropped him at his hotel.
    (d) After she was driven Professor Kumar to the museum she had dropped him at his hotel.
16. I remember my sister taking me to the museum. (IBPS, 2013)
    (a) I remember I was taken to the museum by my sister.
    (b) I remember being taken to the museum by my sister.
    (c) I remember myself being taken to the museum by my sister.
    (d) I remember taken to the museum by my sister.
17. Who is creating this mess? (L&T, 2014)
    (a) Who has been created this mess?
    (b) By whom has this mess been created?
    (c) By whom this mess is being created?
    (d) By whom is this mess being created?

Directions: *In each question, an incomplete statement (stem) followed by fillers is given. Pick out the most appropriate one which can complete the incomplete stem correctly and meaningfully.*

18. Despite his best efforts to conceal his anger _________. (TCS, 2011)

(a) we could detect that he was very happy
(b) he failed to give us an impression of his agony
(c) he succeeded in camouflaging his emotions
(d) people came to know that he was annoyed

19. Even if it rains I shall come means _________. (TCS, 2010)
    (a) if I come it will not rain
    (b) if it rains I shall not come
    (c) I will certainly come whether it rains or not
    (d) whenever there is rain I shall come
20. His appearance is unsmiling but _________. (IBPS, 2013)
    (a) his heart is full of compassion for others
    (b) he looks very serious on most occasions
    (c) people are afraid of him
    (d) he is uncompromising on matters of task performance

SOLUTIONS WITH EXPLANATIONS

1. (d) CORPULENT: OBESE, BULKY
    - Lean: Thin/Bend
    - Gaunt: Very Thin
    - Emaciated: Feeble/Weak/to waste away physically
    - Obese: Very fat
2. (d) BRIEF: short duration, not long lasting
    - Limited: restricted in size, finite
    - Small: few numbers of size
    - Little: small in size
    - Short: period
3. (a) EMBEZZLE: steal money, misappropriate/belonging to organisation for which one works.
    - Misappropriate
    - Balance
    - Remunerate: pay someone for work done
    - Clear
4. (a) VENT: to allow gas to though an opening, to express in angry manner
    - Opening
    - Stodge: food that is heavy, high in carbohydrates
    - End: the point at which something no longer continues.
    - Past tense of go: gone
5. (c) AUGUST: respected, distinguished, impressive quality
    - Common
    - Ridiculous: Extremely silly
    - Dignified

- Petty: little important, trivial

6. (d) Have to move out of a window & go inside a car
7. (a) Climb up the stairs, same direction along the corridor
8. (b)
   - In: within something
   - On: on the surface (television is noun)
9. (a) Go inside the door (through), inside a window
10. (c) out of/in
11. (c) ENORMOUS: Very large in size
12. (d)
    - COMMISSIONED: To bring into working condition, group of people given official job to do something.
    - Terminated: Disqualify, Out of working order
13. (b) Natural
14. (a)
    - EXODUS: Mass departure of people
    - Influx: Arrival of large number of people.
    - Home coming: Arrival of 1-2 persons.
    - Return: come back
    - Restoration : Repair
15. (a)
    - Passive Voice to Active Voice Conversion
    - Driving becomes being taken
    - Kumar is subject; She is object
16. (b)
    - Passive Voice to Active Voice Conversion
    - Taking becomes being taken
    - I: subject, Sister: object, Taking: verb
17. (d)
    - Active Voice to Passive Voice Conversion
    - Creating becomes being created
    - Is: auxiliary verb (option d)
18. (d)
    - Conceal: to hide, keep secret
    - He tried to hide his anger but people came to know he was annoyed.
    - He could definitely come.
20. (a)
    - Unsmiling: serious
    - b, c, d give the same meaning, so they are eliminated

PRACTICE SET 14

Directions: *Read the passage and answer the questions that follow. (CoCubes)*

In the mid-80s, while travelling with friends along Italy's Amalfi coast, I observed a seagull gliding above the rocky cliffs. There was nothing particularly unusual about the seagull but on this occasion, I noted with some surprise that it travelled hundreds of yards with little effort. A mere tilt of its wing and a slight shift of its body took it up or down, right or left. But for expended body heat, minor muscle exertion, a turn of the head, the distance covered by the gull was accomplished with little or no waste.

At the same time, I remembered the camera footage of the space shuttle launching from Cape Canaveral, Florida, and the great plume of smoke exhausted by it. Human waste, to a certain extent, defines human evolution. We have become what we are in accordance with our waste and what we waste has prevented us from evolving to where we could be without waste.

Many a tale has been told of ascetics who eat one meal a day, drink a glass of milk several times a month or eat only leaves on several occasions. Whether true stories or not, such tales do focus on the basic inadequacies of the human digestive system and suggest it can be improved upon by 'conscious' effort and conditioning.

Beyond this and within the reach of the average man are day-to-day episodes of forgetfulness, anger, and dishonesty that may constitute wasted energy which, if made available to us, would assist a personal and collective rise in evolutionary possibilities. Waste in relation to man refers to all energy-baring quantities which pass by us or through us without our exerting a controlled intention over them.

1. What did the author find unusual about the seagull?
   (a) It soared to different heights effortlessly
   (b) It could move up or down with a little tilt of its wing to either direction
   (c) It was able to glide great distances without any pollution or wastage of energy
   (d) None of these
2. What did the blast-off of the space shuttle remind the author about?
   (a) Human excess is expendable
   (b) Whenever the space shuttle blasts off, it results in a lot of smoke
   (c) Our digestive systems have not evolved sufficiently and are too much for our planet to hold
   (d) Our waste has hampered our becoming better beings
3. How can we evolve as better humans?
   (a) Control our digestive systems and develop minimal waste
   (b) Contain all unnecessary and negative thoughts and emotions as these too expend energy
   (c) Become angry only when provoked
   (d) Only eat one meal a day and drink a glass of milk occasionally

Directions: *In each of the following questions, out of the given alternatives, choose the one which is closest in meaning to the given word.*

4. Badger (InfoTech, 2011)
   (a) Attempt (b) Convince (c) Pester (d) Persuade
5. Cautiously (InfoTech, 2011)
   (a) Genuinely (b) Carefully (c) Secretly (d) Somewhat
6. Neutra (Mindtree, 2013)
   (a) Unbiased (b) Non-aligned (c) Undecided (d) Indifferent

7. Shallow (Mindtree, 2013)
   (a) Artificial (b) Superficial (c) Foolish (d) Worthless

Directions: *The sentences below are in direct or indirect speech and are followed by four alternatives of the opposite form of narration to that of the sentence. Choose the correct alternative.*

8. They said, 'He deserved our thanks for all he has done'. (CoCubes)
   (a) They said that he deserved their thanks for all he had done
   (b) They said that he had been deserving their thanks for all he had done
   (c) They said that he has deserved their thanks for all he has done
   (d) They said that he was deserving their thanks for all he was doing
9. I told him that he was not working hard. [Oracle, 2011(2)]
   (a) I said to him, 'You are not working hard'
   (b) I told to him, 'You are not working hard'
   (c) I said, 'You are not working hard'
   (d) I said to him, 'He is not working hard'

Directions: *For the following questions, find a word that is opposite (antonym) to the capitalised word.* (IBM, 2012)

10. Sentient
    (a) Abnormal (b) Irregular (c) Unconscious (d) Elemental
11. Prodigious
    (a) Implicit (b) Constant (c) Premature (d) Slight
12. Pristine
    (a) Ruthless (b) Seductive (c) Contaminated (d) Coarse

Directions: *In questions below, each passage consists of six sentences. The first and sixth sentences are given in the beginning. The middle four sentences in each have been removed and jumbled up. These are labelled as P, Q, R, and S. Find out the proper order for the four sentences.* (Oracle, 2011)

13. S1: The cooperative system of doing business is a good way of encouraging ordinary workers to work hard.
    P: If the society is to be well-run, it is necessary to prevent insincere officials being elected to the committee which is responsible for the running of business.
    Q: They get this from experienced and professional workers who are not only familiar with the cooperative system, but also with the efficient method of doing business.
    R: To a large extent, many cooperative societies need advice and guidance.
    S: The capital necessary to start a business venture is obtained by the workers' contributions.

S6: The main object is to maintain the interest of every member of the society and to ensure that the members participate actively in the projects of society.

The proper sequence should be:

(a) SQPR (b) PQSR (c) SRQP (d) PSRQ

14. S1: Ants eat worms, centipedes, and spiders.

P: They are usually much quicker than the ant itself.

Q: Nevertheless, these animals do not make easy game for ants.

R: Besides, they have an extraordinary number of ways of escaping.

S: They also eat larvae and insect adults such as flies, moths, and spring tails.

S6: Some jump, and some give out a pungent, repellent substance.

The proper sequence should be:

(a) SQPR (b) SPRQ (c) SQRP (d) SRQP

15. S1: Hungary, with a population of about 10 million, lies between Czechoslovakia to the North and Yugoslavia to the South.

P: Here, a great deal of grain is grown.

Q: In recent years, however, progress has also been made in the field of industrialization.

R: Most of this country consists of an extremely fertile plain, through which the river Danube flows.

S: In addition to grain, the plain produces potatoes, sugar, wine, and livestock.

S6: The new industries derive mainly from agricultural production.

The proper sequence should be:

(a) QRSP (b) RPSQ (c) PRSQ (d) RQSP

16. S1: A gentleman who lived alone always had two plates placed on the table at dinner time.

P: One day just as he sat down to dine, the cat rushed into the room.

Q: One plate was for himself and other was for his cat.

R: She drooped a mouse into her own plate and another into her master's plate.

S: He used to give the cat a piece of meat from his own plate.

S6: In this way, the cat showed her gratitude to her master.

The proper sequence should be:

(a) QSPR (b) PSRQ (c) QRSP (d) RPQS

17. S1: Satyajit Ray made several films for children.

P: Later, film makers have followed his lead.

Q: Today, other nations are making children's films in a big way.

R: This was at a time when no director considered children as a potential audience.

S: Ray was, thus, a pioneer in the field.

S6: But today, few think of Ray as a maker of children's films.

The proper sequence should be:

(a) PSRQ (b) RSQP (c) RSPQ (d) SQRP

Directions: *Fill in the blanks with appropriate words.*

18. The truth is that in a highly capital-intensive business _______ deep pockets, domestic civil aviation is _______ undercapitalised. (Tata Motors, 2014)
    (a) ascertaining, highly (b) requiring, woefully
    (c) sustaining, alarmingly (d) balancing, astonishingly
19. Time has now come for all agencies working in the development sector to launch a multi-pronged _________ to _________ malnutrition. (Tata Motors, 2014)
    (a) system, abjure (b) weapon, annihilate
    (c) policy, deviate (d) strategy, eradicate
20. Fate smiles _________ those who untiringly grapple with stark realities of life. (Wipro, 2014)
    (a) with (b) over (c) on (d) round

SOLUTIONS WITH EXPLANATIONS

1. (a) It soared to different heights effortlessly.
2. (d) • Comparison between smoke & human waste.
   • What we waste has prevented us from becoming good human being.
3. (b) Use of times energy & effort towards particular purpose which is unnecessary.
4. (c) BADGER: to bother someone, annoy someone with comments.
   • Attempt: Try, make effort
   • Convince: to make someone believe
   • Pester: Trouble or annoy someone with frequent interruptions
   • Persuade: plead, convince someone to agree
5. (b) CAUTIOUSLY: careful about risk, danger
   • Cautious: Adjective, cautiously becomes adverb
   • Genuinely: authentically
   • Carefully: cautiously
   • Secretly: confidentially
   • Somewhat: kind of
6. (a) NEUTRA: Impartial
   • Unbiased: not showing unfair tendency, fair
   • Non-aligned: not in straight line
   • Undecided: unsure
   • Indifferent: not concerned
7. (b) SHALLOW: very little depth

- Artificial
- Superficial: outward, close to surface
- Foolish
- Worthless: of no use

8. (a) Some work is done & is successful
9. (a)
   - A: Personally saying to a single person (told)
   - C: to whom?
   - D: He: You
   - Option A is more appropriate than B & C
10. (c) SENTIENT: Responsive, conscious of senses (see, hear, smell taste)
    - Elemental: Basic, Important
    - Abnormal: unusual
    - Irregular: uneven, not following as usual
    - Unconscious: senseless
11. (a) PRODIGIOUS: very big in size, huge
    - Implicit: Tacit, unspoken, implied, not directly expressed.
    - Constant
    - Premature : born before normal time, earlier than usual
    - Slight: small, not considerable
12. (c) PRISTINE: in perfect condition, completely clear, neat
    - ruthless: cruel
    - Seductive: attractive
    - Contaminated: impure
    - Coarse: inferior quality
13. (a)
    - Option S becomes the qualifier (main subject) because the sentence is talking about money to start a business by workers contribution.
    - Option Q: They refers to the workers and their contribution.
    - Option P is talking about the type of worker (unprofessional workers)
14. (a)
    - Option S becomes the qualifier (main subject) because the sentence is talking about what ants eats.
    - Option Q continuation of Option S because it is talking about the animals that ant eats and what they can do to defend themselves.
    - Option P comes after Q because it explains why animals or not easy games for ants.
15. (b)
    - Option R becomes the qualifier (main subject) because the sentence is talking about countries having extremely fertile plain.
    - Option P comes after R because in that area grain is grown.
    - Sentence S comes after P because it explains additional items that is produced in that area.
16. (a)
    - Option Q becomes the qualifier (main subject) because the sentence is talking about the two plates.
    - Option S comes after Q because it explains what is given to that plate.

- Option P comes after S

17. (c) • Option R becomes the qualifier (main subject) because the sentence is talking about a time where no children films were made.
   - Option S comes after R because Ray was the first one to develop the new idea to make children films.
   - Option P follows Option S because other film makers started to produce such films.
18. (b) Requiring, woefully: not at all utilized
19. (d) • system, abjure: reject formally
   - weapon, annihilate: destroy completely
   - policy, deviate: different from what expected
   - strategy, eradicate: remove completely
20. (c) on

Keywords

- Seagull: large bird found near ocean.
- Rocky cliffs: steep surface of rock.
- Expended: use the time, energy and effort for a particular purpose.
- Plume: smoke rises into air.
- Ascetics: simple way of leaving.

PRACTICE SET 15

Directions: *Read the passages given below and answer the questions that follow.*

Passage 1

Growing up in Atlanta during the heyday of the city's baseball team, the Atlanta Braves, gave me a unique perspective of America's national pastime. Witnessing the team and the city win a World Series title in 1996 forever connected my destiny with that of professional baseball; wherever I might be after that point in time, I will always remember the joy and emotion that I was filled with on that day. There are some who denigrate the sport because it does not appear to incorporate a traditional sporting skill set, but it is baseball's unique nature that makes it remarkable. Instead of requiring athletes to run for extended lengths of time, like so many traditional forms of sport, baseball is an exercise in skill and power, one that combines the precision of sports like golf or archery with the pure brawn of sports like weightlifting or the Olympic hammer throw. It is this distinct characteristic of combination that gives baseball its intrigue and singularity, and to those critics who belittle the athletes themselves, I must ask, 'Have you ever played baseball at a competitive level?' While the players themselves make their jobs look incredibly easy, it is only because they have both been born with incredible gifts and trained for their entire lifetimes to develop their skills. Five minutes spent competing against baseball's best would convince any naysayer of the sport's true legitimacy.

Passage 2

The history of American sports is a long and illustrious one, but it is truly foolish to consider professional baseball its 'national pastime'. Baseball is not only not America's national pastime, it should not even be considered a true athletic competition. If the sight of an entire field filled with bloated, steroid-using meatheads is not enough to convince you of its invalidity as a true sport, consider the simple nature of the competition. Nine people stand around an enormous grass field for four hours at a time, barely even breaking a sweat. Over the course of the 'competition', the average player will run a maximum distance of less than a single mile, and spend more than 95 per cent of their time completely uninvolved in the current activity. This is not a sport. A sport is an activity that requires an athlete's focus, determination, strength, endurance, and skill for an extended period of time.

It is certainly no easy thing to be a professional baseball player. But the mere fact that something is difficult does not qualify it as a sport. After all, would training to write your name as many times as possible in a single hour qualify as a sport? One could train for a lifetime, and certainly develop an incredible skill and technique for achieving such a goal, but that would still not make it a sport.

Perhaps, though, it could be considered a 'pastime'.

1. Which of the following best describes the tone of the author of the first passage?
   (a) Personal and opinionated (b) Narrative
   (c) Neutral (d) Ambivalent
2. Which of the following best describes the tone of the author of the second passage?
   (a) Critical and opinionated (b) Neutral and even
   (c) Compliant (d) Bewildered
3. The attitude of the author of the second passage towards baseball players is best characterised as one of __________.
   (a) undisguised veneration (b) contempt
   (c) horror (d) fear
4. The attitude of the author of the first passage towards baseball could best be described as one of __________.
   (a) shock (b) intellectual Inquiry
   (c) nostalgia and admiration (d) questioning doubt
5. The attitude towards baseball players of the author of the first passage is most closely described as one of __________.
   (a) fond recollection (b) respect

(c) worship (d) respite

6. Some say Peter killed his father. That is impossible, he __________ that. (HCL 2011)
   (a) may have done (b) could not have done
   (c) could not done (d) must not have done
7. Despite his best efforts to conceal his anger, ______________________.
   (a) we could detect that he was very happy
   (b) he failed to give us an impression of his agony
   (c) he succeeded in camouflaging his emotions
   (d) people came to know that he was annoyed
8. He has __________ people visiting him at his house because he fears it will cause discomfort to neighbours. (Syntel, 2011)
   (a) curtailed (b) requested (c) stopped (d) warned

Directions: *Fill in the blanks with suitable words:*

9. Although he never learnt to read, his exceptional memory and enquiring mind eventually made him a very __________ man. (Capgemini, 2015)
   (a) dedicated (b) erudite (c) pragmatic (d) benevolent
10. Mary goes ______ school _____ 9 o'clock _____ bus. (PREPOSITIONS) (Accenture, 2011)
   (a) to, at, by (b) to, in, by (c) to, at, by (d) to, in, with
11. Celebrities showed their child-like side (1)/yesterday, as most of them turn up wearing (2)/cartoon T-shirts for the screening of (3)/the latest animated film in the town. (4)/No error (5). (Tech Mahindra, 2014)
   (a) 1 (b) 2 (c) 3 (d) 4
12. The man said, 'No, I refused to, confess guilt'. (Tech Mahindra, 2014)
   (a) The man refused to confess his guilt
   (b) The man said that he did not confess guilt
   (c) The man was stubborn enough to confess guilt
   (d) The man emphatically refused to confess guilt

Directions: *In each of the following questions, a sentence has been given in active (or passive) voice. Out of the four alternatives suggested, select the one which best expresses the same sentence in passive (or active) voice.*

13. I remember my sister taking me to the museum.
   (a) I remember I was taken to the museum by my sister.
   (b) I remember being taken to the museum by my sister.
   (c) I remember myself being taken to the museum by my sister.
   (d) I remember taken to the museum by my sister.
14. You should open the wine about three hours before you use it. (Accenture, 2013)
   (a) Wine should be opened about three hours before use.

(b) Wine should be opened by you three hours before use.
(c) Wine should be opened about three hours before you use it.
(d) Wine should be opened about three hours before it is used.

15. They will inform the police. (Accenture, 2013)
    (a) The police will be informed by them.
    (b) The police will inform them.
    (c) The police are informed by them.
    (d) Informed will be the police by them.

Directions: *In the question given below, each passage consist of six sentences. The first and sixth sentences are given in the beginning. The middle four sentences have been removed and jumbled up. These are labelled as P, Q, R, and S. Find out the proper order for the four sentences.*

16. S1: You know my wife, Madhavi, always urged me to give up smoking.
    P: I really gave it up.
    Q: And so, when I went to jail, I said to myself I really must give it up, if for no other reason, then for being self-reliant.
    R: When I emerged from jail, I wanted to tell her of my great triumph.
    S: But when I met her, there she was with a packet of cigarettes.
    S6: Poor girl.
    The proper sequence should be: (Oracle, 2013)
    (a) PSRQ (b) SPQR (c) QPRS (d) RSPQ

Directions: *In the following questions, choose the word which best expresses the meaning of the given word.*

17. Canny (Triveni Turbine 2014)
    (a) Obstinate (b) Handsome (c) Clever (d) Stout
18. Alert (IBM, 2013)
    (a) Energetic (b) Observant (c) Intelligent (d) Watchful
19. Warrior (Robert Bosch, 2013)
    (a) Soldier (b) Sailor (c) Pirate (d) Spy
20. Distant (Robert Bosch, 2013)
    (a) Far (b) Removed (c) Reserved (d) Separate

SOLUTIONS WITH EXPLANATIONS

1. (a) Personal and opinionated
   The author gives his own perspective about baseball
2. (a) Critical and opinionated: The author expresses criticism/ makes a careful judgement about good and bad Baseball (positive and negative of the game baseball). It is his self opinion.
3. (b) • Undisguised veneration : Respect : Dignity, Wisdom, Dedication
   • Contempt : Lack of respect

- Horror: Fear/Shock
- Fear: Afraid
- Baseball is always considered as a partime not a national sport. No one could give importance to professional players

4. (c) Nostalgia and Admiration
   - Atlanta won the title in 1996. Baseball has its own singularity.
5. (b) Respect
6. (b) could not have done
   - Killed is verb
7. (d) People came to know that he was annoyed
   - Conceal which mean hide. He tried to hide his anger but people came to know he was annoyed.
8. (a) Curtailed – To reduce or limit
9. (b)
   - Dedicated – Loyalty or support to a person
   - Erudite – Having great knowledge
   - Pragmatic – Dealing with problems in a logical way
   - Benevolent – Kind and generous
10. (a) Where : School, When : 9'o Clock, How : Bus
11. (b) Turned up instead of turn up
12. (d)
    - Direct speech is converted into indirect speech
    - Past tense
    - Said in a forceful way
    - Option (d) relates to speaking in a forceful way
13. (b)
    - It is in passive voice which is converted to active voice
    - Taking is converted to being taken
    - I subject and sister is object and taking is verb
14. (d)
    - It is in active voice which is converted to a passive voice
    - You is subject, open is verb and wine is direct object
15. (a)
    - It is in active voice which is converted to a passive voice
    - Will inform is converted to will be informed
16. (c)
    - Q is the qualifier because it is talking about the reason as to why I should give up smoking.
    - P follows Q because after thinking I realized not to smoke
    - R comes after Q because after coming out of jail, I wanted to inform my wife that I have quitted smoking
    - S is the last sentence
17. (c) CANNY: Shrewd
    - Obstinate : Stubborn, unreasonable
    - Handsome
    - Clever: Cunning and witty
    - Stout: Bulky, fat
18. (d) ALERT: Think clearly and notice things, watchful

- Observant: Good at watching and listening
- Intelligent: brilliant
- Energetic: robust
- Watchful: alert

19. (a) Soldier
20. (a) Far

Keywords

- Denigrate: To say unfair things
- Maysayer: A person who denies, refuses something; opposes
- Invalidity: Invalid
- Ambivalent: continual fluctuation, uncertainty to which approach to follow

PRACTICE SET 16

Directions: *Read the passage carefully and answer the questions that follow.*

But I did not want to shoot the elephant. I watched him beating his bunch of grass against his knees, with the preoccupied grandmotherly air that elephants have. It seemed to me that it would be murder to shoot him. I had never shot an elephant and never wanted to (somehow it always seems worse to kill a large animal). Besides, there was the beast's owner to be considered. But I had got to act quickly. I turned to some experienced-looking Burmas who had been there when we arrived, and asked them how the elephants had been behaving. They all said the same thing; he took no notice of you if you left him alone, but he might charge if you went too close to him.

1. The author did not want to shoot the elephant because he __________. (Dell, 2011)
   (a) was afraid of it
   (b) did not have the experience of shooting big animals
   (c) did not wish to kill an animal which was not doing anybody any harm
   (d) did not find the elephant to be ferocious
2. The phrase 'preoccupied grandmotherly air' signifies __________.
   (a) being totally unconcerned
   (b) pretending to be very busy
   (c) a very superior attitude
   (d) a calm, dignified, and affectionate disposition
3. From the passage, it appears that the author was __________.
   (a) an inexperienced hunter (b) kind and considerate
   (c) possessed with fear (d) a worried man

Directions: *In the following questions, choose the word which best expresses the meaning of the given word.*

4. Sacrosanct (ABB, 2014)
   (a) Too important (b) Worship (c) Sacrifice (d) Best
5. Whimsical (GE, 2013)
   (a) Victorious (b) Swift (c) Fanciful (d) Momentary

Directions: *Read the following sentences carefully. Decide which answer is the most inappropriate in the sentence (pick the wrong word).* (Larsen & Turbo 2013)

6. The *truculent* stance adopted by both the countries will not further world peace
   (a) Obstinate (b) Belligerent (c) Pugnacious (d) Antagonistic
7. Caste discrimination remains a *canker* in the society.
   (a) Scourge (b) Mystery (c) Pestilence (d) Blight

Directions: *One sentence is divided into four different statements. Identify the correct statement.* (Capgemini 2013)

8. (a) The brakes and steering failed
   (b) and the bus ran down the hill
   (c) without anyone being able control it
   (d) No error
9. (a) Another reason for pharmaceutical companies beefing up their
   (b) OTC (Over the Country) divisions is that prescription drugs with proven safety records which have been reached
   (c) the end of the their patent protection period are
   (d) Allowed to be sold without a prescription.
   (e) No error.
10. (a) The brand proposition now therefore had to be that Keokarpin Antiseptic Cream is more effective
    (b) because it penetrates deep-down (being light and non-sticky) and works from within
    (c) (because of its ayurvedic ingredients) to keep skin blemish-free and helps cope with cuts nicks, burns, and nappy rash
    (d) No error

Directions: *Arrange the sentence order: Jumbled sentences.* (Mphasis, 2012)

11. A. With the time spent eating, sleeping, taking care of household chores, and looking after the family, there is little time left for leisure activities for many Americans.
    B. Results of a 2001 Harris Poll on free time conducted in the United States showed that the average workweek for many Americans is fifty hours.

C. People today seem to have increasingly hectic lifestyles.
D. In addition, many people spend up to two or three hours a day commuting to and from work

(a) ABCD (b) CBDA (c) ACBD (d) CADB

12. A. The most popular activity for Americans was gardening. (Mphasis-2012)
B. We can see from the above examples that in different countries and cultures around the world, free time is spend in different ways.
C. In the U.K., it was going to the pub, followed by visiting the cinema.
D. In Japan, it was very different from the first two countries. Going to bars and pubs ranked eighth in popularity, and gardening ranked ninth.
E. There were differences in the most popular outdoor pursuits between the following three countries.

(a) EADCB (b) BEACD (c) EACDB (d) CEABD

13. A. Passivity is not, of course, universal. (Robert Bosh 2013)
B. In areas where there are no lords or laws, or in frontier zones where all men go armed, the attitude of the peasantry may well be different.
C. So, indeed it may be on the fringe of the unsubmissive.
D. However, for most of the soil-bound peasants the problem is not whether to be normally passive or active, but when to pass from one state to another.

(a) BDAC (b) CDAB (c) DBAC (d) ABCD

14. A. Similarly, turning to caste, even though being lower caste is undoubtedly a separate cause of disparity, its impact is all the greater when the lower-caste families also happen to be poor. (Robert Bosh 2013)
B. Belonging to a privileged class can help a woman to overcome many barriers that obstruct women from less thriving classes.
C. It is the interactive presence of these two kinds of deprivation—being low class and being female—that massively impoverishes women from the less privileged classes.
D. A congruence of class deprivation and gender discrimination can blight the lives of poorer women very severely.
E. Gender is certainly a contributor to societal inequality, but it does not act independently of class.

(a) EABDC (b) EBDCA (c) DAEBC (d) BECDA

Directions: *In each of the following questions, there is a certain relationship between two given words on one side of :: and one word is given on another side of ::, while another word is to be found from the given alternatives, having the same relation with this word as the words of the given pair bear. Choose the correct option.* (L&T InfoTech, 2011)

15. Tile : Mosaic :: Knot : __________

(a) Embroidery (b) Abacus (c) Macrame (d) Easle

Directions: *Each question consists of two words which have a certain relationship to each other followed by four pairs of related words, Select the pair which has the same relationship.*

16. Wan : Colour (Analogy) (Mindtree, 2013)
    (a) Corpulent : Weight (b) Insipid : Flavour
    (c) Pallid : Complexion (d) Enigmatic : Puzzle
17. Pork : Pig (ABB, 2011)
    (a) Rooster : Chicken (b) Mutton : Sheep
    (c) Steer : Beef (d) Lobster : Crustacean

Directions: *Complete the sentences with suitable words.*

18. Guilherme wanted to visit _______ European city so he decided to go to Paris. (Tech Mahindra, 2014)
    (a) an (b) a (c) the (d) no article
19. Fate smiles _______ those who untiringly grapple with stark realities of life. (ABB, 2011)
    (a) with (b) over (c) on (d) round
20. The miser gazed _______ at the pile of gold coins in front of him. (GE, 2012)
    (a) avidly (b) admiringly (c) thoughtfully (d) earnestly

SOLUTIONS AND EXPLANATIONS

1. (b) did not have the experience of shooting big animals
2. (d) calm, dignified and affectionate disposition
    - The elephant was relaxing at ease. Disposition means nature, characteristics, qualities, tendency to active in a particular way.
3. (b) kind and considerate
    Option B is true and others are false statement
4. (a) too important
    - SACROSANCT: Sacred, too important and valuable to be interfered with.
    - Worship – Devotion
    - Sacrifice – Give up something
    - Best: finest
5. (c) WHIMSICAL: Sudden illogical changes in mind, ideas, unusual in a playful or amusing way, not serious. Ex: Whimsical sense of humor
    - Victorious
    - swift: Fast
    - Fanciful: Over imaginative, freakish which means strange
    - Momentary: Lasting for a moment/short time
6. (a) TRUCULENT: Aggressive, defiant, destructive
    - Obstinate: Stubborn and head strong means does not change ideas

- Belligerent: Aggressive, threatening
- Pugnacious: Quarrel, fight
- antagonistic: Resistant, opposition

7. (b) CANKER (verb): Spreading sore/bitterness/disease
    - Scourge: Cause great suffering
    - Mystery: difficult to understand and explain, puzzle
    - Pestilence: Epidemic disease
    - Blight: Plant disease
8. (c) Without being controlled by any one (it is a grammatical error)
9. (b) Been is the error
10. (d) No error
11. (b)
    - It is about the hectic life style where there is average work hours per week which is 55 hours so option C is the qualifier (main sentence)
    - Option B follows C because it is talking about that particular hectic life style
    - Option D follows B
12. (c)
    - Option E is the main subject because it is according to the position of the countries in the globe: America, UK, Japan (west to east countries).
    - It is talking about outdoor pursuits among the three countries
    - Option B is the conclusion
13. (a)
    - Option B is the qualifier of the main subject because it is talking about peasantry and its laws which may vary in different areas.
    - Option D is continuation of B because it is talking about the soil bound peasants
    - Option A comes after option D because it is talking about passivity which is mentioned option D
14. (b)
    - It is talking about gender, inequality, poor-rich differences.
    - E is the qualifier of the main subject and A is the conclusion
    - D and C talks about discrimination
15. (c) Tile : Mosaic :: Knot : ? : Tile and Mosaic is used for flooring and knot is used for tying purpose
    - Embroidery: Thread work
    - Abacus: Calculating tool
    - Macrame: It is the textile making using knotting rather than weaving
    - Easle: Frame for printing
16. (c) WAN: COLOUR (Analogy): Dull/Pale (complexion)
    - Corpulent: Weight: Obese: Weight can be lower or high
    - Insipid: flavour: Insipid means tasteless, flavor can be of any type
    - Pallid: complexion: Pale complexion
    - Enigmatic: puzzle: Mysterious
17. (b) PORK:PIG: Meat of pig is pork
    - Rooster: chicken

- Mmutton: sheep
- Steer: beef: Beef is from Bull, steer : Male bull
- Lobster: crustacean: Lobster is prawn: Crustacean is class of arthropod like crab
- shrimp, lobster. Lobster belongs to crustacean

18. (b) European is pronounced as with an initial of Y sound which is a consonant. (YU)
    Ex: Hotel: 'O'tel so it becomes vowel. An hour: 'O'ur: Vowel
19. (c) Upon/on
20. (b) • Avidly: Very Eager
    • Admiringly: To look at something with enjoyment
    • Thoughtfully: Careful, serious thinking
    • Earnestly: Serious state

PRACTICE SET 17

Directions: *Read the passage below and answer the questions that follow:*

The Great Wall of China's walls and wall building have played a very important role in Chinese culture. These people, from the dim mists of prehistory, have been wall-conscious; from the Neolithic period—when ramparts of pounded earth were used—to the Communist Revolution, walls were an essential part of any village. Not only towns and villages; the houses and the temples within them were somehow walled, and the houses also had no windows overlooking the street, thus giving the feeling of wandering around a huge maze. The name for 'city' in Chinese (*cheng*) means wall, and over these walled cities, villages, houses, and temples presides the God of walls and mounts, whose duties were, and still are, to protect and be responsible for the welfare of the inhabitants. Thus, a great and extremely laborious task such as constructing a wall, which was supposed to run throughout the country, must not have seemed such an absurdity. However, it is indeed a common mistake to perceive the Great Wall as a single architectural structure, and it would also be erroneous to assume that it was built during a single dynasty, for the building of the wall spanned various dynasties, and each of these dynasties somehow contributed to the refurbishing and the construction of the wall, whose foundations had been laid many centuries ago. It was during the fourth and third centuries BC that each warring state started building walls to protect their kingdoms, both against one another and against the northern nomads. Especially three of these states: the Chin, the Chao and the Yen, corresponding respectively to the modern provinces of Shensi, Shanzi, and Hopei, over and above building walls that surrounded their kingdoms, also laid the foundations on which Chin Shih Huang Di would build his first continuous Great Wall. The role that the Great Wall played in the growth of Chinese economy was an important one. Throughout the centuries, many settlements were established along the new border. The garrison troops were instructed to reclaim wasteland and to plant crops on it, roads and canals were built, to mention just a few of the works carried out. All these undertakings greatly helped to increase the country's trade and cultural exchanges with many remote areas and also with the southern, central, and western parts of Asia—the formation of the Silk Route. Builders, garrisons, artisans, farmers, and peasants left behind a trail of objects, including inscribed tablets, household articles, and written work, which have become extremely valuable archaeological evidence to the study of defense institutions of the Great Wall and the everyday life of these people who lived and died along the wall.

1. Chinese cities resembled a mazen ____________. (IBM, 2012)
   (a) because they were walled
   (b) because the houses had no external windows
   (c) because the name of the cities means 'wall'
   (d) because walls have always been important there
2. Constructing a wall that ran the length of the country ____________.
   (a) honoured the God of walls and mounts
   (b) was an absurdly laborious task
   (c) may have made sense within Chinese culture
   (d) made the country look like a huge maze
3. The Great Wall of China ____________.
   (a) was built in a single dynasty
   (b) was refurbished in the fourth and the third centuries BC
   (c) used existing foundations
   (d) was built by Chin, the Chao, and the Yen
4. Crops were planted ____________.
   (a) on wasteland (b) to reclaim wasteland
   (c) on reclaimed wasteland (d) along the canals
5. The Great Walls ____________.
   (a) helped build trade only inside China
   (b) helped build trade in China and abroad
   (c) helped build trade only abroad
   (d) helped build trade only to remote areas

Directions: *One sentence has been divided into four parts. One part has an error. Choose the option that contains the error.* (Robert Bosch, 2014)

6. (a) We entered (b) into the room
   (c) after the class was over (d) No Error
7. (a) Your account should (b) have been credited
   (c) with three month's interest (d) No error
8. (a) Idli and sambar (b) make the breakfast
   (c) in the south (d) No error

9. (a) He is (b) too intelligent
   (c) to make a mistake (d) No error
10. (a) The single biggest gainer in this process
    (b) was ITCs Gold Flake Kings sales are estimated
    (c) to have moved up from 50 million to 200 million sticks per month during 1987 and last year
    (d) No error

Directions: *Rearrange the sentences given below:* (Robert Bosch, 2013)

11. A. But in the industrial era, destroying the enemy's productive capacity meant bombing the factories which were located in the cities.
    B. So, in the agrarian era, if you needed to destroy the enemy's productive capacity, what you needed to do was burn his fields, or if you were really vicious, salt them.
    C. Now in the information era, destroying the enemy's productive capacity means destroying the information infrastructure.
    D. How do you do battle with your enemy?
    E. The idea is to destroy the enemy's productive capacity, and depending upon the economic foundation, that productive capacity is different in each case.
    F. With regard to defense, the purpose of the military is to defend the nation and be prepared to do battle with its enemy.
    (a) FDEBAC (b) FCABED (c) DEBACF (d) DFEBAC
12. A. When identity is thus 'defined by contrast', divergence with the West becomes central.
    B. Indian religious literature such as the Bhagavad Gita or the Tantric texts, which are identified as differing from secular writings seen as 'western', elicits much greater interest in the West than do other Indian writings, including India's long history of heterodoxy.
    C. There is a similar neglect of Indian writing on non-religious subjects, from mathematics, epistemology, and natural science to economics and linguistics.
    D. Through selective emphasis that point up differences with the West, other civilisations can, in this way, be redefined in alien terms, which can be exotic and charming, or else bizarre and terrifying, or simply strange and engaging.
    E. The exception is the *Kamasutra*, in which western readers have managed to cultivate an interest. (Mphasis, 2012)
    (a) BDACE (b) DEABC (c) BDECA (d) BCEDA

Directions: *In the following questions, choose the word which best expresses the meaning of the given word.* (Capgemini, 2011)

13. Candid
    (a) Frank (b) Close (c) Dignity (d) Happy
14. Specification
    (a) Pointing (b) Documentation
    (c) Reasoning (d) Advertising
15. Extradite
    (a) Addiction (b) Logical (c) Deport (d) Important

Directions: *Read the following sentences carefully. Decide which answer is the most inappropriate in the sentence (pick the wrong word).* (Larsen and Turbo, 2013)

16. Harbouring *vindictive* thoughts about somebody can obstruct a person's spiritual growth.
    (a) Vengeful (b) Villainous (c) Rancorous (d) Malevolent
17. The opposition party questioned the rationale of discussing the vexed issue every session.
    (a) Contentious (b) Contested (c) Impertinent (d) Problematic

Directions: *In each of the following questions, there is a certain relationship between two given words on one side of :: and one word is given on another side of :: while another word is to be found from the given alternatives, having the same relation with this word as the words of the given pair bear. (Choose the correct alternative.)* (L&T InfoTech, 2011)

18. Appraiser : Building :: Critic : ___________
    (a) Book (b) Masterpiece (c) Judge (d) Gold

Directions: *Each question consist of two words which have a certain relationship to each other followed by four pairs of related words, Select the pair which has the same relationship.*

19. Thrust : Spear [Oracle, 2011(2)]
    (a) Mangle : Iron (b) Scabbard : Sword
    (c) Bow : Arrow (d) Fence : *Epee*
20. Wan : Colour (Oracle, 2013)
    (a) Corpulent : Weight (b) Insipid : Flavour
    (c) Pallid : Complexion (d) Enigmatic : Puzzle

SOLUTIONS WITH EXPLANATIONS

1. (b) because the houses has no external windows
    - Like maze houses in cities were constructed like a maze with no partition or separation.
2. (c) May have made sense within Chinese culture
    - All the architecture in China were walled. So building a wall across entire country is possible only in China
3. (c) Used existing foundations

4. (c) on reclaimed wasteland
5. (b) Helped build trade in China and abroad
6. (b) into the room
   - When you walk into a room, you `enter' it. You do not `enter into' it. You normally `enter' a room, building or country.
   - We entered the room
7. (d) No error
8. (b) Instead of make the use comprises of / constitutes the break fast
9. (d) No error
10. (b)
   - was ITCs Gold Flake Kings sales are estimated
   - Sales becomes a new sentence
11. (a)
   - F becomes the qualifier or the main subject. F is the introduction followed by option D because it is talking about different ways of battle.
   - Option no B is followed by A is followed by C because it is talking about eras of doing battle
12. (d)
   - Option no B becomes the qualifier or the main subject because it is talking about religious literature.
   - Option C is a continuation to option no B because it deals with different kinds of Indian writing on literature
13. (a) Frank
   - Candid means expressing opinions and feelings in an honest and sincere way
   - Frank used to say that someone is speaking or writing in a very direct and honest way
14. (b)
   - Specification : Detail description of work / precise requirement
   - Documentation : Written instruction to prove something or make something official
   - Pointing: referring
   - Reasoning: rational, think logically
   - Advertising: commercial
15. (c)
   - Extradite: Surrender of offender to the country where the offence was committed
   - Addiction: Need to have something, habit, dependence
   - Logical: To agree to with rules of logic
   - Deport: To force a person who is not a citizen of the country to leave it
   - Important: Main, Major
16. (b) Vindictive: Revengeful, grudge, vengeful
   - Vengeful: Seeking to harm someone
   - Villainous: Detest, headful, evil
   - Rancorous: Vindictive, bitter, resentful

- Malevolent: Hatred, wish to do evil to do others

17. (c) Vex: Make someone feel annoyed, worried on trivial matters
    - Contentious : Likely to cause arguments, dispute, vexed
    - Contested : Oppose as mistaken or wrong
    - Impertinent : Not showing proper respect
    - Problematic : troublesome
18. (a)
    - Appraiser : Estimates value of assets like building
    - Critic: person who judges or comments the merit of literary work. They give vetting to books
19. (d) THRUST: SPEAR: Action and equipment. Spear is the pole weapon consisting of shaft (pointed head) with the help of spear we perform action.
    - Mangle: iron : Mangle is destroy completely by the use of iron
    - Scabbard: sword: Sheath for sword made of leather. You keep sword in a scabbard.
    - Bow: arrow
    - Fence: epee : Epee is a French term of sword (epee fencing) which is a sport
20. (c)
    - Corpulent : Obese, Weight : Low or Hight
    - Insipid : flavour : Tasteless : Flavour can be of any type
    - Pallid : Complexion : Dull/Pale complexion
    - Enigmatic : Puzzle : Mysterious : Confused

Keywords

- Absurdity: Silly, foolish
- Erroneous: Not correct
- Refurbishing: Renovate
- Reclaim: Taken possession
- Silk Route: Trade routes

PRACTICE SET 18

The strength of the electronics industry in Japan is the Japanese ability to organise production and marketing rather than their achievements in original research. The British are generally recognised as a far more inventive collection of individuals, but never seem able to exploit what they invent. There are many examples, from the TSR Z hovercraft, high speed train and Sinclair scooter to the Triumph, BSA and Norton Motorcycle which all prove this sad rule. The Japanese were able to exploits their strengths in marketing and development many years ago, and their success was at first either not understood in the West or was dismissed as something which could have been produced only at their low price. They were sold because they were cheap copies of other people's ideas churned out of a workhouse which was dedicated to hard grind above all else.

1. It is evident from the passage that the strength of a country's industry depends upon
   (a) original research (b) international cooperation
   (c) dedicated workforce (d) electronic development
2. The sad rule mentioned in this passage refers to
   (a) the inability of the Japanese to be inventive like the British
   (b) the inability of the British to be industrious like the Japanese
   (c) the lack of variety in Japanese inventions
   (d) the poorer marketing ability of British
3. The TSR Z hovercraft, high speed train, Sinclair scooter etc. are the symbols of
   (a) Japanese success (b) British failure
   (c) British success (d) Japanese failure
4. According to the passage, prosperity in industry depends upon
   (a) productivity (b) inventiveness
   (c) marketing ability (d) official patronage
5. The main theme of this passage is
   (a) electronic industry in Japan
   (b) industrial comparison between Japan and Britain
   (c) the role of marketing efficiency in industrial prosperity
   (d) the importance of original research in industry

Directions: *Fill in the blanks with suitable articles.*

6. _____ apple a day keeps the doctor away. (Accenture, 2011)
   (a) An (b) The (c) A (d) No
7. Mount Everest is in _____ Himalayas. (Dell, 2014)
   (a) a (b) the (c) an (d) All of these

Directions: *In the questions given below the sentences have been given in Direct/ Indirect speech. From the given alternatives, choose the one which best expresses the given sentence in the opposite form of speech as the original sentence.*

8. The man said, 'No, I refused to confer guilt'. (Infosys, 2012)
   (a) The man emphatically refused to confers guilt.
   (b) The man refused to confers his guilt.
   (c) The man told that he did not confers guilt.
   (d) The man was stubborn enough to confer guilt.
9. Nita ordered her servant to bring her a cup of tea. (Accenture, 2011)
   (a) Nita told her servant, 'Bring a cup of tea'.
   (b) Nita said, 'Bring me a cup of tea'.
   (c) Nita said to her servant, 'Bring me a cup of tea'.

(d) Nita told her servant, 'Bring her that cup of tea'.

10. My cousin said, 'My roommate had snored throughout the night'. (Cape Gemini, 2014)
    (a) My cousin said that her roommate snored throughout the night.
    (b) My cousin told me that her roommate snored throughout the night.
    (c) My cousin complained to me that her roommate is snoring throughout the night.
    (d) My cousin felt that her roommate may be snoring throughout the night.

Directions: *Choose the correct answer for each question.*

11. Look, that car is ______ fire. (ABB, 2012)
    (a) through (b) with (c) on (d) into
12. He saw a parking space ______ two cars and drove ______ it. (ABB, 2012)
    (a) over/into (b) between/into (c) along/up (d) by/on
13. Harry comes to work _____ car but I prefer to come ____ foot. (GE, 2011)
    (a) at/into (b) beside/next to (c) by/on (d) in/next to
14. He took the book ______ the shelf and put it ______ his bag. (GE, 2012)
    (a) from/into (b) beside/next to (c) at/into (d) by/on

Directions: *In the following questions, choose the word which best expresses the meaning of the given word.*

15. Adversity (HP, 2013)
    (a) Failure (b) Helplessness (c) Misfortune (d) Crisis
16. Fake (Dell, 2014)
    (a) Original (b) Imitation (c) Trustworthy (d) Loyal
17. Indict (IBPS, 2013)
    (a) Condemn (b) Reprimand (c) Accuse (d) Allege

Directions: *In the following questions, choose the word which is the exact OPPOSITE meaning of the given words.*

18. Enormous (Cognizent, 2014)
    (a) Soft (b) Average (c) Tiny (d) Weak
19. Commissioned (Cognizent, 2014)
    (a) Started (b) Closed (c) Finished (d) Terminated
20. Artificial (L&T, 2012)
    (a) Red (b) Natural (c) Truthful (d) Solid

SOLUTIONS WITH EXPLANATIONS

1. (c) Japanese were able to use their marketing and development skill as they had dedicated (devoted, committed) workforce which us didn't have.
2. (d) Britishers were innovative but did not exploit their innovativeness through their marketing starting.

3. (b) • TSR Z hovercraft: vehicle that moves above the surface.
 • All these are products of British ere and they invented it but could not market it.
4. (c) Apart from production you need to have marketing ability.
5. (c) Importance of marketing ability.
6. (b) The (The is used for specific purposes)
7. (b) The (The is used for specific purposes)
8. (a) • Confer: to discuss something important in order to make decision
 • Emphatically: speaking in forceful way
9. (c) Order was given to the servant to give her a cup of tea
10. (a) The main sentence is in past perfect tense. To whom it is to be said is not specified
11. (c) On
12. (b) between / into
13. (c) by / on
14. (a) from / into
15. (c) ADVERSITY: Difficult situation, tragedy, misfortune, calamity
 • Misfortune: bad luck
 • Crisis: Dangerous situation that needs serious attention
 • Failure: defeat
 • Helpless: powerless
16. (b) • Fake: Artificial or false
 • Imitation: Duplicate, copy, replica
 • Trustworthy: Able to be relied on
 • Loyal: Faithful, showing constant support
 • Original: primal
17. (c) INDICT: To formally decide that someone should be put on trial.
 • Condemn: Say in definite way that someone is wrong, criticise someone, charge someone
 • Reprimand: Blame
 • Accuse: Guilty of crime
 • Allege: To state without definite proof
18. (c) Enormous: Huge, large in size
19. (d) • Commissioned: A certificate / formal warrant / for granting power to perform certain task.
 • Terminated Wind up
20. (b) Artificial: Not natural / not real / man made

PRACTICE SET 19

To those who do listen, the desert speaks of things with an emphasis quite different from that of the shore, the mountain, the valley, or the plains; whereas these invite action and suggest limitless opportunity and exhaust less resources, the implications and the mood of the desert are something different. For one thing, the desert is conservative and not radical. It is more likely to provide awe than to invite conquest. The heroism which it encourages is the heroism of endurance, not that of conquest. It brings man up against this limitation, turns him upon himself, and suggests values which more indulgent regions suppress. Sometimes it includes contemplation in men who have never contemplated before: And of all the answers to the question—what is a desert good for—'contemplation' is perhaps the best. The last half of my life was spent at one of those painful epochs of human history, during which the world was getting worse and past victories which had seemed to be definitive turned out to be only temporary. When I was young, Victorian optimism was taken for granted. It was thought that freedom and prosperity would spread gradually throughout the world through an orderly process, and it was hoped that cruelty, tyranny, and injustice would continually diminish. Hardly anyone thought of the nineteenth century as a brief interlude between past and future barbarism. (Oracle, 2013)

1. In order to receive the desert's message, the beholder needs to __________.
   (a) be contemplation (b) indolence
   (c) heroic endeavour (d) adventurous Spirit
2. If one responds with insight to the mood of the desert, it evokes ________.
   (a) an inclination for deep thought
   (b) the possibility of unending resources
   (c) the desire for heroic conquest
   (d) a sense of intense revulsion
3. The writer calls the desert conservative rather than radical because it provides an environment that __________.
   (a) inspires man to explore it
   (b) offers unlimited opportunity to conquer
   (c) tests ones endurance
   (d) makes one gloomy
4. What does the phrase 'it brings man up against his limitations' mean?
   (a) It makes man feel hopeless about his limitations.
   (b) It makes man aware of his limitations.
   (c) It compels man to fight against his limitations.
   (d) It persuades man to overcome his limitations.
5. The desert is unique among landscapes because it encourages only _______.
   (a) contemplation (b) indolence
   (c) heroic endeavour (d) adventure spirit

Directions: *In the questions below, the sentences have been given in Direct/Indirect speech. From the given alternatives, choose the one which best expresses the given sentence in the opposite form of speech.*

6. 'If you do not keep quiet, I shall shoot you', he said to her in a calm voice. (Cognizent, 2013)
   (a) He warned her to shoot if she did not keep quiet calmly.
   (b) He said calmly that I shall shoot you if you do not be quiet.
   (c) He warned her calmly that he would shoot her if she did not keep quiet.
   (d) Calmly he warned her that is quiet or else he will have to shoot her.
7. I told him that he was not working hard. (Capgemini 2014)
   (a) I said to him, 'You are not working hard'.
   (b) I told to him, 'You are not working hard'.
   (c) I said, 'You are not working hard'.
   (d) I said to him, 'He is not working hard'.
8. His father ordered him to go to his room and study. (Capgemini 2012)
   (a) His father said, 'Go to your room and study'.
   (b) His father said to him, 'Go and study in your room'.
   (c) His father shouted, 'Go right now to your study room'.
   (d) His father said firmly, 'Go and study in your room'.
9. He said to his father, 'Please increase my pocket-money.' (Mphasis, 2012)
   (a) He told his father, 'Please increase the pocket-money'.
   (b) He pleaded his father to please increase my pocket money.
   (c) He requested his father to increase his pocket-money.
   (d) He asked his father to increase his pocket-money.

Directions: *Choose the correct answer for each question.*

10. She took the key ______ her pocket and put it ________ the lock. (Robert Bosch, 2013)
    (a) over/into (b) between/into
    (c) out of/in (d) by/on
11. He drove ______ me without stopping and drove off ______ the center of town. (Tata Motors, 2011)
    (a) from/into (b) towards/over
    (c) along/up (d) past/towards
12. I took the old card ______ the computer and put ______ the new one. (HP, 2014)
    (a) through/in (b) out of/in
    (c) out of/between (d) out of/into
13. I went ____ him and asked him the best way to get _____ town. (GE, 2011)
    (a) from/into (b) towards/over
    (c) along/up (d) up to/out of

Directions: *In the following the questions, choose the word which best expresses the meaning of the given word.*

14. Stringent (L&T, 2013)

(a) Dry (b) Strained (c) Rigorous (d) Shrill

15. Lament (CoCubes, 2013)
    (a) Complain (b) Comment (c) Condone (d) Console
16. Hesitated (CoCubes, 2013)
    (a) Stopped (b) Paused (c) Slowed (d) Postponed

Directions: *In the following questions, choose the word which is the exact opposite of the given words.*

17. Exodus (AMCAT, 2012)
    (a) Influx (b) Home-coming
    (c) Return (d) Restoration
18. Relinquish (AMCAT, 2012)
    (a) Abdicate (b) Renounce (c) Possess (d) Deny
19. Expand (Mindtree, 2013)
    (a) Convert (b) Condense (c) Congest (d) Conclude
20. Mortal (Accenture, 2013)
    (a) Divine (b) Immortal (c) Spiritual (d) Eternal

SOLUTIONS WITH EXPLANATIONS

1. (a) Contemplation
    - Does not provide awe rather than conquest.
2. (a) An inclination for deep thought
    - Insight: View thoroughly
    - Evokes: Brings out
    - When we view a desert intensively it brings out contemplation
3. (c) Tests ones Endurance
    - There is no question of conquest or action, hence it brings about tolerance (endurance)
4. (d) It persuades man to overcome his limitations
    - It does not supplies man with opportunities or resources which man is used to. At this stage a person has to face this limitation and finally with endurance he has to overcome.
5. (a) Up to / out of
6. (c) In direct-indirect speech, present tense must be changed to past, here option A & option C is in past, option B & C is removed and in option A, CALM is not mentioned. So OPTION C is Accurate.
7. (a) Because, whenever 'told to' comes we have to change it to as 'said'.
8. (a) In the sentence, 'his room' becomes 'your room' and 'ordered' has been converted into 'said'
9. (c) As in question we find word please so it's kind of request so option c is right answer and pledged is begging.

10. (c) Contemplation: observation
11. (d) First blank: Left him and second blank: went to town
12. (b) out of / in
13. (d) up to / out of
14. (c) STRINGENT : Strict, firm and rigorous
    - Strained: Tiredness
    - Rigorous: Strict, extremely thorough
    - Shrill: High speed sound, very loud
    - Dry: water less, parched
15. (a)
    - Lament: A complaint, express regret / complaint about something
    - Condone: To dismiss as of little importance / ignore
    - Console: Comfort some at a time of grief
    - Complain: grumble, protest
    - Comment: remark
16. (b) Hesitated : Pause in indecision / delay
17. (a) Exodus: mass departure of people
    - Homecoming: return to home
    - Restoration: Repair work, reconstruction
    - Influx: sudden arrival of large number of people.
    - Return: to come back
18. (c)
    - Relinquish: to give up something, give away (position of power)
    - Abdicate: to leave a position (fail to do your duty)
    - Renounce: to say in definite way that you refuse to follow, obey support someone any longer
    - Possess: to have or own something
    - Deny: refuse
19. (b) Congest: Concentrate on small space
20. (b)
    - Mortal : Certain to die
    - Immortal : Living forever
    - Divine : of the very best kind, formless
    - Eternal : No beginning and no end
    - Spiritual : sacred, divine

Keywords

- Conservative: Traditional value
- Awe: Astonished
- Conquest: Conquer
- Endurance: Tolerance
- Contemplation: Thoughtful
- Epochs: Period of time
- Optimism: Positive thinking

- Interlude: Passage, Interval
- Barbarism: Cruelty

PRACTICE SET 20

Work expands to fill the time available for its completion. The general recognition of this fact is shown in the proverbial phrase, 'It is the busiest man who has time to spare.' Thus, an elderly lady at leisure can spend the entire day writing a postcard to her niece. An hour will be spent in writing a postcard, another hunting for spectacles, half an hour to search for the address, an hour and a quarter in composition and twenty minutes in deciding whether or not to take an umbrella when going to the pillar-box in the street. The total effort that could occupy a busy man for 3 minutes, all told may in this fashion leave another person completely exhausted after a day of doubt, anxiety, and toil. Accidents on roads can be prevented, provided the quality of roads is improved and the drivers are instructed in safety rules which they must follow for their protection. It is also necessary that the illumination on the roads is adequate to prevent accidents at night. The surprisingly abundant life of the Indian Ocean is confined to the upper layers; the deeper and especially the bottom waters are devoid of oxygen and are often permeated with hydrogen sulphide. It is not luck but labour that makes a man. Luck, says an American Writer, is ever waiting for something to turn up; labour with keen eyes and strong will always turn up something. Luck lies in bed and wishes the postman would bring him news of legacy; labour turns out at six and with busy pen ringing hammer lays the foundation of competence. Luck whines, labour watches. Luck slips downwards to self-indulgence; labour strides upwards and aspires to independence. The conviction, therefore, is extending that diligence is the mother of good luck. In other words, a man's success in life will be proportionate to his efforts, industry, and attention to small things. (Genpact, 2012)

1. What is the total time spent by the elderly lady in writing a postcard?
   (a) 3 minutes (b) 4 hours and 5 minutes
   (c) Half day (d) The entire day
2. Which one of the following words in the passage indicate that the writer does not ultimately reject the element of luck:
   (a) Luck ... is ever waiting.
   (b) Luck whines.
   (c) Diligence is the mother of good luck.
   (d) Luck... wishes the postman would bring him the news.
3. Labour turns out at six and with a busy pen ringing hammer lays the foundation of competence. What does this statement mean?
   (a) Hard work of all kinds makes people efficient.
   (b) Labour lays the foundation of the building.

(c) The writer and the labourer are the true eyes of society.
(d) No worker works so hard as the labourer who begins.

4. Which one of the following words in the passage indicate that the writer does not ultimately reject the element of luck:
(a) Luck... is ever waiting.
(b) Luck whines.
(c) Diligence is the mother of good luck.
(d) Luck... wishes the postman would bring him news.

5. Despite of their differences on matters of principles, they all agree on the demand for a hike in salary.
(a) Despite their
(b) Despite of the
(c) Despite for their
(d) Despite off their

Directions: *In the following questions, the sentences have been given in direct/ indirect speech. From the given alternatives, choose one option which best expresses the given sentence in direct/indirect speech.*

6. She said that her brother was getting married. (Medhaj, 2013)
(a) She said, 'Her brother is getting married.'
(b) She told, 'Her brother is getting married.'
(c) She said, 'My brother is getting married.'
(d) She said, 'My brother was getting married.'

7. The boy said, 'Who dare call you a thief?' (Accenture, 2011)
(a) The boy enquired who dared call him a thief.
(b) The boy asked who called him a thief.
(c) The boy told that who dared call him a thief.
(d) The boy wondered who dared call a thief.

8. She exclaimed with sorrow that was a very miserable plight. (Accenture, 2011)
(a) She said with sorrow, 'What a pity it is.'
(b) She said, 'What a mystery it is.'
(c) She said, 'What a miserable sight it is.'
(d) She said, 'What a miserable plight it is.'

9. Dhruv said that he was sick and tired of working for that company. (Capgemini, 2013)
(a) Dhruv said, 'I am sick and tired of working for this company.'
(b) Dhruv said, 'He was tired of that company.'
(c) Dhruv said to me, 'I am sick and tired of working for this company.'
(d) Dhruv said, 'I will be tired of working for that company.'

Directions: *Choose the correct answer for each question.*

10. It is unlucky to walk ______ a ladder in my culture. I always walk ______ them. (Oracle, 2011)
    (a) through/in (b) out of/in
    (c) under/around (d) out of/into
11. The restaurant is ______ the High Street, ______ the cinema. (GE, 2012)
    (a) through/in (b) out of/in
    (c) under/around (d) in/next to
12. Sally left school ______ the age of 16 and went to work ______ a bank. (Amazon, 2014)
    (a) through/in (b) at/in
    (c) under/around (d) in/next to
13. He jumped ______ the wall and ______ the garden. (Cognizent, 2014)
    (a) over/into (b) towards/over
    (c) along/up (d) by/on

Directions: *In the following questions, choose the words which best express the meaning of the given words.*

14. Rescue (CoCubes, 2013)
    (a) Command (b) Help (c) Defense (d) Safety
15. Attempt (CoCubes, 2013)
    (a) Serve (b) Explore (c) Try (d) Explain
16. Foray (AMCAT, 2014)
    (a) Maraud (b) Contest (c) Ranger (d) Intuition

Directions: *In the following questions, choose the word which is the exact opposite of the given words.*

17. Quiescent (CoCubes, 2013)
    (a) Active (b) Dormant (c) Weak (d) Unconcerned
18. Obeying (GE, 2013)
    (a) Ordering (b) Following (c) Refusing (d) Contradicting
19. Fraudulent (Accenture, 2011)
    (a) Candid (b) Direct (c) Forthright (d) Genuine
20. Flagitious (Mphasis, 2013)
    (a) Innocent (b) Vapid (c) Ignorant (d) Frivolous

SOLUTIONS WITH EXPLANATIONS

1. (d) the entire day
    - It takes full day to complete the work
2. (c) Diligence is the mother of good luck
    - Good luck comes after hard work. Hence, author is supportive of good luck through hard work

3. (d) There is no worker who works so hard as the labourer who begins
    - Labourer rises early in the morning to work, busy throughout the day to achieve success
4. (c) Diligence is the mother of good luck
5. (a) Despite their
    - Despite will not be followed by 'of'
6. (c) She said, 'My brother is getting married.'
    - 'Her brother' become 'my brother' while converting into direct speech in present tense.
7. (a) The boy enquired who dared call him a thief.
    - There is no object with reporting verb. So you can't use told in place of said
8. (d) She said, 'What a miserable plight it is.'
    - Plight: A dangerous, difficult, or otherwise unfortunate situation. Option D is the only sentence which talks about the miserable plight
9. (a) Dhruv said, 'I am sick and tired of working for this company.'
    - Always direct speech should be in 'present tense'.
    - Here in answer stated as 'this company'. In direct speech, have to point out directly. So come this company.
10. (c) Under/around
11. (d) In/next to
12. (b) At/in
13. (a) Over/into
14. (b) Rescue: Save/Help from difficult situation
15. (c)
    - Attempt: Make an effort
    - Serve: Perform duties
    - Explore: Travel through unfamiliar area in order to learn
    - Try: Attempt
    - Explain: describe
16. (a)
    - Foray: Sudden attack, raid
    - Maraud: People to attack, raid, plunder/raid in search of plunder (destroy)
    - Ranger: Keeper of park/forest
    - Intuition: Instinct, ability to understand instinctively
    - Contest: competition
17. (a)
    - Quiescent: Period of inactivity
    - Dormant: Temporarily inactive
    - Unconcerned: Not interested
    - Active: Lively, Agile
    - Weak: Feeble
18. (c)
    - Obeying: Carry out/perform/submit to authorities/to follow order
    - Ordering: to give command

- Refusing: Disobey
- Contradicting: Disagree
- Following: backing

19. (d) Fraudulent: Something done involving deception, dishonest, cheating
    - Candid: Frank, direct
    - Forthright: Outspoken, frank, direct
    - Direct: straight
    - Genuine: original
20. (a)
    - Flagitious: Criminal, marked by scandalous crime, villainous
    - Vapid: Insipid, dull, off, not lively
    - Ignorant: Lacking knowledge
    - Frivolous: Not serious, not important, silly
    - Innocent: guiltless

Keywords

Diligence: Careful work, effort.

PRACTICE SET 21

The strength of the electronics industry in Japan is the Japanese ability to organise production and marketing rather than their achievements in original research. The British are generally recognised as a far more inventive collection of individuals, but never seem able to exploit what they invent. There are many examples, from the TSR Z hovercraft, high-speed train, and Sinclair scooter to the Triumph, BSA, and Norton Motorcycle which all prove this sad rule. The Japanese were able to exploit their strengths in marketing and development many years ago, and their success was at first either not understood in the West or dismissed as something which could have been produced only at their low price. They were sold because they were cheap copies of other people's ideas churned out of a workhouse that was dedicated to hard grind above all else. (Oracle, 2011)

1. It is evident from the passage that the strength of a country's industry depends on
   (a) original research
   (b) international cooperation
   (c) dedicated workforce
   (d) electronic development
2. The sad rule mentioned in this passage refers to
   (a) the inability of the Japanese to be inventive like the British.
   (b) the inability of the British to be industrious like the Japanese.
   (c) the lack of variety in Japanese inventions.
   (d) the poorer marketing ability of the British.
3. The TSR Z hovercraft, high speed train, Sinclair scooter, etc., are the symbols of

(a) Japanese success
(b) British failure
(c) British success
(d) Japanese failure

4. According to the passage, prosperity in an industry depends on
   (a) productivity
   (b) inventiveness
   (c) marketing ability
   (d) official patronage
5. The main theme of this passage is an
   (a) electronic industry in Japan.
   (b) industrial comparison between Japan and Britain.
   (c) the role of marketing efficiency in industrial prosperity.
   (d) the importance of original industry research.

Directions: *In the questions given next, the sentences have been given in direct/indirect speech. From the given alternatives, choose the one which best expresses the given sentence in direct/indirect speech.*

6. 'Are you alone, my son?' asked a soft voice close behind me. (GE, 2012)
   (a) A soft voice asked that what I was doing there alone.
   (b) A soft voice said to me are you alone son.
   (c) A soft voice from my back asked if I was alone.
   (d) A soft voice behind me asked if I was alone.
7. She said to him, 'Why do you not go today?' (Mphasis, 2013)
   (a) She asked him why he did not go that day.
   (b) She said to him why he does not go that day.
   (c) She asked him not to go that day.
   (d) She asked him why he did not go today.
8. He exclaimed with joy that India had won the Sahara Cup. (CoCubes, 2013)
   (a) He said, 'India has won the Sahara Cup.'
   (b) He said, 'India won the Sahara Cup.'
   (c) He said, 'How! India will win the Sahara Cup.'
   (d) He said, 'Hurrah! India has won the Sahara Cup.'
9. The little girl said to her mother, 'Did the sun rise in the East?' (Oracle, 2011)
   (a) The little girl said to her mother that the sun rose in the East.
   (b) The little girl asked her mother if the sun rose in the East.
   (c) The little girl said to her mother if the sun rises in the East.
   (d) The little girl asked her mother if the sun is in the East.

Directions: *Choose the correct answer for each question.*

10. He was driving ______ 180 miles per hour when he crashed ______ the central barrier. (Sail, 2013)
    (a) at/into
    (b) out of/in
    (c) under/around
    (d) in/next to

11. She ran ______ the corridor and ______ the stairs to the second floor. (L&T, 2013)
    (a) from/into (b) towards/over (c) along/up (d) by/on
12. John is the person standing ______ the window, ______ the woman with the long blonde hair. (GE, 2014)
    (a) at/into (b) beside/next to
    (c) under/around (d) in/next to
13. When the bull ran ______ me, I jumped ______ the fence. (Mphasis, 2014)
    (a) from/into (b) towards/over
    (c) beside/next to (d) by/on

Directions: *In the following questions, choose the word which best expresses the meaning of the given word.*

14. Reckless (CoCubes, 2014)
    (a) Courageous (b) Rash (c) Bold (d) Daring
15. Consequences (Mphasis, 2013)
    (a) Results (b) Conclusions (c) Difficulties (d) Applications
16. Improvement (AMCAT, 2013)
    (a) Advancement (b) Betterment (c) Promotion (d) Preference

Directions: *In the following questions, choose the words which are the exact opposite of the given words.*

17. Belittle (Oracle, 2014)
    (a) Criticise (b) Flatter (c) Exaggerate (d) Adore
18. Startled (Triveni Turbine, 2015)
    (a) Amused (b) Relaxed (c) Endless (d) Astonished
19. Busy (Spaneos, 2015)
    (a) Occupied (b) Engrossed (c) Relaxed (d) Engaged
20. Fresh (IBPS, 2014)
    (a) Faulty (b) Sluggish (c) Disgraceful (d) Stale

SOLUTIONS WITH EXPLANATIONS

1. (c) dedicated workforce
2. (d) the poorer marketing ability of British
3. (b) British failure
4. (c) marketing ability
5. (c) the role of marketing efficiency in industrial prosperity
6. (d) Behind is more flexible than from my back so we are using option (d)
7. (a) Here the 'today' changed to past tense 'as that day'
8. (d) Hurrah means happy or joy. Hurrah is used in exclamation sentence
9. (b) Present tense is converted into past tense in indirect speech

10. (a) at/into
11. (c) One has to climb along the corridor and climb up the stairs
12. (b) beside/next to
13. (b) towards/over
14. (b)
    - Reckless: Carless, lack of caution
    - Courageous: Very brave
    - Rash: Hasty, reckless
    - Bold Very confident, fearless, not afraid of danger
    - Daring: Adventurous (adj)
15. (a)
    - Consequences: Result/effect/outcome
    - Conclusions: verdict, end, decision, end result
    - Applications: Act of putting to use
    - Result: End product
    - Difficulties: Inconvenience
16. (a) Improvement: Act of making something better
    - Advancement: Act of moving forward
    - Betterment : the act of making something better
    - Promotion: designation hike
    - Preference : liking, choice, priority
17. (c) Belittle: Something of little importance / unimportant
    - Criticize: Blame, to express disapproval
    - Flatter: to praise too much
    - Exaggerate: Over state, to describe something as larger or greater than it really is
    - Adore: to love deeply, to like very much
18. (b) Startled: Astonish, to surprise some one, dumb found
    - Amused: to make some one laugh / smile
    - Relaxed: Comfortable, peaceful
    - Endless: without limits
    - Astonished: Surprised
19. (c) Active
    - Giving all the attention
    - Comfortable, peaceful
    - Involved in something
20. (d) Fresh: Clean and pure
    - Faulty: Defect
    - Sluggish: Slow / inactive
    - Disgraceful: Shameful
    - Stale: Lost freshness

Practice Sets Type – II

PRACTICE SET 1

Direction: *Read the following passage and answer the questions based on it.*

Jyoti, a gardener's son, was once was invited to attend a marriage ceremony of a Brahmin friend. As he loved his friend dearly, he attended the function. The bridegroom was being led in a procession to the bride's house. The procession consisted of men, women, and children—mostly Brahmins. Jyoti was also walking along with the procession.

One orthodox Brahmin recognised him and was annoyed at the sight of a low-caste boy walking with the Brahmins in the marriage procession. Unable to contain himself, he shouted, '"How dare you walk along with us? You are not our equal. Get behind!" Otherwise, go away.' Jyoti felt insulted. He left the procession and went home.

He narrated the whole incident to his father with anger in his eyes. However, his father advised him to observe old customs. That night, Jyoti could not sleep. He was assailed by the insult he had suffered as a result of discrimination inflicted on lower castes. He felt compelled to find a way to end caste discrimination. As the lower-caste people were not educated, they had accepted this mental slavery for ages. Jyoti therefore resolved to revolt against this mental slavery and educate the lower-caste people. He became the first Indian to start a school for the untouchables as well as a girls' school in Maharashtra. We recognise him today as Mahatma Phule.

1. According to the passage, what has made low-caste people accept mental slavery?
   (a) Poverty (b) Old customs (c) Apathy of change
   (d) Lack of education (e) Supremacy of Brahmins
2. What did Jyoti do after he was insulted?
   (a) Left the procession and went to his friend
   (b) Tried to take revenge on his friend
   (c) Decided not to join any such marriage processions in future
   (d) Involved himself actively in the Freedom Movement
   (e) Engaged himself in social service
3. Why did Joti not sleep that night?
   (a) He had to attend the marriage of his friend
   (b) He wanted to do something to the lower-caste people
   (c) The Brahmins insulted in his friend
   (d) His father was sick

(e) He was not getting any help from his school

4. According to the passage, why did Jyoti quit the marriage procession?
   (a) He was asked accordingly by his friend
   (b) He could not tolerate his insult
   (c) He had to see his ailing father
   (d) His father warned him against attending that marriage
   (e) He had no faith in customary rituals.
5. What does the author highlight in the passage?
   (a) Jyoti's contribution to the upliftment of the people of the lower-castes
   (b) Poverty of lower-class people in India
   (c) Need for separate schools for girls
   (d) Merits of the caste system in India
   (e) Need for unity among different sections of people in India

Directions: *In the following the questions, four words are given of which, two are most nearly the same or opposite in meaning. Find out the two words which are most nearly the same or opposite in meaning.*

6. A. Perfunctory B. Deep C. Wanton D. Compassionate
   (a) A-C (b) A-B (c) B-D (d) C-D (e) B-C
7. A. Diminutive B. Intelligent C. Large D. Prolific
   (a) A-D (b) B-C (c) A-C (d) A-B (e) C-D
8. A. Serene B. Jealous C. Identical D. Calm
   (a) A-B (b) A-C (c) A-D (d) B-C (e) B-D
9. A. Eudemonia B. Extol C. Eulogise D. Euhemerise
   (a) A-B (b) B-C (c) B-D (d) A-D (e) C-D
10. A. Enormous B. Malign C. Absorb D. Slander
    (a) A-C (b) B-C (c) C-D (d) B-D (e) A-D

Directions: *Read each sentence to find out whether there is any error in it. Identify the part of the sentence with the error. If there is no error, the answer is 'No error'.*

11. This laboratory of physics is (a)/not only equipped with (b)/all state of the art instruments (c)/but also with outstanding physicists. (d)/No error (e).
12. No method of making (a)/other people agree to (b)/your view point is (c)/as effective as this method. (d)/No error (e).
13. I was pretty sure that (a)/he would support my views (b)/for changing the age old (c)/and static structure of our organisation. (d)/No error (d).
14. I did not like this (a)/comments on my paper (b)/but I had no alternative (c)/as I had agreed to keep quiet. (d)/No error (e).
15. The report is candid in admitting (a)/that the investment by the government (b)/in health and family planning (c)/have been eroded considerably. (d)/No error. (e)

Directions: *In the questions below, each passage consist of six sentences. The first S1 and the sixth S6 sentences are given in the beginning. The middle four sentences have been removed and jumbled up. These are labelled as P, Q, R, and S. Find out the proper order for the four sentences.*

16. S1: In the middle of one side of the square sits the Chairman of the committee, the most important person in the room.
    P: For a committee, is not just a mere collection of individuals.
    Q: On him rests much of the responsibility for the success or failure of the committee.
    R: While this is happening, we have an opportunity to get the 'feel' of this committee
    S: As the meeting opens, he runs briskly through a number of formalities.
    S6: From the moment its members meet, it begins to have a sort nebulous life of its own.
    The proper sequence should be:
    (a) RSQP (b) PQRS (c) SQPR (d) QSRP
17. S1: A force exists between everybody in the universe.
    P: Normally, it is very small but when the one of the bodies is a planet, like the earth, the force is of considerable magnitude.
    Q: It has been investigated by many scientists including Galileo and Newton.
    R: Everything on or near the surface of the earth is attracted by the mass of the earth.
    S: This gravitational force depends on the mass of the bodies involved.
    S6: The greater the mass, the greater is the earth's force of attraction on it. We can call this the force of attraction gravity.
    The proper sequence should be:
    (a) PRQS (b) PRSQ (c) QSRP (d) QSPR
18. S1: Calcutta, unlike other cities, kept its trams.
    P: As a result, there is horrendous congestion.
    Q: It was going to be the first in South Asia.
    R: They run down the centre of the road
    S: To ease in, the city decided to build an underground railway line.
    S6: The foundation stone was laid in 1972.
    The proper sequence should be:
    (a) PRSQ (b) PSQR (c) SQRP (d) RPSQ
19. S1: For some time in his youth, Abraham Lincoln was a manager for a shop.
    P: Then a chance customer would come.
    Q: Young Lincoln's way of keeping the shop was entirely unlike anyone else's
    R: Lincoln would jump up and attend to his needs and then return to his reading.

S: He used to lie full-length on the counter of the shop eagerly reading a book.

S6: Never before had Lincoln had so much time for reading as he had then.

The proper sequence should be:

(a) SRQP (b) QSPR (c) SQRP (d) QPSR

20. S1: All the land was covered by the ocean.

P: The leading God fought the monster, killed it, and chopped its body in to two halves.

Q: A terrible monster prevented the Gods from separating the land from the water.

R: God made the sky out of the upper part of the body and ornamented it with stars.

S: God created the earth from the lower part, grew plants on it and populated it with animals.

S6: God moulded the first people out of clay according to his own image and mind.

The proper sequence should be:

(a) PQRS (b) PQSR (c) QPSR (d) QPRS

SOLUTIONS WITH EXPLANATIONS

1. (d) Lack of education
2. (e) Engaged himself in social service
3. (b) He wanted to do something to the lower-caste people
4. (b) His father warned him against attending that marriage
5. (e) Need for unity among different sections of people in India
6. (b) Antonyms
7. (c) Antonyms
8. (c) Synonyms
9. (b) Synonyms
10. (d) Synonyms
11. (b) not only equipped with
12. (a) No method of making
13. (c) for changing the age old
14. (c) but I had no alternative
15. (d) have been eroded considerably
16. (d) QSRP
17. (d) QSPR
18. (d) RPSQ
19. (b) QSPR
20. (d) QPRS

PRACTICE SET 2

Directions: *Read the following passage and answer the questions that follow.*

The assault on the purity of the environment is the price that we pay for many of the benefits of modern technology. For the advantages of automotive transportation, we pay a price in smog-induced diseases; for the powerful effects of new insecticides, we pay a price in dwindling wildlife and disturbances in the relation of living things and their surroundings; for nuclear power, we risk the biological hazards of radiation. By increasing agricultural production with fertilisers, we increase water pollution.

The highly developed nations of the world are not only the immediate beneficiaries of the good that technology can do, they are also the first victims of the environmental diseases that technology breeds. In the past, the environmental effects which accompanied technological progress were restricted to a small place and a relatively short time. The new hazards are neither local nor brief. Modern air pollution covers vast areas of continents. Radioactive fallout from nuclear explosions is worldwide. Radioactive pollutants now on the earth's surface will continue to exist for generations, and in the case of Carbon-14, for thousands of years.

1. The widespread use of insecticides has ___________.
   (a) reduced the number of wild animals
   (b) caused an imbalance in the relationship between living beings and their environment
   (c) eliminated diseases by killing mosquitoes and flies
   (d) caused biological hazards
2. The passage emphasis that modern technology ___________.
   (a) is an unmixed blessing
   (b) has caused serious hazards to life
   (c) has produced powerful chemicals
   (d) has benefited highly developed nations
3. According to the passage, the increasing use of fertilisers is responsible for ___________.
   (a) abundance of food (b) disturbance in the ecological system
   (c) water pollution (d) increase in diseases
4. The harmful effects of modern technology are ___________.
   (a) widespread but short-lived (b) widespread and long-lasting
   (c) limited and long-lasting (d) severe but short-lived
5. Radioactive pollutants ___________.
   (a) are limited in their effect
   (b) will infect the atmosphere for thousands of years
   (c) will be on the surface of the earth for a very long time
   (d) will dissipate in a short span of time

Directions: *In each of the following questions, there is a sentence of which some parts have been jumbled up. Rearrange these parts, which are labelled P, Q, R, and S, to produce the correct sentence. Choose the proper sequence.*

6. When he ____________.

   P: did not know

   Q: he was nervous and

   R: heard the hue and cry at midnight

   S: what to do

   The proper sequence should be:

   (a) RQPS (b) QSPR (c) SQPR (d) PQRS

7. It has been established that ____________.

   P: Einstein was

   Q: although a great scientist

   R: weak in arithmetic

   S: right from his school days

   The proper sequence should be:

   (a) SRPQ (b) QPRS (c) QPSR (d) RQPS

8. Then ____________.

   P: it struck me

   Q: of course

   R: suitable it was

   S: how eminently

   The proper sequence should be:

   (a) SPQR (b) QSRP (c) PSRQ (d) QPSR

9. I read an advertisement that said ____________.

   P: posh, air-conditioned

   Q: gentleman of taste

   R: are available for

   S: fully furnished rooms

   The proper sequence should be:

   (a) PQRS (b) PSRQ (c) PSQR (d) SRPQ

10. Since the beginning of history ____________.

    P: have managed to catch

    Q: the Eskimos and the Red Indians

    R: by a very difficult method

    S: a few specimens of this aquatic animal

    The proper sequence should be:

    (a) QRPS (b) SQPR (c) SQRP (d) QPSR

Directions: *Read each sentence to find out whether there is any error in it.*

11. He is certainly a man (a)/whom I know very well (b)/is trust worthy beyond doubt (c)/and meticulous in his habits. (d)/No error (e)

12. No sooner did (a)/we reach the station (b)/than the train had (c)/started moving out of the station. (d)/No error (e)
13. I am sure about it, (a)/nobody has lived (b)/in that house (c)/for a hundred years. (d)/No error (e)

Directions: *Pick out the most effective word(s) from the given words to fill in the blank to make the sentence meaningfully complete.*

14. Fate smiles _____ those who untiringly grapple with stark realities of life.
    (a) with (b) over (c) on (d) round
15. The miser gazed __________ at the pile of gold coins in front of him.
    (a) avidly (b) admiringly (c) thoughtfully (d) earnestly
16. Catching the earlier train will give us the ________ to do some shopping.
    (a) chance (b) luck (c) possibility (d) occasion

Directions: *In the following questions, choose the word which best expresses the meaning of the given word.*

17. Canny
    (a) Obstinate (b) Handsome (c) Clever (d) Stout
18. Indict
    (a) Condemn (b) Reprimand (c) Accuse (d) Allege

Directions: *In the following questions, choose the word which is the exact opposite in meaning of the given words.*

19. Commissioned
    (a) Started (b) Closed (c) Finished (d) Terminated
20. Quiescent
    (a) Active (b) Dormant (c) Weak (d) Unconcerned

SOLUTIONS WITH EXPLANATIONS

1. (b) caused an imbalance in the relationship between living beings and their environment
2. (b) has caused serious hazards to life
3. (c) water pollution
4. (b) widespread and long-lasting
5. (c) will be on the surface of the earth for a very long time
6. (a) RQPS
7. (b) QPRS
8. (c) PSRQ
9. (b) PSRQ
10. (d) QPSR
11. (c) is trust worthy beyond doubt
12. (c) started moving out of the station.

13. (b) nobody has lived
14. (c) on
15. (a) avidly
16. (a) chance
17. (c) Clever
18. (c) Accuse
19. (d) Terminated
20. (a) Active

PRACTICE SET 3

Direction: *Read the given passage and the answer the questions that follow.*

The Devil's Interval enjoyed great popularity among composers in the 19th Century, when 'you have got lots of presentations of evil built around the tritone'. 'It can sound very spooky. It depends on how you orchestrate it. It is also quite exciting,' says Professor Deathridge. 'Wagner's Gotterdammerung has one of the most exciting scenes—a "pagan", evil scene, the drums and the timpani. It is absolutely terrifying; it is like a black mass.' There is a big connection between heavy rock music and Wagner. They have cribbed quite a lot from nineteenth century music. 'A more modern advocate of the tritone is Black Sabbath—the rock outfit led by Ozzy Osbourne—particularly in their signature song, Black Sabbath, a milestone in the genesis of heavy metal. But this link between heavy metal and musical conjuring of the Devil in the Middle Ages comes as a bit of a surprise to the band's guitarist, Tony Iommi. When I started writing Sabbath stuff it was just something that sounded right. I did not think I was going to make it Devil music,' says Iommi.

He says he was aiming for 'something that sounded really evil and very doomy' but admits he may have been unconsciously influenced by other music and was certainly not aiming to summon the Devil. 'Beforehand we were doing jazzy blues. It certainly was not something I thought about. I did not read music. I had no terms for anything. 'I like all sorts of classical stuff—various sorts of music, jazz, blues, to classical played a big part in my writing.' There are, however, plenty of bands who consciously use tritones, including the notorious metal act Slayer, who offered their tribute in an album simply entitled Diabolus in Musica. (Mphasis, 2012)

1. Why does the link between heavy metal and musical conjuring of the Devil come as a surprise to Tony Iommi?
   (a) Because he did not believe in the Devil
   (b) Because he did not believe that the Devil could be conjured through music
   (c) Because he was not aiming to write something that sounded evil and doomy

(d) Because he had played only jazz and blues

2. According to Tony Iommi, what influenced his playing style?
   (a) Only jazz, blues and classical
   (b) Solely a desire to create evil-sounding music
   (c) Both jazz, blues, classical, and a desire to create evil sounding music
   (d) Slayer
3. Which of the titles given below best expresses the ideas of this passage?
   (a) The History of the Tritone
   (b) The Devil's Note in Modern Music
   (c) Diabolus in Musica
   (d) Heavy Metal and Wagner
4. What is the antonym of the word 'Pagan' given in the passage?
   (a) Infidel (b) Atheist (c) Agnostic (d) Religious
5. As per the passage, the timpani can be inferred as ________.
   (a) a loud cry (b) a musical instrument
   (c) the orchestra conductor (d) a purring cat
6. Which of the following words is spelt correctly?
   (a) Remenisent (b) Reiminisent (c) Riminisint (d) Reminiscent

Directions:

7. Construe
   (a) Interpret (b) Promote (c) Reserve (d) Erect
8. Contaminate
   (a) Arrest (b) Prepare (c) Pollute (d) Beam
9. Choose the odd one among the following. (CoCubes, 2013)
   (a) Niche (b) Angst (c) Trepidation (d) Disquiet

Directions: *Given below are the sentences which, when arranged logically, form a coherent passage. Identify the correct sequence of sentences.* (Accenture, 2012)

10. A. The alternative was a blitz by the health workers to popularise preventive measures
    B. But the information in mass media was not sufficient
    C. People have been reading about AIDS in the mass media
    D. But nobody is sure as to how effective even this would be, as
    E. People are not being influenced enough to take preventive measures
    (a) CBADE (b) ABCDE (c) BACDE (d) CDABE
11. A. Combining supportiveness with openness produces a cumulative effect that characterises the most successful teams
    B. Present day work consists almost only completely of team work
    C. We can use openness as an excuse for being caustic, insulting, psychologically cold, and distant

D. The combination is the key, because openness can go in either of the two basic directions

(a) BADC (b) ABCD (c) BACD (d) CDAB

12. The sentence below is in direct or indirect speech and is followed by four alternatives of the opposite form of narration. Choose the correct alternative, which is in opposite narration. (Accenture, 2010)

She asked me, 'Have you been to Amritsar before'?

(a) She asked have you been to Amritsar before.
(b) She asked had you been to Amritsar before.
(c) She said I had been to Amritsar before.
(d) She asked if I had been to Amritsar before.

Directions: *Fill in the blank(s) with the most suitable options.*

13. Previous studies have shown that drinking tea is a boon __ cardiovascular health, but now researchers have found that the beneficial effects __ the drink are totally wiped out__ putting milk __ it. (Oracle, 2014)

(a) for, of, by, into (b) of, for, to, in
(c) by, at, for, on (d) on, in, by, in

14. _____ teacher who takes our mathematics lessons is on leave today. He may not be available for _____ coming week. (Oracle, 2014)

(a) An, the (b) A, the (c) The, the (d) The, a

15. He lives near a lovely _______ of countryside. (Oracle, 2014)

(a) length (b) piece (c) section (d) stretch

Directions: *Find the error.*

16. The government needs to provide (1)/specific regulations that create an environment (2)/where trained scientific personnel enjoyed space and freedom (3)/to design new products benefiting society. (4)/No error (5) (Tech Mahindra, 2014)

(a) 1 (b) 2 (c) 3 (d) 4 (e) 5

17. Conventionally speaking, (1)/men are supposed to earn while (2)/women are supposed to sit at home, (3)/do housework, and discipline the children. (4)/No error (5) (Tech Mahindra, 2014)

(a) 1 (b) 2 (c) 3 (d) 4 (e) 5

Directions: *Pick out the most effective word from the given words to fill in the blank to make the sentence meaningfully complete.*

18. Your friend died _____ over work. (Syntel, 2011)

(a) of (b) from (c) due to (d) with

19. It is not easy to beat ______ a swarm of wasps if they attack you. (Syntel, 2011)

(a) out (b) up (c) down (d) off

20. What a sensation it would cause if it _____ now discovered that such a man had left behind a diary. (Syntel, 2011)
    (a) is (b) be (c) was (d) were

SOLUTIONS WITH EXPLANATIONS

1. (d) Because he had played only jazz and blues
2. (c) Both jazz, blues, classical, and a desire to create evil sounding music
3. (b) The Devil's Note in Modern Music
4. (d) Religious
5. (b) a musical instrument
6. (d) Reminiscent
7. (a) Interpret
8. (c) Pollute
9. (a) Niche
10. (a) CBADE
11. (a) BADC
12. (d) She asked if I had been to Amritsar before
13. (a) for, of, by, into
14. (c) The, the
15. (d) stretch
16. (c) 3
17. (a) 1
18. (a) of
19. (d) off
20. (d) were

PRACTICE SET 4

Directions: *Read the passage and answer the questions that follow.*

Harold, a professional man who had worked in an office for many years, had a fearful dream. In it, he found himself in a land where small slug-like animals with slimy tentacles lived on people's bodies. The people tolerated the loathsome creatures because after many years, they grew into elephants which then became the nation's system of transport, carrying everyone wherever they wanted to go. Harold suddenly realised that he himself was covered with these things, and he woke up screaming. In a vivid sequence of pictures this dream dramatised for Harold what he had never been able to put in to words; he saw himself as letting society feed on his body in his early years so that it would carry him when he retired. He later threw off the 'security bug' and took up freelance work. (Mphasis, 2013)

1. In his dream, Harold found the loathsome creatures ___________.
    (a) in his village (b) in his own house

(c) in a different land (d) in his office

2. Which one of the following phrases best helps to bring out the precise meaning of 'loathsome creatures'?
   (a) Security bug and slimy tentacles
   (b) Fearful dream and slug-like animals
   (c) Slimy tentacles and slug-like animals
   (d) slug-like animals and security bug
3. The statement 'he later threw off the security bug' means that __________.
   (a) Harold succeeded in overcoming the need for security
   (b) Harold stopped giving much importance to his dreams
   (c) Harold started tolerating social victimisation
   (d) Harold killed all the bugs that troubled him
4. Harold's dream was fearful because __________.
   (a) it brought him face to face with reality
   (b) it was full of vivid pictures of snakes
   (c) he saw a huge elephant in it
   (d) in it, he saw slimy creatures feeding on people's bodies
5. Choose the odd one among the following.
   (a) Rubric (b) Stricture (c) Label (d) Caption
6. Choose the word from the following options which is spelt correctly.
   (a) Connosseur (b) Connoisseur (c) Conniseur (d) Conoissur

Directions: *Consider the given sentence and identify the part which contains an error.*

7. There are people who book domain names for the sole purpose of profit from the domain by either selling advertisements or selling the domain name at a later date for a higher amount.
   (a) There are people who book domain names
   (b) for the sole purpose of profit from the domain
   (c) by either selling advertisements or sell the domain name
   (d) at a later date for a higher amount.

Directions: *Given below are the sentences which when arranged logically form a coherent passage. Identify the correct sequence of sentences.* (Mphasis, 2012)

8. A. The word Piazza, of course reminds us of Italy
   B. It is leaning to one side with the celebrated inclination—that daring challenge to the laws of statics and is a unique building of its kind, both for its great art, historical value and for its peculiar situation,
   C. In the context of the vast and similarly distinctive area known as the Piazza dei Miracoli
   D. The Tower of Pisa is the bell tower of the Cathedral
   (a) ABCD (b) DBCA (c) BACD (d) BCAD

9. A. But the difficulty for anyone carrying out such an investigation is finding people known to have dieted rigorously enough for a sufficiently long time
   B. Scientists have inferred that diets have an impact on our body
   C. Findings like this have led scientists to wonder if strict dieting can help humans live longer
   D. Now, a team from Washington State University has overcome that obstacle by recruiting volunteers from an American group dedicated to serious low-calorie eating
   (a) ABCD (b) CBAD (c) BCAD (d) CADB

Directions: *Fill in the blank(s) with the most suitable option.* (Mphasis, 2014)

10. It is impossible ______ Ravi to do away _____ his extravagant ways.
    (a) to, for (b) for, with (c) for, into (d) to, with
11. I took _____ book from the pile of books on your table. _____ book was very interesting to read.
    (a) a, The (b) the, A (c) an, The (d) some, The

Directions: *The sentence below is in direct or indirect speech and is followed by four alternatives of the opposite form of narration. Choose the correct alternative, which is in opposite narration.*

12. 'How old is your mother?', he asked her.
    (a) He asked how old her mother was.
    (b) He asked how old is your mother.
    (c) He asked how old your mother was.
    (d) He asked how old was your mother.
13. Fill in the blank(s) with the most suitable option. (Mphasis, 2013)
    The no-frills airline, Air Deccan, is offering a ticket worth five lakh for free, but _____ taxes and surcharges. In an effort _____ stimulate air travel _____ the lean season.
    (a) without, for, at (b) from, to, for
    (c) with, to, during (d) instead, on, from

Directions: *Find the error.*

14. The movement, which aims to (1)/raise awareness about climate change hopes (2)/to bring people together to think about (3)/what they can do for reduce harmful pollution. (4)/No error. (5) (Tech Mahindra, 2014)
    (a) 1 (b) 2 (c) 3 (d) 4 (e) 5
15. Six Women achievers, who continue (1)/ to inspire the younger lot, were honored (2)/with their contributions in their chosen fields (3) / on the occasion of women's day. (4)/No error. (5) (Tech Mahindra, 2014)
    (a) 1 (b) 2 (c) 3 (d) 4 (e) 5

Directions: *Read the sentences given below and answer the questions that follow.*

The surprisingly abundant life of the Indian Ocean is confined to the upper layers; the deeper, and especially, the bottom waters, are devoid of oxygen and are often permeated with hydrogen sulphide.

16. The sentence gives the information about ________.
    (a) the life of the people near the Indian Ocean
    (b) the reason why life exists in particular water layers
    (c) the reason why oxygen is found in the bottom layers
    (d) the reason why hydrogen sulphide is found in the bottom layers
17. The bottom waters of the Indian Ocean ________.
    (a) have no oxygen
    (b) have large amounts of oxygen
    (c) have no hydrogen sulphide
    (d) contain oxygen and hydrogen sulphide
18. The waters of the Indian Ocean ________.
    (a) are devoid of life
    (b) are always permeated with hydrogen sulphide
    (c) have life only in the lower layers
    (d) lack life, and it is very surprising
19. Which of the following is opposite in meaning to the word 'abundant', as used in the passage?
    (a) Plentiful (b) Minute (c) Insufficient (d) Tiny
20. The sentence suggests that ________.
    (a) observers are surprised at how little life exists in the Indian Ocean
    (b) hydrogen sulphide is necessary for life to exist
    (c) both oxygen and hydrogen sulphide are necessary for life to exist
    (d) oxygen is not necessary for marine life

SOLUTIONS WITH EXPLANATIONS

1. (c) in a different land
2. (c) Slimy tentacles and slug-like animals
3. (a) Harold succeeded in overcoming the need for security
4. (a) it brought him face to face with reality
5. (b) Stricture
6. (b) Connoisseur
7. (c) by either selling advertisements or sell the domain name
8. (b) DBCA
9. (c) BCAD
10. (b) for, with
11. (a) a, The
12. (a) He asked how old her mother was.

13. (c) with, to, during
14. (d) 4
15. (c) 3
16. (d) the reason why hydrogen sulphide is found in the bottom layers
17. (a) have no oxygen
18. (d) lack life, and it is very surprising
19. (d) Tiny
20. (a) observers are surprised at how little life exists in the Indian Ocean

PRACTICE SET 5

Directions: *Read the passage and answer the questions that follow.*

There was a marked difference of quality between the personages who haunted near the bridge of bricks and the personages who haunted the far one of stone. Those of lowest character preferred the former, adjoining the town; they did not mind the glare of the public eye. They had been of no account during their successes; and though they might feel dispirited, they had no sense of shame in their ruin. Instead of sighing at their adversaries, they spat, and instead of saying the iron had entered into their souls, they said they were down in their luck. The miserable who would pause on the remoter bridge of politer stamp persons who did not know how to get rid of the weary time. The eyes of his species were mostly directed over the parapet upon the running water below. While one on the town ward bridge did not mind who saw him so, and kept his back to the parapet to survey the passer-by, one on them never faced the road, never turned his head at the coming foot-steps, but, sensitive on his own condition, watched the current whenever a stranger approached, as if some strange fish interested him, though every finned thing had been poached out of the rivers years before. (Accenture, 2010)

1. In this passage, the author is trying to __________.
   (a) explain the difference between the construction of the two bridges
   (b) describe the way different sections of people like to dress
   (c) explain the variety of ways in which strangers can be treated
   (d) describe how people of different classes behaved when unhappy
2. People belonging to the lower strata in their moments of distress ________.
   (a) the days of glory
   (b) dressed shabbily to earn sympathy
   (c) visited the brick made bridge
   (d) felt ashamed of their failures
3. The attitude of lowly and genteel towards the strangers was
   (a) virtually the same
   (b) entirely different
   (c) completely indifferent

(d) virulently hostile

4. Choose the word from the following options which is spelt correctly.
(a) Fisticoughs (b) Fisticoups (c) Fisticuffs (d) Fisticuphs
5. Haughty
(a) Clear (b) Simple (c) Arrogant (d) Teetotaller

Directions: *Fill in the blank(s) with the most suitable option.*

6. During the ________ election week in May, last year, ________ politicians were busy dodging the issue of incomplete work they had done in the previous five years while promising a lot to the poor. (Capgemini, 2013)
(a) final, terse (b) tumultuous, unscrupulous
(c) pitched, ineffective (d) showy, unseasonable
7. Hiatus : Gap :: ______ : ______
(a) Imbecile : Smart (b) Greenfield : Project
(c) Zenith : Pinnacle (d) Nuptial : Cornucopia
8. Consider the following four words and identify the two which have the same meaning.
1. Choleric 2. Inept 3. Irascible 4. Indentation
(a) 1, 4 (b) 1, 3 (c) 3, 4 (d) 1, 2

Directions: *Fill in the blank(s) with the most suitable option.* (Capgemini, 2015)

9. He ran away by jumping _______ a window and jumping ________ a waiting car.
(a) over, into (b) up to, into (c) out of, into (d) between, into

Directions: *Frame a proper sentence.*

10. The actor, who plays (1)/a detective in the film, alleged to have pushed the director (2)/when he asked him to get into his costume (3)/as it was getting late. (4)/No error (5) (Tech Mahindra, 2014)
(a) 1 (b) 2 (c) 3 (d) 4 (e) 5
11. Manish was advised an operation (1)/more than thirty years back, but (2)/ due to his financial condition he (3)/could not undergoes the procedure. (4)/No error (5) (Tech Mahindra, 2014)
(a) 1 (b) 2 (c) 3 (d) 4 (e) 5
12. Many of the young people (1)/studying abroad agreed that (2)/returning home was always (3)/an attractive option. (4)/No error (5) (Tech Mahindra, 2014)
(a) 1 (b) 2 (c) 3 (d) 4 (e) 5

Directions: *Pick out the most appropriate word from the given words to fill in the blank and make the sentence meaningfully complete.* (Capgemini, 2013)

13. Madan _______ the first prize in this competition. (Syntel, 2011)
(a) bore up (b) bore with (c) bore out (d) bore away

14. In large cities, people are cut ________ from nature. (Syntel, 2011)
    (a) down (b) out (c) off (d) away

Directions: *Frame proper sentence.*

15. Have you been more careful, the accident could have been averted. (Cognizant, 2012)
    (a) If you have been (b) Had you been
    (c) Have you been (d) If you could have been
    (e) No correction required
16. The prices of essential commodities has risen unprecedentedly, causing a lot of hardship to the common man. (Cognizant, 2012)
    (a) has Rosen (b) has rising (c) have risen
    (d) have rose (e) no correction required
17. The two belligerent nations decided to come to a compromise and resolve the issue amicably. (Cognizant, 2012)
    (a) to make a compromise (b) making a compromise
    (c) for a compromise (d) on compromising
    (e) No correction required

Directions: *In the following questions, choose the words which are the exact opposite in meaning of the given words.*

18. Evasive (Oracle, 2014)
    (a) Free (b) Honest (c) Liberal (d) Frank
19. Rarely (Oracle, 2014)
    (a) Hardly (b) Definitely (c) Frequently (d) Periodically
20. Malicious (Oracle, 2013)
    (a) Kind (b) Boastful (c) Generous (d) Indifferent

Directions: *In the following questions, choose the word which best expresses the meaning of the given word.*

21. Shallow (Oracle, 2014)
    (a) Artificial (b) Superficial (c) Foolish (d) Worthless

SOLUTIONS WITH EXPLANATIONS

1. (d) describe how people of different classes behaved when unhappy
2. (b) dressed shabbily to earn sympathy
3. (c) completely indifferent
4. (c) Fisticuffs
5. (c) Arrogant
6. (b) tumultuous, unscrupulous
7. (c) Zenith : Pinnacle
8. (b) 1,3

9. (c) out of, into
10. (b) 2
11. (d) 4
12. (e) 5
13. (a) bore up
14. (c) off
15. (b) Had you been
16. (c) have risen
17. (e) No correction required
18. (d) Periodically
19. (a) Hardly
20. (a) Kind
21. (b) Superficial

PRACTICE SET 6

Directions: *Read the passage and answer the questions that follow.*

The biggest house of cards, the longest tongue, and of course, the tallest man: these are among the thousands of records logged in the famous *Guinness Book of Records*. Created in 1955 after a debate concerning Europe's fastest game bird, what began as a marketing tool sold to pub landlords to promote Guinness, an Irish drink, became the bestselling copyright title of all time (a category that excludes books such as the Bible and the Koran). In time, the book would sell 120 million copies in over 100 countries—quite a leap from its humble beginnings.

In its early years, the book set its sights on satisfying man's innate curiosity about the natural world around him. Its two principal fact finders, twins Norris and Ross McWhirter, scoured the globe to collect empirical facts. It was their task to find and document aspects of life that can be sensed or observed, things that can be quantified or measured. But not just any things. They were only interested in superlatives: the biggest and the best. It was during this period that some of the hallmark Guinness Records were documented, answering such questions as "What is the brightest star?" and "What is the biggest spider?" Once aware of the public's thirst for such knowledge, the book's authors began to ranch out to cover increasingly obscure, little-known facts. They started documenting human achievements as well. A forerunner for reality television, the *Guinness Book* gave people a chance to become famous for accomplishing eccentric, often pointless tasks. Records were set in 1955 for consuming 24 raw eggs in 14 minutes and in 1981 for the fastest solving of a Rubik's Cube (which took a mere 38 seconds). In 1979, a man yodelled non-stop for ten and quarter hours.

In its latest incarnation, the book has found a new home on the internet. No longer restricted to the confines of physical paper, the Guinness World Records website contains seemingly innumerable facts concerning such topics as the most powerful combustion engine, or the world's longest train. What is striking, however, is that such facts are found sharing a page with the record of the heaviest train to be pulled with a beard. While there is no denying that each of these facts has its own, individual allure, the latter represents a significant deviation from the education-oriented facts of earlier editions. Perhaps there is useful knowledge to be gleaned regarding the tensile strength of a beard, but this seems to cater to an audience more interested in seeking entertainment than education. Originating as a simple bar book, the *Guinness Book of Records* has evolved over decades to provide insight into the full spectrum of modern life. And although one may be more likely now to learn about the widest human mouth than the highest number of casualties in a single battle of the Civil War, the Guinness World Records website offers a telling glimpse into the future of fact-finding and record-recording. (Infosys, 2013)

1. Which of the following statements would best serve as the headline for this passage?
   (a) The encyclopaedia of the extremes reflects the changing interests of modern society.
   (b) A book of simple origins makes it to the top as sales total a staggering 120 million copies.
   (c) Facts are often displayed in a boring, uninteresting manner, but not in the *Guinness Book of Records*.
   (d) The Guinness World Records website proves itself a valuable resource for insight into the full spectrum of modern life.
   (e) Where other books fall short, the index of superlative sciences never ceases to amaze.
2. According to the author, the most significant difference between the older editions of the *Guinness Book of Records* and the new Guinness World Records website involves ___________.
   (a) an end to the use of facts as a means to promote Guinness
   (b) an overall increase in the total number of facts presented
   (c) a move from fact-finding to the recording of achievements
   (d) a shift in focus from educational to entertaining material
   (e) a departure from book sales being limited to local pubs and bars
3. As used in paragraph 2, which is the best definition for empirical?
   (a) Natural (b) Derived from experience
   (c) Recordable (d) Excellent or unmatched
   (e) Convenient or handy
4. Based on its use in paragraph 2, which of the following best describes something that is superlative?

(a) Students give presentations about their favorite subjects for a grade. Amy Newhouse receives an 87 per cent for her presentation, while Dustin Lincoln receives a 92 per cent.
(b) Although sharks are significantly bigger and have razor-sharp teeth, dolphins are smarter and can therefore successfully evade attack.
(c) The lake holds a contest to see who can catch the biggest fish. Tommy wins, having caught a 6 lb. 5 oz. smallmouth bass.
(d) A man built an enormous house of cards. It took him 44 days and 218,792 individual playing cards to complete.
(e) Ichiro likes tennis and practices every day. In his last tournament, he placed 3rd of over 350 competitors, winning the bronze trophy.

5. Using the passage as a guide, it can be inferred that the author most likely believes reality television to be ________.
(a) corrupt (b) absurd (c) idiotic (d) invaluable (e) shallow

6. Which of the following best summarises the organisation of this passage?
(a) Introduction, history, conclusion
(b) History, examples, explanations, conclusion
(c) Exposition, history, conclusion
(d) Introduction, thesis, supporting paragraphs, conclusion
(e) Introduction, history, exposition, conclusion

Directions: *Fill in the blanks.*

7. Some say peter killed his father that is impossible he ________ that. (HCL, 2011)
(a) may have done (b) could not have done
(c) could not done (d) must not have done

8. Let us go ______ get some petrol. (HCL, 2011)
(a) for (b) and (c) we (d) together

9. One _____ the new scheme is that it might actually _____ just those applicants that it was intended to encourage. (Tech Mahindra, 2014)
(a) highlight of, rouse (b) feature of, attract
(c) problem with, provoked (d) attraction of, intimidate
(e) drawback of, daunt

10. His characteristically ____ views on examination methods at university level have aroused ____ in those who want to introduce innovative and flexible patterns of assessment. (Tech Mahindra, 2014)
(a) hidebound, antagonism (b) moderate, anger
(c) reactionary, admiration (d) rigid, support
(e) accommodating, annoyance

Directions: *Each question consist of two words which have a certain relationship to each other followed by four pairs of related words, Select the pair which has the same relationship.* (Mindtree, 2013)

11. After : Before
    (a) First : Second (b) Present : Past
    (c) Contemporary : Historic (d) Successor : Predecessor
12. Indigent : Wealthy
    (a) Angry : Rich (b) Native : Affluent
    (c) Gauche : Graceful (d) Scholarly : Erudite
13. Distance : Mile
    (a) Liquid : Litre (b) Bushel : Corn
    (c) Weight : Scale (d) Fame : Television

Directions: *Arrange the sentences in the correct order.* (Infosys, 2012)

14. A. With the time spent eating, sleeping, taking care of household chores, and looking after the family, there is little time left for leisure activities for many American.
    B. Results of a 2001 Harris Poll on free time conducted in the United States showed that the average workweek for many Americans is fifty hours.
    C. People today seem to have increasingly hectic lifestyles.
    D. In addition, many people spend up to two or three hours a day commuting to and from work.
    (a) ABCD (b) CBDA (c) ACBD (d) CADB
15. A. The most popular activity for Americans was gardening.
    B. We can see from the above examples tat in different countries and cultures around the world, free time is spend in different ways.
    C. In the U.K., it was going to the pub, followed by visiting the cinema.
    D. In Japan, it was very different from the first two countries. Going too bars and pubs ranked eighth in popularity, and gardening ranked ninth.
    E. There were differences in the most popular outdoor pursuits between the following three countries.
    (a) EADCB (b) BEACD (c) EACDB (d) CEABD
16. A. When identity is thus 'defined by contrast', divergence with the West becomes central.
    B. Indian religious literature such as the Bhagavad Gita or the Tantric texts, which are identified as differing from secular writings seen as 'western', elicits much greater interest in the West than do other Indian writings, including India's long history of heterodoxy.
    C. There is a similar neglect of Indian writing on non-religious subjects, from mathematics, epistemology and natural science to economics and linguistics.

D. Through selective emphasis that point up differences with the West, other civilizations can, in this way, be redefined in alien terms, which can be exotic and charming, or else bizarre and terrifying, or simply strange and engaging.
E. The exception is the Kamasutra in which western readers have managed to cultivate an interest.
(a) BDACE (b) DEABC (c) BDECA (d) BCEDA

17. A. This is now orthodoxy to which I subscribe—up to a point.
B. It emerged from the mathematics of chance and statistics.
C. Therefore the risk is measurable and manageable.
D. The fundamental concept: Prices are not predictable, but the mathematical laws of chance can describe their fluctuations.
E. This is how what business schools now call modern finance was born.
(a) ADCBE (b) EBDCA (c) ABDCE (d) DCBEA

Directions: *Each of the following sentences has been divided into four parts. There is an error in one of the parts. Point out the part which has an error.*

18. (A) he has broken his pen,/(B) and his paper is not yet complete,/(C) but you can help him/(D) if you give him your for an hour./(E) no error. (InfoTech, 2011)
(a) A (b) B (c) C (d) D (e) E
19. (A) This book is quite different/(B) than the one I gave you,/(C) because it is an old edition/(D) and does not cover the whole course./(E) no error. (InfoTech, 2011)
(a) A (b) B (c) C (d) D (e) E
20. (A) He could come/(B) if you invite him/(C) well in time/(D) in writing./(E) no error. (InfoTech, 2011)
(a) A (b) B (c) C (d) D (e) E

SOLUTIONS WITH EXPLANATIONS

1. (a) The encyclopaedia of the extremes reflects the changing interests of modern society
2. (d) a shift in focus from educational to entertaining material
3. (b) Derived from experience
4. (c) The lake holds a contest to see who can catch the biggest fish. Tommy wins, having caught a 6 lb. 5 oz. smallmouth bass.
5. (e) Shallow
6. (e) Introduction, history, exposition, conclusion
7. (b) could not have done
8. (b) and
9. (e) drawback of, daunt

10. (a) hidebound, antagonism
11. (d) Successor : Predecessor
12. (c) Gauche : Graceful
13. (a) Liquid : Litre
14. (b) CBDA
15. (c) EACDB
16. (d) BCEDA
17. (b) EBDCA
18. (d) D
19. (b) B
20. (b) B

PRACTICE SET 7

Directions: *Read the passage. Then, answer the questions that follow.*

The Alaska pipeline starts at the frozen edge of the Arctic Ocean. It stretches south-ward across the largest and northern-most state in the United States, ending at a remote ice-free seaport village nearly 800 miles from where it begins. It is massive in size and extremely complicated to operate. The steel pipe crosses windswept plains and endless miles of delicate tundra that tops the frozen ground. It weaves through crooked canyons, climbs sheer mountains, plunges over rocky crags, makes its way through thick forests, and passes over or under hundreds of rivers and streams. The pipe is 4 feet in diameter, and up to 2 million barrels (or 84 million gallons) of crude oil can be pumped through it daily. Resting on H-shaped steel racks called "bents", long sections of the pipeline follow a zigzag course high above the frozen earth. Other long sections drop out of sight beneath spongy or rocky ground and return to the surface later on. The pattern of the pipeline's up-and-down route is determined by the often harsh demands of the Arctic and sub-Arctic climate, the tortuous lay of the land, and the varied compositions of soil, rock, or permafrost (permanently frozen ground).

A little more than half of the pipeline is elevated above the ground. The remainder is buried anywhere from 3 to 12 feet, depending largely upon the type of terrain and the properties of the soil. One of the largest in the world, the pipeline cost approximately US$ 8 billion and is by far the biggest and most expensive construction project ever undertaken by private industry. In fact, no single business could raise that much money, so 8 major oil companies formed a consortium in order to share the costs. Each company controlled oil rights to particular shares of land in the oil fields and paid into the pipeline-construction fund according to the size of its holdings. Today, despite enormous problems of climate, supply shortages, equipment breakdowns, labor disagreements, treacherous terrain, a certain amount of mismanagement, and even theft, the Alaska pipeline has been completed and is operating. (Infosys, 2011)

1. The passage primarily discusses the pipeline's __________.
   (a) operating costs (b) employees (c) consumers (d) construction
2. The word 'it' in line 4 refers to the __________.
   (a) pipeline (b) ocean (c) state (d) village
3. According to the passage, 84 million gallons of oil can travel through the pipeline each __________.
   (a) day (b) week (c) month (d) year
4. The phrase "Resting on" in line 13 is closest in meaning to __________.
   (a) consisting of (b) supported by
   (c) passing under (d) protected with
5. The author mentions all of the following as important in determining the pipeline's route EXCEPT the __________.
   (a) climate (b) lay of the land itself
   (c) local vegetation (d) kind of soil and rock
6. The word 'undertaken' in line 26 is closest in meaning to __________.
   (a) removed (b) selected (c) transported (d) attempted
7. How many companies shared the costs of constructing the pipeline?
   (a) 3 (b) 4 (c) 8 (d) 12
8. The word 'particular' in line 29 is closest in meaning to __________.
   (a) peculiar (b) specific (c) exceptional (d) equal
9. Which of the following determined what percentage of the construction costs each member of the consortium would pay?
   (a) How much oil field land each company owned
   (b) For how long each company had owned land in the oil fields
   (c) How many people worked for each company
   (d) How many oil wells were located on each company's land
10. Where in the passage does the author provide a term for an earth covering that always remains frozen?
   (a) Line 3 (b) Line 13 (c) Line 19 (d) Line 32

Directions: *Fill in the blanks.*

11. ________ a beautiful present ________ expensive it must be. (HCL, 2011)
   (a) Such, what (b) What, such
   (c) What, how (d) Such, what
12. There is no reason ________ anyone should behave so cruelly. (HCL, 2011)
   (a) for which (b) that (c) why (d) because
13. Your friend died ________ over work. (Syntel, 2011)
   (a) of (b) from (c) due to (d) with
14. It is not easy to beat ________ a swarm of wasps if they attack you. (Syntel, 2011)
   (a) out (b) up (c) down (d) off

15. Some critics maintain that Tennyson's poetry is uneven, ranging from the _______ to the _______. (Tech Mahindra, 2014)
    (a) magnificent, elevated (b) trite, inspired
    (c) vacuous, inane (d) succinct, laconic
    (e) resonant, voluble

Directions: *In the questions given below, each passage consist of six sentences. The first and the sixth sentences are given in the beginning. The middle four sentences have been removed and jumbled up. These are labelled as P, Q, R, and S. Find out the proper order for the four sentences.* (Mindtree, 2011)

16. S1: You know my wife, Madhavi, always urged me to give up smoking.
    P: I really gave it up.
    Q: And so, when I went to jail, I said to myself, 'I really must give it up, if for no other reason than of being self-reliant'.
    R: When I emerged from jail, I wanted to tell her of my great triumph.
    S: But when I met her, there she was with a packet of cigarettes.
    S6: Poor girl. The Proper sequence should be
    (a) PSRQ (b) SPQR (c) QPRS (d) RSPQ
17. S1: When a satellite is launched, the rocket begins by slowly going upwards through the air.
    P: However, the higher it goes, the less air it meets.
    Q: As the rocket goes higher, it travels faster.
    R: For the atmosphere becomes thinner.
    S: As a result, there is less friction.
    S6: Consequently, the rocket still does not become too hot.
    The proper sequence should be:
    (a) QPRS (b) QSPR (c) PQRS (d) PQSR

Directions: *In the following questions, choose the word which is the exact opposite in meaning of the given words.*

18. Evasive (Oracle, 2013)
    (a) Free (b) Honest (c) Liberal (d) Frank
19. Embezzle (Oracle, 2013)
    (a) Misappropriate (b) Balance (c) Remunerate (d) Clear
20. Gregarious (Oracle, 2013)
    (a) Antisocial (b) Glorious (c) Horrendous (d) Similar

SOLUTIONS WITH EXPLANATIONS

1. (d) Construction
2. (a) Pipeline
3. (a) day
4. (b) supported by

5. (c) local vegetation
6. (d) attempted
7. (c) 8
8. (b) specific
9. (a) How much oil field land each company owned
10. (c) Line 19
11. (c) What, how
12. (a) for which
13. (a) of
14. (d) off
15. (b) trite, inspired
16. (c) QPRS
17. (a) QPRS
18. (b) Honest
19. (a) Misappropriate
20. (a) Antisocial

PRACTICE SET 8

Directions: *Read the passage and answer the questions that follow.*

At this stage of civilization, when many nations are brought in to close and vital contact for good and evil, it is essential, as never before, that their gross ignorance of one another should be diminished, that they should begin to understand a little of one another's historical experience and the resulting mentality. It is the fault of the English to expect the people of other countries to react as they do, to political and international situations. Our genuine goodwill and good intentions are often brought to nothing, because we expect other people to be like us. This would be corrected if we knew the history, not necessarily in detail but in broad outlines, of the social and political conditions which have given to each nation its present character. (Oracle, 2011)

1. According to the author, the 'mentalitly' of a nation is mainly a product of its ___________.
   (a) present character (b) international position
   (c) politics (d) history
2. The character of a nation is the result of its ___________.
   (a) gross ignorance (b) cultural heritage
   (c) socio-political conditions (d) mentality
3. The need for a greater understanding between nations ___________.
   (a) is more today than ever before (b) was always there
   (c) is no longer there (d) will always be there
4. Englishmen like others to react to political situations like ___________.
   A. others (b) us (c) themselves (d) each other

5. According to the author, his countrymen should ___________.
   (a) read the story of other nations
   (b) not react to other's actions
   (c) have a better understanding of other nations
   (d) have vital contacts with other nations

Directions: *In the following questions, choose the word which best expresses the meaning of the given word.*

6. Inebriate
   (a) Dreamy (b) Stupefied (c) Unsteady (d) Drunken
7. Sterile
   (a) Barren (b) Arid (c) Childless (d) Dry
8. Abject
   (a) Challenge (b) Miserable (c) Deny (d) Disobey
9. Moving
   (a) Taking (b) Toying (c) Shifting (d) Turning

Directions: *Read each sentence to find out whether there is any grammatical error in it or not. The error, if any, will be in one part of the sentence. Identify which part of the sentence has the error. If there is no error, the answer is (d). Ignore the errors of punctuation, if any.*

10. (a) We discussed about the problem so thoroughly
    (b) on the eve of the examination
    (c) that I found it very easy to work it out
    (d) No error
11. (a) An Indian ship (b) laden with merchandise
    (c) got drowned in the Pacific Ocean (d) No error
12. (a) I could not put up in a hotel
    (b) because the boarding and lodging charges
    (c) were exorbitant
    (d) No error
13. (a) The Indian radio
    (b) which was previously controlled by the British rulers
    (c) is free now from the narrow vested interests.
    (d) No error
14. (a) If I had known (b) this yesterday
    (c) I will have helped him (d) No error

Directions: *In each question, an incomplete statement (stem), followed by fillers is given. Pick out the most appropriate filler which can complete the incomplete stem correctly and meaningfully.*

15. Despite his best efforts to conceal his anger ___________,

(a) we could detect that he was very happy
(b) people came to know that he was annoyed
(c) he succeeded in camouflaging his emotions
(d) he could succeed in doing it easily

16. Even if it rains I shall come means ________.
(a) if I come it will not rain
(b) if it rains I shall not come
(c) I will certainly come whether it rains or not
(d) whenever there is rain I shall come

17. His appearance is unsmiling but ________.
(a) his heart is full of compassion for others
(b) he looks very serious on most occasions
(c) people are afraid of him
(d) he is uncompromising on matters of task performance

18. She never visits any zoo because she is a strong opponent of the idea of ________.
(a) holding the animals in captivity for our joy
(b) feeding the animals while others are watching
(c) watching the animals in their natural abode
(d) going out of the house on a holiday

19. I felt somewhat more relaxed ________.
(a) but tense as compared to earlier
(b) and tense as compared to earlier
(c) as there was already no tension at all
(d) and tension-free as compared to earlier

20. In order to raise the company's profit, the employees ________.
(a) demanded two additional increments
(b) decided to go on paid holidays
(c) requested the management to implement new welfare schemes
(d) offered to work overtime without any compensation

SOLUTIONS WITH EXPLANATIONS

1. (d) history
2. (c) socio-political conditions
3. (a) is more today than ever before
4. (c) themselves
5. (c) have a better understanding of other nations
6. (d) Drunken
7. (a) Barren
8. (b) Miserable
9. (c) Shifting

10. (a) We discussed about the problem so thoroughly
11. (c) got drowned in the Pacific Ocean.
12. (a) I could not put up in a hotel
13. (c) is free now from the narrow vested interests.
14. (c) I will have helped him.
15. (b)
16. (c)
17. (a)
18. (a)
19. (d)
20. (d)

PRACTICE SET 9

Directions: *Read the passage and answer the questions that follow.*

What needs to be set right is our approach to work. It is a common sight in our country of employees reporting for duty on time, and at the same time doing little work. If an assessment is made of time they spent in gossiping, drinking tea, eating *pan* and smoking cigarettes, it will be shocking to know that the time devoted to actual work is negligible. The problem is the standard which the leadership in administration sets for the staff. Forget the ministers because they mix politics and administration. What do top bureaucrats do? What do their junior officials do? The administration set up remains weak mainly because the employees do not have the right example to follow and they are more concerned about being in the good books of the bosses than doing work. (Oracle placement paper, 2011)

1. According to the writer, the administration in India ___________.
   (a) is by and large effective
   (b) is very strict and firm
   (c) is affected by red tape
   (d) is more or less ineffective
2. The central idea of the passage could be best expressed by which of the following?
   (a) The employee-outlook towards work is justified
   (b) The employees must change their outlook towards work
   (c) The employees would never change their work culture
   (d) The employer-employee relationship is far from healthy
3. The leadership in administration ___________.
   (a) sets a fine example for the employees
   (b) is of a reasonably high standard
   (c) is composed of idealists
   (d) is of a very poor standard

Directions: *In the following questions, choose the word which best expresses the meaning of the given word.*

4. Ironic
   (a) Inflexible (b) Bitter
   (c) Good-natured (d) Disguisedly sarcastic
5. Timid
   (a) Fast (b) Slow (c) Medium (d) Shy
6. Extricate
   (a) Pull (b) Free (c) Tie (d) Complicate
7. Neutral
   (a) Unbiased (b) Non-aligned (c) Undecided (d) Indifferent
8. Shallow
   (a) Artificial (b) Superficial (c) Foolish (d) Worthless

Directions: *Read each sentence to find out whether there is any grammatical error in it or not. The error, if any, will be in one part of the sentence. Identify which part of the sentence has the error. If there is no error, the answer is (d). Ignore the errors of punctuation, if any.*

9. (a) A lot of travel delay is caused
   (b) due to the inefficiency and lack of good management
   (c) on behalf of the railways.
   (d) No error
10. (a) One of the members (b) expressed doubt if
    (c) the Minister was an atheist. (d) No error
11. (a) I have got (b) my M.Sc. degree
    (c) in 1988 (d) No error
12. (a) Having received your letter (b) this morning, we are writing
    (c) to thank you for the same. (d) No error
13. (a) If you lend him a book (b) he will lend it to someone else
    (c) and never you will get it back. (d) No error

Directions: *In each question, an incomplete statement (stem), followed by fillers, is given. Pick out the most appropriate filler which can complete the incomplete stem correctly and meaningfully.*

14. It is not easy to remain tranquil when those around you ______.
    (a) behave in a socially acceptable manner
    (b) exhibit pleasant mannerisms
    (c) are losing their heads
    (d) agree to whatever you say
15. 'The food in this hotel is no match to what we were forced at late hours in Hotel Kohinoor', means the ______.
    (a) the food in this hotel is quite good compared to what we ate at Kohinoor

(b) Hotel Kohinoor served us better quality food than what we get here
(c) both hotels have maintained good quality of food
(d) both hotels serve poor quality of food

16. Although initial investigations pointed towards him, ______.
    (a) the preceding events corroborated his involvement in the crime
    (b) the additional information confirmed his guilt
    (c) the subsequent events established that he was guilty
    (d) the subsequent events proved that he was innocent
17. The weather outside was extremely pleasant, and hence, we decided to ____.
    (a) utilise our time in watching television
    (b) refrain from going out for a morning walk
    (c) refrain from going out for a morning walk
    (d) employ this rare opportunity for writing letters
18. 'It is an uphill task but you will have to do it', means that ______.
    (a) the work is above the hill and you will have to do it
    (b) it is a very easy task but you must do it
    (c) it is very difficult task but you have to do it
    (d) this work is not reserved for you but you will have to do it
19. 'To end in smoke' means ______.
    (a) to make completely understand (b) to ruin oneself
    (c) to excite great applause (d) to overcome someone
20. 'To be above board' means ______.
    (a) to have a good height (b) to be honest in any business deal
    (c) to have no debts (d) to try to be beautiful

SOLUTIONS WITH EXPLANATIONS

1. (d) is more or less ineffective
2. (b) The employees must change their outlook towards work
3. (d) is composed of idealists
4. (d) Disguisedly sarcastic
5. (d) Shy
6. (b) Free
7. (a) Unbiased
8. (b) Superficial
9. (c) on behalf of the railways
10. (b) expressed doubt if
11. (a) I have got
12. (d) No error
13. (c) and never you will get it back
14. (c) are losing their heads
15. (b) Hotel Kohinoor served us better quality food than what we get here

16. (d) the subsequent events proved that he was innocent
17. (b) refrain from going out for a morning walk
18. (c) it is very difficult task but you have to do it
19. (b) to ruin oneself
20. (b) to be honest in any business deal

PRACTICE SET 10

Directions: *Read the following passage and answer the questions that follow:*

Work expands to fill the time available for its completion. The general recognition of this fact is shown in the proverbial phrase'. It is the busiest man who has time to spare'. Thus, an elderly lady at leisure can spend the entire day writing a post card to her niece. An hour will be spent in writing a postcard, another hunting for spectacles, half an hour to search for the address,an hour and a quarter in composition, and 20 minutes in deciding whether or not to take an umbrella when going to the pillar box in the street. The total effort that could occupy a busy man for 3 minutes, all told may in this fashion leave another person completely exhausted after a day of doubt, anxiety, and toil. Accidents on roads can be prevented, provided the quality of roads is improved and the drivers are instructed in safety rules which they must follow for their protection. It is also necessary that the illumination on the roads is adequate to prevent accidents at night. The surprisingly abundant life of the Indian Ocean is confined to the upper layers; the deeper and especially the bottom waters are devoid of oxygen and are often permeated with hydrogen sulphide. It is not luck but labour that makes the man. Luck, says an American Writer, is ever waiting for something to turns up; labour with keen eyes and strong will always turns up something. Luck lies in bed and wishes the postman would bring him news of legacy; labour turns out at six and with busy pen ringing hammer lays the foundation of competence. Luck whines, labour watches. Luck slips downwards to self-indulgence; labour strides upwards and aspires to independence. The conviction, therefore, is extending that diligence is the mother of good luck. In other words that a man's success in life will be proportionate to his efforts, industry, and attention to small things. (Cognizent, 2014)

1. What is the total time spent by the elderly lady in writing a postcard?
   (a) 3 minutes (b) 4 hours and 5 minutes
   (c) Half an hour (d) The entire day
2. Which one of the following words in the passage indicates that the writer does not ultimately reject the element of luck?
   (a) 'Luck ... is ever waiting.'
   (b) 'Luck whines.'
   (c) Diligence is the mother of good luck.
   (d) Luck ... wishes the postman would bring him the news.

3. 'Labour turns out at six and with busy pen ringing hammer lays the foundation of competence.' What does this statement mean?
   (a) Hard work of all kinds makes people efficient.
   (b) Labour lays the foundation of the building.
   (c) The writer and the labourer are the true eyes of society.
   (d) There is no worker who works so hard as the labourer who begins.
4. Which one of the following words in the passage indicate that the writer does not ultimately reject the element of luck?
   (a) 'Luck ... is ever waiting.'
   (b) 'Luck whines.'
   (c) Diligence is the mother of good luck.
   (d) Luck ... wishes the postman would bring him news.
5. Despite of their differences on matters of principles, they all agree on the demand of a hike in salary?
   (a) Despite their (b) Despite of the
   (c) Despite for their (d) Despite off their

Directions: *In the following questions, choose the word which is the exact opposite of the given words.*

6. Culpable
   (a) Defendable (b) Blameless (c) Careless (d) Irresponsible
7. Evasive
   (a) Free (b) Honest (c) Liberal (d) Frank
8. Hirsute
   (a) Scaly (b) Bald (c) Erudite (d) Quiet

Directions: *Read each sentence to find out whether there is any grammatical error in it or not. The error, if any, will be in one part of the sentence. Identify which part of the sentence has the error. If there is no error, the answer is '(d)'. (Ignore the errors of punctuation, if any).*

9. According to the Bible, it is meek and humble who shall inherit the earth.
   (a) According to the Bible. (b) It is meek and humble.
   (c) who shall inherit the earth. (d) No error.
10. Do the roses in your garden smell more sweetly than those in ours?
    (a) Do the roses in your garden smell (b) more sweetly
    (c) than those in ours? (d) No error.
11. Block of residential flats is coming up near our house.
    (a) Block of Residential flats (b) are coming up
    (c) near our house (d) No error
12. You can get all the information that you want in this book.
    (a) You can get (b) all the information that you want
    (c) in this book. (d) No error.

13. The students were waiting for the arrival of the chief guest.
    (a) The students were
    (b) awaiting for
    (c) the arrival of the chief guest
    (d) No error.

Directions: *In each question, an incomplete statement (stem), followed by fillers is given. Pick out the best one which can complete the incomplete stem correctly and meaningfully.*

14. 'You are thinking very highly about Ravi but he is not so' means that ______.
    (a) Ravi is as good as you think about him
    (b) You have a good opinion about Ravi but he is not as good as you think
    (c) Your view about Ravi is philosophical, keep it up
    (d) Ravi is much better than what you think of him
15. 'Anand stuck up a friendship with Mahesh in just 2 days' means that ______.
    (a) Anand's friendship with Mahesh came to an end recently
    (b) Anand became a friend of Mahesh's in less than 2 days
    (c) Anand fixed a deal with Mahesh in 2 days
    (d) Anand's friendship with Mahesh lasted for 2 years
16. Although, he is reputed for making very candid statements, ______.
    (a) his today speech was not fairly audible
    (b) his promises had always been realistic
    (c) his today's statements were very ambiguous
    (d) people follow whatever he instructs them
17. 'The manager would like you to help Dhiraj' means that ______.
    (a) the manager would like you if you help Dhiraj
    (b) the manager desires you to help Dhiraj
    (c) the manager likes you because you help Dhiraj
    (d) Dhiraj expects the manager to tell you to help him
18. Owing to the acute power shortage, the people of our locality have decided to the ______.
    (a) resort to the use of electricity only when it is inevitable
    (b) resort to abundant use of electricity for illumination
    (c) switch off the electrical appliances when not in use
    (d) explore other avenues for utilising the excess power
19. To have an axe to grind ______.
    (a) a private end to serve
    (b) to fail to arouse interest
    (c) to have no result
    (d) to work for both sides
20. To cry wolf ______.
    (a) to listen eagerly
    (b) to give a false alarm
    (c) to turn pale
    (d) to keep off starvation

SOLUTIONS WITH EXPLANATIONS

1. (d) The entire day
2. (c) Diligence is the mother of good luck.
3. (d) There is no worker who works so hard as the labourer who begins.
4. (c) Diligence is the mother of good luck.
5. (a) Despite their
6. (b) Blameless
7. (b) Honest
8. (b) Bald
9. (b) It is meek and humble.
10. (b) more sweetly
11. (a) Block of residential flats
12. (b) all the information that you want.
13. (b) awaiting for.
14. (b) You have a good opinion about Ravi but he is not as good as you think.
15. (b) Anand became a friend of Mahesh's in less than 2 days.
16. (c) his today's statements were very ambiguous.
17. (b) The manager desires you to help Dhiraj.
18. (a) resort to the use of electricity only when it is inevitable.
19. (a) a private end to serve
20. (b) To give false alarm

PRACTICE SET 11

Directions: *Read the following passage and answer the questions that follow:*

Male lions are rather reticent about expanding their energy in hunting. More than three-quarters of kills are made by lionesses are in front, tensely scanning ahead, the cubs lag playfully behind and the males bring up the rear, walking slowly, their massive heads nodding with each step as if they were bored with the whole matter. But slothfulness may have survival value. With lionesses' busy hunting, the males function as a guard for the cubs, protecting them particularly from hyenas. (Oracle placement paper, 2011)

1. According to the passage, male lions generally do not go hunting because
   (a) they do not like it.
   (b) they want lionesses to get trained.
   (c) they wish to save their vigour for other things.
   (d) they are very lazy.
2. Male lions protect their cubs
   (a) from the members of their species.
   (b) from hyenas only.
   (c) from hyenas as much as from other enemies.

(d) more from hyenas than from other animals.

3. When the lionesses go in search of their prey, they are very
   (a) serious (b) cautious (c) playful (d) sluggish

Directions: *In the following questions, choose the words which are the exact opposite of the given words.*

4. Shrink
   (a) Contract (b) Spoil (c) Expand (d) Stretch
5. Common
   (a) Rare (b) Small (c) Petty (d) Poor
6. Comfort
   (a) Uncomfort (b) Miscomfort (c) Discomfort (d) None Of These
7. Dear
   (a) Priceless (b) Free (c) Worthless (d) Cheap
8. Arrogant
   (a) Humble (b) Cowardly (c) Egotistic (d) Gentlemanly

Directions: *Read each sentence to find out whether there is any grammatical error in it or not. The error, if any, will be in one part of the sentence. Identify the part of the sentence that has the error. If there is no error, the answer is (d). Ignore the errors of punctuation, if any.*

9. Sixty miles are a good distance.
   (a) Sixty miles (b) Are (c) a good distance (d) No error
10. They have been very close friends until they quarrelled.
    (a) They have been (b) very close friends
    (c) until they quarrelled (d) No error
11. When the dentist came in my tooth was stopped aching out of fear that I might lose my tooth.
    (a) When the dentist came in
    (b) my tooth was stopped aching
    (c) out of fear that I might lose my tooth.
    (d) No error
12. It is the duty of every citizen to do his utmost to defend the hardly-won freedom of the country.
    (a) It is the duty of every citizen to do his utmost
    (b) to defend the hardly-won
    (c) freedom of the country
    (d) No error
13. No sooner did I open the door when the rain, heavy and stormy, rushed in making us shiver from head to foot.
    (a) No sooner did I open the door
    (b) when the rain, heavy and stormy, rushed in

(c) making us shiver from head to foot
(d) No error

Directions: *In each question, an incomplete statement (stem), followed by fillers is given. Pick the best one which can complete the incomplete stem correctly and meaningfully.*

14. He has no money now ______
    (a) although he was very poor once.
    (b) as he has given up all his wealth.
    (c) because he was very rich once.
    (d) because he has received a huge donation.
15. He is so lazy that he ______
    (a) cannot depend on others for getting his work done.
    (b) cannot delay the schedule of completing the work.
    (c) can seldom complete his work on time.
    (d) dislikes to postpone the work that he undertakes to do.
16. Dinesh is as stupid as he is lazy. This means that ______
    (a) Dinesh is equally stupid and lazy.
    (b) Dinesh is lazy because he is stupid.
    (c) Dinesh is either stupid or lazy.
    (d) Dinesh is hardly stupid but he is lazy.
17. Practically, very little work could be completed in the last week as it was ______
    (a) full of working days. (b) a very hectic week.
    (c) full of holidays. (d) a very busy week.
18. Because he believes in democratic principles, he always ______
    (a) decides all the matters himself.
    (b) listens to others' views and enforces his own.
    (c) shows respect to others' opinions if they match his own.
    (d) reconciles with the majority views and gives up his own.
19. To catch a tarter ______
    (a) to trap wanted criminals with great difficulty.
    (b) to catch a dangerous person.
    (c) to meet with disaster.
    (d) to deal with a person who is more than one's match.
20. To drive home ______
    (a) to find one's roots. (b) to return to the place of rest.
    (c) back to the original position. (d) to emphasize.

SOLUTIONS WITH EXPLANATIONS

1. (c) they wish to save their vigour for other things.

2. (d) more from hyenas than from other animals.
3. (b) cautious
4. (c) Expand
5. (a) Rare
6. (c) Discomfort
7. (d) Cheap
8. (a) Humble
9. (b) Are
10. (a) They have been
11. (b) my tooth was stopped aching
12. (b) to defend the hardly-won
13. (b) when the rain, heavy and stormy, rushed in
14. (b) as he has given up all his wealth.
15. (c) can seldom complete his work on time
16. (a) Dinesh is equally stupid and lazy.
17. (c) full of holidays.
18. (d) reconciles with the majority views and gives up his own.
19. (b) to catch a dangerous person.
20. (d) to emphasize

PRACTICE SET 12

Directions: *Read the following passage and answer the questions that follow:*

Laws of nature are not commands but statements of acts. The use of the word 'law' in this context is rather unfortunate. It would be better to speak of uniformities in nature. This would do away with the elementary fallacy that a law implies a law giver. If a piece of matter does not obey a law of nature, it is punished. On the contrary, we say that the law has been incorrectly started. (Oracle placement paper, 2011)

1. If a piece of matter violates nature's law, it is not punished because
   (a) it is not binding to obey it.
   (b) there is no superior being to enforce the law of nature.
   (c) it cannot be punished.
   (d) it simply means that the facts have not been correctly stated by the law.
2. Laws of nature differ from man-made laws because of
   (a) the former state facts of nature.
   (b) they must be obeyed.
   (c) they are natural.
3. The author is not happy with the word law, because
   (a) it connotes rigidity and harshness.
   (b) it implies an agency that has made them.
   (c) it does not convey the sense of nature's uniformity.

(d) it gives rise to false beliefs.

Directions: *In the following questions, choose the words which are the exact opposite of the given words.*

4. Victorious
   (a) Defeated (b) Annexed (c) Destroyed (d) Vanquished
5. Graceful
   (a) Rough (b) Expert (c) Miserable (d) Awkward
6. Nadir
   (a) Modernity (b) Zenith (c) Liberty (d) Progress
7. Extravagance
   (a) Luxury (b) Poverty (c) Economical (d) Cheapness
8. Pertinent
   (a) Irrational (b) Irregular (c) Insistent (d) Irrelevant

Directions: *Read each sentence to find out whether there is any grammatical error in it or not. The error, if any, will be in one part of the sentence. Identify the part of the sentence that has an error. If there is no error, the answer is (d). Ignore the errors of punctuation, if any.*

9. If a man diligently seeks to come into the contact with the best that has been thought and said in this world.
   (a) If a man diligently seeks to come into the contact
   (b) with the best that has been thought and said in this world
   (c) he will become simple and unselfish.
   (d) No error.
10. You must remember me to post this letter.
    (a) You must (b) remember me
    (c) to post this letter. (d) No error.
11. I shall certainly write you when I shall reach New Delhi.
    (a) I shall certainly (b) write you
    (c) when I shall reach New Delhi. (d) No error.
12. On the busy Ring Road, we witnessed collision between a truck and an auto.
    (a) On the busy Ring Road (b) we witnessed a collusion
    (c) Between a truck and an auto. (d) No error.
13. Mr. Praful Patel is not attending his office for the last one month.
    (a) Mr. Praful Patel (b) is not attending his office
    (c) for the last one month (d) No error

Directions: *In each question, an incomplete statement (stem), followed by fillers is given. Pick out the best one which can complete the incomplete stem correctly and meaningfully.*

14. With great efforts, his son succeeded in convincing him not to donate his entire wealth to an orphanage ______

(a) and lead the life of a wealthy merchant.
(b) but to a home for forsaken children.
(c) and make an orphan of himself.
(d) as the orphanage needed a lot of donations.

15. The employer appeared to be in such an affable mood that Rohit ______
(a) decided to ask for a raise in his salary.
(b) was scared to talk to him about his leave.
(c) felt very guilty for his inadvertent slip.
(d) promised him that he would not commit any mistake again.

16. He always stammers in public meetings, but his today's speech ______
(a) was fairly audible to everyone present in the hall.
(b) was free from that defect.
(c) could not be understood properly.
(d) was not liked by the audience.

17. Even though it is a very large house, ______
(a) there is a lot of space available in it for children.
(b) there is hardly any space available for children.
(c) there is no dearth of space for children.
(d) the servants take a long time to clean it.

18. It was an extremely pleasant surprise for the hutment-dweller when the Government officials told him that ______
(a) he had to vacate the hutment which he had been unauthorised occupying.
(b) he had been gifted with a furnished apartment in a multistoried building.
(c) he would be arrested for wrongfully encroaching on the pavement outside his dwelling.
(d) they would not accede to his request.

19. To make clean breast of ______
(a) to gain prominence. (b) to praise oneself.
(c) to confess without reserve. (d) to destroy before it blooms.

20. To keep one's temper ______
(a) to become hungry. (b) to be in good mood.
(c) to preserve ones energy. (d) to be aloof from.

SOLUTIONS WITH EXPLANATIONS

1. (b) there is no superior being to enforce the law of nature.
2. (a) the former state facts of nature.
3. (a) it connotes rigidity and harshness.
4. (a) Defeated
5. (d) Awkward
6. (b) Zenith

7. (c) Economical
8. (d) Irrelevant
9. (a) If a man diligently seeks to come into the contact
10. (b) remember me
11. (c) when I shall reach New Delhi
12. (b) we witnessed a collusion
13. (b) is not attending his office
14 (c) and make an orphan of himself
15. (a) decided to ask for a raise in his salary
16. (b) was free from that defect
17. (b) there is hardly any space available for children
18. (b) he had been gifted with a furnished apartment in a multistoried building
19. (c) to confess without reserve
20. (b) to be in good mood

PRACTICE SET 13

Reading Comprehension

Directions: *Read the following passage and answer the questions given below.*

The pioneers of the teaching of science imagined that its introduction into education would remove the conventionality, artificiality, and backward-lookingness which were characteristics of classical studies, but they were gravely disappointed. So, in their time had the humanists thought that the study of the classical authors in the original would banish at once the dull pedantry and superstition of medieval scholasticism? The professional schoolmaster was a match for both of them and has almost managed to make the understanding of chemical reactions as dull and dogmatic an affair as the reading of Virgil's *Aeneid.* The chief claim for the use of science in education is that it teaches a child something about the actual universe in which he is living, in making him acquainted with the results of scientific discovery, and at the same time teaches him how to think logically and inductively by studying scientific method. A certain limited success has been reached in the first of these aims, but practically none at all in the second. Those privileged members of the community who have been through a secondary or public school education may be expected to know something about the elementary physics and chemistry of a hundred years ago, but they probably know hardly more than any bright boy can pick up from an interest in wireless or scientific hobbies out of school hours. As to the learning of the scientific method, the whole thing is palpably a farce. Actually, for the convenience of teachers and the requirements of the examination system, it is necessary that the pupils not only do not learn scientific method but learn precisely the reverse, that is, to believe exactly what they are told and to reproduce it when asked, whether it seems nonsense to them or not. The way in which educated people respond to such quackeries as spiritualism or astrology, not to say more dangerous ones such as racial theories or currency myths, shows that fifty years of education in the method of science in Britain or Germany has produced no visible effect whatever. The only way of learning the method of science is the long and bitter way of personal experience and, until the educational or social systems are altered to make this possible, the best we can expect is the production of a minority of people who can acquire some of the techniques of science and a still smaller minority who are able to use and develop them. (Mindtree, 2013)

1. The author implies that the 'professional schoolmaster' (line 7) has
   (a) no interest in teaching science
   (b) thwarted attempts to enliven education
   (c) aided true learning
   (d) supported the humanists
   (e) been a pioneer in both science and humanities.
2. The author's attitude to secondary and public school education in the sciences is
   (a) ambivalent (b) neutral (c) supportive
   (d) satirical (e) contemptuous
3. The word 'palpably' (line 24) nearly means
   (a) empirically (b) obviously (c) tentatively
   (d) markedly (e) ridiculously
4. The author blames all of the following for the failure to impart scientific method through the education system except
   (a) poor teaching (b) examination methods
   (c) lack of direct experience (d) the social and education systems
   (e) lack of interest on the part of students
5. If the author were to study current education in science to see how things have changed since he wrote the piece, he would probably be most interested in the answer to which of the following questions?
   (a) Do students know more about the world than them?
   (b) Do students spend more time in laboratories?
   (c) Can students apply their knowledge logically?
   (d) Have textbooks improved?
   (e) Do they respect their teachers?
6. Astrology (line 31) is mentioned as an example of
   (a) a science that needs to be better understood.
   (b) a belief which no educated people hold.
   (c) something unsupportable to those who have absorbed the methods of science.
   (d) the gravest danger to society.

(e) an acknowledged failure of science.

7. All of the following can be inferred from the text except
   (a) at the time of writing, not all children received a secondary school education.
   (b) the author finds chemical reactions interesting.
   (c) science teaching has imparted some knowledge of facts to some children.
   (d) the author believes that many teachers are authoritarian.
   (e) it is relatively easy to learn the scientific method.

Directions: *Fill in the blanks.*

8. In large cities, people are cut _____ from nature. (Syntel, 2011)
   (a) down (b) out (c) off (d) away
9. My parents had tried to make an artist of me, but I refused to be made___. (HCL, 2011)
   (a) that (b) him (c) a (d) one

Directions: *In the questions below, each passage consists of six sentences. The first and sixth sentences are given in the beginning. The middle four sentences have been removed and jumbled up. These are labelled as P, Q, R, and S. Find out the proper order for the four sentences.* (Mindtree, 2013)

10. S1: A father having offered to take the baby out in a perambulator, was tempted by the sunny morning to slip into a pub for a glass of beer.
    P: Indignant at her husband's behaviour, she decided to teach him a lesson.
    Q: She wheeled away the pram.
    R: A little later, his wife came by, where to her horror, she discovered her sleeping baby.
    S: Leaving the pram outside, he disappeared inside the bar.
    S6: She waited for him, anticipating the white face and quivering lips that would soon appear with the news that the baby had been stolen.
    The proper sequence should be:(Arrangement)
    (a) SRPQ (b) RQPS (c) SPQR (d) PQSR
11. S1: While crossing a busy road, we should obey the policeman on duty.
    P: We should always cross the road at the zebra crossing.
    Q: We must look at the signal lights and cross the road only when the road is clear.
    R: If there are no signal lights at the crossing, we should look to the right, then to left, and again to the right before crossing the road.
    S: If the road is not clear we should wait.
    S6: We should never run while crossing the road.
    The proper sequence should be:
    (a) PSRQ (b) PQRS (c) RQSP (d) QRPS

Directions: *Fill in the blanks with suitable words.*

12. Rajeev failed the examination because none of his answers were ________ to the questions asked. (Syntel, 2011)
    (a) allusive (b) revealing (c) pertinent (d) referential
13. There are __________ views on the issue of giving bonus to the employees. (Syntel, 2011)
    (a) independent (b) divergent (c) modest (d) Adverse
14. A man who has committed such an ________ crime must get the most severe punishment. (Syntel, 2011)
    (a) injurious (b) uncharitable
    (c) unworthy (d) admirable
15. The British were able to establish an empire in India, largely because the ruling Indian princess were
    (a) disunited (b) disintegrated (c) disjointed (d) disoriented

Directions: *In each of the following questions, find out which part of the sentence has an error. If there is no mistake the answer is 'no error'.*

16. It is rude for the young making fun of their elders. (Syntel, 2011)
    (a) It is rude (b) for the young
    (c) making fun of their elders (d) No error
17. Meerabai was sent away from her home because she spend most of the time in the company of holy men. (Syntel, 2011)
    (a) Meerabai was sent away from her home
    (b) because she spends most of the time
    (c) in the company of holy men
    (d) No error

Directions: *A sentence is written in four different ways. Only one of these is grammatically correct. (Select the correct sentence).* (Larsen & Turbo 2013)

18. (a) The jury are not unanimous in their verdict.
    (b) The jury is not unanimous in its verdict.
    (c) The jury are not unanimous by their verdict.
    (d) The jury are not unanimous in its verdict.
19. (a) The Himalayas form a great barrier on the north of India.
    (b) Himalayas form a great barrier in the north of India.
    (c) Himalayas form a great barrier on the north of India.
    (d) The Himalayas form a great barrier in the north of India.
20. (a) Each of the participants were given a gift.
    (b) Everyone of the participants were given a gift.
    (c) All of the participants was given a gift.
    (d) Each of the participants was given a gift.

SOLUTIONS WITH EXPLANATIONS

1. (b) thwarted attempts to enliven education
2. (c) supportive
3. (c) tentatively
4. (d) the social and education systems
5. (d) Have textbooks improved?
6. (c) something unsupportable to those who have absorbed the methods of science
7. (e) it is relatively easy to learn scientific method.
8. (c) off
9. (d) one
10. (a) SRPQ
11. (d) QRPS
12. (c) pertinent
13. (b) divergent
14 (a) injurious
15. (a) disunited
16. (c) making fun of their elders
17. (b) because she spends most of the time
18. (a) The jury are not unanimous in their verdict.
19. (a) The Himalayas form a great barrier on the north of India.
20. (d) Each of the participants was given a gift.

PRACTICE SET 14

Directions: *Read the following passage and then answer the questions given next.*

All the sound reasons ever given for conserving other natural resources apply to the conservation of wildlife and with three-fold power. When a spendthrift squanders his capital it is lost to him and his heirs, yet it goes somewhere else. When a nation allows any one kind of natural resource to be squandered it must suffer a real, positive loss; yet substitutes of another kind can generally be found. But when wildlife is squandered it does not go elsewhere, like squandered money; it cannot possibly be replaced by any substitute, as some inorganic resources are: it is simply an absolute, dead loss, gone beyond even the hope of recall. The public still has a hazy idea that nature has an overflowing sanctuary of her own, somewhere or the other, which will fill up the gaps automatically. The result is that poaching is commonly regarded as a venial offence, poachers taken red-handed are rarely punished, and willing ears are always lent to the cry that rich sportsmen are trying to take the bread out of the poor settler's mouth. The poor settler does not reflect that he himself, and all other classes alike, really have a common interest in the conservation of any wildlife that does not conflict with legitimate human development. (Cognizent, 2013)

1. The author probably uses the expression 'three fold power'
   (a) because there are three-times as many reasons for conserving wildlife.
   (b) to be more dramatic than saying 'double-power'.
   (c) to emphasise the contrast between the loss of money, loss of other resources, and wildlife.
   (d) to stress the need for saving money, resources, and time.
   (e) to indicate the magnitude of the problem without intending the expression to be taken literally.
2. From the context, the word 'venial' (in paragraph two) most nearly means
   (a) major (b) criminal (c) frequent
   (d) trivial (e) natural
3. Both paragraphs imply that
   (a) there is no source from which wildlife, once exterminated, can be replaced.
   (b) poachers must be punished.
   (c) wildlife has much in common with other natural resources.
   (d) conservation is in conflict with human development.
   (e) preserving wildlife is expensive.
4. It can be inferred that the spendthrift in paragraph one and the poor settler mentioned in paragraph two are alike in that they are
   (a) in conflict with the aims of conservation.
   (b) inclined to waste natural resources.
   (c) more concerned with the present than the future.
   (d) unable to control their spending.
   (e) unaware of conservation.

Direction: *Fill in the Blanks*

5. We are not in a position to do __________we promised to do.
   (a) all thing (b) the whole (c) all (d) it all
6. She will no doubt feed the cat when she _________. (HCL, 2011)
   (a) will come (b) would come
   (c) will have come (d) comes
7. At the end of the speech, the whole assembly gave the speakers a standing _________. (HCL, 2011)
   (a) ovation (b) applause (c) cheering (d) support
8. It is much ________ than I expected. (HCL, 2011)
   (a) best (b) good (c) better (d) the better
9. Joanna killed _________ because they no longer saw ______. (HCL, 2011)
   (a) him, themselves (b) herself, each other
   (c) herself, themselves (d) her, them
10. He lives ____ Hyderabad. He lives ____ 48 tilak street. (HCL, 2011)
    (a) in, at (b) in, in (c) at, in (d) at, at

Directions: *In the following questions, choose the words which are the exact opposite of the given words.*

11. Evasive (Oracle, 2013)
    (a) Free (b) Honest (c) Liberal (d) Frank
12. Embezzle (Oracle, 2013)
    (a) Misappropriate (b) Balance (c) Remunerate (d) Clear
13. Gregarious (Oracle, 2013)
    (a) Antisocial (b) Glorious (c) Horrendous (d) Similar

Directions: *Each of the following sentences has been divided into four parts. There is an error in one of the parts. Point out the part which has an error.*

14. We entered into the room after the class was over. (Robert Bosch, 2014)
    (a) We entered (b) into the room
    (c) after the class was over (d) no error
15. Your account should have been credited with three months' interest. (Robert Bosch, 2014)
    (a) Your account should (b) have been credited
    (c) with three month's interest (d) no error
16. Idli and sambar make the breakfast in the south. (Robert Bosch, 2014)
    (a) make the breakfast (b) in the south
    (c) no error (d) choose the correct answer
17. We discussed about the politics in the class room. (Robert Bosch, 2014)
    (a) about the politics (b) in the class room
    (c) no error (d) choose the correct answer

Directions: *Fill in the Blanks.*

18. My parents will ________ for Canada tomorrow. (Tech Mahindra, 2013)
    (a) Leave (b) Leaving (c) Leaves (d) Left
19. I will be _______ in the park tomorrow. (Tech Mahindra, 2013)
    (a) sing (b) sang (c) sung (d) singing
20. We ________ not coming over. (Tech Mahindra, 2013)
    (a) is (b) are (c) am (d) has

SOLUTIONS WITH EXPLANATIONS

1. (e) to indicate the magnitude of the problem without intending the expression to be taken literally.
2. (e) natural
3. (c) wildlife has much in common with other natural resources.
4. (c) more concerned with the present than the future.
5. (c) all
6. (d) comes

7. (a) ovation
8. (a) best
9. (b) herself, each other
10. (a) in, at
11. (b) Honest
12. (a) Misappropriate
13. (a) Antisocial
14. (b) into the room
15. (d)
16. (b) in the south
17. (b) in the class room
18. (b) leaving
19. (d) Singing
20. (b) Are

PRACTICE SET 15

Directions: *Read the passage and then answer the questions given next.*

The word euthanasia is of Greek origin and means 'a good death'. The *American Heritage Dictionary* defines it as 'the act of killing a person painlessly for reasons of mercy'. Such killing can be done through active means, such as administering a lethal injection, or by passive means, such as withholding medical care or food and water.

In recent years in the United States, there have been numerous cases of active euthanasia in the news. They usually involve the deliberate killing of ill or incapacitated persons by relatives or friends who plead that they can no longer bear to see their loved ones suffer. Although such killings are a crime, the perpetrators are often dealt with leniency by our legal system, and the media usually portrays them as compassionate heroes who take personal risks to save another from unbearable suffering. The seeming acceptance of active forms of euthanasia is alarming, but we face a bigger, more insidious threat from passive forms of euthanasia. Every year, in hospitals and nursing homes around the country, there are growing numbers of documented deaths caused by caregivers withholding life-sustaining care, including food and water, from vulnerable patients who cannot speak for themselves.

While it is illegal to kill someone directly, for example with a gun or knife, in many cases the law has put its stamp of approval on causing death by omitting needed care. Further, many states have 'living will' laws designed to protect those who withhold treatment, and there have been numerous court rulings that have approved of patients being denied care and even starved and dehydrated to death. Because such deaths occur quietly within the confines of hospitals and nursing homes, they can be kept hidden from the public. Most euthanasia victims are old or very ill, so their deaths might be attributed to a cause other than the denial of care that killed them. Further, it is often relatives of the patient who request that care be withheld. In one case, the court held that decisions to withhold life-sustaining care may be made not only by close family members but also by a number of third parties and that such decisions need not be reviewed by the judicial system if there is no disagreement between the decision-makers and the medical staff. The court went so far as to rule that a nursing home may not refuse to participate in the fatal withdrawal of food and water from an incompetent patient!

'Extraordinary' or 'heroic' treatment need not be used when the chance for recovery is poor and medical intervention would serve only to prolong the dying process. But to deny customary and reasonable care or to deliberately starve or dehydrate someone because he or she is very old or ill should not be permitted. Most of the cases coming before the courts do not involve withholding heroic measures from imminently dying people, but rather they seek approval for denying basic care, such as administration of food and water, to people who are not elderly or terminally ill, but who are permanently incapacitated. These people could be expected to live indefinitely, though in an impaired state, if they were given food and water and minimal treatment.

No one has the right to judge that another's life is not worth living. The basic right to life should not be abridged because someone decides that someone else's quality of life is too low. If we base the right to life on the quality of life standards, there is no logical place to draw the line. To protect vulnerable patients, we must foster more positive attitudes towards people with serious and incapacitating illnesses and conditions. Despite the ravages of their diseases, they are still our fellow human beings and deserve our care and respect. We must also enact positive legislation that will protect vulnerable people from those who consider their lives meaningless or too costly to maintain and who would cause their deaths by withholding life-sustaining care such as food and water.

(Mindtree, 2014)

1. The tone of the author can best be described as
   (a) pleading (b) argumentative (c) compassionate
   (d) emphatic (e) empathetic
2. In Paragraph 3, the author finds starvation and dehydration-induced euthanasia is to be 'more insidious' because
   (a) euthanasia is legally considered to be a criminal act.
   (b) the public's attitude toward euthanasia is becoming more positive.
   (c) it often involves those who cannot protest.
   (d) the patient has asked to die with dignity.
   (e) its perpetrators are viewed as kindly caregivers.
3. As used in Paragraph 3, what is the best synonym for insidious?
   (a) mischievous (b) treacherous (c) seductive

(d) apparent (e) cumulative

4. The author maintains that death by withholding care is
   (a) largely confined to hospitals.
   (b) largely confined to the terminally ill.
   (c) often requested by family members.
   (d) approved by living wills.
   (e) difficult to prove if prosecuted.
5. As used in paragraph 7, what is the best definition of abridged?
   (a) trimmed (b) curtailed (c) lengthened
   (d) extended (e) compressed
6. Using the passage as a guide, it can be inferred that the author would find euthanasia less objectionable in cases in which
   (a) the patient's death is imminent.
   (b) the patient has left instructions in a living will to not be provided with care.
   (c) the patient refuses to accept nourishment.
   (d) All of the above.
7. The main idea of Paragraph 7 is that
   (a) lawyers will be unable to prosecute or defend caregivers.
   (b) no comprehensive right or wrong definition of euthanasia will exist.
   (c) using a subjective standard will make the decision to end an individual's life arbitrary.
   (d) no boundary will exist between euthanasia and care omission.
   (e) 'quality of life' will no longer be able to be rigidly defined.

Directions: *Fill in the Blanks.*

8. She bakes her bread so they all eat ______bread at lunch. (HCL, 2011)
   (a) homemade (b) house making
   (c) making at home (d) made home
9. It is raining ______ she wants to go out. (HCL, 2011)
   (a) although (b) unless (c) and yet (d) since
10. I cannot stand ____________ the house work. (HCL, 2011)
   (a) me to do (b) do (c) doing (d) that I do
11. She is not here today, she ________ be ill. (HCL, 2011)
   (a) must (b) cannot (c) has to (d) can

Directions: *Each of the following sentences has been divided into four parts. There is an error in one of the parts. Point out the part which has an error.*

12. Had, the doctor reached an hour earlier and gave him proper medicine his life would have been saved without any doubt. (InfoTech, 2011)
   (a) Had, the doctor reached an hour earlier
   (b) and gave him proper medicine

(c) his life would have been saved
(d) without any doubt (e) no error

13. He ought to have tried his best from the very beginning because the goal he set before him was not an ordinary one. (InfoTech, 2011)
    (a) He ought to have tried his best (b) from the very beginning
    (c) because the goal he set before him (d) was not an ordinary one
    (e) no error

Directions: *In each of the following questions, out of the given alternatives, choose the one which is nearest in meaning to the given word (synonym).* (InfoTech, 2011)

14. Error
    (a) Blunder (b) Misadventure
    (c) Ambiguity (d) Misgiving
15. Acrid
    (a) Dirty (b) Pungent (c) Unripe (d) Bitter
16. Requite
    (a) Servile (b) Trashy (c) Ferocious (d) Juicy
17. Badger
    (a) Attempt (b) Convince (c) Pester (d) Persuade
18. Cautiously
    (a) Genuinely (b) Carefully (c) Secretly (d) Somewhat.

Directions: *Fill in the blanks with appropriate words.*

19. The truth is that in a highly capital-intensive business _______ deep pockets, domestic civil aviation is _______ undercapitalised. (Tata Motors, 2014)
    (a) ascertaining, highly (b) requiring, woefully
    (c) sustaining, alarmingly (d) balancing, astonishingly
20. The time has now come for all agencies working in the development sector to launch a multi-pronged ________ to _______ malnutrition. (Tata Motors, 2014)
    (a) system, abjure (b) weapon, annihilate
    (c) policy, deviate (d) strategy, eradicate

SOLUTIONS WITH EXPLANATIONS

1 (c) compassionate
2. (c) it often involves those who cannot protest.
3. (b) treacherous
4. (c) often requested by family members
5. (b) curtailed
6. (d) All of the above.
7. (c) using a subjective standard will make the decision to end an individual's life arbitrary.

8. (a) homemade
9. (c) and yet
10. (c) doing
11. (a) must
12. (b) and gave him proper medicine
13. (d) was not an ordinary one
14. (a) Blunder
15. (d) Bitter
16. (b) Trashy
17. (c) Pester
18. (b) Carefully
19. (b) requiring, woefully
20. (d) strategy, eradicate

PRACTICE SET 16

Directions: *Read the passage carefully and answer the questions given next.*

In the world today we make health and end in itself. We have forgotten that health is means to enable a person to do his work and do it well. A lot of modern medicine and this includes many patients as well as many physicians pays very little attention to health but very much attention to those who imagine that they are ill. Our great concern with health is shown by the medical columns in newspapers, the health articles in popular magazines, and the popularity of television programmes and all those books on medicine. We talk about health all the time. Yet, for the most part, the only result is more people with imaginary illnesses. A healthy man should not be wasting time talking about health: he should be using health for work. The work does the work that good health possible. (Dell, 2011)

1. A healthy man should be concerned with
   (a) his work which good health makes possible.
   (b) looking after his health.
   (c) his health which makes work possible.
   (d) talking about health.
2. The passage tells us
   (a) how medicines should be manufactured.
   (b) what a healthy man should or should not do.
   (c) what television programmes should be about.
   (d) how to best imagine illness.
3. Talking about health all the time makes people
   (a) always suffer from imaginary illness.
   (b) sometimes suffer from imaginary illness.
   (c) rarely suffer from imaginary illness.

(d) often suffer from imaginary illness.
4. The passage suggests that
   (a) health is an end in itself.
   (b) health is a blessing.
   (c) health is the only means to an end.
   (d) we should not talk about health.

Directions: *Choose the word nearest in meaning to the word in italics from the given options.*

5. The notice said that the meeting would begin *precisely* at 9.00 AM. (Accenture, 2011)
   (a) Exactly (b) Accurately (c) Concisely
   (d) Approximately (e) None of these

Directions: *Correct the italicised part in the sentences given next.*

6. The golden crab of the Gulf of Mexico has not been fished commercially in great numbers, primarily *on account of living* at great depths 2,500 to 3,000 feet down. (Tech Mahindra, 2014)
   (a) on account of living (b) on account of their living
   (c) because it lives (d) because it living
7. John is absent *today. Because he is ill.* (Infosys, 2012)
   (a) today. Because he is ill. (b) today because he is ill.
   (c) today, because he is ill. (d) today: because he is ill.
8. She always seemed to be acting, but she had the theatre *in her blood*, and performing was as natural for her as breathing. (Infosys, 2014)
   (a) bleeding on getting wounded
   (b) having a natural interest to do something
   (c) as a basic part of your qualities and characteristics
   (d) hatred against something

Directions: *In the following questions, choose the word which best expresses the meaning of the given word.*

9. Stringent (Oracle, 2014)
   (a) Tense (b) Stringy
   (c) Strict (d) Causing to Shrink
10. Value (Capgemini, 2015)
   (a) Good (b) Price (c) Worth (d) Number
11. Stringent (GE, 2014)
   (a) Dry (b) Strained (c) Rigorous (d) Shrill
12. Extortionate (Tech Mahindra, 2014)
   (a) excessive (b) kidnapped
   (c) extinguishable (d) extractable

Directions: *Pick out the most effective word from the given words to fill in the blank to make the sentence meaningfully complete.*

13. What a sensation it would cause if it _____ now discovered that such a man had left behind a diary. (Syntel, 2011)
    (a) is (b) be (c) was (d) were
14. Although he never learnt to read, his exceptional memory and enquiring mind eventually made him a very _______ man. (Syntel, 2013)
    (a) Dedicated (b) Erudite (c) Pragmatic (d) Benevolent
15. Fate smiles _______ those who untiringly grapple with the stark realities of life. (ABB, 2014)
    (a) with (b) over (c) on (d) round
16. Corruption is ________ in our society; the integrity of even the senior officials is _________. (Tech Mahindra, 2014)
    (a) Endangered, disputed (b) Pervasive, integral
    (c) Rare, corrupted (d) Rife, suspect
17. Because King Philip's desire to make Spain the dominant power in the sixteenth century Europe ran counter to Queen Elizabeth's insistence on autonomy for England, _______ was_______. (Tech Mahindra, 2014)
    (a) Ceasefire, assured (b) Warfare, avoidable
    (c) Ruination, impossible (d) Conflict, inevitable

Directions: *The following question consists of two words, each that have a certain relationship to each other, followed by four lettered pairs of words. Select the lettered pair that has the same relationship as the original pair of words.*

18. Bread : Bakery : : Brick : ? (Wipro, 2014)
    (a) Mint (b) Kiln (c) Furnace (d) Mine

Directions: *In the question given next, the sentences have been given in active/passive voice. From the given alternatives, choose the one which best expresses the given sentence in passive/active voice.* (Wipro, 2014)

19. After driving Professor Kumar to the museum she dropped him at his hotel.
    (a) After being driven to the museum, Professor Kumar was dropped at his hotel.
    (b) Professor Kumar was being driven dropped at his hotel.
    (c) After she had driven Professor Kumar to the museum she had dropped him at his hotel.
    (d) After she was driven Professor Kumar to the museum she had dropped him at his hotel.

Directions: *In the following question one sentence is divided into four parts. Identify the part that has an error.* (Tech Mahindra, 2014)

20. The study focusing exclusively to critically-ill children found that children with chronic illnesses, especially respiratory illnesses, are most likely, to develop influenza that requires critical care.
    (a) The study focusing exclusively to
    (b) critically-ill children found that children with chronic illnesses
    (c) especially respiratory illnesses, are most likely
    (d) to develop influenza that requires critical care.

SOLUTIONS WITH EXPLANATIONS

1. (a) his work which good health makes possible.
2. (b) what a healthy man should or should not do.
3. (d) often suffer from imaginary illness.
4. (c) health is the only means to an end.
5. (a) Exactly
6. (c) because it lives
7. (b) today because he is ill.
8. (c) as a basic part of your qualities and characteristics
9. (c) Strict
10. (c) Worth
11. (c) Rigorous
12. (a) Excessive
13. (d) were
14. (b) Erudite
15. (c) on
16. (d) Rife, suspect
17. (d) Conflict, inevitable
18. (b) Kiln
19. (a) After being driven to the museum, Professor Kumar was dropped at his hotel.
20. (a) The study focusing exclusively to

PRACTICE SET 17

Directions: *Read the passage carefully and answer the questions given below.*

At this stage of civilization, when many nations are brought in to close and vital contact for good and evil, it is essential, as never before, that their gross ignorance of one another should be diminished, that they should begin to understand a little of one another's historical experience and resulting mentality. It is the fault of the English to expect the people of other countries to react as they do, to political and international situations. Our genuine goodwill and good intentions are often brought to nothing, because we expect other people to be like us. This would be corrected if we knew the history, not necessarily in detail but in broad outlines, of the social and political conditions which have given to each nation its present character. (Dell, 2011)

1. The need for a greater understanding between nations
   (a) was always there (b) is no longer there
   (c) is more today than ever before (d) will always be there
2. The character of a nation is the result of its
   (a) mentality (b) cultural heritage
   (c) gross ignorance (d) socio-political conditions
3. According to the author his countrymen should
   (a) read the story of other nations
   (b) have a better understanding of other nations
   (c) not react to other actions
   (d) have vital contacts with other nations
4. Englishmen like others to react to political situations like
   (a) us (b) themselves (c) others (d) each other's

Directions: *Choose the word nearest in meaning to the word in italics from the given options.*

5. The man *vehemently* denied all the charges of corruption that were leveled against him. (Accenture, 2011)
   (a) Forcefully (b) Serenely (c) Devoutly
   (d) Hysterically (e) None of these

Directions: *Correct the italic part in the sentences given below.*

6. My *apartment which is air conditioned* is cool in the summer. (Infosys, 2012)
   (a) Apartment which is air conditioned
   (b) Apartment, which is air conditioned
   (c) Apartment, which is air conditioned,
   (d) Apartment which is air conditioned,
7. In addition to having more protein than wheat does, *the protein in rice is higher quality than that in* wheat, with more of the amino acids essential to the human diet. (Tech Mahindra, 2014)
   (a) rice has protein of higher quality than that in
   (b) the protein in rice is higher in quality than it is in
   (c) rice protien is higher in quality than it is in
   (d) rice has a protein higher in quality than
8. They were almost *at each other's throats* during their argument. (Infosys, 2014)
   (a) holding each other's throats (b) trying to kill each other

(c) concluding the argument (d) fighting or arguing heavily

Directions: *Pick out the most effective word from the given words to fill in the blank to make the sentence meaningfully complete.*

9. The miser gazed ____________ at the pile of gold coins in front of him. (ABB, 2014)
   (a) avidly (b) ddmiringly
   (c) thoughtfully (d) earnestly
10. Traffic problems in Bombay are as serious as in any other city in India, and they are complicated by digging of roads by corporations on this or that ________. (Syntel, 2013)
   (a) reason (b) instance (c) aspect (d) pretext
11. Has this work been done ____ you? (Capgemini, 2015)
   (a) from (b) by (c) to (d) with
12. Although ancient tools were _____ preserved, enough have survived to allow us to demonstrate, an occasionally interrupted but generally _____ progress through prehistory. (Tech Mahindra, 2014)
   (a) partially, noticeable (b) superficially, necessary
   (c) unwittingly, documented (d) rarely, continued

Directions: *In the following questions, choose the word which best expresses the meaning of the given word.*

13. Shy (Capgemini, 2015)
   (a) Timid (b) Silent (c) Distant (d) Strange
14. Lament (GE, 2014)
   (a) Complain (b) Comment (c) Condone (d) Console
15. Demeanor (Tech Mahindra, 2014)
   (a) demarcation (b) way of behaving
   (c) detection (d) liability

Directions: *The following questions consist of two words each that have a certain relationship to each other, followed by four lettered pairs of words. Select the lettered pair that has the same relationship as the original pair of words.*

16. Sword : Slaughter : : Scalpel : ? (Wipro, 2014)
   (a) Murder (b) Stab (c) Surgery (d) Chopping

Directions: *In the questions gien below, the sentences have been given in Active/ Passive voice. From the given alternatives, choose the one which best expresses the given sentence in Passive/Active Voice. (Wipro, 2014)*

17. They greet me cheerfully every morning.
   (a) Every morning I was greeted cheerfully.
   (b) I am greeted cheerfully by them every morning.
   (c) I am being greeted cheerfully by them every morning.

(d) Cheerful greeting is done by them every morning to me

18. What do you want from me? (Tech Mahindra, 2014)
    (a) He asked me if I wanted anything from him.
    (b) He asked me what I wanted from him.
    (c) He asked me what did I want from him.
    (d) He asks me what I want from him.

Directions: *Following sentences are given in direct/indirect speech. Covert the sentence to its respective speech.*

19. The boy said, 'Who dare call me a thief?' (Tech Mahindra, 2014)
    (a) The boy enquired who dared call him a thief.
    (b) The boy asked who called him a thief.
    (c) The boy told that who dared call him a thief.
    (d) The boy wondered who dared call a thief.
20. She said to him, 'Why don't you go today?" (Tech Mahindra, 2014)
    (a) She asked him why he did not go that day.
    (b) She said to him why he don't go that day.
    (c) She asked him not to go that day.
    (d) She asked him why he did not go today.

SOLUTIONS WITH EXPLANATIONS

1. (c) is more today than ever before
2. (d) socio-political conditions
3. (b) have a better understanding of other nations
4. (d) each other's
5. (a) Forcefully
6. (b) apartment, which is air conditioned
7. (a) rice has protein of higher quality than that in
8. (d) fighting or arguing heavily
9. (a) avidly
10. (a) reason
11. (b) by
12. (d) rarely, continued
13. (a) Timid
14. (a) Complain
15. (b) way of behaving
16. (c) Surgery
17. (b) I am greeted cheerfully by them every morning.
18. (b) He asked me what I wanted from him
19. (a) The boy enquired who dared call him a thief.
20. (a) She asked him why he did not go that day.

PRACTICE SET 18

Directions: *Read the passage carefully and answer the questions given below.*

The strength of the electronics industry in Japan is the Japanese ability to organize production and marketing rather than their achievements in original research. The British are generally recognized as a far more inventive collection of individuals, but never seem able to exploit what they invent. There are many examples, from the TSR Z hovercraft, high speed train and Sinclair scooter to the Triumph, BSA and Norton Motorcycle which all prove this sad rule. The Japanese were able to exploits their strengths in marketing and development many years ago, and their success was at first either not understood in the West or was dismissed as something which could have been produced only at their low price. They were sold because they were cheap copies of other people's ideas churned out of a workhouse which was dedicated to hard grind above all else.

1. It is evident from the passage that the strength of a country's industry depends upon
   (a) original research (b) international cooperation
   (c) dedicated workforce (d) electronic development
2. According to the passage, prosperity in industry depends upon
   (a) productivity (b) inventiveness
   (c) marketing ability (d) official patronage
3. The main theme of this passage is
   (a) electronic industry in Japan
   (b) industrial comparison between Japan and Britain
   (c) the role of marketing efficiency in industrial prosperity
   (d) the importance of original research in industry

Directions: *Choose the option which best expresses the given sentence in Passive/ Active voice.* (Dell, 2013)

4. They have built a perfect dam across the river.
   (a) Across the river a perfect dam was built.
   (b) A perfect dam has been built by them across the river.
   (c) A perfect dam should have been built by them.
   (d) Across the river was a perfect dam.
5. Sam: Did they arrive on time? (Tech Mahindra, 2014)
   (a) Sam asked had they arrived on time
   (b) Sam wanted to know if they arrive on time
   (c) Sam questioned about their arrival time
   (d) Sam wondered if they had arrived on time

Directions: *Select the word from the options given below that is the closest in meaning to the word in the question.*

6. Pusillanimous (Tech Mahindra, 2014)

(a) Timorous (b) Courageous (c) Wise (d) Punctual

7. Reckless (GE, 2014)
   (a) Courageous (b) Rash (c) Bold (d) Daring
8. Exodus (ABB, 2014)
   (a) Influx (b) Home-coming (c) Return (d) Restoration

Directions: *Fill the blanks with the appropriate words to complete the sentences.*

9. Many people at that time believed that spices help preserve food; however, Hall found that many marketed spices were ________ bacteria, moulds and yeasts. (Tech Mahindra, 2014)
   (a) devoid of (b) teeming with (c) improved by
   (d) shattered by (e) active against
10. Archaeology is a poor profession; only ____ sums are available for excavating sites and even more ____ amounts for preserving the excavations. (Tech Mahindra, 2014)
   (a) trifling, meager (b) miniscule, substantial
   (c) average, augmented (d) judicious, penurious
   (e) modest, munificent
11. Summit distributed the sweets _______ his friends. (Capgemini 2015)
   (a) among (b) for (c) to (d) with
12. This train travels from London ______ Paris. (Accenture, 2012)
   (a) at (b) to (c) over (d) below
13. Albert Einstein was _____ famous scientist. Einstein won _______ Nobel Prize for Physics in 1921. Einstein left his country and lived in _______ States until he died in 1955. (Accenture, 2013)
   (a) A, the, an (b) A, the, the
   (c) A, an, the (d) An, an, the

Directions: *In the questions given below, each passage consist of six sentences. The first and sixth sentences are given in the beginning. The middle four sentences in each have been removed and jumbled up. These are labelled as P, Q, R, and S. Find out the proper order for the four sentences.*

14. S1: You know my wife, Madhavi, always urged me to give up smoking.
   P: I really gave it up.
   Q: And so when I went to jail I said to myself I really must give it up, if for no other reason than of being self-reliant.
   R: When I emerged from jail, I wanted to tell her of my great triumph.
   S: But when I met her, there she was with a packet of cigarettes.
   S6: Poor girl. The Proper sequence should be: (Oracle, 2013)
   (a) PSRQ (b) SPQR (c) QPRS (d) RSPQ
15. S1: The city is almost a slum and stinks most of the time.
   P: The slush on the road did not deter them.

Q: The occasional slips and falls were considered a small price to pay for the trip.

R: They were excited, fascinated by the sight of fresh snow on the roads.

S: Even so, it looked beautiful to tourists of various categories.

S6: But some visitors came away with the unforgettable sight of young labors scantily clad.

The proper sequence should be: (Oracle, 2014)

(a) RQPS (b) QPRS (c) RSQP (d) SPQR

Directions: *Each question consist of two words which have a certain relationship to each other followed by four pairs of related words, Select the pair which has the same relationship.*

16. Pork : Pig (Oracle, 2013)
    (a) rooster : chicken (b) mutton : sheep
    (c) steer : beef (d) lobster : crustacean
17. Indigent : Wealthy (Oracle, 2014)
    (a) angry: rich (b) native: affluent
    (c) gauche: graceful (d) scholarly: erudite

Directions: *Which of the phrases (a), (b), (c) and (d) given below each sentence should replace the phrases printed in bold in the following sentences to make the sentences grammatically correct.*

18. Outrunning the other players on the football **field, I saw Jack score** the winning touchdown. (Infosys, 2012)
    (a) Field, I saw Jack score (b) Field, I saw Jack scoring.
    (c) Field, Jack scored (d) Field, Jack scoring
19. The Navy used the nuclear submarine accident off the coast of Hawaii **to show that everyone must be held responsible for their actions.** (Infosys, 2014)
    (a) To show that everyone must be held responsible for their actions.
    (b) To demonstrate their belief that everyone must be held responsible for their actions.
    (c) To demonstrate its belief that everyone must be held responsible for their actions.
    (d) To signal how no one should be able to get away with committing acts of terrible negligence.
    (e) To show that everyone must be held responsible for his/her actions.

Directions: *Choose the correct meaning of the bold phrases.*

20. They were almost **at each other's throats** during their argument. (Infosys, 2014)
    (a) Holding each other's throats (b) Trying to kill each other
    (c) Concluding the argument (d) Fighting or arguing heavily

SOLUTIONS WITH EXPLANATIONS

1. (c) dedicated workforce
2. (c) marketing ability
3. (c) the role of marketing efficiency in industrial prosperity
4. (b) A perfect dam has been built by them across the river.
5. (d) Sam wondered if they had arrived on time
6. (a) Timorous
7. (b) Rash
8. (a) Influx
9. (b) teeming with
10. (a) trifling, meager
11. (a) among
12. (b) to
13. (b) a, the, the
14. (c) QPRS
15. (d) SPQR
16. (b) Mutton : Sheep
17. (c) Gauche : Graceful
18. (c) field, Jack scored
19. (e) To show that everyone must be held responsible for his/her actions.
20. (d) fighting or arguing heavily

PRACTICE SET 19

Direction: *Read the passage carefully and answer the questions given below.*

To those who do listen, the desert speaks of things with an emphasis quite different from that of the shore, the mountain, the valley or the plains, whereas these invite action and suggest limitless opportunity and exhaust less resources, the implications and the mood of the desert are something different. For one thing, the desert is conservative not radical. It is more likely to provide awe than to invite conquest. The heroism which it encourages is the heroism of endurance, not that of conquest. It brings man up against this limitation, turns him upon himself and suggests values which more indulgent regions suppress. Sometimes it includes contemplation in men who have never contemplated before: And of all the answers to the question—what is a desert good for—'contemplation' is perhaps the best. The last half of my life was spent at one of those painful epochs of human history, during which world was getting worse and past victories which had seemed to be definitive have turned out to be only temporary. When I was young, Victorian optimism was taken for granted. It was thought that freedom and prosperity would spread gradually throughout the world through an orderly process, and it was hoped that cruelty, tyranny and injustice would continually diminish. Hardly anyone thought of the nineteenth century as a brief interlude between past and future barbarism.

1. In order to receive the desert's message, the beholder needs to be?
   (a) Contemplation (b) Indolence
   (c) Heroic Endeavor (d) Adventurous Spirit
2. If one responds with insight to the mood of the desert, it evokes?
   (a) An inclination for deep thought.
   (b) The possibility of unending resources.
   (c) The desire for Heroic conquest.
   (d) A sense of intense revulsion.
3. The writer calls the desert conservative rather than radical because it provides an environment that
   (a) Inspires man to explore it
   (b) offers unlimited opportunity to conquer
   (c) tests ones Endurance
   (d) makes one gloomy
4. What does the phrase 'it brings man up against his limitations', mean?
   (a) It makes man feel hopeless about his limitations.
   (b) It makes man aware of his limitations.
   (c) It compels man to fight against his limitations.
   (d) It persuades man to overcome his limitations.
5. Which of the following represents a methodological handicap in the field of astronomy?
   (a) The difficulty of formulating predictive theories.
   (b) The impossibility of evaluating data collected by early observers.
   (c) The difficulty of correlating observed data with theoretical predictions.
   (d) The difficulty of testing hypotheses through experimentation.

Directions: *Choose the option which best expresses the given sentence in Passive/ Active voice.*

6. You can play with these kittens quite safely. (Tech Mahindra, 2014)
   (a) These kittens can played with quite safely.
   (b) These kittens can play with you quite safely.
   (c) These kittens can be played with you quite safely.
   (d) These kittens can be played with quite safely.

Directions: *Select the word from the options given below that is the closest in meaning to the word given in the question.*

7. Mendacious (Tech Mahindra, 2014)
   (a) Meaningful (b) Trustworthy
   (c) Melancholic (d) Perfidious
8. Relinquish (ABB, 2014)

(a) Abdicate (b) Renounce (c) Posses (d) Deny

Directions: *Fill in the Blanks.*

9. The study of history leads one away from the extremes of belief, thus allowing one to develop conviction without dogmatism, devotion without ___________. (Tech Mahindra, 2014)
   (a) Comprehension (b) Realism (c) Moderation
   (d) Fanaticism (e) Skepticism
10. I have not seen him ______ yesterday. (Capgemini 2015)
   (a) from (b) till (c) since (d) beside
11. Are you shopping for ________ health club to join so you can get in shape? Shop wisely! You could end up choosing _______ wrong club and losing more money than pounds. (Accenture, 2013)
   (a) the, an (b) the, the (c) A, the (d) An, the

Directions: *In the questions given below, each passage consists of six sentences. The first and sixth sentences are given in the beginning. The middle four sentences have been removed and jumbled up. These are labelled as P, Q, R, and S. Find out the proper order for the four sentences.*

12. S1: When a satellite is launched, the rocket begins by going slowly upwards through the air.
   P: However, the higher it goes, the less air it meets.
   Q: As the rocket goes higher, it travels faster.
   R: For the atmosphere becomes thinner.
   S: As a result there is less friction.
   S6: Consequently, the rocket still does not become too hot. The Proper sequence should be: (Oracle, 2013)
   (a) QPRS (b) QSPR (c) PQRS (d) PQSR
13. A. The most popular activity for Americans was gardening.
   B. We can see from the above examples tat in different countries and cultures around the world, free time is spend in different ways.
   C. In the U.K., it was going to the pub, followed by visiting the cinema.
   D. In Japan, it was very different from the first two countries. Going too bars and pubs ranked eighth in popularity, and gardening ranked ninth.
   E. There were differences in the most popular outdoor pursuits between the following three countries. (Robert Bosch, 2013)
   (a) EADCB (b) BEACD (c) EACDB (d) CEABD
14. S1: A gentleman who lived alone always had two plates placed on the table at dinner time.
   P: One day just as he sat down to dine, the cat rushed in to the room.
   Q: One plate was for himself and other was for his cat.

R: She drooped a mouse into her own plate and another into her master plate.
S: He used to give the cat a piece of meat from his own plate.
S6: In this way the cat showed her gratitude to her master. (Oracle, 2014)
The Proper sequence should be:
(a) QSPR (b) PSRQ (c) QRSP (d) RPQS

Directions: *Each question consist of two words which have a certain relationship to each other followed by four pairs of related words. Select the pair which has the same relationship as the pair of words given in the question.*

15. After : Before (Oracle, 2013)
    (a) First : Second (b) Present : Past
    (c) Contemporary : Historic (d) Successor : Predecessor
16. Symphony : Composer (Oracle, 2014)
    (a) Leonardo : Music (b) Fresco : Painter
    (c) colours : Pallet (d) Art : Appreciation

Directions: *Which of the phrases [(a), (b), (c), and (d)] given below each sentence should replace the phrases printed in bold to make the sentence grammatically correct?*

17. When you **pay with a stolen credit card**, this is known as larceny. (Infosys, 2012)
    (a) When you pay with a stolen credit card, this
    (b) You pay with a stolen credit card, this
    (c) Paying with a stolen credit card, this
    (d) Paying with a stolen credit card
18. Your admission into this university **will be dependent** on the marks you score in the entrance examination. (Cognizent, 2012)
    (a) is depending (b) depends (c) will depend
    (d) depending (e) No correction required
19. Each of the movies **were great and the choice for the best one among all three was very difficult indeed.** (Infosys, 2014)
    (a) were great and choosing the best one among the three was very difficult indeed.
    (b) was great and choosing the best one among the three was very difficult indeed.
    (c) were great and choosing the best one between the three was very difficult indeed.
    (d) was great and choosing the best one between the three was very difficult indeed.
    (e) were great and the choices among all three were very difficult indeed.

Directions: *Choose the correct meaning of the bold phrases.*

20. He was **fishing for compliments** on his culinary skills. (Infosys, 2014)

(a) receiving compliments on cooking fish
(b) putting oneself down hoping that others will contradict them and in the process compliment them
(c) waiting for people to compliment
(d) running away from compliments

SOLUTIONS WITH EXPLANATIONS

1. (a) contemplation
2. (a) An inclination for deep thought
3. (c) Tests ones endurance
4. (d) It persuades man to overcome his limitations
5. (d) The difficulty of testing hypotheses through experimentation.
6. (a) These kittens can played with quite safely.
7. (d) Perfidious
8. (c) Posses
9. (d) fanaticism
10. (c) since
11. (c) A, the
12. (a) QPRS
13. (c) EACDB
14. (a) QSPR
15. (d) Successor : Predecessor
16. (b) Fresco : Painter
17. (d) Paying with a stolen credit card
18. (c) will depend
19. (d) was great and choosing the best one between the three was very difficult indeed.
20. (b) Putting oneself down hoping that others will contradict them and in the process compliment them

PRACTICE SET 20

Directions: *Read the passage carefully and answer the questions given below.*

In the world today we make health and end in itself. We have forgotten that health is really means to enable a person to do his work and do it well. a lot of modern medicine and this includes many patients as well as many physicians pays very little attention to health but very much attention to those who imagine that they are ill. Our great concern with health is shown by the medical columns in newspapers. The health articles in popular magazines and the popularity of television programmes and all those books on medicine. We talk about health all the time. Yet for the most part the only result is more people with imaginary illness. The healthy man should not be wasting time talking about health: he should be using health for work. The work does the work that good health possible. (Dell, 2011)

1. A healthy man should be concerned with
   (a) his work which good health makes possible.
   (b) looking after his health.
   (c) his health which makes work possible.
   (d) talking about health.
2. The passage tells us
   (a) how medicine should be manufactured.
   (b) what healthy man should or should not do.
   (c) what television programs should be about.
   (d) how best to imagine illness.
3. Talking about the health all time makes people
   (a) always suffer from imaginary illness.
   (b) sometimes suffer from imaginary illness.
   (c) rarely suffer from imaginary illness.
   (d) often suffer from imaginary illness.
4. The passage suggests that
   (a) health is an end in itself. (b) health is blessing.
   (c) health is only means to an end. (d) we should not talk about health.

Directions: *Choose the option which best expresses the given sentence in Passive/ Active voice.*

5. They have built a perfect dam across the river. (Tech Mahindra, 2014)
   (a) Across the river a perfect dam was built.
   (b) A perfect dam has been built by them across the river
   (c) A perfect dam should have been built by them.
   (d) Across the river was a perfect dam.

Directions: *Select the word from the options given below that is the closest in meaning to the word in the question.*

6. Expostulate (Tech Mahindra, 2014)
   (a) Express (b) Dissuade (c) Pursue (d) Explain
7. Recuperate
   (a) Mend (b) Endorse (c) Persist (d) Worsen

Directions: *Fill the blanks with the appropriate words to complete the sentences.*

8. In that era, painters believed that human beauty was a _______ of divine beauty, just as human intellect was a microcosm of the universal mind. (Tech Mahindra, 2014)
   (a) supposition (b) rejection (c) reflection

(d) misconception (e) revision

9. He has been here _____ yesterday. (Capgemini, 2015)
   (a) by (b) from (c) since (d) at
10. My home town ___ California is a wonderful place to live. I live ______ a suburb not far from a busy city. ______ a fast pace. (Prepositions) (Accenture, 2011)
   (a) at, in (b) in, at (c) in, in (d) at, on
11. It is pleasant to have ______ sleep in ______ afternoon. (Articles) (Accenture, 2011)
   (a) a, a (b) a, an (c) an, the (d) a, the

Directions: *In the following questions, choose the words which are the exact opposite of the given words.*

12. Mortal (GE, 2014)
   (a) Divine (b) Immortal (c) Spiritual (d) Eternal
13. Torpor (ABB, 2013)
   (a) Alacrity (b) Sloth (c) Dormancy (d) Chagrin

Directions: *In the questions given below, each passage consists of six sentences. The first and sixth sentences are given in the beginning. The middle four sentences have been removed and jumbled up. These are labelled as P, Q, R, and S. Find out the proper order for the four sentences.*

14. S1: A father having offered to take the baby out in a perambulator, was tempted by the sunny morning to slip into a pub for a glass of beer.
   P: Indignant at her husband's behavior, she decided to teach him a lesson.
   Q: She wheeled away the pram.
   R: A little later, his wife came by, where to her horror, she discovered her sleeping baby.
   S: Leaving the pram outside, he disappeared inside the bar.
   S6: She waited for him, anticipating the white face and quivering lips which would soon appear with the news that the baby had been stolen.
   (Oracle, 2013)

   The proper sequence should be:
   (a) SRPQ (b) RQPS (c) SPQR (d) PQSR
15. S1: Ants eat worms, centipedes and spiders.
   P: They are usually much quicker than the ant itself.
   Q: Nevertheless, these animals do not make easy game for ants.
   R: Besides, they have an extraordinary number of ways of escaping.
   S: They also eat larvae and insect adults such as flies, moths and spring tails.
   S6: Some jump, and some give out a pungent repellent substance.
   (Oracle, 2014)

The proper sequence should be:
(a) SQPR (b) SPRQ (c) SQRP (d) SRQP

Directions: *Each questions consist of two words which have a certain relationship to each other followed by four pairs of related words. Select the pair which has the same relationship as the pair of words given in the question.*

16. Indigent : Wealthy (Oracle, 2013)
    (a) Angry : Rich (b) Native : Affluent
    (c) Gauche : Graceful (d) Scholarly : Erudite
17. Corporeal : Spiritual (Oracle, 2014)
    (a) Mesa: Plateau (b) Moron: Savant
    (c) Foreigner: Immigrant (d) Pedagogue: Teacher

Directions: *Which of the phrases [(a), (b), (c), and (d)] given below each sentence should replace the phrases printed in bold to make the sentence grammatically correct?*

18. In southern United States, many indigenous native **tribes still perform** traditional rites and ceremonies. (Infosys, 2012)
    (a) do still perform (b) they still perform
    (c) are still performed (d) were still performed
19. Never fail to get frustrated **on the golf course: nonetheless, I always resolve to continue my involving in the game**. (Infosys, 2014)
    (a) on the golf course: nonetheless, I always resolve to continue my involving in the game.
    (b) on the golf course: yet nonetheless I always resolve to continue my involvement in the game.
    (c) on the golf course; nonetheless, I always resolve to continue my involvement in the game.
    (d) on the golf course; yet nonetheless I always resolve to continue being involved in the game.

Direction: *Choose the correct meaning of the bold sentences.*

20. While in a concert with Sandeep, Amrita pointed at Vinay and said **two's a company and three's a crowd**. (Infosys, 2014)
    (a) a way of asking the third person to leave because you want to be left alone with someone else
    (b) a way of defining the crowd
    (c) a way of adding on to the company
    (d) a way of inviting people to be a part of the crowd

SOLUTIONS WITH EXPLANATIONS

1. (a) his work which good health makes possible
2. (b) what healthy man should or should not do

3. (d) often suffer from imaginary illness
4. (c) health is only means to an end
5. (b) A perfect dam has been built by them across the river
6. (b) Dissuade
7. (a) Mend
8. (c) reflection
9. (c) since
10. (c) in, in
11. (c) an, the
12. (b) Immortal
13. (a) Alacrity
14. (a) SRPQ
15. (d) SRQP
16. (c) Gauche : Graceful
17. (b) Moron : Savant
18. (c) are still performed
19. (c) on the golf course; nonetheless, I always resolve to continue my involvement in the game.
20. (a) A way of asking the third person to leave because you want to be left alone with someone else

PRACTICE SET 21

Direction: *Read the passage carefully and answer the questions given next:*

Harold a professional man who had worked in an office for many years had a fearful dream. In it, he found himself in a land where small slug-like animals with slimy tentacles lived on people's bodies. The people tolerated the loathsome creatures because after many years they grew into elephants which then became the nation's system of transport, carrying everyone wherever he wanted to go. Harold suddenly realized that he himself was covered with these things, and he woke up screaming. In a vivid sequence of pictures this dream dramatized for Harold what he had never been able to put in to words; he saw himself as letting society feed on his body in his early years so that it would carry him when he retired. He later threw off the "security bug" and took up freelance work.

1. Which one of the following phrases best helps to bring out the precise meaning of loathsome creatures?
   (a) Security bug and slimy tentacles
   (b) Fearful dream and slug-like animals
   (c) Slimy tentacles and slug-like animals
   (d) slug-like animals and security bug
2. The statement that, he later threw off the security bug, means that
   (a) Harold succeeded in overcoming the need for security

(b) Harold stopped giving much importance to dreams
(c) Harold started tolerating social victimization
(d) Harold killed all the bugs troubled him

3. Harold's dream was fearful because
   (a) it brought him face to face with reality
   (b) it was full of vivid pictures of snakes
   (c) he saw huge elephant in it
   (d) in it he saw slimy creatures feeding on peoples bodies

Directions: *Choose the option which best expresses the given sentence in Passive/Active voice.*

4. You should open the bottle about three hours before you use it. (Tech Mahindra, 2014)
   (a) Bottle should be opened about three hours before use.
   (b) Bottle should be opened by you three hours before use.
   (c) Bottle should be opened about three hours before you use it.
   (d) Bottle should be opened about three hours before it is used.

Directions: *Select the word from the options given below that is the closest in meaning to the word in the question.*

5. Conglomerate (Tech Mahindra, 2014)
   (a) Single (b) Asunder (c) Motley (d) Contradict
6. Commissioned
   (a) Started (b) Closed (c) Finished (d) Terminated

Directions: *Fill the blanks with the appropriate words to complete the sentences.*

7. The world is not _____, but _____, which means that every economic event that takes place somewhere in the world is felt virtually everywhere in the world. (Tech Mahindra, 2014)
   (a) static, changing (b) cohesive, discrete
   (c) complete, imperfect (d) isolated, unified
   (e) fragmented, integrated
8. Do you want me to help you ______ this? (Capgemini, 2015)
   (a) by (b) before (c) for (d) with
9. In the evening, all the kids _____ our neighborhood play ball on the street. Some play basketball _______ a court marked by chalk. Others play Ping-pong ______ a neighbor's garage. (Accenture, 2011)
   (a) at, out, in (b) in, on, in (c) at, on, in (d) in, on, at
10. The US is ______ open economy and _____ strong proponent of free trade globally. (Accenture, 2011)
    (a) an, a (b) The, the (c) a, the (d) in, the

Directions: *Choose the word nearest in meaning to the word in italics from the given options.*

11. The art movie I watched this evening has put me in a *pensive* mood. (Accenture, 2011)
    (a) Confused (b) Depressed (c) Cheerful (d) Reflective

Directions: *In the following questions, choose the words which are the exact opposite of the given words.*

12. Quiescent (GE, 2014)
    (a) Active (b) Dormant (c) Weak (d) Unconcerned

Direction: *In the questions given below, each passage consist of six sentences. The first and sixth sentence are given in the beginning. The middle four sentences have been removed and jumbled up. These are labelled as P, Q, R, and S. Find out the proper order for the four sentences.*

13. S1: While crossing a busy road, we should obey the policeman on duty.
    P: We should always cross the road at the zebra crossing.
    Q: We must look to the signal lights and cross the road only when the road is clear.
    R: If there are no signal lights at the crossing, we should look to the right, then to left and again the right before crossing the road.
    S: If the road is not clear we should wait.
    S6: We should never run while crossing the road. (Oracle, 2013)
    The proper sequence should be:
    (a) PSRQ (b) PQRS (c) RQSP (d) QRPS
14. S1: Satyajit Ray made several films for children.
    P: Later film makers have followed his lead.
    Q: Today other nations are making the children's film in a big way.
    R: This was at a time when no director considered children as potential audience.
    S: Ray was, thus, a pioneer in the field.
    S6: But today few think of Ray as a maker of children's films. (Oracle, 2014)
    The proper sequence should be:
    (a) PSRQ (b) RSQP (c) RSPQ (d) SQRP

Directions: *Each question consist of two words which have a certain relationship to each other followed by four pairs of related words. Select the pair which has the same relationship as the pair of words given in the question.*

15. Distance : Mile (Oracle, 2013)
    (a) Liquid : Litre (b) Bushel : Corn
    (c) Weight : Scale (d) Fame : Television
16. Hope : Aspires (Oracle, 2014)

(a) Love : Elevates
(b) Film : Flam
(c) Fib : Lie
(d) Fake : Ordinary

Directions: *Which of the phrases [(a), (b), (c), and (d)] given below each sentence should replace the phrases printed in bold to make the sentence grammatically correct?*

17. We were exhausted from our long journey **and decided** to go straight to bed. (Infosys, 2012)
    (a) as we were
    (b) we decided
    (c) we were deciding
    (d) we decided and went
18. The information presented in the most recent reports **indicate that turbulent times lie ahead for those who have invested only in NASDAQ stocks.** (Infosys, 2014)
    (a) indicate that turbulent times lie ahead for those who have invested only in NASDAQ stocks.
    (b) indicate that turbulent times should lie ahead for those who have invested only in NASDAQ stocks.
    (c) indicate that turbulent times are laying ahead for those who have invested only in NASDAQ stocks.
    (d) indicates that turbulent times lie ahead for those who have invested only in NASDAQ stocks.
19. When it was decided to send the rescue team **in the colliery**, the experts showed their reluctance.
    (a) into the colliery
    (b) inside the colliery
    (c) under the colliery
    (d) underneath the colliery

Directions: *Choose the correct meaning of the bold phrases.*

20. I had to **go out on my limb** for my colleague's absence at work. (Infosys, 2014)
    (a) stand on one leg
    (b) go against someone strongly
    (c) put oneself in a tough position in order to support someone/thing
    (d) act as a replacement

SOLUTIONS WITH EXPLANATIONS

1. (c)
2. (a)
3. (a)
4. (d) Bottle should be opened about three hours before it is used.
5. (c) Motley
6. (d) Terminated
7. (e) fragmented, integrated
8. (d) with

9. (b) in, on, in
10. (a) an, a
11. (d) Reflective
12. (a) Active
13. (d) QRPS
14. (c) RSPQ
15. (a) Liquid : Litre
16. (c) Fib : Lie
17. (b) we decided
18. (a) indicate that turbulent times lie ahead for those who have invested only in NASDAQ stocks.
19. (a) into the colliery
20. (c) Put oneself in a tough position in order to support someone/thing

Group Discussion

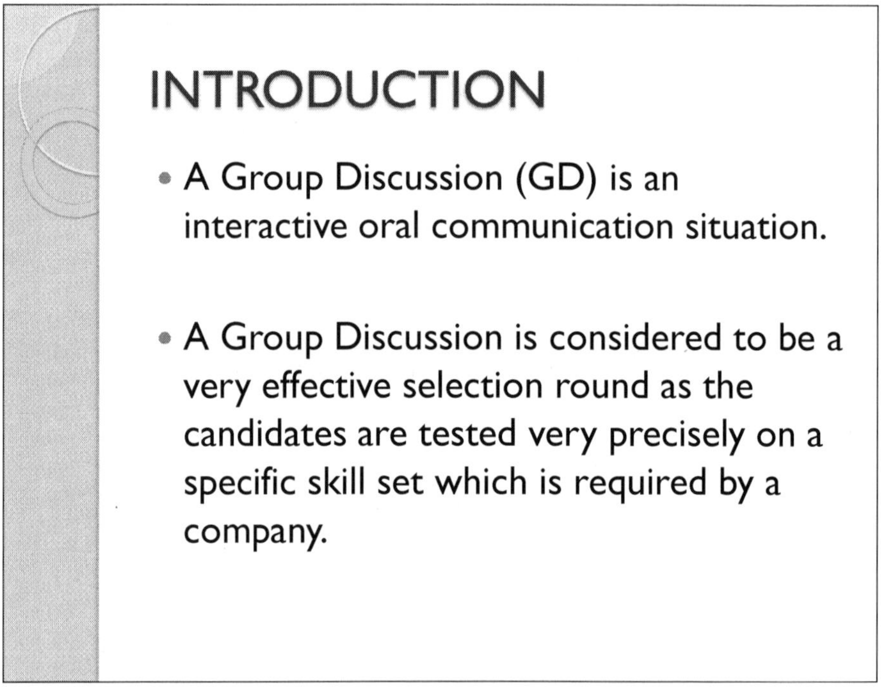

- Group means a number of persons gathered together.
- Discussion is the process of talking about something.
- A GD is a cooperative activity with in a framework of ground rules.
- Monologue: Long speech by one actor in a play/ film as a part of a theoretical or broadcast programme.
- Dialogue : Discussion between two or more persons in a play/film.
- Conversation: Informal talk between two or more persons.
- Debate: A formal discussion on a particular matter in a public meeting, or legislative assembly, in which opposing arguments are put forward and then votes are cast.
- Group Discussion: Focused conversation on a particular topic.

WHY COMPANIES CONDUCT GD

- Organisation wants to make sure that the candidate is suitable for that particular job.
- It is a process in which the participants sit together, discuss a topic, and try to reach a consensus.
- If it is an administrative/HR job, and they have to display confidence.

Eg: If it is a sales job, then the candidate must have a right mix of assertiveness and willingness to serve the customers.

- Different managerial traits are spotted in this discussion. Eg: leadership abilities, planning, negotiation skills.
- Consensus : General agreement on something
- Ex. : Whenever a company visits for a campus drive, it means there is a vacant position to be filled by a fresher.
- HR jobs candidates have to display confidence as they have to deal with different segments of people.

TYPES OF GD

1. Topic-Based Discussion
   - A controversy
   - A descriptive topic
   - An abstract topic

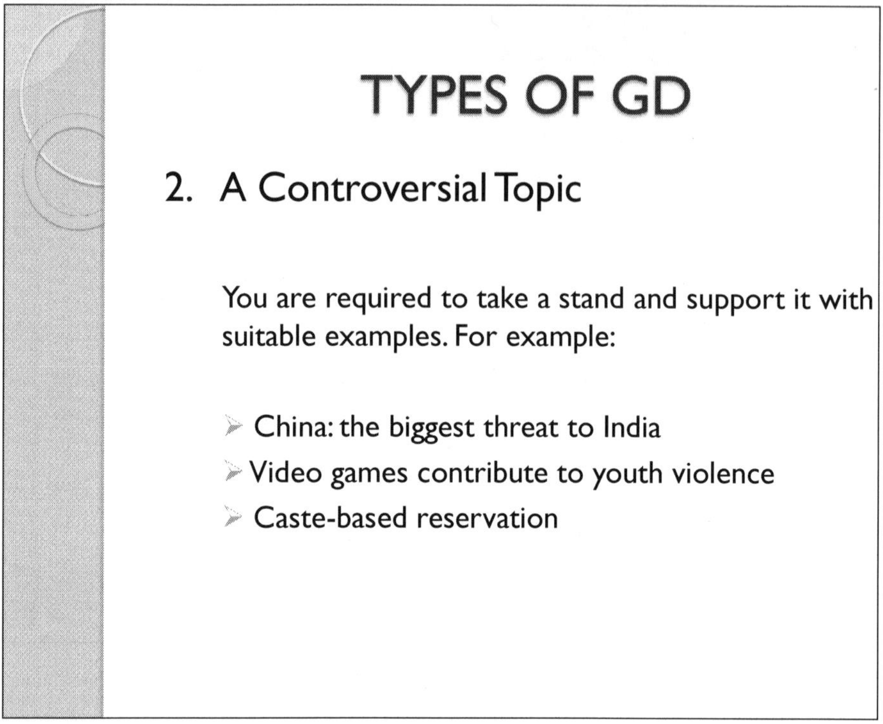

- What should the approach be: For/Against

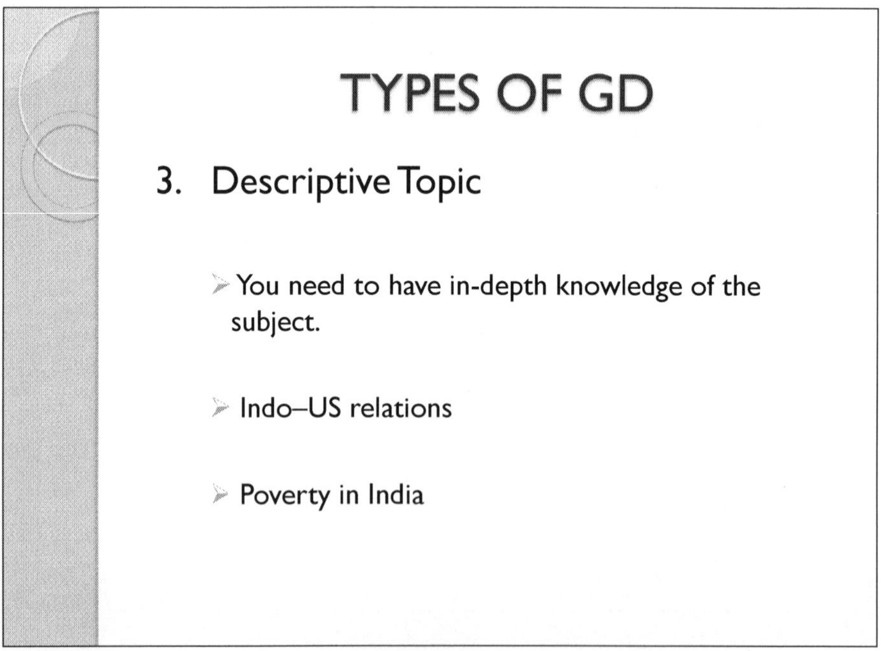

- Support with suitable facts and figures and mention the source.

- You simply say what you think about the topic.
- Companies conduct JAM sessions.

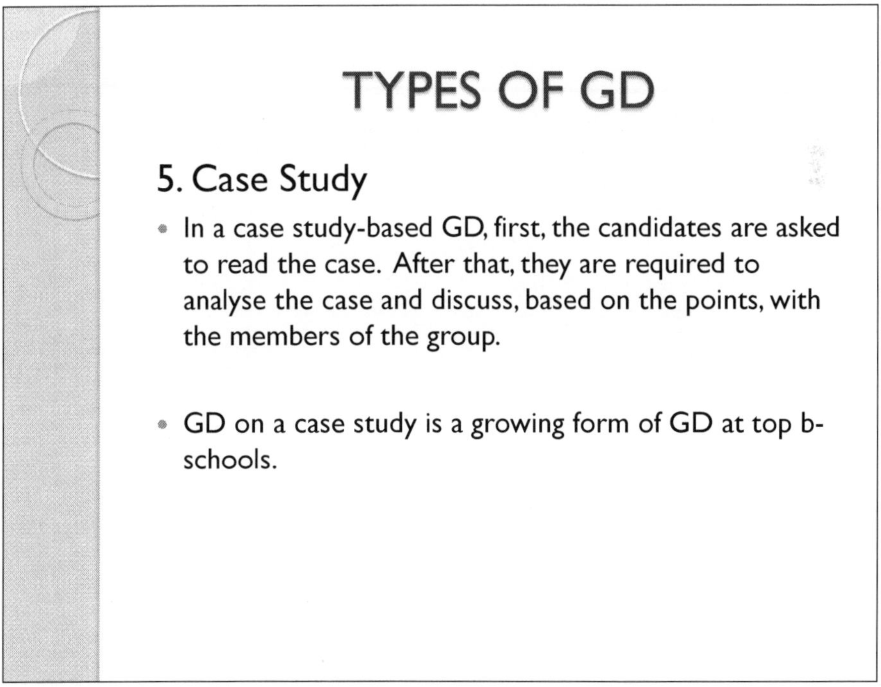

- You would be given real life situations/imaginary cases.

- You have to present your opinion in the given situation.
- Eg: Scene at a police station, hospital, flood hit areas.

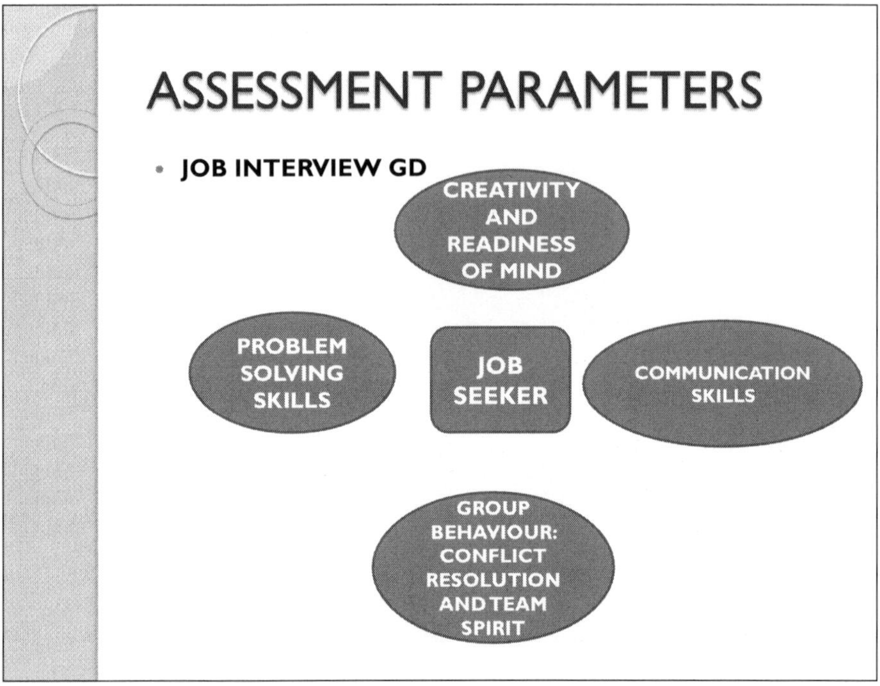

GD TEMPLATE								
				Level 1	*Level 2*	*Level 3*	*Level 4*	*Level 5*
S. No.	*Name*	*Registration Number*	*Branch*	*Body Language*	*Communication skills*	*Leadership skills*	*Negotiation skills*	*Content*

Note: Communication skills: Pronunciation, Fluency; Body Language: Posture, Eye contact

CHARACTERISTICS OF A CANDIDATE

- Body Language
- Eye contact
- Grab the opportunity to speak first
- Maintain your stand

- Knowledge – content regarding the subject. One has to be a voracious reader and increase their knowledge by reading newspapers, magazines and watching TV.
- Leadership skills may include initiation, adaptability, decision making skills, ability to reach to common consensus.
- Leadership skills: Ability to moderate the discussion
- **Confidence level:** Your confidence level adds a lot of value to your candidature.
- **Communication skills:** Pronunciation and fluency. If you have good points to put across but if you do not communicate them effectively, you do not have the chance to impress the evaluators.
- To improve communication skills, one needs to read books on communication and general subjects.
- This would improve the vocabulary strength of the individual.
- One needs to pick up good phrases and try to use them in day-to-day discussions.
- **Listening skills:** You are incorporating words and their meanings by comprehending the same.
- Hearing does not involve understanding.
- So, active listening, which is acquired with attention and understanding of ideas and facts, is essential in GDs.
- Candidate is always alert.
- **Body Language:** Posture.
- **Eye contact:** A candidate should make eye contact with other candidates while expressing their point of view.
- **Initiate the discussion:** Nobody will ask you to speak. You have to take your own opportunity to speak and be confident.

- Maintain your stand: You should not change your stand and give logical justification in support–facts and figures.
- A person cannot be evaluated of they do not speak.
- Participants need to ignore the observer.

NON-VERBAL COMMUNICATION

- Hands on lap, right hand on top of left – Logical person
- Frequent hand movements – distractive person
- Occasional hand movements – Emphasis
- Legs firmly on the ground - Alertness
- Shaking legs – Frustration
- Raising eyebrows – Curiosity

INTERACTIVE STRATEGIES AND USEFUL EXPRESSIONS

1. To Begin a GD
   - It is a thought provoking topic, let us start the discussion
   - I feel that . . .
2. To give opinion
   - In my opinion
   - I am of the view
3. To accept others' views
   - I am strongly in favour of that
   - This is a good idea

- These are the phrases to begin a GD.
- Use your thinking ability.

INTERACTIVE STRATEGIES AND USEFUL EXPRESSIONS

4. To disagree with others:
   - I do not agree with you on this point
   - I am afraid I think differently
5. To focus on the discussion:
   - I think we are off the track
   - I am afraid we are diverting from the topic
6. To interrupt politely:
   - Sorry to interrupt you but can I add a point here
   - Excuse me, I have a point to convey.

- To focus on the discussion: it shows leadership quality.

Do's of participating in a GD

- Listen to the subject carefully.
- Put down your thoughts on a paper.
- Initiate the discussion if you know the subject well.
- Listen to others if you do not know the subject.
- Support your point with some facts and figures.
- Make short contributions of 25–30 seconds 3–4 times.
- Give others a chance to speak.
- Speak politely and pleasantly. Respect the contribution from other members.
- Disagree politely and agree with what is right.
- Summarise the discussion if the group has not reached a conclusion.

- Initiation.
- It makes other people realise that you are well-versed with the topic.
- It gives the impression.
- Give quotes and definitions, facts and figures.

Don'ts of participating in a Group Discussion

- Over speaking, interrupting, and snatching someone's chance to speak.
- Arguing and shouting during the GD.
- Looking at the evaluators.
- Talking about irrelevant things and diverting from the discussion.
- Displaying negative body gestures like touching the nose, leaning back on the chair, knocking the table with a pen, etc.
- Bringing in erratic statistics.
- Displaying low self confidence with a shaky voice and trembling hands.
- Trying to dominate the discussion.
- Putting others in an embarrassing situation by asking them to speak if they do not want to.

- Mention erratic statistics: facts and figures should be correct.

Personal Interview

PREPARING FOR THE INTERVIEW

MINIMUM RULES IN THE RESUME

How it looks

- Consistency of information
- Use lowercase everywhere, unless otherwise stated
- Spelling and grammar checks
- Neat and proper alignment

Content

- Include all your achievements, interests, strong points, projects, internships
- Write a few sentences on projects/activities you are proud of
- Highlight all those activities and projects about which you want your interviewer to ask you questions

- CONSISTENCY: Stability or uniformity in resume (CV).
  — Information given in the CV should be maintained.
  — E.g. font size and percentage mentioned in educational qualification.

- Unnecessary use of upper case letters should be avoided.
- Grammatical errors should be avoided.
- Uniformity in alignment should be there throughout the CV.

- Content: Ingredients of a CV.
  - Include projects, besides academics, extra-curricular activities, and co-curricular activities.
  - Whatever information is provided, the candidate must be prepared to answer questions asked by the interviewer.

CONSISTENCY

Consistency of information

- Cannot have 73% at one place and 73.8% at another, for the same exam
- Cannot write B.Tech. /MBA/ PGDM at a place and B.E. MBA/ PGDM elsewhere
- Consistency of fonts

  Cannot *have* multiple fonts without reason, as in this sentence.
- Consistency of font size

- Percentage: While writing the percentage under educational qualification, one should consider till one decimal place or make it a round figure.
- Need to maintain uniformity in writing.
- One should use the same font and size throughout the CV.

MINIMUM RULES: UPPERCASE AND LOWERCASE

Must know when to use uppercase, and when to use lowercase

- Proper nouns are always in uppercase
- e.g. your guide's name, or your father's name
- Abbreviations must be in uppercase
- e.g. RCM/ CUTM
- Beginning of a paragraph or sentence – use uppercase
- I or God – always uppercase. Always.

When such rules do not apply, one must use lowercase

- Never use uppercase without reason.
- Writing long sentences in uppercase looks ugly.

- The candidate should know where to use uppercase and lowercase.
- E.g. Project title/objective: The entire should not be in uppercase.

SPELLING AND GRAMMAR CHECKS

Spelling and grammar mistakes create a bad impression

- These can easily be corrected in MS Word.
- If your CV shows mistakes that can be easily identified by MS Word, it would mean that you are casual about your CV and possibly about other things as well

- Spelling and grammatical errors can be fixed using MS word.
- Green and red colour are shown as an error in Word documents which can be corrected.

LOOKS AND ALIGNMENT

Comma, full stop, and other punctuation marks, must come immediately after the word. There should be a space after the punctuation mark.

- Mark, mark is ok but mark ,mark does not look ok.

- The alignment should be left or in the centre.
- Use the same alignment throughout the CV.
- These are common errors that students make while writing CVs.

CONTENT

What to include?

- Include all areas where you want interviewer to ask you questions (this means that you are expected to be well prepared especially on those areas to answer questions)
- Where you have done something really well (e.g. a robotics competition, some programming assignment, or some internship or project), highlight it with 2 or 3 sentences.
- Must include interests and hobbies like painting, dance, debate, etc.
- Awards, if any, should find a place in a CV

What to avoid

- Highlighting areas where you don't want questions
- Frivolous stuff like net surfing, chatting with friends, etc.

Be honest in anything you include.

- Projects, summer internships: Objective, learning, outcome, work done, and duration should be mentioned in the CV.
- In hobbies, one should know different kinds of dance forms, types of art forms, famous dancers, famous painters, etc.
- Frivolous: Not of much value/purpose.

PREPARING FOR THE INTERVIEW

Come well prepared with 5 sentences on some open questions, e.g.

- Introduce yourself
- What are your interests?
- What are your strengths?
- What are your weaknesses?
- Why do you want to join our company?
- Why a software career? (for those not in CS, and appearing for an IT job)

If you make statements, be prepared to explain:

- "Accenture has got many awards" – you must know at least 2 awards
- "Accenture has good culture" – be prepared to explain what is good culture

- One should be prepared with answers to frequently asked questions.

- One should give good examples to support the statements given.
- Good culture means working environment and working hours.

WHEN THINGS GO WRONG

During the interview:

- Avoid criticizing your teacher or family or University or friends
- Avoid mentioning wrong information which would indicate your ignorance
- Avoid appearing helpless or ignorant (no one will give you a job out of pity)
- When you make a mistake, take responsibility – don't defend obvious mistakes
  - If you have written you have got 6.8% marks in B.Tech., avoid defending it. You lose even if you win.
- Don't make excuses
  - "I came to this interview because my University asked me to come."

- Do not blame anyone at the time of the interview.
- For any certification course you have done, you need to show the project with the certificate to the interviewer.
- Do not make excuses: You need a job so you appear for the interview.

HOMEWORK BEFORE THE INTERVIEW

Read the company web-site

- Find some connections that you like
- Prepare some questions on the company's technologies or customers, in case they ask you "Do you have any questions?"

Brush up fundamental concepts

Read your CV, and brush up possible questions on all areas you have written on your CV

If you have charts, diagrams of your Project, bring a hard copy of that to the interview. Make use of it to illustrate your project.

Give your CV to a friend and ask him/her to interview you

- After preparation of CV before appearing for the interview.

- While going through the company's website, have a look at the vision statement, mission statement, clients' and partners' names, products, and technologies.
- Brush up fundaments concepts: It deals with the candidate's technical field. One should be thorough with their subject knowledge.
- One should carry a hard copy of their projects during interviews.

MORE TIPS

Show commitment and seriousness

- No one will recruit you if you seem you do not really care for the job.

Avoid making disclosures of ignorance, or excuses, e.g.

- I know only basics of C
- I studied this 2 years back ...
- "As I have heard, it's like" ...
- We did not have good lab facilities

Accept mistakes when you don't know

When you are wrong, listen to their explanation.

- It's ok to ask the interviewer what the right answer is.

Don't look away from the interviewer while answering questions

- Be serious and attentive during the interview.
- Be a good listener.
- Make eye contact with the interviewer during the interview.

INTERVIEW QUESTIONS

1. Tell me something about yourself / Introduce yourself.
2. Where do you see yourself 5 years down the line?
3. What are your greatest strengths? Support it with live evidence.
4. What are your hobbies?
5. What do you know about our company?
6. Why should we hire you?
7. Why do you want to join our company?
8. What do you look in a job?
9. How much do you expect if we offer you this position?
10. Give examples where you have taken initiative & shown leadership traits.
11. Describe a situation where you have worked under pressure & met deadlines.

- Tell me something about yourself/introduce yourself.
  - Qualification, objective, project title, and strengths.
- Where do you see yourself 5 years down the line?
  - Long-term commitment, realistic progression.
- What are your hobbies?
  - Dance, painting, debate, reading books.
- What do you look for in a job?
  - Relate your objective with the achievement of organisation goals. 'I look for an environment where I can use my knowledge and skills to achieve organisations objectives.'
- How much remuneration do you expect if we offer you this position?
  - Fair salary as per job responsibilities. Career goals match with organisation goals.

FREQUENTLY ASKED QUESTION'S (FAQ's)

1. Tell me something about yourself/introduce yourself.
2. Where do you see yourself 5 years down the line?
3. What are your greatest strengths? Support it with live examples.
4. What are your hobbies?
5. What do you know about our company?
6. Why should we hire you?
7. Why do you want to join our company?
8. What do you look for a job?
9. How much remuneration do you expect if we offer you this position?
10. Give examples where you have taken initiative and shown leadership traits.
11. Describe a situation where you have worked under pressure and met deadlines.

Sample Interview Questions

1. Tell me something about yourself.
   - I am ________ currently working as ________. My objective in life is to exploit my technical and managerial skills in a good working environment where there is enough scope for growth.
   - I am an engineering graduate and have done MBA (HR). I have worked on projects like 'Title 1' and 'Title 2'.

   How you would describe yourself? (Greatest strength)
   - I believe my greatest strength lies in my honesty, integrity, and positive attitude towards life.
   - I am a wonderful team player, a great communicator, and a skilled builder of relationships and networks.

   I am energetic, enthusiastic, and able to shoulder responsibilities.

Weaknesses

   - No one is perfect, I too have my weaknesses.
   - I am impatient in achieving results.
   - I am a workaholic (a person who works excessively hard).
2. Where do you see yourself 5 years down the line?
   - I believe in making a long-term commitment. In terms of my future carrier, I expect a realistic progression.
   - In quantifiable terms, I wish to become an HR Director.
3. What are your hobbies?
   - I spend my time surfing the internet.
   - My hobbies relate to playing and watching lawn tennis.
4. Why should we hire you?
   - I believe I have technical and managerial skills. I am a wonderful team player, a great communicator, and a skilled builder of relationships and networks—a perfect fit for the organisation as my career goals match with the organisational goals.
5. You may be over qualified. After engineering, you could have gone in for a job. Why did you opt to peruse an MBA?
   - I am not just looking for a job.
   - I am looking for a place where I can use my skills to contribute to the benefit of the organisation.

- The industry prefers an engineer with an MBA degree to an ordinary graduate. (Technically strong)

6. What is the importance of Human Resources (HR) in today's scenario?
   - HR is contributing a lot towards the growth of the organisation.
   - HR is contributing to improving quality of life.
   - Before HR was record-keeping, satisfying trade union wants.
   - Today, HR has transformed itself from HR to Human Resource Department (HRD).
   - More emphasis is given to identifying the competencies of the individual.
   - There is a transformation from reactive HR to proactive HR.
   - Emphasis on building employee brand. (Employee first)
7. Why do you want to join our company? (Why you are looking for a change?)
   - It is a challenging job and brings the best out of people, and I am a skilled builder of relationships and networks.
   - The scope of growth is high.
8. What is competency mapping? Explain the competency model.
   - Competency is the underlying characteristic of an individual that is related to effective and superior job performance (KSA).
     K – Core
     S – Conviction
     A – Capabilities
   - Competency mapping refers to the mapping of KSA with organisational objects.

MODEL

- BLOOMS MODEL
  - Knowledge
  - Application
  - Analysis
  - Synthesis
  - Evaluation
  - Knowledge: Knowledge of facts and figures.
  - Skills: Behaviour skills, listening skills.
  - Abilities: Capability of an individual.
- **Job Analysis:** (a.r.t)
  - It is defined as the basic technical procedure that defines the accountabilities and responsibilities, it takes to do a particular job.
  - It is of three types: Job Description, Job Specification, and Job Evaluation.
- **Job Description**
  - It is defined as the factual description of the job content, working conditions, and working environment.
  - Job title, employee code, reporting manager, joining number, duties to be performed
- **Job Specification**
  - It is the minimum acceptable human qualities and qualifications that the individual should possess to perform a job successfully.
  - It includes KSA, soft skills, experience level, and education.
- **Job Evaluation:** It defines the relative value of the job in the organisation.
- **Job Enrichment:** It is an attempt to motivate the employees by giving them opportunities to use their KSA to do a particular job.
- **Job Enlargement**
  - Increases the number of tasks to be performed.
  - Job enrichment is the vertical loading of the job and job enlargement is the horizontal loading of the job.
- RECRUITMENT
  - It is a process for searching potential candidates in large numbers and ensuring quality so that the organisation selects the best candidate according to the job needs.

YIELD RATIO

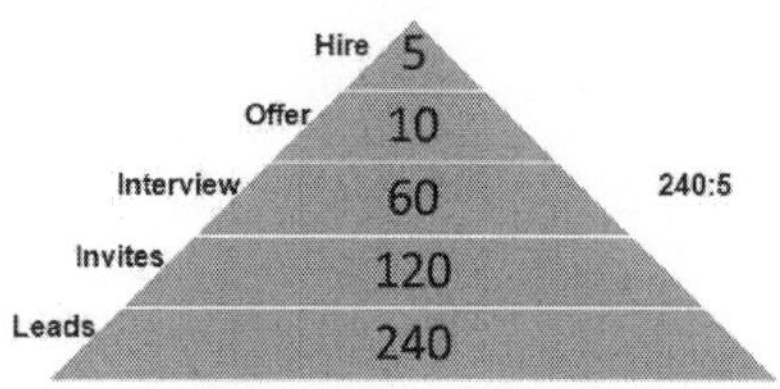

Internal Sources (JPE UPM RLI)

1. **Job Posting:** If there is a vacant post in the organisation, then it is posted on the notice board of the company.
2. **Personal Records:** It contains the work done by the employee, details of the particular employee.
3. **Employee Referral:** It is a recommendation by the current employee regarding a job applicant.
4. **Union Hall:** It is a gathering of peers and supervisors where there is a discussion about the vacant position.
5. **Promotion and Transfer**
    - Promotion refers to progress in one's position and responsibilities.
    - It may take place inside the organisation (promotion in) or outside the organisation (promotion out).
    - Transfer refers to the individual going to another place at the same position.
6. Mobilising management staff
7. Rehiring retired employees
8. **Laying Off Employees:** It involves rehiring employees that were once a part of the organisation.
9. **Inside Moonlighting:** It involves employees doing a particular work and other work.

Advantages of Internal Sources

- Cost effective
- Builds morale
- Individuals already know the organisation

External Sources of Recruitment (ACC, EEE, MUP)

1. **Advertisement**
    - If there is a vacant position in the organisation then it is advertised in newspapers, magazines, and through broadcast messages.
    - There is a blind box advertisement where the name of the organisation is not disclosed.
2. **Computer Data Banks:** It is a database containing information about the employees.
3. **College Recruitment:** Most educational institutions offer college recruitment where representatives of organisations come and review the credentials and interview the candidates.
4. **Employment Agencies**
    - Employment agencies can be public, private, and head hunters.

- Individuals have to get registered in these agencies.
- Public agencies do not charge any money from candidates.
- Private agencies charge some amount, but now it is given by organisations if candidates are selected.
- Head hunters specialise in middle and top-level positions.

5. **Employee Leasing**
   - Employees working in one firm are sent to work in another firm for a specific time duration.
   - When an organisation requires employees with a specific skill set, it brings employees from leasing firms.
6. **E-recruitment**
   - It refers to web portals like Naukri.com.
   - It includes job postings.
   - The detailed job description is provided along with education, and experience level.
   - Aggressive candidates post their web pages called 'websumes' to sell their job candidacy.
7. **Military Organisation:** Professional well-trained employees.
8. **Voluntary Organisation**
9. **Professional Trade Association**

Selection

1. **Intial Screening:** In this, job applicants are sorted on the basis of the job description and job specifications.
2. **Application Blank:** It is the employment form that is used to get specific information from the candidates that the organisation wants.
3. **Priminary Interview:** It is the first round of interviews taken by the HRD.
4. **Employee Test:** It refers to job-related tests.
5. **Second Round of Interview:** It is a selection device used to gain in-depth information about the candidate. (Behavioural, realistic job preview)
6. **Reference Check:** It is used to determine the fitness level of candidates for essential job performance.
7. **Final Selection:** Here, a job offer is given.
9. **Medical Examination:** It is used to determine the fitness level of candidates for essential job performance.

SELECTION PREDICATORS (RELIABILITY AND VALIDITY)

- **Training:** It is defined as the art of increasing the knowledge, skills, and abilities of the employees to do a particular job.
- **Training Need Analysis**

- It is a model to know why actual performance expected performance.
- It helps in identifying present the KSA of employees.

- **Training Methods**
- **Off the Job Training**

1. Lectures, Discussions, Conferences
   - It is the oldest form of training which may be oral or written.
   - Discussion is a way of communication.
   - In the conference method, the number of trainees can be increased and it is the sales company's cost.
2. Computer-based Training (CBT)
   - It reduces training costs.
   - It reduces learning time.
   - It has manuals to learn from.
   - Eg: Interactive media.
3. Games and Simulation
   - Here, trainees are assigned a situation and asked to react to it.

- **On the Job Training**

1. Coaching
   - It is one-to-one teaching and guidance provided by seniors.
2. **Under Study**
   - The chosen trainee is asked to perform a task as per the instructions given.
3. **Job Instruction**
   - A trainee is asked to perform a task as per the instructions given.
4. **Job Rotation**
   - It is a method to increase the job responsibilities of EMP through horizontal and vertical leading so that they improve their KSA.
5. **Special Meeting with the Staff**
   - It is used to understand problems faced by the staff members.
6. **Internship**
   - Educational institutes have agreements with organisations to help students gain practical knowledge.
7. **Stipend**
   - It is given to trainees who have come to learn or get training in an organisation.

- **Training Evaluation**

  KIRK–PATRIX EVALUATION MODEL

  Level 1: Reaction

  - Here, learning takes place and there is no transfer of learning.

  Level 2: Learning

  - Knowledge is gained
  - Assessment test: questionnaire, criterion reference test.

Level 3: Behaviour

– What is learnt in training is applied at the job.

Level 4: Result

– Productivity increases.

– Profit increases.

- **Performance Management System (PMS) and Performance Appraisal (PA)**
    - PMS is a process of managing people to maximise the success rate.
    - PA is a 'historic approach' which tells what the individual has done.

  There are three pillars of PMS. These are as follows:
    - **Strength Finder:** Build a system where employees work according to their strengths.
    - **Planned Work Allocation:** Inspire employees to invest a minimum of 80 per cent effort to get 100 per cent compensation/result.
    - **Position Person to Future:** There should be quarterly feedback on what employees are doing and how they can do better.

Appraisal

↓ Annual/bi-annual informal

↓ Takes place before time

Outcome

1. **Management by Objective (MBO Approach)**
    - It is an organisation-wide intervention technique where there is a joint goal-setting between the employee and the manager.
    - It is two-way communication.
    - There are participants in the decision-making process.
    - There are no role conflicts.
    - Employees are clear about what is expected from them.
2. **360° Feedback**
    - It is also known as 'multi ratter feedback' where feedback comes from subordinates, peers, and managers as per the hierarchy of the organisation.
    - The employees become aware of their present competencies.
    - They also know what others think about them.
    - The disadvantage is that there can be dishonest feedback.

Management of Industrial Relations (Labour Laws)

1. Factories Act, 1948
    - It is used to amend labour laws and rules in factories.
    - Broad areas of coverage are wages, working hours, health, and safety.
    - Factory means where 20 of more workers are working or where working in the preceding 12 months without the aid of power.

- Canteens: This facility is available if a factory employs more than 250 workers.
- Creaches: The facility is available if 30 women workers are employed and there are children of younger than 6 years.
- Welfare Officers: These officers are needed if a factory employs more than 500 workers.
- Working Hours: For a dult workers = 9 hours per day, 54 hours for a week. Interval after 5 hours of work.
- Wage: If a worker works more than 9 hours per day, he is entitled to overtime less than or equal to two times of the ordinary wage.
- Penalty: 2 years imprisonment and 1 lakh fine.

2. Employees State Insurance Act, 1948
    - Established by the government to provide medical facilities, sickness facilities, maternity benefits, disablement benefits, and dependent benefits.
    - Employee State Insurance = 4.75 per cent of (gross income)
    - Employee = 1.75 per cent of wage.
3. Employees Provident Fund Act, 1952
    - It provides provident fund, pension fund, unit linked insurance to the employees employment in factories and other establishments.
    - PF = 12 per cent (basic)
    - Pension Scheme = Minimum Basic Wage Rs. 6,500 (Super annulation, retiring scheme)
    - Insurance = 1 per cent (Basic + D/A + Retaining Allowance)
4. Payment of Gratuity Act, 1972
    - It is applicable to workers employed in factories and other establishments employing more than 10 persons in the preceding 12 months.
    - Employees who have completed 5 years of service are eligible to get gratuity (Maximum of Rs. 10,00,000)
    - Gratuity = Last Wage * 15 * Service Period / 26
    - Penalty: 6 months imprisonment and Rs. 10,000 fine

What is Meant by a Strike and How to Prevent It?

- STRIKE: Work coming to a halt by the actions of persons employed in the industry.
- CAUSES
    - Company policy, salary and increment, dispute.
    - Dismissal of employees, wages, working hours.
    - One should create an employee-friendly atmosphere, employees should participate in the decision-making process, build trust.

- STEPS TO AVOID:
  - **Strike Breaking:** Some companies negotiate with the trade unions and others try to eliminate them.
  - **Union Busting:** Elimination of unions with the help of labour relation consultants.
  - **Lock Outs:** Employees causing strikes are not allowed to work by their employers. They hire other candidates to work in their place.
  - **Collective Bargaining:** There is a negotiation between employer and employee, employer and employer, employee and employer. It is a bipartite process where there is no intervention of any third party in the negotiation relating to working conditions and terms of employment.

How will you look into the competencies of the candidate at the time of recruitment?

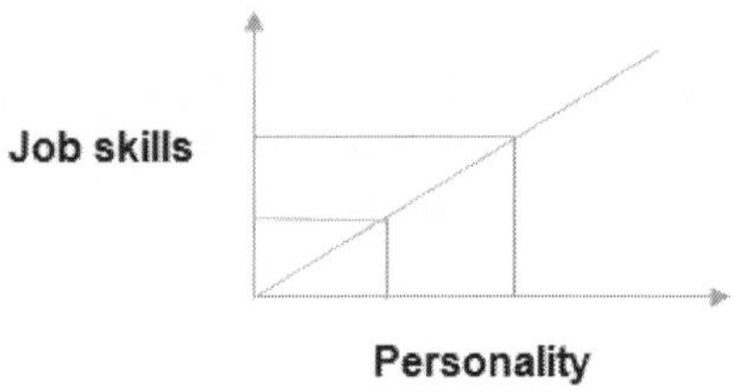

- Identify the job skills.
- Identify the personality traits.
- Match the job skills and personality traits.
- Test those personality traits through life experience and just experience.

How to motivate the employee and retain an employee when he is leaving?

MOTIVATION: Give importance to motivating factors like:

- Feeling of achievement
- Recognition
- Increased responsibilities
- MBO: Set joint goal settings between the employees and employer
- Link performance with rewards, thereby increasing expectations
- Emphasis on team work
- Provide training to improve the KSA of employees needed for career growth
- Pleasant working environment.

RETENTION:

- Involve employees in the decision-making process.
- Job Enrichment: It is vertical loading of job, enables employees to work on their present KSA utilise it in their particular job.

- Quality Circle: Influence the management by saying that workers can provide ideas and that they should be consulted in decision-making.
- Quality Work Life: It is used to increase the involvement of employees and employers, leading to better relations, thereby improving productivity.
- Gain Sharing: Increased employee involvement.
- Link performance with rewards.
- Have relevant O/A, reward structure, compensation levels.

Competency Mapping of Marketing Agents:

1. Master Thinker: One who thinks strategically and out of the box.
2. Energetic leaders who initiate, influence, inspire to achieve results (Leadership competencies)
3. A great communicator, skilled builder of relationships and networks understands communication dynamics, builds networks at the workplace.
4. A wonderful team player who knows about team dynamics.
5. Example of acting, deciding, delivering, staying fast, lesser processes, less paperwork, fast delivery of goods and services.
6. Lifelong learner of high technical expertise.

Leadership Competencies

- It is noteworthy what Warren Buffet looks for before he invests in the organisation.
- He looks into two factors.
- He wants to invest in businesses he understands.
- He looks into the leadership teams, if he believes in the leadership, he believes in the organisation.
- Organisation explicitly if implicitly design L.D.P.
- Two questions that stifle any HR professionals are:
- Despite having leadership competencies, the survivors pass all the tests but fail to deliver to the future challenges.
- Despite having a pool of leaders, organisations fail to develop a leadership pipeline.
- To answer these two questions, Ulrich in 'leadership brand' said that the leadership field is more enamoured with competencies and traits of leaders, as a results, the main function of leaders is to deliver result. It is almost forgotten.
- LEADER: Personal identity/brand
- LEADERSHIP: Personal identity + organisational identity
- ANALOGIES: Mother versus motherhood

  A mother is a powerful figure in the family, but motherhood deals with building next-generation children.

- LEADERS ARE BORN/MADE
  A recent study has put it 50–50. It means half the leadership trait is from heritage and the other half is from experience.
- **Analogy:** Why do some people in the organisation have to be spoon-fed information about how to serve customers, while others do not need any spoon-feeding.

Leadership Competencies (MICEE)

- **Model the Way:** Find your voice.
- **Inspire a Shared Vision**: Vision is shared among all employees.
- **Challenge the Process**: Capitalise on opportunities, take risks.
- **Enable Others to Act**: Foster collaboration.
- **Enable the Heart**: Celebrate victories, rewards, recognition.

What do you know about the organisation? (vision, mission, products)

According to your definition of success, how successful have you been so far?

- Success is achieving the desired outcome. I have been successful in most of the tasks assigned to me.

What do you look for in a job?

- I look for an environment where I can use my technical and managerial skills for the benefit of the organisation. Teamwork is key.

What kind of people do you find difficult to work with?

- People who are not team players and do not perform.

How long would it take you to make a meaningful contribution to our firm?

- Not long because of my transferrable skills and abilities.

What are you doing/done to achieve your career objectives?

MBA:

- SUMMER TRAINING: Competency skill mapping of marketing agents covering 13 organisations.
- F.R.P.: Competency-based training design leadership.
- Technical: C, C++, Java, satellite communication through VSTA, wireless communication of computers.

What kind of hours would you like to work?

I could work for as many hours as it takes to get my job done.

Give examples where you have taken initiatives and shown leadership traits.

- I have been an effective leader/born leader.
- During my college days, I had organised conferences, invited speakers, and coordinated entire functions.
- Arranged football matches and cricket matches and led them in my office days.
- Effective monitor for 5 years in school.

Describe a situation where you have worked under pressure and met deadlines.

- Have arranged seminars when semester examinations were going on.
- Arranged cricket matches in short spans of time.
- Mustered roll attendance of 1 year in a month.

How will you handle rejection?

- Rejection is part of the business.
- It is an opportunity and I learn from it.
- Failures are pillars of success.

How much remuneration do you expect if we offer you this position?

- I expect a fair salary as per the job responsibilities.
- I feel I am a perfect fit for the organisation as my career goals match the organisational goals.
- Salary does not determine my worth in the new job as job responsibilities might differ.

How dedicated and aggressive are you in relationship building?

- I feel I am dedicated and proactive in relationship building.
- For example, I organised seminars and invited speakers and HR professionals to attend.
- Relationship building takes time and I am a skilled builder of relationships and networks.

How will you contribute to our organisation if you are hired? / Which of the companies do you like working for?

- The main priority of an HR professional is to build a cohesive unit where there is the maximisation of human potential.
- Be the foundation that integrates the vision, mission, and values of the organisation to create an environment where there is maximisation of human potential.
- I would monitor every individual and device strategies to increase the potential of individuals by providing T&D programmes on various technical and soft skills.
- I am here to establish an HR system since HR is a strategic function in the competitive battle for acquiring talent.
- Finding the right people for the right job and doing things that would benefit the organisation.

NAME: ______________________ B. Tech. Mechanical Engineering	ADDRESS: C/o:
Email:	Contact No : + 91

PERSONAL SUMMARY

- A team player and a communicator who can establish rapport with members of diverse groups and promote team cohesiveness.
- With good presentation skills, an honest speaker as well a patient listener who believes in creating a positive and healthy atmosphere at the workplace.
- Believes that knowing every answer is not important, but having a never-quit attitude to find out the answer to every problem is important.
- Seeking opportunities to earn a challenging job where I can use my capabilities to achieve the organisationals goals and, in the process, gain some knowledge and a sense of fulfillment.

EDUCATIONAL QUALIFICATIONS

Name of the Course	*Name of the Institution*	*Board/ University*	*Year of Passing*	*Percentage/ CGPA*
B. Tech. (Mechanical Engineering)			2015	7.5
XII	Ispat English Medium School, Rourkela	ICSE Board	2010	72
X	Ispat English Medium School, Rourkela	ICSE	2008	93

TECHNICAL KNOWLEDGE

Operating Systems : WINDOWS-8, 7, XP, 98
Microsoft Packages : MS-EXCEL, MS-Word, MS-PowerPoint
Languages : C

AREAS OF INTERESTS

- Computer Programming
- Refrigeration Systems
- Hydraulic Machines
- Non-conventional Energy Resources

EXTRA CURRICULAR ACTIVITIES

- Conducting learning programmes for the unprivileged students
- Programming
- Organising various programmes, events, and tournaments
- Entrepreneurship projects

- Acquired training in Odishi classical music for 2 years
- Trained swimmer (specialisation in freestyle)
- Trained dancer (locking poping)
- Reading

PROJECTS

Project Title: 'Motivational Factors Influencing a Student's Performance'

- **Functionality of the Project:** This project aimed at redefining the education system with motivation as an integral part of it and raising the efficiency of the students academically to their personal best. The basic objectives were to create awareness about the importance of motivation and identify and evaluate the effects of the motivational factors.
- **What was Achieved**
  - Creation of a blueprint for a new education system.
  - Growth in students' outlooks and intellects.
  - Factors like 'glamorising and popularising of topics' were identified.

  Role in the Project: Group Leader

  Project Team Size: 5

  Duration of the Project: 6 Months

  Responsibilities: Team Management, Data Analysis, Survey, Interviews, Seminars.

Project Title: 'Mechanical Analysis of CNT/PMMA'

- **Functionality of the Project:** This project involved the fabrication of composites containing Polymethyl Methacrylate (PMMA) in the matrix phase and multi-walled Carbon nanotubes in the reinforcement phase. Different compositions of PMMA and CNT were taken into consideration while fabrication. Tensile and hardness tests were performed on the material.

  Role in the Project: Group Leader

  Project Team Size: 6

  Duration of the Project: 6 Months

  Responsibilities: Data Analysis, Material Fabrication, Team Management

INDUSTRIAL TRAINING

15 days of Industrial Training at Rourkela Steel Plant

- Unit of the Plant Studied: Steel Melting Shop
- Processes sSudied: Melting of steel in a furnace, pouring of hot metal into ingot moulds, and solidification of ingots.

ACHIEVEMENTS

- Initiated an evening school for the kids of construction workers.

- 2nd Prize in Debate Competition.
- 1st Prize in Pictorial Representation Competition.
- 3rd Prize in Anchoring Competition.

PERSONAL INFORMATION

Date of Birth: 14 April 1992
Gender: Male
Nationality: Indian
Driving License: ________________________
AADHAR Card No: ________________________

DATE:
SIGNATURE:
PLACE:

NAME:	**ADDRESS:**
Email:	Contact No : +91

PERSONAL SUMMARY

- A team player with excellent communication skills and academic qualifications, who will graduate with a degree in Electronics and Communications Engineering.
- Focused on an in-depth understanding of designing, developing, and maintaining electrical systems and components according to the required specifications.
- Currently seeking a suitable **electronics design engineer** (*needs to be changed with each job)* position with a reputable company

EDUCATIONAL QUALIFICATION

Name of the Course	*Name of the Institution*	*Board/ University*	*Year of Passing*	*Percentage/ CGPA*
B.Tech. (Electronics and Communication Engineering)	Centurion Institute of Technology, Jatni	Centurion University of Technology & Management	2015	7.5
XII	Bhairaba Mahabidyalaya, Borigumma	CHSE (Odisha)	2009	66

X	Government High School, Borigumma, Koraput	BSE (Odisha)	2007	83

TECHNICAL KNOWLEDGE

Operating Systems: MS-DOS, WINDOWS-7, XP
Databases: MS EXCEL, MY SQL
Languages: C, C++, Data Structure, Java, Java Script.

AREAS OF INTERESTS

- Antenna systems and satellite communication
- Mobile computing and mobile communication

INDUSTRIAL TRAINING

- Four weeks of industrial training from Bharat Sanchar Nigam Limited, Vizag
  - Please include things done, learnt and works completed.

EXTRA-CURRICULAR ACTIVITIES

- Participated in college cultural programme and received prizes in various running races.
- Participated in national-level paper presentations and quiz competitions.
- Winner of the Football Tournament in 2012, during the annual function.
- Participated in skits.

PROJECT

Project Title: Novel Antenna System Design for Satellite Communication and Multimedia Services

Functionality of the Project: This system consists of the design and simulation of the hybrid antenna using MATLAB software. The main aim of this project is to reduce the noise level from signal transmission in satellite communication and multimedia services and increase the Gain, Beam Scanning Capacity of the Antenna System.

Role in the Project: Group Leader
Project Team Size: 3
Tools and Technique Used in the Project: MATLAB, HFSS
Duration of the Project: 6 Months

ACHIEVEMENTS

- Selected for LBW merit scholarship provided by Vikash Charitable Trust, New Delhi.
- Participated in national-level paper presentations.
- Achieved the NCC A-certificate as an SGT rank holder at the school level.
- I was selected as a president in RED RIBBON CLUB in junior college (+2).

PERSONAL INFORMATION

Date of Birth : 7 July 1992
Gender : Male
Nationality : Indian
Driving License :
Passport No :
PAN Number :

REFERENCES

Available on request.

DATE:
SIGNATURE:
PLACE:

Group Discussion Topics

1. Hard work or Smart work – Which is important?
2. Degree or skill – what is more important?
3. WhatsApp is killing minds!
4. Android versus iOS
5. Clean India – Attitude is more important than the movement.
6. China market – a threat to the Indian market.
7. Tablets should replace textbooks in the Indian education system.
8. Virat Kohli is world's best ODI batsman
9. Social Media is killing the book reading habit!
10. Yoga is a science of inner well-being, not a religion
11. Women are better managers
12. Should Internet freedom be curtailed?
13. Do we really need smart cities?
14. English should continue to be the official language of India.
15. M-governance: Will it be the panacea for all the problems of India in the next decade?
16. Beauty or Brain – who can rule the world?
17. PM's vision to make India a Manufacturing hub – a dream or a practical possibility?
18. Life imprisonment is a good alternative to capital punishment
19. Net Neutrality – Advantages and Disadvantages
20. Digital India's and initiatives & their advantages
21. T20 is killing the real cricket!
22. Should India get back its *Kohinoor* from the British?
23. The weak can never forgive, forgiveness is the attribute of the strong!
24. Should male sports persons earn more money than their female counterparts?
25. Managers are born, not trained
26. Which is more informative: electronics media or print media?
27. Which of them do you support – Love marriage or arranged marriage?
28. Returning Sahitya Akadami Awards, is it a right kind of protest by writers?
29. Social media is killing book reading habit!
30. Rising petrol prices – Can the government control it?
31. Sould the Nirbhaya juvenile be realised?
32. Tablets should replace text books in Indian education
33. National wealth decides individual happiness!

34. Net neutrality – advantages and disadvantages.
35. Examinations – have they killed education?
36. Impact of COVID-19 (Coronavirus) on the global economy
37. How COVID-19 deepens the digital education divide in India
38. Work from home: pros and cons.

GROUP DISCUSSION TOPICS

1. HARD WORK OR SMART WORK - WHICH IS IMPORTANT?

Introduction

Work is important to do as it takes us to the next level of success. The most important question you should ask at this point is what kind of work will take you to that level: is it hard work or smart work.

For (smart work)

- Smart work is really the need of the hour.
- Smart work saves a lot of time and allows you to be more organised.
- Through smart work, your goals can be reached faster.
- Doing smart work allows you to save time for other things which you might not get by doing hard work, like, exercise, spending time with family, etc.
- Smart work brings you lots of recognition from the society and allows you to grow more in the industry you are in.

Against

- Hard work takes a lot of time just to make things correct.
- It is a time consuming and exhausting experience, as after doing a lot of work, you are left with less energy to do anything else.
- Hard work does not allow you to fully use your brain and it pushes you for more physical work.
- In terms of determination and persistence, hard work is really important but not lot can be achieved.
- Working hard is not enough as it might not bring the best results.

Conclusion

I would like to conclude that smart work is really important as it saves time and allows you to reach your goals faster than hard work does.

2. WHATSAPP IS KILLING MINDS!

A Saudi man divorced his wife after she ignored his WhatsApp messages. The husband said that his wife used to spend all her time on WhatsApp. Due to the addiction, she even ignored her children. WhatsApp is not a new thing in the market. Even people who are not educated are well aware of the messaging platform. The messaging app that started as a boon can turn into a bane, if not used carefully. It is killing the minds of people. Do you agree?

Yes

- Youngsters are getting addicted to the messaging platform like other addictive substances. It is more of an addiction rather than convenience.
- People are not using the messaging platform for connecting with friends or relatives instead, they just want to check out the their presence on the messaging platform.
- A messaging platform connects people, but WhatsApp is creating bridges between people. The app, in many cases, is creating unnecessary doubts in relationships.
- The day begins and ends with WhatsApp. And, if people don't find any messages, they start feeling low.
- People are so occupied with the use of whatsapp that they are unable to differentiate between real and factual relationships. We can easily notice that while you are talking all the time to your friends on WhatsApp, you hardly have an interaction with your immediate family. This also points out the fact that while people have a lot of friends on WhatsApp. There is hardly any friend available to whom they can talk their heart out face-to-face.

No

- WhatsApp has become the largest messaging app, and it is just because it has allowed people to come closer to each other.
- There are some people who are not involved in any work, and only such people are addicted to WhatsApp, not everyone.
- WhatsApp has allowed the school friends and distant relatives to come and talk at one place. It does not kill minds but helps people to cherish the old, good memories and relationships.
- In a world where people do not have the time to meet friends, Whatsapp has allowed people to share their problems with friends on the messaging platform regardless of time and location.
- WhatsApp is now even used by many firms and organisations for sharing of important information among employees.

- If used properly, WhatsApp can help generate new business opportunities and close the existing deals faster.

Conclusion

Every thing in this world has two sides, one positive and one negative. The use of WhatsApp is no different. It is not a black or white app, but a grey app whose pros and cons are decided by the user himself. People are more isolated than before in the present world. Some make their world better by using the app, and some make themselves more isolated after using this app. In all the cases, balance is the key.

3. ANDROID VERSUS iOS

Are you looking to buy a smartphone? You will then have a tough time to decide whether to buy an iOS- or Android-powered Smartphone. Both the companies are launching new upgrades of their operating system. Apple has already launched the latest version iOS with improved features in September. Google is gearing up to launch its latest upgrade, Android L, soon. So, in the fierce battle of Android and iOS, what you prefer? Which one is better: Android or iOS?

Android

- Android is the most vastly used Smartphone platform in the world. It is used by several phone manufacturers whereas iOS runs only on Apple devices.
- Android always offers better battery life versus iOS, especially when users play with its apps for longer periods of time.
- Google is very much connected to the web, and therefore it becomes easy for users to choose browser tabs, document files, and other content. The synchronisation feature of Android beats iOS.
- Android provides a single icon to clear all active items on all devices whereas it is not the same case with iOS notifications.

iOS

- When it comes to security, iOS offers much enhanced security features as compared to Android. Google's operating system is believed to be more vulnerable to mobile malware infiltration.
- The latest upgrade of iOS has got the feature of interactive notifications that allows users to see the new updates without any external app. Android tried to implement the same feature but failed to match the level of iOS.
- The buttons on the new version of iOS appear to be expanded all the time. However, it has got quick-reply capability. iOS native functionality beats Android here.

- The design has remained the power point of iOS, and the new version has got a clean look with the glass effect staying prevalent.

Conclusion

It is clear that both Android and iOS are trying hard to fetch a larger pie of the market share by improving their older versions. The battle continues and can get fierce in the near future. Both the operating platforms have got their own sets of own set of pros and cons. However, the utility largely depends on the user and his personal perception. Still, Android occupies first slot in the United States with a 51.5 per cent market share, whereas iOS trails Android with a 42.4 per cent market share.

4. SPICEJET: ANOTHER KINGFISHER IN THE MAKING?

The aviation industry, SpiceJet employees, common public, and government bodies have started comparing SpiceJet with Kingfisher. Many of the participants believe that the financial situation of SpiceJet is indeed very alarming. The aviation industry has always remained a tough and challenging industry. It has to deal with internal as well as external variables. So, let us share our views on the topic – SpiceJet: Another Kingfisher in the making?

Yes

- Although SpiceJet is a low-cost carrier, it is showing the same problems as faced by Kingfisher in its early problem days. The employees have not received allowances and even the foreign travel allowances are on decline.
- SpiceJet hasn't deposited TDS and it is the first signal of a serious financial problem in any company. It was the same case with Kingfisher.
- SpiceJet posted a huge loss of USD 170 million in fiscal 2013, and if it continues it will not be able to survive in the competitive industry.
- When the crisis of Kingfisher started, the airline first compromised on its equipment list, and it is the same case with SpiceJet, where the spare parts are minimised, compromising safety.
- SpiceJet still has a pending order of 42 Boeing 737s worth USD 4.3 billion, and any financial mess will force it to cut pending orders.

No

- The financial woes of SpiceJet have not worsened so much that salaries have become an issue. The airline is meeting its payroll obligations on time.
- Most of the problems for SpiceJet are due to the weakening rupee, that declined against the dollar late last year. However, under the new government, things are expected to change soon.

- The most important factor for any airline company is crude oil, and SpiceJet is set to benefit from plummeting crude oil prices.
- The airline company is ready to pay interest or penalties that it will incur on personal tax filings of employees, once the matter with the tax department is resolved.
- SpiceJet is smartly launching new deep discount plans for the customers to generate cash for fulfilling its working capital requirements.

Conclusion

All the companies face some financial problem or the other at some point in time. However, it depends on the management how it deals with the financial woes. Does the management take steps to solve the problem or mismanages worsening the problems? There is no denial that SpiceJet is showing similar signs as those of Kingfisher, but it has other positive factors it can use for improving its financial condition.

5. DEGREE OR SKILL – WHAT IS MORE IMPORTANT?

Degree and skill are two sides of the same coin. To succeed in the race of life, a person needs to have a degree along with skills. A degree without skills would be as empty as skills without degree. Both need to go hand-in-hand in order to ensure the survival of the fittest. A degree is nothing but the certified documentation of a skill within the individual. Every person having the skill may not manage to attain a degree. Similarly, every degree holder is not necessarily skilled. The requirement of a degree or skill depends upon the organisation, the nature of the post, etc. On a general outlook, which criterion carries more weightage – a degree or a skill?

Degree

- A degree is an authentic certificate states that the person applying for a post has the knowledge of the work requirement and has the ability to manage the functioning and justify the post.
- A degree makes a person more confident in his approach and outlook. These things are an essential part of personality development.
- A degree can make a person more polite, humble, and wise. This could be in order to take charge of the job or to climb the success ladder. But these things are difficult to manage without a degree in hand.
- A degree earns respect and social reputation. A person is assessed through his qualifications, which are reflected by his degree.
- A degree earns money and status for its master. The more specialised the degree, the higher the post, status, and salary package.

Skill

- Every degree holder is not necessarily skilled. It is the skill that helps to achieve the target and not the degree.
- A skill is an abstract term which cannot be evaluated on bits of paper. It is a broad spectrum which is groomed within the individual and nurtured through the repeated practical implications in life.
- It is not the degree but the skill that helps one achieve success. A degree can just earn the job, but it cannot help one to grow further without the skill.
- It is skill which attracts employers, clients, and management which lifts or drops the person. Without the skill, the person would not be able to catch hold of the interest of their superiors and attain success.
- The great people from the history were all skilled people, but they did not have the certifications for their knowledge.

Conclusion

A degree is the theoretical evaluation of an abstract concept which is virtually not possible. It is the skill that helps the person to grow up both materially/financially and immaterially with respect to the status, importance, social respect, and recognition, etc. Degree definitely has its own importance, as a person needs to have some skill in order to achieve a degree. A completely dumb individual cannot qualify to attain a degree. Hence, we can summarise by saying that a degree is the first step in the ladder of skills, which leads to success in life.

6. CLEAN INDIA – ATTITUDE CHANGE IS MORE IMPORTANT THAN MOVEMENT

Prime Minister Modi has laid a lot of emphasis on cleanliness. In this direction, he launched the *Swachh Bharat Abhiyan*. This movement envisages a clean India through the participation of every Indian. A lot of suspicion prevails over the success of this campaign, as many are arguing that until the attitude and mentality of people changes, no campaign can clean India. So, should the government have launched a mass awareness mission to change the mentality prior to the *Swachh Bharat Abhiyan*?

Yes

- There will be no expected participation unless people's attitude towards cleanliness and its importance changes.
- Indians generally care very less about hygiene. Most of them even spit where ever they want, as they are unaware of the health implications. Their habits will not change unless they are aware.

- Workers who indulge in cleaning jobs hardly get any respect in the society. Most of them are from Scheduled castes. Unless the mentality towards these workers and their job changes, we cannot expect mass participation.
- People keep their homes clean, but when it comes to their surroundings like streets, parks, etc., nobody cares because they perceive it as the duty of the government even though they themselves are responsible for throwing garbage and making their surroundings dirty.

No

- Launching this mission with active participation of the PM, the ministers, and the officials itself motivates citizens to participate.
- The mission highlights the importance of cleanliness very well, making them aware is an integral part for this mission.
- The issue of cleanliness was not given enough priority during the last many decades. This campaign will prioritise this issue.
- We cannot wait for changing mentalities and attitudes as the burden of diseases on the economy due to lack of cleanliness is increasing.
- Most importantly, taking action for making India clean through this campaign itself is the first necessary step towards realising this dream.

Conclusion

Making people aware is important, but more important is that this awareness is converted to actions. As the government itself has taken the initiative, this will definitely motivate people and make them realise that cleanliness is not just the government's responsibility. On its part, the government can introduce a separate awareness drive too, so that more and more people join this campaign. Ultimately, these efforts will not only force people to change their attitude of "nothing will change" but also ensure their participation.

7. GIRLS MUST HAVE ACCESS TO MAULANA AZAD LIBRARY OF AMU

The students union at the women's college, which is a part of Aligarh Muslim University (AMU) has often raised the issue of girls not being issued a membership of the Maulana Azad Library, which is a part of AMU. Recently, while addressing the demands of the students union, the vice-chancellor of AMU, Lieutenant General (retired) Zameeruddin Shah, said that allowing girls in the library would increase the number of boys visiting the library to four times than usual. He also said that this would lead to disciplinary issues. Should girls be denied access to the library just because boys would crowd it to see them?

Yes, girls must be provided access to the library

1. The students of the women's college are also a part of AMU and according to reports, the Maulana Azad Library is better stocked with books than the library at the women's college. It is the right of the girls there to have access to the best of knowledge and information that is provided by the university.
2. The idea of banning girls from the library is not only denying them equal right to education but also treating them like distracting objects. This is the same kind of thought that states that women invite rapes when they wear provocative clothes.
3. Right from the inauguration of the library, women were not allowed membership. We do not expect educational institutes to be making such discriminations on grounds of gender. For whatever reason the library initially did not allow women, it is time when these rules be amended and the university must make provisions for allowing students of the women's college proper access to the library.
4. The VC later modified his comment stating that it is not discrimination, but the lack of space, which is the real problem. This statement cannot be taken to be true as the library has 12 seats reserved for women students of AMU. 1,300 for boys and just 12 for girls is an odd ratio to consider equal and leaves behind no space for false excuses being made in the name of space.
5. With 1,300 boys in there, the university is able to handle all disciplinary issues and things seem to be running smooth when we all know violence and indiscipline is more of a boy's thing. How can allowing girls inside the library create disciplinary issues? Is the university not safe enough for girls to share the space of the library with boys? These questions clearly have an answer and that shows the biased nature of the rules.

No, the issue is being wrongly interpreted:

1. With only 1,300 seats, it is quite obvious that there is shortage of space in the library and suddenly allowing girls also in the library, which is usually very crammed with boys, might lead to disciplinary issues like eve-teasing, etc. If there is no adequate space, it is wise to avoid more students from cramming the same place.
2. The rule is not at all about alienating girls and the media misinterpreted it on wrong grounds. The college supports women empowerment and thirty five per cent girls study in AMU, which is much more than any other college.
3. Only undergraduate girls are not issued membership of the library. Girls of postgraduate courses and research have access to the library, which makes it clear that it is not about gender discrimination.
4. With the introduction of online catalogues in the library, any student of the women's college can order any book from the Maulana Azad Library, and

on the next day, the book is delivered to the student. All the books of the Maulana Azad Library are available online and the students are provided those books whenever they ask for them.

Conclusion

It can be considered that the lack of space is a genuine issue at the library and that allowing girls at the same time might lead to overcrowding of the library, but instead of stopping girls from accessing the library, the university must find solutions to solve this issue. However, not allowing access of the library to girls for any reasons is something that is not acceptable in the society.

8. AVIATION INDUSTRY – CAN INDIA LEAD?

India's Aviation sector is one of the fastest growing sectors in the world. There are about 450 airports and 1100 registered aircrafts in India. This sector has a compound annual growth rate of about 18 per cent. The Indian aviation industry made a total revenue of USD 14.2 billion in 2011. These figures reflect the growing potential of Indian aviation sector. But we need to analyse if this sector has the ability to emerge as a future world leader in the aviation industry.

Yes

- With the increase in per capita income, more and more Indians are now able to travel through airlines.
- The government has allowed FDI in the aviation industry. So, collaboration with foreign players will enhance Indian airlines' global reach.
- Interest shown by foreign airlines in buying stakes in domestic airlines has shown the faith and confidence of foreign industries in the Indian airline sector.
- Also, Indian companies, through these collaborations, will get the much needed global exposure in the airlines sector.
- FDI in the aviation sector will bring in foreign capital as well as technology, which transform the domestic aviation industry and can turn India into the preferred destination for aircraft planes manufacturing.

No

- Most of the civil air carriers in India are under severe financial strain. For instance, Air India has a debt of approximately USD 6.4 billion.
- Indian airlines are operating with high fuel costs because of the PSU's monopoly in finalising the price of ATF (Air Turbine Fuel).
- Volatility in Rupee's price against USD is yet another problem, which impacts airline companies' long-term planning.

- Kingfisher's debacle has proved to be disastrous for airline companies. They are already facing complex taxation and bureaucratic controls. Now, this new episode has made it more difficult for these players to raise funds from markets.

Conclusion

The high-on-optimism Indian airline industry has crossed new milestones and is progressing to achieve new targets. Unfortunately, domestic rules are pulling back this sector from realising its potential to the fullest. With new opportunities being opened up for foreign players, these domestic hurdles need to be eradicate, only then can we expect India to emerge as the world leader in the aviation industry.

9. INDIAN CULTURE DOES NOT BREED LEADERS

For

- From a very small age, we are never given the rights to make our own decisions. It has always been our parents and our teachers who get a say in all our matters.
- We Indians have always backed away from taking responsibilities for ourselves and for others.
- We are always taught to let the superior person make decisions for us and never to question their ability and judgment.
- We lack confidence in our ability of achieving anything and everything, which is a very important quality in shaping a leader.
- We lack the desire and the drive to lead, which are very essential factors that define a leader.

Against

- It is a very wrong conception induced by people that leaders are born but the correct notion is that they are made, not born. Thus, we can say that India does not breed leaders, it helps people become leaders.
- Indian culture is a very rich culture, it is because of our culture that we are called 'Incredible India'. So, if we cannot breed leaders, no other nation can.
- We are well renowned for our intelligence and our influential nature, which are trademarks of a potent leader.
- Not every individual born can lead. But everyone can be effective. Thus, it is right to say that in India, everyone is not a born leader, but everyone is effective enough to become one.

10. THE CHINESE MARKET: A THREAT TO INDIAN MARKET

Against

- China has always been compared to India in terms of population and technological advancement. China undoubtedly has a humongous software market, but is definitely not a threat.
- India has its own unique power and intelligence.
- Indian IT companies have captured Japan is in Asia only.
- India is becoming one of the world's largest internet and mobile users' country.
- India's mobile market is growing by leaps and bounds.
- Most countries prefer employees from India rather than China because of their communication barrier. English is spoken by almost all IT industries in India.
- India has a large consumer and industrial market, all thirsting for products, with great brands and distribution networks.

For

- There is no doubt that India may take many years to have a market like China.
- China has a huge population. Moreover people, there are advancing with each passing day.
- China launches new mobiles, technologies, and automobiles almost everyday.
- China's automobile industry is much bigger than India's, it can therefore serve quality products at a lower cost.
- China has a string support from the government. Indian IT industries have negligible support.
- China launches many products like gadgets, etc., everyday. Because of this, they can sell them at a cheaper rate.

Conclusion

China's market cannot be a threat until India considers it one. India must work on each opportunity that comes its way. It should efficiently make use of all possible resources and infrastructure to welcome foreign investment and manpower hiring.

11. PARIS ATTACK: WHO IS RESPONSIBLE?

Introduction

7 January 2015, Paris witnessed barbarity and ruthless killing in the name of vengeance. Gunmen, or more specifically, terrorists, claiming to be followers of Islam, stormed into the the office of Charlie Hebdo's satirical magazine and killed 12 people brutally. This is not the first time when Charlie's weekly was attacked. Back in November 2011, there was firebomb attacks on the headquarters of his office. Threats were given by mad extremists to yet another bunch of mad cartoonists who abuse and offend people through their cartoons. Who is actually responsible for this barbarism and the loss of 12 lives?

Terrorists are Responsible

1. Media has the freedom of expression and though they misuse the freedom to offend the religious beliefs of people, nothing justifies killing of people. It is terrorism and fanaticism and everyone should condemn the act for the sake of humanity. These terrorists are no friends of any religion. They are the biggest enemies of peace and humanity, have crossed every limit of barbarism, and should be punished.
2. There is no vengeance in Islam and those hypocrites who shouted out after the killing that they avenged Prophet Muhammed are actually nowhere near the teachings of the Prophet. The greatest prophets of Islam do not need mere humans to take revenge for them. Islam teaches tolerance and these extremists know nothing of the same, and yet call themselves followers of the Prophet.
3. Protesting against the media and condemning the obscene caricatures of Hebdo could be done in a peaceful way too. There is no denying that his cartoons are indescribably offending to our Prophet and raised anger everywhere, not only amongst the Muslims, but other religions as well (it is not only Islam that Cynic Charlie offends) but such acts of terrorism are not justified in any way.
4. Freedom of press and democracy cannot be stabbed to silence by these means of inhuman acts. Intimidation by religious extremists and politicians is at its height and these terrorists are born out of it. They might take a stand that their act is justified, given that they were offended by the press' publication and they did not agree to it. But you do not need to agree to everything they write and publish and power does not give you the authority to punish them for what they wrote or drew.
5. Islamic minorities in France are living in a unpleasant situation with Islamophobia getting them discriminated against. To add to their despair, their economic crisis makes them an easy target to intimidation by the

so called jihadists. But instead of resorting to violence, these people can protest in other peaceful ways where there would be more space for sensible discussions and that would yield effective results too.

Charlie Hebdo Shares the Partnership in Crime

1. The role of the media is to bring forth the truth, free from intimidation and fear. Lampooning shariah laws and offending a religion is what media does when they have nothing else left to cover their pages. Without thinking of the consequences or the kind of response such offensive cartoons could draw, Hebdo continued the business of hurting sentiments of people worldwide. This is not meant to defend the terrorists or their act of terrorism, but there is no denying that such content is like oil on fire for those already ready to kill and die intimidated by the leaders of the terror groups.
2. According to Florence Noiville, a French novelist, there is a keyword in France – *laicite* – which means public life should be separated from religion. Does this rule not apply to the French media? Terrorists hurt people physically in the name of religion. We can them hypocrites. Media cartoonists like Hebdo hurt the sentiments of millions intentionally in the name of democracy and freedom of press. We call this strategy. How are people like Hebdo any different from those of the likes of ISIS? Both are ruthless in different ways.
3. Other than the followers of these terror groups, every Muslim condemns the atrocities and fundamentalism of these extremists. The terror act was condemned by Muslims across the globe. Did Charlie's media think of the sentiments of these people when they drew the obscene cartoons of one of the greatest prophets of a religion? Common people like us could get angry over it and condemn the cartoons with words but what else had Charlie expected from these terrorists? Opponents would call this a strategy to gain sympathy and outspread messages of Islamophobia – we expect Charlie to be expecting this too.
4. Meaningless and obscene cartoons of Charlie Hebdo are just meant to anger people of a religion and they have nothing in it that calls for freedom of press of democracy. They are drawn just to offend people. Is that so difficult to stop? If we cannot expect sensible media people to understand that their content is hurting people's sentiments, there is no expecting these fanatics to feel the pain of people.

Conclusion

For Hebdo, it is just a cartoon he created one fine day when he was retarder and had no news to play around with. His cartoons were failing to get attention so he decided to play safe with the matter that would get him into the limelight for no good reason. Muslims across the globe were offended (mission accomplished), but then came the unexpected blow from another bunch of retards. Both of these groups insulted the Prophet. More than the cartoonist, these terrorists offended his teachings. Our heart goes out to the families of the victims of this massacre.

12. DO YOU SUPPORT *PK* OR BOYCOTT *PK*?

The much-hyped movie, *PK*, has performed well on the box-office in last three days. However, the movie has also attracted controversies as it happens when anyone in India touches a sensitive topic like religion. Just like all the other participants, the social media world is also divided into two parts. There are two hashtags trending on Twitter, the first one is #WeSupportPK and the second one is #BoycottPK. So, which category do you belong to? Would you support *PK* or boycott *PK*?

Support *PK*

- The movie is not against religion, God, or his existence. The movie just wants people to know that God exists and therefore, God men should not.
- The movie talks about the most important principle of love and that is sacrifice and happiness of other person. It teaches that letting go your love is the toughest thing, but then it is the form of true love.
- The so-called managers of God use fear of the people to sell their marketing gimmicks and make money. The people blindly follow them.
- The message is clear, it is essential to have faith in God who created us, not in the God created by people to fulfill their personal motives.
- The movie highlights the hypocrisy of people where everyone claims the fallen money but everyone avoids to claim the condoms fallen out of their pockets.
- The movie focuses on prejudices where the liking for a person suddenly converts into hatred as soon as he comes to know about the caste or nationality of other person.
- The movie is made from an alien's point of view and therefore, it was justified to question the beliefs and values of religion.
- The movie has a scientific aspect which states that aliens exist and even they like to challenge every concept and question everything.
- The movie does not mock religion but only tries to remove the cover from hidden religious conservatism.

Boycott *PK*

- There are many scenes in the movie that clearly mock Hindu traditions and ceremonies, hurting the sentiments of people.

- Secularism does not give the right to abuse the majority. The right thing is to abuse unjustified dogmas irrespective of religion.
- The movie states that the person who is a coward or harbors fear goes to religious places. Well, the maker of the movie has really not done his homework before stating the concept in the movie. The half-truth is nothing but a lie.
- Director Rajkumar Hirani has always made fun of the system. He mocked at the education system in *Munna Bhai MBBS* and even did the same in *3 Idiots*.
- The movie has mixed the terms religion and superstition. It failed to highlight the difference between faith in religion and blind faith in superstition.
- The movie has just focused on one religion, namely, Hinduism. It has given rise to unwanted religious controversies across the nation.
- The movie *Oh My God* was well directed as it questioned God men and their unjustified activities. The movie did not question religion.

Conclusion

It is the high time that people should figure out the flaws that they conceive and not enter into arguments based on indifferences in ideologies. There are many flaws and drawbacks in the system. The movie just wants to highlight them. However, there is no denying that the movie mocked Hindu religion and their practices in some of the scenes, which the director should take note of and apologise to the segment.

13. YOGA IS A SCIENCE OF INNER WELL-BEING, NOT A RELIGION

What is Yoga?

Yoga is a practice which involves your body, mind and soul. The origin of yoga is dated back to the Vedic age. Today, some people also practice it as a religion. But the fact is yoga is not a religion, it is a practice which is adopted by many people to attain peace and maintain bodily harmony. Yoga involves meditation and it has been a part of the society since ages.

Recently, in a speech in the US, Narendra Modi stated that yoga should be widely practiced across the globe. The United Nations declared 21 June as International Yoga Day.

Many people are of the view that yoga is a part of Hinduism. It has also led to several controversies. The fact is that people from this religion (the early ascetics) were the first to practice it. It does not mean that yoga belongs to this religion. Patanjali, the inventor of yoga, did not teach that yoga is as a Hindu or Muslim practice.

Yoga is a Science

Science has proved that the whole of the universe depends on one energy and yoga means to get united. Practicing yoga brings all your energy forms together and keeps you healthy. We have many machines and tools to repair damaged things. In the same way, yoga is used to repair and maintain your body and mind.

Yoga does not give you a religion, but a methodology to follow. It helps you understand your mind, body, actions, and emotions. Yoga is used for medicinal purposes. It helps cure ailments like asthma. In a recent study by researchers, it was found that yoga reduces the BMI (Body Mass Index), cholesterol, and the risk of heart attack. Yoga costs less than the huge amount you spend on machines in a gym. It is particularly helpful for people for whom exercising at the gym is difficult.

Yoga is a process wherein you modify yourself continuously. It is a science that teaches us how to remove our physical and mental problems and improve our attitude towards life. Thus, yoga is the solution to retain your inner well being, and anything which does all this is beneficial for all human beings on the earth and cannot be bound be religion.

14. WOMEN ARE BETTER MANAGERS

For

- Women are the ones who are expected to handle various responsibilities from their childhood, which makes them good multi-taskers.
- Be it managers in the top companies or the ones who are managing their homes, women, in all areas manage their work flawlessly.
- Their inherent qualities make them good managers as they are more patient in difficult situations and are able to manage situations better with their positive attitude and calm mind as compared to their male counterparts.
- They have the quality of managing their children and are simultaneously able to concentrate on their career.

Against

- Women are very emotional and soft-hearted, which is considered as a weakness in managing things. They are not practical about the situations.
- They might be good at managing things at home, but this same strategy cannot be applied in the external environment where they have to work for an organisation.
- They might have all the qualities of managing like courage, patience, understanding, etc., but these are not the only key qualities required to manage a vast workforce or other difficult situations.

- Today we have progressed a lot, but there are many women who are not given a chance to prove themselves or are not given enough responsibilities to showcase their potential.
- A woman alone will not be able to manage things if she is not supported by her family members.

Conclusion

We all are born with some weakness and strengths. In the same way, women also have some strengths and weakness. They have the power to change their weakness into their strengths. If they do that, then there is no stopping them.

15. SHOULD INTERNET FREEDOM BE CURTAILED?

Introduction

With Russia and Turkey playing hard to restrain internet freedom, there is no short of countries as more and more join the clash to retrain giants like Facebook, Twitter, and Google to censor their content. Both Russia and Turkey tried curtailing these internet companies at different times of the year to remove controversial content and pages from the internet. The result, however, was the same in both the cases. Facebook and Twitter respectably removed the content but copies of the same documents were circulated in various ways, and hence, censoring the content was worthless. India and Pakistan has also been in the imbroglio of internet censorship to fight terrorists from manipulating youths for joining the ISIS. Pakistan, however, had a different kind of story to censor with ban of YouTube.

Yes, Internet Freedom should be Curtailed

1. Controversies never spread faster until they started going online. Anti-government protests, terrorism blurts, defaming of persons, false rumours, and allegations have all been a prominent part of the viral content on the internet in the gone year. Even before companies were contacted for censoring or removing the content or videos, copies were uploaded the very next moment.
2. In the European Union, a court ruling last year established a 'right to be forgotten', which includes freedom to access search engines like Google to remove links of content of negative material about oneself. This is important to safeguard against personal information going online after being hacked and leaked. 2014 saw many incidences of nude pictures of renowned celebrities going viral over the internet. Internet freedom should not include the right to leak private content of any person without their consent.

3. Talking of freedom of expression, not everything shared on the internet is intended for good reasons. Leaked MMS defame women. Racial content creates imbroglio. Misleading information harms youngsters. Manipulative videos and articles create revolutions that are harmful for the world at large. The sharing of this type of content cannot be included in freedom of expression.
4. Censoring content on the internet is difficult, but that does not mean that the government should not even try to do so. The further spread of such content could be stopped by asking companies to remove or censor videos or any sort of content. Graphics and videos on the internet are far more influential in affecting the minds of people, and hence, it is important to put restraint on these.
5. The biggest challenge that the world is currently facing the spread of terrorism, and to prevent further more youths from being manipulated by the fundamentalists, it is important that interaction of this sort be censored from the internet.
6. Internet access is available to children below the maturity age limit. For preventing children from viewing inappropriate content, it has become even more important to censor hard core pornography and other disturbing content on the internet. India is still lagging behind in retraining such content from the access of minors.

No, Internet Freedom should not be Curtailed

1. Freedom of speech and press is being advocated in support of Charlie Hebdo, but the same is being censored on the internet. Every individual has the right to express their ideas and to propagate what they believe to be true on the basis of recorded evidences in the form of audio or video. Why cannot the government apply the same rule before asking internet companies to cut out the controversial content? Free speech can either be curtailed to certain limits or given complete freedom to circulate any sort of crap over the web.
2. Censoring content creates that curiosity that compels people to do what they are prevented from doing. Copies of such content go viral after they are removed or blocked from the main pages. These copies contents add to the trouble with the addition of baseless rumours to them, and hence, are more awkward that the original content could be.
3. Censoring will become the right exercised by the government at its call. This might prevent information containing the truth of any situation from reaching the public. There will hidden secrets which the public would have no access to.

Conclusion

It is necessary to go by the demand of the present situation, and the present day challenges that the world at large has been dealing with call for restraining freedom of internet and to limit its extent of publishing content to only those that are non-harmful and do not involve larger controversies that could affect lives of people. Facebook has always been very cooperative in this matter. In the year ahead, we expect all the other big internet companies to follow the same prospect.

16. DO WE REALLY NEED SMART CITIES?

Introduction

The rate of migration from rural to urban areas is increasing across the world day by day. By 2050, around 70 per cent of the people will be living in cities and India is no exception in this regard.

There is an emerging need for the cities to get smarter in India so that they can tackle the issues related with the large scale urbanisation.

A smart city can be defined as a city which is equipped with basic infrastructure to give a decent quality of life.

Recently, PM Modi has announced his vision to set up around 100 smart cities across the nation. The 100 smart city mission tends to promote the adoption of smart solutions for the proper use of available resources and infrastructure.

But, does a country like India require smart cities? Let us take a look.

Yes – Smart Cities are Required

1. Good infrastructure – The main aim of constructing a smart city is to provide good infrastructure to the residents, such as water and sanitation services, 24 × 7electricity supply, etc. Information will be collected through the detectors – gas, electricity, and other government analytics, which will be carefully complied into small grids, and then, will be fed into the computers. This process can focus on making cities efficient.
2. Smart solutions – Smart cities are required as they would also provide smart solutions, such as providing public data, electronic service delivery, 100 per cent treatment of water waste, monitoring water quality, etc.
3. Promotes development – Smart cities enhance the developmental activities of a region. A lot of developmental activities, such as building schools, organisations, and shopping malls can take place. These activities benefit everybody, including citizens, businesses, the government, and the environment.

4. Housing for all – The main aim of a smart city is 'housing for all'. More than 70 per cent of the Indian population would be living in cities by 2050. Due to rising urbanisation, a better standard of living is required. To support this rising shift, a sustainable model of housing should be developed.
5. Provides employment – A smart city is an economy of agglomeration. It provides various opportunities and advantages to its residents. India is expanding rapidly and the emergence of smart cities can provide employment to many. The construction of a smart city requires a lot of manpower.

No – Smart Cities are not Required

1. Dumb administration – The politicians of India have picked up the term 'smart city' to woo the youngsters. In the past few months, we have witnessed the real face of the corrupt ministers who rule our country. Corruption has become a part of our country's identity. Talking about a smart city and creating a plan under the corrupt minsters is a waste of time and resources. A smart city is not possible with a set of dumb administrators and politicians.
2. Unable to afford – In a smart city, people have to build their own houses according to their financial capacity. A lot of people would not be able to afford a place in a smart city as it would be very costly. Thus, people from middle classes and poor sections of the society will not be able to enjoy the benefits of a smart city.
3. Better utilisation of space – A large expanse of land would be wasted for the construction of a smart city. If properly utilised, this area can be turned into a biodiversity park. Cities which are rich on river beds and hilly regions can be utilised to avoid ecological degeneration.
4. Proper use of funds – India is a country which is better known for its increasing poverty rate. Only a certain part of the city would be utilised for constructing a smart city whereas, the other part of the city would still be still under the shadow of poverty. We should understand that smart cities will not be able to solve the basic issues of an entire state or city. If the funds which are planned to be spent for a smart city are utilised for decreasing the poverty rate, India would be much ahead of other countries.

Conclusion

India is a developing country and the Modi government is trying its best to develop India into a powerful nation.

Introducing the concept of smart cities in India is a great idea but due to increasing poverty rate, and lack of infrastructure and basic amenities, the cities might have to face a lot of challenges. Before initiating the project, the government should try to attend to the basic issues of the nation, such as implementing a proper drainage system, providing good water, sanitation, and health care facilities, etc.

A nation with a strong infrastructure would be successful in creating numerous smart cities.

17. ONLY MAHATMA GANDHI DESERVES TO BE FEATURED ON THE CURRENCY NOTES

In the 20th Lalit Doshi Memorial Lecture, RBI Governor Raghuram Rajan said that no one but only Mahatma Gandhi should feature on the currency notes. He said that undoubtedly, there are many great Indians, but no one can match Mahatma Gandhi. Getting anyone else on the currency notes can be controversial. Do you agree with the RBI Governor? Do you think only Mahatma Gandhi should be featured on the currency notes?

Yes

- He is the man who led the fight of independence. It would have been impossible for India to achieve its freedom without *Bapu*.
- It needs courage to leave worldly pleasures and work for the people who are living a miserable life, which Mahatama Gandhi could do.
- Mahatma Gandhi advocated that if you want to change the world, first change yourself. He is the only one who is respected all over the world.
- There are a number of famous people, but all of them failed to impress a large chunk of people.
- Any kind of change made at this time will only create chaos and political disorder in the country.

No

- There are many other freedom fighters who contributed equally to the freedom fight of India.
- Bal Gangadhar Tilak, who was known as the 'Father of the Indian Movement', worked as a social reformer and laid the foundation of modern India.
- The contributions of other revolutionaries, including Bhagat Singh, in the national movement cannot be ignored.
- Lal Bahadur Shastri was a world-known leader whose efforts for the development of India are still admired. Why does he not deserve to be on Indian notes?

Conclusion

It is a bitter truth that no one is perfect in this world. Considering the contributions of Mahatma Gandhi, it is not wrong to feature him on the currency notes, but there are many other great people who contributed in the development process of India. And, in any case, their contributions cannot be ignored. If an opportunity arises to feature any more people on the currency of India, other people can also be given a chance

18. ARE NOKIA AND MICROSOFT A PLANNED ALLIANCE OR IS IT A DESPERATE MOVE?

For

- Nokia and Microsoft are a planned alliance as they both require each other to make something new of substantial quality.
- Nokia has the technology to make a better smartphone whereas, Microsoft has the support of online features that are required for the promotion of this new technology.
- They are forming an alliance just to ensure their power and collective leadership in the market.
- It is a very good strategy adopted by these two power companies to match the innovative smartphone made by other companies such as Apple and Android.
- These two companies, if brought together, will bring in some tremendous products which will help them compete on the global scale.

Against

- It is a desperate move as both these are companies are giants in their own world and they do not need an alliance to promote themselves.
- Nokia's attempts to create better and innovative smartphones have been all but in vain.
- Microsoft on the other hand has also been unsuccessful in taking the world by storm by the launch of its mobile OS, which was termed as ridicule.
- Apple and Android are two massive brands that stand as the main dominant forces in the market of smartphones. Thus, making huge companies like Nokia and Microsoft to combine forces to dominate the market.

19. RISING PETROL PRICES – CAN THE GOVERNMENT CONTROL IT

Rising petrol prices is a big reason for worry as it has a direct effect on the prices of our basic needs. During the last 1 year, the petrol prices have seen a steep increase, which is a big worry for the society. Can the government take some steps to contain these prices or will they keep burning holes in our pockets in the same way?

For

- The government can start using alternative sources of energy such as electric energy, solar energy, wind energy, hydroelectric energy, etc., as solutions to curb the rising prices of petrol.
- The government can make some efforts in order to minimise the use of petrol, which will ultimately reduce the price of petrol.
- It can reduce the price of petrol to a large extent by lowering various taxes imposed on petrol prices. The price of petrol is increased due to the taxes which are added to it.
- Better roads and handling traffic can help in saving the petrol we burn. This can lead to saving petrol and the government will not be required to raise the prices so fast.
- Better public transport can motivate people to reduce the usage of personal vehicles, which can again help in saving petrol and containing the prices.
- Providing subsidies on diesel further aggravates the problem.

Against

- The main reason for regular hikes in petrol prices is corruption, imbalanced Indian economy, fluctuating dollar value, dependency on imports, price of crude oil in the international market, rising population, etc. Many of these are external factors and not under the control of the government.
- The other main reason for the increase in petrol price is the increase in demand compared to low supply of petrol, which cannot be controlled by the government alone.
- The government alone will not be able to control the price of petrol, we as individuals should make an effort to save as much petrol as we can. We all should use these scare resources carefully.
- We can use public transport to go to places instead of our using own vehicles. We need to think individually in order to save petrol for ourselves as well as for the future generations.

20. ENGLISH SHOULD CONTINUE TO BE THE OFFICIAL LANGUAGE OF INDIA

English is used as the official language in India. Recently, when PM Modi used Hindi for his diplomatic talks, it surged agitation in non-Hindi states, especially Tamil Nadu. Also, NDA government's recent proposal for giving importance to Hindi language on social media accounts faced stiff opposition by the Tamil Nadu CM and other regional parties. It is considered a violation of Official Languages Act, 1963. In the country where most of the people understand Hindi, is it okay to continue with English as the official language of the country?

Yes

- English is a language that is understood by people from different castes and states, and therefore deserves to be the official language of India.
- If any other language is tried to make the official language, all the regional parties will start the battle of making their state's language the official language of India.
- If Hindi is given priority, then it will create differences among the people who don't speak it, making them feel like second-class citizens.
- Region C, which forms an important part of India, got agitated when PM Modi used Hindi for his diplomatic talks.
- The use of English language is as per the requirement of being a part of globalisation, and there is nothing wrong in it.

No

- Forget about all the different castes and religions as Indians have their own national language that is Hindi, and that should be the official language of India.
- It is the duty of the government to take measures to ensure that people all over in India can read, write, and speak in Hindi.
- India has already adopted the western culture in many ways. If it continues, there will be no personal, or rather, national identity of India.
- In this case, India should learn something from Pakistan, who made Urdu its official language after the division of the country.
- The small steps are the ways that we can make sure that the people from different religions have at least something in common as Indians.
- English might be used as the official language of India, but is the unofficial *lingua franca* in South Asia. When it is not official for the region, why make it official for the country.

21. M-GOVERNANCE: WILL IT BE THE PANACEA FOR ALL THE PROBLEMS OF INDIA IN THE NEXT DECADE?

Introduction

M-governance means mobile governance. It ensures that services are available to the people with the help of mobile phones. M-governance is a subset of E-governance. The government has emphasised that the service delivery mechanism should move from e-governance to m-governance. It can revolutionise the way public services are delivered to the citizens today because of its various benefits like accessibility, low cost, transparency and reach to the inaccessible areas of the country. Certainly, if implemented effectively, it can turn out to be the panacea for all the problems of India.

Advantages of M-governance

1. It is transparent and provides a direct interface between the citizens and the government, which will make the government accountable.
2. Use of mobiles is increasing day-by-day and the penetration of mobile phones is ever-increasing phenomenon in rural India. It will create opportunities for the government to deliver public services to the people anytime, anywhere.
3. The cost of mobile technology is much cheaper than internet technology. Therefore, it will be an effective tool for the poor people because people will adopt this technology for its low cost.
4. To avail the facilities of the internet, there is need for infrastructure which is lacking in various areas of the country. In these areas, M-governance will work better.

Challenges to M-governance

1. The cost on the part of the government to implement the facilities of M-governance together with E-governance will be a challenge.
2. There is a lack of knowledge and training among the rural people about operating mobile phones, which needs to be addressed.
3. The security of mobile transactions needs to be maintained by the people.
4. There is also a need for the basic infrastructure for continuous access to mobile technology. For example, telecommunication signals should be present in the rural and inaccessible areas.

Conclusion

M-governance will not only solve many problems of public service delivery but also help in strengthening the democracy. It will help in increasing the interaction between the citizens and the government. M-governance will not only give power to the citizens of the country but also help in empowering the people of India.

22. THE GOVERNMENT SHOULD STOP FUNDING IIT'S AND IIM'S AND, INSTEAD DIVERT THE FUNDS TO PRIMARY EDUCATION (12-30-2011)

Primary education is losing its importance in the time of growing IIT's and IIM's and the efforts made towards enlightening individuals with primary education are hampered by lack of funds. Can a student go to IIT's and IIM's without proper primary education?

For

- Primary education is compulsory for a person to build his/her personality, but due to the under-developed nature of India, not every individual receives primary education.
- Government should make a conscious effort to make more people literate rather than concentrating their sum on a small and confined population.
- Students from IITs and IIMs are migrating from India to other countries for better jobs, leaving a sour taste in everyone's mind.
- Illiterate people in India are incapable of meeting the expenses of primary schools, let alone IITs and IIMs. So, the government should divert the funds on educating them with primary education rather than giving it to IITs and IIMs.
- Students going to IITs and IIMs are self-capable of paying expenses that are required for these colleges.
- Compulsory primary education is necessary for the overall growth of the country.

Against

- India, being a developing nation, needs these institutes to polish the young talent to perform on the international front.
- Students migrating from these institutes result in an increase of our economy while connecting us globally.
- The growth of young talent in India requires better education and reorganisation as the talent pool is vast and ever-growing in India.
- IITs and IIMs produce brilliant minds that can help in shaping India democratically and make it a better democratic country.
- Students are coming to these institutes from other countries, thus generating revenue for India.
- It is the students of IIMs, IITs and other big institutes who help in creating employment opportunities in India.

Primary education is compulsory and it is not to be mixed with IITs and IIMs as they are restricted to a very small area. IITs and IIMs can be self-financed by the students, but primary education should not be neglected and funds should be used to literate people from the grass-root level.

23. BEAUTY OR BRAINS – WHO CAN RULE THE WORLD?

Introduction

The combination of beauty and brain is not very common. The one who has got both brains and beauty is by far the most lucky person on earth. Every person has his own strengths and weaknesses, and the good traits definitely speak out in some or the other way. A beautiful person with his wrong deeds cannot excel; similarly an ugly person with a beautiful soul struggles throughout his life to prove himself. When we come to the discussion about who can rule the world – beauty or brains, there come a plenty of points both in favour of and against the notion. Let us discuss a few of them.

Beauty

- Let us start with the saying 'True beauty lies in the eyes of its beholder'. The beauty which holds the eyes of the one who perceives, rules the entire globe with its attraction.
- Beauty paves a faster way to success with its charm and charisma.
- Brains without beauty finds it difficult to withstand the initial phase of interaction, as 'the first impression is the last impression'.
- Beauty not only implies the external looks but also the inner beauty of the soul. Inner beauty marks refined thoughts and soul, which could win millions of hearts.
- Inner beauty is the requirement for the 'higher purpose of existence and survival'. It is the internal beauty of the soul which helps in the self-growth and development of the society.
- Beauty implies captivity, and the world today follows appearances and external looks.
- We call women to be the most beautiful creation of God, and by far the women have a strong say worldwide, which implies that beauty is ruling the world.

Brain

- Brains are ultimate. Beauty would fade away with time, but brains is eternal and get polished and shine more with time and increasing age.
- Beauty can glow only if the person has good luck, conversely brains have the capacity to mould and shape fortune and win hearts.
- The adverse times being the right ones to judge; brains shine like a diamond and pave its way out from difficult situations, however, beauty gets tugged up in trouble.
- Beauty is God's creation, which cannot be made better, whereas, brains can be developed through human efforts and gaining worldly knowledge. The true efforts definitely succeed and rule the world.
- Brains have the capacity to retain career and gain recognition. They retain relationships and knit the world into a single entity.
- Beauty might not be there with the brainy, but brains is present in every human in varying capacity. Even the not-so-beautiful people may possess a

sharp intellect and the capacity to rule the world, but a beautiful brainless idiot cannot even stand up in the race of life.

- Even beauty contests like Miss World and Miss Universe are won on the basis of their intellect and not beauty alone.

Conclusion

Beauty and brains are undoubtedly a unique and nice combination to excel in the life arena. When coming to the debate, the brains has an upper say over beauty. The inner beauty of a person is very close to the brains, but the external looks alone cannot excel in life. Brains undoubtedly have strong domination to rule the world in comparison to the external outlook and beauty.

24. PM'S VISION TO MAKE INDIA A MANUFACTURING HUB – A DREAM OR A PRACTICAL POSSIBILITY?

Introduction

In the Independence day speech from Red Fort, PM Narendra Modi gave delivered a new approach for Indians to cease exporting raw materials and importing the manufactured products. He gave a new vision of converting India into a 'Manufacturing Hub'. He boosted up our good spirit to come forward and show our excellence and team spirit and earn the credit for self and gain the fame for the nation. This approach means a lot for the economy of the country in addition to the development of the industrial sector in the country. His initiative towards starting up the manufacturing of products with the raw materials that we have been exporting for a long time is worth giving a bold thought. Yet, these things are far more complicated than just building a dream vision. Is the PM's vision of making India a Manufacturing Hub a dream, or is that a practical possibility that could be accomplished with our best efforts?

Dream

- Indians are used to the lifestyle of earning their living by exporting raw materials and importing manufactured goods. It is difficult to change their mind-set.
- It is not very practical to set up these many manufacturing units for all the raw materials that we export. Setting up these units demands infrastructure.
- We need a good amount of funds for machineries and other requirements for establishing industries and starting the manufacturing process.
- We need to train the employees and staff for the organisations/manufacturing industrial set-up who can work and deliver the products on International Standards.

- We are already fighting our best to gear the prevailing industries in order to nurture them with global-level technology and deliver the end products on International standards. It would be a much far-off dream to start on with a lot many manufacturing units.

Practical Possibility

- India is very rich in manpower, which is the top-most requirement to start with a new industrial set-up for the manufacturing process.
- Indians are hardworking. We have talents and efficiency to deliver the best output with minimal input. It is one of the reasons that Indians are hired universally for employment. If we can work for some other nation, then why can we not join hands together to uplift our own dooming economy?
- Our brain power is very famous throughout the world. We have new ideas and layout plans for all types of tasks and also have the efficiency to implement the same in practical way.
- If we can curb corruption, then we would end up saving plenty funds to accommodate and initiate many new employment opportunities.
- All we need is to boost the 'Young India' to have faith and confidence in their outlook and approach, who are our future stepping stones.
- The only reason that we have not been able to excel in this field is because we have never tried seriously. If we decide to start manufacturing, we can for sure do it.

Conclusion

We have arguments both in favour of and against the setting up of new industries. With the corruption level in our country at present, the task of turning ourselves into a manufacturing hub is undoubtedly a heavy and difficult one. But there is a very nice proverb that we have learnt since childhood – 'Where there is will, There is a way'. If we can join hands to give ourselves this new outlook, then we can not only check corruption, but also make the PM's vision come true. Making India a manufacturing hub could be the vision of PM Modi, but it will be a matter of pride for every Indian.

25. LIFE IMPRISONMENT IS A GOOD ALTERNATIVE TO CAPITAL PUNISHMENT

We talk about punishments for the criminals, thieves, or people who commit serious mistakes. Do we ever ask ourselves that what is the purpose of these punishments is it always necessary to punish people for every mistake? And what are the parameters to decide which punishment is better for which crime.

For

- If a person commits a mistake which has a deep impact on the victim or the victim's family, then life imprisonment is an appropriate punishment.
- Capital punishment takes the life of a person, which is not real justice to any crime.
- Life imprisonment gives a chance to the criminals to realise their mistakes.

Against

- Life imprisonment is not a good alternative to capital punishment as no mistake is big enough for life imprisonment.
- Capital punishment is the best way to pass a message to the society.
- It removes dangerous criminals from the society, making it a safer place for people.
- It will help remove the discrimination, which should be corrected by giving capital punishment to murderers.
- Life imprisonment is still far better than capital punishment because it is better to live then die as everyone loves to live.

26. VIRAT KOHLI IS THE WORLD'S BEST ODI BATSMAN

For

- He has been the most consistent batsman in the ODI and the statistics are also in his favor to support the fact that he is the world's best batsman now.
- He has shown the ability, hunger and perseverance that is necessary to excel at the international level.
- He has been the story behind India's success in almost all the important fixtures.
- He has outclassed the little master in the few years that he has played and has proved a strong force to reckon with.
- He has scored under pressure and the manner in which he has fetched these runs is what makes him the best batsman in the world as of now.

Against

- Just scoring a few brilliant centuries does not make him the best player in the world.
- He has not excelled under different and difficult conditions, i.e. he has not been put under testing conditions yet.
- Virat has the capability and attitude to make it to the top, but it is still a long way to go and we should not overestimate his recent performances.
- He is still raw and temperamental and he should overcome all these to become the world's best batsman.

27. MALL SHOPPING, STREET SHOPPING, OR ONLINE SHOPPING – WHICH IS BETTER?

Shopping is one word that brings smiles on women's faces. Shopping is loved by everyone. Even if people do not want to buy anything, they love to opt for window shopping. Previously, it was all about street shopping. Then was introduced the whole new world of malls and entertainment. And now, it is more about online shopping. So, which is your most preferred form of shopping?

Mall Shopping

- It offers availability of a range of merchandise and brands in a single place. Buyers can explore a variety of designs and styles under one roof.
- It saves time and efforts as there is no need to move from one street to another in search of the products.
- Mall shopping comes with entertainment. There are cinema halls and gaming zones included in shopping malls.
- Most of the shopping malls have a complete supermarket and grocery retailers where products are available at discounted rates.
- There is the easy option to try and feel the products in real time. There is no need to wait for the products to come home.
- The quality of products is much better than the products found in street shops.

Online Shopping

- There is no need to search for any physical space to showcase the products. Shopping is not restricted by area constraints.
- Online shopping provides immense comfort to the working people, who do not have much time to go out and shop for products.
- With the advent of online stores, it has become easy to buy products required in day-to-day life, including groceries.
- Online shopping allows buyers to find the best quality products at affordable prices. Compare the prices and then buy the products.
- Online shopping can be done without worrying about time restrictions or location constraints.

Street Shopping

- Street shopping is all about the independent shops where shoppers can find unique and innovative stuff. Malls have more or less the same stuff and same brands.

- Street shopping is more about fun, where shoppers can enjoy the real fun of bargaining with the shopkeepers.
- The stuff found it street shops is not expensive. They offer affordable products that can be bought by all classes.
- Street shopping is more about roaming carelessly, having a drink or coffee with friends, or enjoying street food along with shopping.

Conclusion

All people are different with their own sets of tastes and preferences. More options in the form of street shopping, mall shopping and online shopping have made things much easier for people. It has made shopping all the more convenient. All the forms of shopping have their own set of good and bad points. But the fact is that they have made shopping really easy in the always-running world.

28. RETURNING *SAHITYA AKADEMI* AWARDS – IS IT A RIGHT KIND OF PROTEST BY WRITERS?

'The purpose of a writer is to keep civilization from destroying itself.'

– Albert Camus.

There has been a recent spur in the writers returning *Sahitya Akademi* Awards in protest. The number has reached 20. It simply reminds one of the time when Rabindranath Tagore renounced his title of 'Sir' in protest to the Jallianwala Bagh massacre during the British times. Though we are not British times and we have all the freedom which we need, writers still felt that they are facing hostility from some factions of the society and have taken to protests in the form of returning the awards.

But is this protest being done in an appropriate form as *Sahitya Akademi* Awards are among the highest-level literary awards in the country; or is there no truth to the allegations by the writers?

Yes

1. It is an appropriate response to the insecurities felt by writers.
2. It is a symbolic show of protest against what writers feel as a growing disregard for freedom of speech.
3. The writers can use the media or their writings to bring their problems in front of the entire nation. However, they fear that some factions of the society might turn hostile if they are criticised. Writings of the writers might provoke hostilities among those fractions.
4. Thus, we can see what remains with a writer to do, if his writings are bone of contention. This symbolic gesture thus shows the severity of the problem.

5. The violence against murders of writers with very different points of view was another issue. Here, we see that writings and difference of opinions themselve got writers killed. So, there was no other way to protest. A strike might not have the same effect as a strike of petrol pumps or a doctors' strike.
6. This gesture shows that one of the highest literary honors too is insufficient if the writers feel that all spaces of liberal values and thought, all locations of dissent and dialogue, and all attempts at sanity and mutual trust are under assault.
7. This tradition of returning awards is not new in our country and has been going on since the British times. So, frowning at the writers to for using this method is not fair.

No

1. It is irrelevant to return the awards. It will not have much effect.
2. *Sahitya Akademi* Awards were given by the *Sahitya Akademi* to writers and not by the government. If an award is returned as a protest, it does not make sense as the government did not give the awards. Had the award been awarded by the government, it would have made sense to return them.
3. If the writers want to protest they can do so in their writing. Many read what writers write. This way they can reach a majority of the population with their problems. Returning awards is of no use.
4. The writers can also use media to make sure their plights reaches the appropriate authority and even people come to know about them.
5. The writers are feeling that their liberal space is getting reduced. To address this issue, the entire nation is with them. They just need to initiate a dialogue with appropriate authorities to resolve the problem. They need not take such steps.
6. These steps are only making such awards political. This will have ramifications in the future too. This can make these honorable awards political tool.
7. In India, during the British times, whenever there was pressure on the writing space provided to the writers, the writers reacted with their articles and generated public opinion from their side. With the growing use of internet and good communication networks, the writers can reach every nook and corner of the country in a matter of hours. Such avenues of protests must be used.
8. Also, more than returning awards, scathing articles and criticism can do a better job of generating public opinion. If a writer is afraid, then to hide identity, pen names can be used.

'No tears in the writer, no tears in the reader. No surprise in the writer, no surprise in the reader.'

– Robert Frost

Such is the importance of writers. This is how they can have an impact on the people. Various hostilities and problems of India have provoked writers and artists to protest against and condemn the damage done to the social fabric, communal harmony, and the creative life of India. Not doing so will be failing in their duty. Literature in India has been a sort of conscience-keeper of the country. Though returning awards may not be the most appropriate kind of protest, it is a symbolic gesture which only aims to draw attention towards the issues raised by the writers. This protest is not damaging public life, and hence, instead of arguing if the protest is appropriate or not, we must focus on addressing the concerns of the writers.

29. SOCIAL MEDIA IS KILLING THE BOOK READING HABIT!

'A room without books is like a body without a soul.' – Marcus Tullius Cicero

With the growing influence and liking towards social media, it will surely become difficult to fill a room with books. A survey in the U.K. showed that with the increasing age, the tendency to read a book decreases; an effect profoundly seen when a comparison was made between three age groups – six to eight, 12–14, and 15–17 year olds. There have been frowns from parents and many quarters of society towards teen indulgence in Facebook, internet, and other social media websites. They are not happy with the neglect of reading books. Thus, it is worthwhile to discuss whether social media is killing the practice of reading books.

Yes, They are Affecting

1. Social media is unproductive use of time as it only entertains you and gives no food for thought.
2. The amount of education you get from it is very less compared to reading books.
3. It hampers creativity as much of the time is spent on forwarding things to others.
4. Most of the time is spent in searching what others are doing, time can be well spent in reading, which atleast adds knowledge to ones your life.
5. Another prominent example can be the usage of 'new' abbreviations to express oneself on social media. This hampers language development, which in turn affects writing and reading both.

6. Due to the fast changing content on such websites, the attention span of the readers has reduced. So, an important habit of thinking over a thought, giving it time to percolate in your mind, is reduced to a great extent. This is one of the benefits of books. Books cultivate the capacity to understand and think.
7. Good reading habits makes way for a better understanding of one's experiences, however, social media mostly indulges the cravings of people rather than what is good for them.
8. Role models teens follow are more active on social media. Teens try to emulate them.

No, They Do Not Affect

1. Times change and with it, habits. Even if people are moving away from reading, one can always devise better ways to indulge them in reading. One cannot blame everything on change in culture and social media.
2. Teens are just trying to find themselves and prioritise socialisation over reading something alone.
3. They are getting connected instead of being alone.
4. With increasing age there is bound to be changes in the tendency to read as teenagers feel the need to establish one's presence in society, find one's position, and hence, use all the methods available to socialise; an important one being social media.
5. They are learning to find themselves with social media. This is in no way affecting reading.
6. Socialisation is their current priority, but this does not mean that social media is affecting reading of books.
7. There is lack of literature which can suit contemporary needs and thoughts. The classics might be good but do not necessarily suit everyone.
8. Also, disinterest in reading is mostly seen due to no encouragement for reading. For this, parents, peer groups, teachers, etc., could be blamed, rather than social media.

Conclusion

Reading enriches one's intellectual abilities. In-depth reading helps to develop the mind and personality of a person; it provides insights into human problems, and influences attitudes and behaviour. In other words, reading helps to mould a person's character. It is well known that books can be a stimulating agent for building oneself. In this fast changing world, there are going to be lots of distractions. We must innovate to make book-reading relevant again. Encouraging book-reading through social media, incorporating reading in social media, eBooks, developing relevant and quality literature, role models with whom the teens can connect, etc., can be a few starting steps. Instead of blaming we need to work constructively so as to not deny ourselves the benefits of social media.

30. RISING PETROL PRICES – CAN THE GOVERNMENT CONTROL THEM?

Rising petrol prices is a big reason for worry as it has a direct effect on the prices of our basic needs. During the last 1 years the petrol prices have seen a steep increase which is a big worry for the society. Can government take some steps to contain these prices or will they keep burning holes in our pockets in the same way?

For

- Government can start using alternative sources of energy such as electric energy, solar energy, wind energy, hydroelectric energy etc. as solution to curb the rising prices of petrol.
- Government can make some efforts in order to minimize the use of petrol which will ultimately reduce the price of petrol.
- It can reduce the price of petrol to a large extent by lowering various taxes imposed on petrol prices. The price of petrol are increased due to the taxes which are added to it.
- Better roads and handling traffic can help in saving the petrol we burn. This can lead to savinf petrol and the government will not be required to raise the prices so fast.
- Better public transport can motivate people to reduce the usage of personal vehicles which can again help in savind petrol and containing the prices.
- Providing subsidies on diesel further aggravates the problem.

Against

- The main reason for regular hike in petrol prices is corruption, imbalanced Indian economy, fluctuating dollar value, dependency on imports, price of crude oil in the international market, rising population etc. Many of these are external factors and not under the control of government.
- The other main reason for the increase in petrol price is increase in demand compared to low supply of petrol, which cannot be controlled by the Government alone.
- Government alone will not be able to control the price of petrol, we as an individual should make an effort to save petrol as much as we can. We all should use these scare resources carefully.

Conclusion

Government alone cannot control the rising petrol prices. We all as an individual also need to make an effort with the government in order to curb the petrol prices by using our vehicles efficiently. We can use other means of public transport to go to places instead of using own vehicle. We need to think individually in order to save petrol for ourself as well as for the upcoming generation.

31. SHOULD THE NIRBHAYA JUVENILE BE RELEASED?

Nirbhaya was brutally assaulted by six persons, including a juvenile, in a moving bus in South Delhi on 16 December 2012. She had later succumbed to her injuries in a Singapore hospital. Now, the juvenile who committed this heinous and brutal crime is being allowed to walk free as per the Juvenile Justice Act under the custody of an NGO. The juvenile convict is the most brutal of the 6 accused and will be released on 20 December after his term at the observation home ends. As per the Juvenile Justice Act, the maximum punishment which can be given to the juvenile is 3 years and he has completed this term. But does society want such as brutal criminal to be released merely because he is a juvenile? Is it right that he should walk free and be allowed to hold a job after the terrible crime he has committed? Should the government and the SC not intervene and prevent this rapist and killer from being released?

Yes

1. **A juvenile is not the same as an adult:** Juveniles have a lower level of mental development and they are not capable of logical thinking like adults. They are therefore, not fit to be tried as adults.
2. **The juvenile deserves rehabilitation:** As he was a child when he committed the crime, he did not have proper guidance and this led to his heinous act. If he is regulated and placed under observation, he will be able to make a better life for himself.
3. **A Juvenile Court has been established with the crime in mind:** Just because a juvenile has committed a crime means that different rules apply for him or her. In this case, the juvenile court has been formed, keeping the needs and best interests of child criminals in mind along with balancing the need for a fair and just society.
4. **Special Juvenile Justice Board's directive must be respected:** The special Juvenile Justice Board has been established under the Juvenile Justice Act, 2000 to control and prosecute offense committed by persons below 18 years of age on the rationale that such individuals have less clarity of reasoning and thought and are not the masters of their minds.

5. **Kids, not adults:** While committing the crime, the juvenile is held to lack of understanding requisite to constitute the intention necessary to expose him to prosecution under ordinary law, exempting him from this and placing him under the Juvenile Justice Board, manned by child welfare experts.

No

1. **Nirbhaya juvenile is already radicalised:** A government report has held that the juvenile in question has become worse after radicalisation through association with other juveniles. In such a circumstance, releasing the juvenile will be detrimental to the interests the society and will also increase the possibility of harm coming to him once he is out of government jurisdiction.
2. **The crime is a heinous one:** The brutal juvenile has committed a terrible crime and he should be punished for it. On the strength of a mere technicality, he is getting away with a heinous rape and murder. This should not be allowed.
3. **The juvenile is worse than an animal:** Subramanian Swamy has said the juvenile is an animal and he should be denied freedom on the grounds of this. Keeping the gravity of the crime in mind and death penalty awarded to the other rapists. Why is this juvenile criminal and rapist being allowed to walk scot free?
4. **Injustice is served and crime is incentivised if he is released:** If the juvenile is allowed to be released into the society, it serves to incentivise his crime and give the wrong message that lawlessness and heinous crimes are acceptable in society.
5. **Juvenile crime on the rise:** According to the data from the National Crime Records Bureau, a division of the home ministry, juveniles in the age group of 16 to 18 years have committed 60 per cent of the crimes from 2003 to 2013, the highest among all juvenile age groups. Juvenile arrests for rape increased 288 per cent over the period against arrests for theft, which were up by 68 per cent according to the data. Organised crime networks even use minors to exploit legal loopholes and punishing adults exploiting and pushing children into criminal acts is not enough to stop this. Punishment needs to be given to such rapists and killers or the society will become even more lawless.
6. **Number of juvenile crime offenders on the rise:** Crimes committed by juveniles have increased and releasing the Nirbhaya juvenile sends a further wrong message to society. RS was informed that the number of juvenile offenders in the country has seen a rise from 36,822 in 2012 to 48,230 in 2015. The number of juveniles apprehended rose from 43,506 in 2013 to 48,230 in 2014. Using arguments to evade punishment is a denial of justice for the victims.

7. **Surveillance is needed:** A law needs to be passed for mandatory registration of sex offenders and accused who have served punishment to allow surveillance by local police as well as community members. Releasing the convict is a counterproductive move for the interests of society.
8. **Victims are also children:** Do not leave aside the fact that the victims of many of these crimes are also children. It is wrong to shield the criminal by saying he or she lacks the capacity to form a moral judgement regarding the crime. If steps are not taken to imprison the Nirbhaya juvenile convict or ensure he is kept in custody, who will protect the victims, many of whom are also children.

Conclusion

Lack of mental development or moral reasoning are not excuses for a heinous crime, nor are the justifications. Criminals are evil-doers who are aware of their actions and the consequences of them, regardless of their age. Moreover, the Nirbhaya juvenile even tried to get another victim to board the bus, before successfully convincing the victim and her boyfriend to do so. Such evil actions show a premeditated crime and not an act committed without conscious thought or planning. The brutal nature of the crime makes it vital that the punishment sho

32. TABLETS SHOULD REPLACE TEXTBOOKS IN THE INDIAN EDUCATION SYSTEM!

Advanced nations all over the world are equipping children with tablets instead of textbooks. Now, with an increasing emphasis on Digital India, can Indian schools and colleges also look to empower students by providing them with tablets? Can technology be used to bridge the digital divide? Let us examine if Indian educational institutions can provide better learning assistance to children!

Tablets should Replace Textbooks

1. **Multimedia learning provides an edge** – Difficulty in remembering what was taught previously can be eliminated through interactive learning across multiple mediums.
2. **Tablets offer graphical representations that are 3D** – Tablets offer a more complex visual and graphical representation making it easier to understand the subject. You can also cover better illustrations and graphical descriptions using tablets as these provide scope for deeper, richer, more meaningful diagrams.
3. **More affordable** – Using textbooks scores low on affordability. If the entire amount spent on textbooks for a single year is calculated, it will be more

than the price of an average tablet. Also, tablets can be reprogrammed and used across successive years as against textbooks, which can only be used for that particular grade.

4. **Reduce the weight of schoolbags** – Using tablets will reduce the burden of carrying thick textbooks and associated instruments which require separate toolboxes. Research studies have shown students should carry less than 15 per cent of their own weight in terms of schoolbags or backpacks. This is no longer a reality in present day conditions. Using a tablet would lighten the burden on students.
5. **Tablets are eco-friendly** – Taking notes on tablets would save paper. Schools would find the use of tablets more cost effective as well as eco-friendly. Moreover, presentations, tests, assignments, and projects could be interactively handled through tablets, providing a rich and affordable learning experience at nominal costs to the environment.

Tablets cannot be a Replacement for Textbooks

1. **Tablets are distracting** – Addictive games, social networking and media sites, and other distractions would take away from the studying time and act as unnecessary and unrequited distractions for students.
2. **Taking care of tablets is costlier** – Textbooks are easier to maintain. Students will not be able to take care of tablets in schools and public places, especially if they have to travel long distances.
3. **Lost or dead tablets can be a real problem** – Lost notes, textbooks and assignments will be the result of a malfunctioning or misplaced tablet
4. **Tablets require heavy maintenance** – Tablets are gadgets that require extensive maintenance and repair and children would have to get used to studying on tablets rather than textbooks.
5. **Students may face health problems** – Using technology such as tablets for extended hours can lead to health problems such as Computer Vision Syndrome, strain on eyes, and head, blurred vision, as well as carpal tunnel syndrome and orthopaedic problems.
6. **Internet is costly** – In many rural and isolated areas, internet has not yet made its mark and tablets would prove counterproductive. Moreover, internet connections with high bandwidth will make education costlier for parents and create monetary hurdles.
7. **Bad impact on grammar and handwriting** – With the use of tablets, handwriting would be eliminated and grammar rules would be bypassed through spellcheck. This will contribute to the ignorance of students and their inability to work without tablets or technology in the future. Handwriting and grammar would both suffer as a result of extensive tablet use.

Conclusion

'Tablets over textbooks' remains a luxury for the Indian education system. In a system where even the basic infrastructure is not in place, the use of technology to bridge the digital divide remains a distant dream. But if efforts are made to connect parts of India through the internet and tablets do replace textbooks, it will represent a quantum leap in the Indian education system. Technology can make us more capable and using tablets instead of textbooks will utilise the benefits of this scientific innovation. It will also revolutionise education.

33. NATIONAL WEALTH DECIDES INDIVIDUAL HAPPINESS!

Does the prosperity of an individual affect the economic health of his or her nation or vice versa? Does national wealth reflect the individual degree of happiness with the quality of life? Most of us are familiar with phrases like 'Most things in life are free. For the rest, use MasterCard!' or 'Anyone who says money cannot buy happiness just does not know where to shop.' How does national wealth translate into individual happiness of citizens or is the 'rags to riches story' only for a select few? Does the prosperity of a nation determine the prosperity of an individual and his or her consequent happiness? Let us examine both sides of the coin and see where the truth of the matter lies.

Yes

1. **Enough money is needed to cover basic needs:** Fundamental needs such as food, clothing, and shelter can only be met if you have cash. The more money you have, the greater is the amount of products and services you can buy, and these material objects give you a certain amount of satisfaction.
2. **Money makes you happier:** Gross Domestic Product (GDP) has a direct link to individual happiness and Gross National Happiness. Consider studies which show that citizens of developed countries are happier.
3. **Happiness research shows correlation between national wealth and personal happiness:** Studies measuring national wealth and personal levels of happiness have found a robust link between the level of economic development of a country and its people's happiness levels.
4. **Economic growth means longer and healthier lives:** A wealthy nation has more resources to invest in research and development as well as healthcare and this means a better, longer and happier life for its citizens.
5. **Social barriers are removed with economic prosperity:** Greater national wealth reduces income inequalities and erases divisions between communities in society, thereby contributing to peace, happiness, and social harmony.

No

1. **Other considerations matter:** While money makes us happier, other considerations such as how to spend the money, how much wealth you have compared with others, and the way you think about your time also play an important role in the equation.
2. **The paradox of riches:** Income has only a modest effect on happiness, as per the Easterlin Paradox, which found that citizens of rich countries were not much more happier than those of poor or middle income countries.
3. **Money cannot buy happiness:** National wealth is not a reflection of the degree of contentment of a country's citizens because money cannot buy happiness. There are things far more important than money, such as social interaction, community bonds and non material attainments.
4. **Satisfaction with life transcends money:** Political leaders such as David Cameron and Nicholas Sarkozy have said happiness is the best way to gauge living standards of a nation rather than looking at its GDP.
5. **How national wealth is measured varies:** While there may be a robust correlation between individual well-being and national wealth, it does not imply causation. Moreover, national wealth can be measured in a number of ways so it is tough to assess the exact level of economic development of the country.
6. **People in poorer nations are happier:** Studies show that in poor nations also, people are leading happy lives.
7. **Level of wellbeing has not risen with level of income:** In Chile, China, and South Korea, studies have shown that per capital income doubled within 2 decades yet surveys show some amount of decline in life satisfaction of the citizens belonging to these countries.
8. **Relative income matters only on the margins:** Levels of economic development differ across countries and being rich in a rich nation may not be as advantageous as being so in a poor nation.
9. **Spending on little things makes us happy:** Even if you spend money on less expensive things, you may cherish and remember them more. High quality relationships may create a greater degree of happiness than having lots of cash.
10. **People may not get equal shares of the pie:** When it comes to wealth distribution, income inequalities may create a situation where rich get richer and poor get poorer. In such a situation, a rise in national wealth will not impact the happiness and well-being of poor people.
11. **Prosperity is not always equated with happiness:** Well being is a state of the mind and there are many reasons why happiness may be denied to wealthy persons as well. Consequently, a rise in national wealth is not related to the well being of the nation's citizens.

Conclusion

National wealth has an important role to play in individual well-being only if there is distributive justice. In the face of rising economic inequalities and lack of social justice, a country may be very rich but a majority of its citizens could have a poor quality if life. Money may not buy happiness, but it does provide for meeting the basic needs of life and human existence. Provided that income inequality is eliminated, national wealth can influence individual happiness.

34. TABLETS SHOULD REPLACE TEXTBOOKS IN INDIAN EDUCATION SYSTEM!

Advanced nations all over the world are equipping children with tablets instead of textbooks. Now, with an increasing emphasis on Digital India, can Indian schools and colleges also look to empower students by providing them with tablets? Can technology be used to bridge the digital divide? Let us examine if Indian educational institutions can provide better learning assistance to children!

Tablets should Replace Textbooks

1. **Multimedia learning provides an edge** – Difficulty in remembering what was taught previously can be eliminated through interactive learning across multiple mediums.
2. **Tablets offer graphical representations that are 3D** – Tablets offer more complex visual and graphical representation making it easier to understand the subject. You can also cover better illustrations and graphical descriptions using tablets as these provide scope for deeper, richer, more meaningful diagrams.
3. **More affordable** – Using textbooks for students scores low on affordability. If the entire amount spent on textbooks for a single year is calculated, it will be more than the price of an average tablet. Also tablets can be reprogrammed and used across successive years as against textbooks which can only be used for that particular grade.
4. **Reduce the weight of schoolbags** – Using tablets will reduce the burden of carrying thick textbooks and associated instruments which require separate toolboxes. Research studies have shown students should carry less than 15 per cent of their own weight in terms of schoolbags or backpacks. This is no longer a reality in present day conditions. Using a tablet would lighten the burden on the students
5. **Tablets are eco-friendly** – Taking notes on tablets would save paper. Schools would find the use of tablets more cost effective as well as eco-friendly. Moreover, presentations, tests, assignments and projects could

be interactively handled through tablets providing a rich and affordable learning experience at nominal costs to the environment.

Tablets can't be a Replacement for Textbooks

1. **Tablets are distracting** – Addictive games, social networking and media sites and other distractions would take away from studying time and act as unnecessary and unrequited distractions for the students.
2. **Taking care of tablets is costlier** – Textbooks are easier to maintain. Students will not be able to take care of tablets in schools and public places, especially if they have to travel long distances.
3. **Lost or dead tablets can be a real problem** – Lost notes, textbooks and assignments will be the result of a malfunctioning or misplaced tablet
4. **Tablets require heavy maintenance** – Tablets are gadgets that require extensive maintenance and repair and children would have to get used to studying on tablets rather than textbooks.
5. **Students may face health problems** – Using technology such as tablets for extended hours can lead to health problems such as Computer Vision Syndrome, strain on eyes, head and blurred vision as well as carpal tunnel syndrome and orthopaedic problems.
6. **Internet is costly** – In many rural and isolated areas, Internet has not yet made its mark and tablets would prove counterproductive. Moreover, internet connections with high bandwidth will make education costlier for parents and create monetary hurdles.
7. **Bad impact on grammar and handwriting** – With the use of tablets, handwriting would be eliminated and grammar rules would be bypassed through spellcheck. This will contribute to the ignorance of students and their inability to work without tablets or technology in the future. Handwriting and grammar would both suffer as a result of extensive tablet use.

Conclusion

Tablets over textbooks remains a luxury for the Indian education system. In a system where basic infrastructure is not even in place, the use of technology to bridge the digital divide remains a distant dream. But if efforts are made to connect parts of India through the Internet and tablets do replace textbooks, it will represent a quantum leap in the Indian education system. Technology can make us more capable and using tablets instead of textbooks will utilise the benefits of this scientific innovation. It will also revolutionise education.

35. NET NEUTRALITY – ADVANTAGES AND DISADVANTAGES

The net neutrality debate is not only waging in India, but across the world. After all what is net neutrality and why is there so much controversy surrounding the matter? In simplest terms, net neutrality can be defined as the principle that all internet traffic must be treated equally. The supporters of net neutrality are of the view that internet service providers should not have any right to restrict certain forms of internet traffic on their respective networks. Do you agree? Are you in support of net neutrality?

Advantages

- Big telecom companies can provide ways but do not have any right to direct how people should walk on them. They cannot differentiate between different groups.
- Net neutrality has remained a core democratising tenet of the internet since the time it came into existence.
- Net neutrality protects innovation and if big companies like Google and Netflix could pay to get exceptional treatment, more bandwidth, faster speeds, the new start-up firms would be at a disadvantage.
- It will also negatively affect freedom of speech. In the absence of net neutrality, big companies could give priority to TV networks from videos it owns and slow down the signals from its peers.
- Net neutrality supports a competitive marketplace and provides a chance to every firm, from big companies to small start-ups, to take part in it.
- If net was not neutral, Google, Facebook, or Zomato would not have been able to reach where they are today. Curbing netizens' right to a neutral net will be a big blow for budding entrepreneurs.

Disadvantages

- Times have changed. Today, YouTube and Netflix clog the pipes with huge amounts of data. Users download an insane amount of software, music, and movies illegally. The changes will put a restriction.
- Various companies like Google have created services that allow people to make calls for free on networks that telecom companies have spent billions to build. Net neutrality is injustice to these companies.
- Net neutrality does not protect innovation, but stifles it. If telecom companies can charge higher fees to the prime bandwidth hogs, they can also afford to develop advanced fiber networks that support all forms of new internet services.

- Some level of prioritisation or restriction is essential to support the best interest of consumers as a whole.
- Bandwidth is definitely a limited commodity and regulation will help restrict illegal use of the platform.

Conclusion

The internet has grown at an exceptional pace since its inception in the early 1990s, and this extraordinary growth is largely due to the freedom and protection that net neutrality offers. Groundbreaking ideas and novel products like YouTube, Google, eBay, and torrents have reached where they are because of net neutrality. There are thousands of new online stores, start-ups, and simple ecommerce sites that hope to make it big every day. Net neutrality promotes creative expression.

36. DIGITAL INDIA INITIATIVES AND THEIR ADVANTAGES

'All one needs is a computer, a network connection, and a bright spark of initiative and creativity to join the economy.' – Don Tapscott

This is increasingly becoming true nowadays. The Digital India initiative aims to transform India into a digitally empowered society and knowledge economy. It aims to connect entire India digitally in a span of 4 years, i.e. till 2018-19.

Envisaged by the Department of Electronics and Information Technology (DeitY), the vision of Digital India focuses on – Digital Infrastructure as a utility to every citizen, governance and services on demand, and digital empowerment of citizens. It wants to bridge the digital divide and bring India at par with the developed nations. It will combine many existing schemes related to e-governance, an other digital initiatives; restructure them and implement them in a synchronized manner under the umbrella initiative named as 'Digital India'.

Initiatives under Digital India and their Advantages

The main initiative under Digital India is the 'National Optic Fiber Network'. Started much earlier in 2011, it was an ambitious programme to connect 2.5 lakh Gram Panchayats through broadband. It would be pursued with renewed vigor, planning and monitoring.

The Nine pillars of growth areas which would be focused on:

- **Broadband Highways** – High speed connectivity and high speed internet
- **Universal Access to Mobile Connectivity** – To reach inaccessible areas also
- **Public Internet Access Programme** – Connect India to the world and newer ideas. It is a National Rural Internet Mission.

- **E-Governance** – Improving governance using technology. This is to improve the government to citizen interface for various service deliveries.
- **E-Kranti** – Deliver services electronically, and thus, in a faster and time-bound manner. This is helpful in education, healthcare, planning, security, financial inclusion, justice, farmers, etc.
- **Information for all** – This will bring in transparency and accountability by giving easy and open access to documents and information to the citizens.
- **Electronics manufacturing** – This will encourage manufacturing of electronics in India, reduce electronics imports and help in job creation too. This will help in achieving the goals of the 'Make in India' initiative also.
- **IT for jobs** – Employment opportunities will be increased and the training aspect will be focused on under the 'Skill India' programme. Focus will be more on IT training.
- **Early Harvest programme** – This has a number of programmes under it, which are to be implemented within a short timeline. They addresses development in a variety of sectors like education (school as well as university level), weather forecast, telecom, social problems like lost and found children, etc.
  - Cloud facility will be available. Thus, all government documents/certificates will be available on the Cloud.
  - The digital resources/services will be available in Indian languages.
  - 'MyGov.in' will help in participative governance.
  - Financial transactions would become cashless above a threshold.
  - Safe and secure cyber space would be provided.
  - Many other minor initiatives and services will be provided digitally by the government. It has already started providing many online services.
  - All the above initiatives will open up opportunities for Indian manufacturers and entrepreneurs, thus helping create employment in a direct and indirect way.

A Note on Digital India

- Digital India is a modified and expanded version of the national E-governance plan. It seeks to deliver all government services electronically.
- It also will address the issues of public accountability and transparency through a unique ID and E-Pramaan based on authentic and standard government applications. Fully online delivery will help a lot in this venture. It will reduce corruption.
- Though it may not be a new vision, the energy and efforts that are being put in are noteworthy. The budget is increased almost five-folds.

- It will benefit many sectors like IT/ITeS, power sector, education sector, telecom sector, electronics manufacturing sector, banking and financial sectors, etc.
- It will connect the entire expanse of India and bring to the forefront all the hidden talent and entrepreneurs that constitute the country's future.
- It will help in achieving universal digital literacy.
- A dedicated monitoring committee headed by the PM as chairman is constituted to oversee the target achievement in a time bound manner.
- This project will certainly help in improving the ease of doing business. India ranked 134 in terms of ease of doing business in 2014 as per the World Bank.
- The government's resolve to implement such an ambitious programmes can be seen in the JAM trinity solution – Jan Dhan Yojana for financial inclusion and direct benefit transfers based on Aadhaar infrastructure and mobile interface for banking. Tele-medicines, Smart cities, Digital Locker System, eSign, eHospital, Digitize India Platform (DIP) for large scale digitisation of records, etc., are other programmes which will be implemented. This project will definitely help us in increasing productivity and reap our demographic dividend.

37. SHOULD INDIA GET BACK ITS *KOHINOOR* FROM THE BRITISH?

Introduction

Ever since Narendra Modi was sworn in as Prime Minister, there have been three notable pieces of history that have been returned by other countries. The tenth century Indian statue of Goddess Durga from Germany, the 900-year-old 'Parrot Lady' sculpture from Canada, and the antique statue of Hindu deities from Australia. It should be noted that these historical pieces were stolen from India and later found in the museums of these countries.

With hopes high, Indians are looking up to PM Modi for bringing back the famous thirteenth century diamond that was stolen, or perhaps gifted to England under the terms of the Last Treaty of Lahore. It has long been under dispute with various claims from various dynasties and even our neighboring countries are trying to lay hands on the piece of stone that is worth a fortune.

Soon after its independence, India made claims and requests about the diamond being rightfully ours and for its return but each time British government declined the requests with their own excuses. History has only so much to say about the diamond that creates fuss that has no end but with the assurance from Modi Government that it would do everything to bring back Kohinoor, there seems hope.

Yes

1. **Rules of gifting:** History has it that the diamond was gifted to Queen Victoria by the 13-year-old Maharaja Duleep Singh, the last Sikh ruler as a part of treaty to end a conflict. There could have been not much choice of the Giver in this as it would have been laid down as a strict term of the treaty. Surely a 13-year-old child is in no state to give out such huge gifts to anyone, even though he inherited them from his ancestors. Later, he also wrote to the British Government to claim the diamond back, which is evidence enough for the British to return back our heritage.
2. **Origin:** The *Kohinoor* was mined from Gantur in Andhra Pradesh and first owned by the Kakatiya Dynasty in the thirteenth century. It was then passed over, or actually possessed in loot, by the Khilji Dynasty, which later went into the hands of Babar during the reign of the Delhi Sultanate. After being passed, on to various other hands in the same pattern of inheriting and looting, it came to the possession of the Sikh Emperor, Maharaja Ranjit Singh.
3. **Will:** *Maharaja* Ranjit Singh willed the diamond to the Hindu temple of Jagannath in Puri, Odisha. After his death, the East India Company did not execute his will, which was a shame. Instead, after the Second Anglo-Sikh War, when Punjab was annexed by British India, they eyed the diamond and desired to possess it. When the last treaty of Lahore was signed, the British made sure that the soils of war included the famous *Kohinoor*. Rightfully, the diamond should be in possession of the Puri temple, to which it was willed by the last owner.
4. **One of the many looted wealth:** Laying it out in paper and ink does not make a loot any less of a theft possession. During their reign, the British destroyed and plundered our wealth to a great extent. While some countries have showed friendly gestures by returning the artifacts, Britain is still proud and arrogant of its colonialism. Giving back *Kohinoor* or any other artifact that rightfully belongs to our country should not have been so much of a problem for them otherwise.
5. **Holocaust Act:** The group named after *Kohinoor*, 'Mountain of Light', is trying to get back the diamond and they can rightfully base their case on the Holocaust law, which gives national institutions in the U.K. the power to return artefacts that have been stolen from another country.

No

1. **Obsessing over what is lost:** We have been trying so hard since independence to get hands our on what we do not have that we are failing to pay heed to and preserve what we have. The age old monuments are losing their charm, some ancient ones are so ill-managed that they are being depleted to ruins.

Scribbling on walls of these monuments has never ceased and yet we want our artefacts back with made-up excuse of retaining our historical heritage.

2. **What is gifted is not stolen:** Whatever the condition and situation was during the annexation of Punjab, it is said that the last *Maharaja* travelled all the way to the U.K. and presented the Kohinoor to Her Majesty, the Queen. It was given as gift or soils of war if we like to call it but that is not coming back and we have to accept that instead of brooding all over history trying to find facts that could support our views despite knowing the truth to be otherwise.
3. **Multiple claims:** There have been many claims of the diamond being rightfully theirs by Pakistan and Afghanistan. The descendants of Ranjit Singh want it too. Even the Talibans are eyeing it greedily. Next, we might see Iranians making similar claims based on the historical fact that Nader Shah also possessed it once. And even if we get back the *Kohinoor*, what next? The priests of Puri will want to have it as per the will. The *Dalits* will be agitated for they have long accused that it was harsh the *Brahmins* of Puri who gave the diamond to the British. Hyderabad will also claim it to be returned to its origin in Golconda. The Telugu priests of Warangal will want it in their temple. Dwarka Priests have their own claim of the diamond belonging originally to Krishna. The government might put it on display under high security, and yet there will be many who will try to trespass, and hence, we will have a new lot of problems to deal with. Does India really want it back?
4. **Breaking relations with UK:** We do need better relations with all other countries at such crucial times when we are trying for better days for our people and, at the same time fighting terrorism and corruption. Making constant claims on a diamond that was given away long before any evidences could mark their origin will only loosen ties with the U.K., which is not something we look forward to. What is gone is gone. We need to get over it already.

Conclusion

The Modi government earlier made the statement that the *Kohinoor* was gifted and could not be brought back which was very apt but unfortunately, there was controversy on that and the government had to take its famous U-turn and make the promise of trying to bring the diamond back, which is not going to be possible unless and until Britain gets inexplicably impressed by our PM and decides to gift it back. We do not see that happening, and hence, there does not seem to be any point in making claims and bringing up lawsuits. There is lack of evidence of its being stolen while there are testimonies of its being gifted. It may have belonged to us once, but it does not anymore, which we need to accept and take care of what we have.

38. WEAK CAN NEVER FORGIVE; FORGIVENESS IS THE ATTRIBUTE OF THE STRONG!

Introduction

Vengeance brings plunder and distress to one's soul whereas forgiveness brings peace, both to others and you. In the present day world, when we are so easily frustrated to revenge and hit back at someone who could have done us wrong in any way, forgiveness does not come easy.

When Mahatma Gandhi said, 'The weak can never forgive; forgiveness is the attribute of the strong,' he meant it with his heart and soul, but we talk of forgiveness only in vague terms. We do not really want to forget, forgive, and move on. We keep holding grudges, either to retaliate when the time is right or take it our graves with us. Are we really getting weaker and weaker if Mahatma Gandhi is to be believed?

It does take a big heart to forgive someone for his past mistakes and give him a chance to prove that he really is regretful and wants to make things better with you. It should not classify you as weak or strong, but the fact remains that forgiving does not come easy. The world will indeed be so much of a better place if people could learn to let go of grudges instead of letting go of the relationship they have with the person in question.

For

1. **Being secure:** An insecure person cannot forgive. Unless you are confident and secure in yourself and you position, you cannot have it in you to come forth and forgive someone. You have to be contended with the fact that the person does not have the strength over you to keep you stressed forever. Even if you are hurt, you have to understand that it is only temporary and in the long run, it would not really matter to you. Whatever the person did to you shouldn't have the power to keep you begrudged forever.
2. **Focus on important things:** You cannot focus your mind on anything else when you are carrying the anger of hurt and wanting revenge from someone. If you have other important things in life to concentrate on, it is best for you to forgive the person and shift your focus to things that are more important for you. If you give the person that power over you to keep you from doing essential things in life, you are definitely not strong enough to prioritise your things.
3. **Makes you a better person:** Forgiving not just makes you a stronger person, but a better person at heart. You feel lighter as if a burden has been lifted off you. Your mind gets to have its much needed peace and this brings positivity in life. Brooding on negative thoughts of vengeance and rivalry brings negative vibes in life, which is not something that could make you

strong as a person. You have to realise that you do not want to get even with the person who has hurt you, not to fall low to his standards, but to rise above him. This definitely takes strength.

4. **Breaking the ice:** If you hold on to past conflicts, you lose a friend or someone who was once close to you. Maybe your friend too would be waiting to talk to you, but does not have it in him to make the first move. To be the first one to initiate remaking a connection takes strength. If you are strong and confident, you can go forth and try to talk to the person. Initiating conversation, hearing his views on what went wrong in the past, and if he is willing to make up for it, putting forth your views will go help ahead to make things better.
5. **Hatred does no good:** Holding anger and grudges is a poison. It eats you from inside. We think that hating is a weapon that attacks the person who annoyed us, but it is, in fact, a curved blade and the harm we do, we do to ourselves. Hurting yourself for someone else's mistake is definitely a weakness. You are giving the person the power to affect you in the long run. If you are strong enough, you will be able to realise that it is not worth holding onto anger and hurting yourself with it. Life has so much more to offer. What you cannot change the past, your future lies in your hands to be shaped the way your actions choose to.

Against

1. **Learning from mistake:** If we keep forgiving people for the wrong they did to us, we give them the opportunity to repeat it with us or with anyone else. You cannot forgive and let go of a thief without teaching him a lesson or making him pay for his deeds. He will only get encouraged and try bigger crimes if you simply see him one fine day and say, 'It is okay, I forgave you for it.' That will be like saying, 'you are welcome for another burglary session in my house.'
2. **Intentions matter:** Some mistakes get made unintentionally or because of negligence, but there are others who do it knowingly to make other people suffer. There are psychopaths and sadists who derive pleasure from harming others. They should not and cannot be forgiven. Forgiving them would not make you any stronger, but only an ignorant person. A girl cannot forgive someone who molested her in the past, even if that person happens to be a closely related man.
3. **Do not torture yourself but do not live in denial too:** You may want to come out of the tragic incident, and that you must do, but at the same time you cannot simply forgive the person and pretend that it never happened to you. It was not your mistake so you should not dwell on it to give you nightmares, but in order not to trust in those kind of people again, you need

to stay reminded at the back of your mind that it is not worth relying on such kind of people. It is precautionary behavior and not weakness.

4. **Not unless he is sorry and he means it:** People play with your trust, use your good nature to plot their evil plans. These kind of people are not just few in number. If you act like a sheep, there will be thousands of lions to tread you down. Do not forgive the person and grant him access to your life unless you are sure that he is guilty and would not think of repeating the same mistake twice. Marriages that should have ended long back due to domestic violence continue to stay mended because the innocent wife was too forgiving every time he asked for a last chance. We all know it sometimes ends badly in tragic deaths and irreparable damage.
5. **Your rights:** He made a grave mistake and you had to deal with the consequences. When the turmoil is over and you begin to sort out your life, he comes back for forgiveness at your feet. You must know that it is your rights, whether you want to forgive him or not. Do not be bound by morals that teach you what to do for they were written in a certain context and yours could be a totally different one. If you are not free of the traumatic effect of the hurt, do not forgive him.

Conclusion

Yes, forgiveness makes your heart and soul free. You feel better when you forgive but it is also important to know if the person really deserves to be forgiven or not.

If someone hurts you, forgive him for his deed as it will ultimately make you feel lighter, but at the same, time do not be *naïve* to let them misuse your goodness again.

Every unpleasant experience should give you a lesson in life and then you should move on!

39. SHOULD MALE SPORTSPERSONS EARN MORE MONEY THAN THEIR FEMALE COUNTERPARTS?

Introduction

At BNP Paribas Open tennis tournament, the real game started off the court when CEO Raymond Moore made sexist comments at the expense of women tennis players asking them to thank God for all the publicity that the sports gets due to famous players like Roger Federer and Rafa Nadal. This did not go down well with Serena Williams and other female tennis players, who aptly answered Moore to the extent of making him apologise for his poor words.

If that was not enough of a controversy, world's top men's player, Novak Djokovic, added more fuel to fire by saying that men should fight for more money since their matches were more popular compared to the female counterparts.

There have been outcry from various sports to support equal pay money for both men and women but it cannot be said that every sport advocates it. However, tennis does advocate equal prize money for male and female players to a great extent. But since top notch players are asking for inequality, is there a point in advocating the same in this sport?

Yes

1. **Popularity:** The revenue generated out of a game does come out from the popularity of the match and the number of spectators worldwide. If it is a proven theory that men's matches are more popular, watched and liked by more people around the world, it puts more pressure on players to perform better, and there is nothing wrong in asking for more pay compared to the female counterparts whose the matches are comparatively less lucrative.
2. **Because all other sports do the same:** Most sports do offer more money to male players as compared to women players owing to the same fact that there is less profit being raised from female sports matches. Well, Djokovic did go on to say that women should be paid more if their tennis could one day go on to become more popular and profitable. The popularity of cricket, for instance, is confined to the matches of men and hence they are paid more than women playing cricket. How is it that no one even brought this up with cricket?
3. **Sheer business:** Everyone has the right to fight for what they think is correct. Women players, at many levels, have fought for their rights and have rightfully claimed what they should be getting. If Novak feels he needs to fight for more pay because of generating more spectators, selling more tickets, being more profitable for the tennis associations, it is up to him to raise such requests. There is no harm coming from doing pure business, which does call for distribution of pay, owing to their contribution in generating profit from ticket sales and TV viewing figures.
4. **The same could go for women:** There are times when women's tennis matches have more spectators compared to men's, like the US Open last year, when women's finals tickets sold out before men's. If pay is distributed on the basis of profit generation, there could be times when women will earn more than men. It is also to be mentioned that men play five sets at the Grand Slams, while in all other matches, both men and women play three sets.

No

1. **Wrong data:** The popularity and success of tennis as a sport is an equal contribution of both men and women. It would be absolutely wrong to say that men like Federer and Djokovic alone contribute to the popularity of

this sport. The William sisters, Maria Sharapova, Kim Clijsters, Sania Mirza, and many more are much more popular and most spectators can attest to the fact that they watch tennis only for these players.

2. **Strength and stamina:** It is a misconception that women are made of delicate stuff, and hence, they are unable to play longer matches like the five sets. It is in fact in the rules book that has defined the sets at Grand Slams and neither men nor women have any say in that. As far as the endurance and body limits of women are concerned, as stated by Novak, women have always proved that they are made of sterner stuff and do not, in any way, treat their body as a weakness, be it the harshest time of the month.
3. **Popularity on rise:** It is a clear statistical fact that the popularity of women's tennis and the inspiration that girls draw from them it on the constant escalation. Recent figures have shown that tickets for women's matches have sold out faster than those of men. Moreover, pay should not depend of popularity figures at all. US female soccer stars earn comparatively less than their male counterparts, even though their popularity is far higher than those of men's matches.
4. **Equal pay in other sports:** Figure skating and gymnastics attract more spectators and viewers worldwide for their women's competitions as compared to their male counterparts and yet, the pay statistics are equal, which is the reason why players of both genders are equally inspired to work harder for the sport, regardless of popularity. Equal pay does help in attracting players from both sides to aspire for the sport and pursue it with motivation.
5. **Media support:** The fact that women's matches garner less support is owing to the fact that media often provides them with lesser coverage and publicity as compared to men's matches, where sponsorship is also high owing to high publicity. They are less endorsed and hence suffer from the problem of publicity. Lowering the pay would only lessen the popularity and decrease motivation of those aspiring to be sportswomen in years to come.

Conclusion

They work equally harder, they face equal problems sometimes, even more yet never complain or ask for special care, they are equally talented and have struggled their way to the top – there is no reason why women should be thought of as the weaker sex and paid lesser than their male counterparts.

Tennis has always been an inspiration for all sportswomen who believe that equality could be achieved in times to come. Examples of tennis are given when people advocate for equal pay and that makes the sport shine in both the matches – of men and women. Creating bias on basis of popularity would make it sheer business and lessen the sport spirit that prevails in the game.

Raising the pay of male players would only take us back to time where women were considered less competitive and weaker enough to not try and be at par with men.

40. MANAGERS ARE BORN, NOT TRAINED

Managing is an art. It cannot be acquired overnight.

For

- There are numerous management schools. The schools and college exist are because none of the managers are born trained.
- Like every professional today goes through his respective studies, managers need to as well.
- No one is a born an actor, actress, doctor, or engineer. Neither are managers.
- Management may be a very general term. However, each manager needs to excel in his stream. Different forms of managerial skills are required for each stream. They need to be trained.
- Management does not merely include managing people and work; it requires administrative techniques as well. These cannot be inbuilt.
- Management involves professionalism as well. This can certainly not be inbuilt. It needs to be taught.

Against

- Looking at people around (especially mothers), few people get the art of management.
- Management is quite a practical aspect. It can not be taught through theory in colleges.
- Most of us, through daily experiences, can become managers. It cannot be taught through training.
- Most of the successful businessmen today may not have a management degree. This is simply because management is not something that can be taught. It is inbuilt.
- Even though training may impart some knowledge, the skill of management can be influenced from people around.

Hence, even though managers may be born trained or not, professionalism, respect to others is what matters the most. If all of this is acquired, a manager will always excel.

41. EXAMINATIONS – HAVE THEY IT KILLED EDUCATION?

It is true that examinations help to evaluate an individual academically, however following are some negative aspects:

- Exams unnecessarily pressurise students.
- In India especially, there are many exams annually. Students have barely any time for extra curricular activities.
- Most of the exams' structures and designs are not sufficient to evaluate the real capabilities of the student.
- Exams in India are based on marks. Grades can be an appropriate mechanism.

If exams can be a curse, they can also help a child:

- It help the students stay connected to their books and keep them on their toes.
- Exams help students understand pressure, which they will face in their professional lives.
- Exams help in facing competition.
- If students are only taught, there is no way to judge if they have understood what is being taught.

Exams should not be theoretical. Most questions should be multiple choice and objective to really understand the analytical ability of the child.

As long as exams are not very theoretical and are prepared to evaluate a student's understanding ability rather than marks, examinations are definitely important. Moreover, it should be understood that judging a student merely on marks cannot be justified.

42. IMPACT OF COVID-19 (CORONAVIRUS) ON THE GLOBAL ECONOMY

- COVID-19 (Coronavirus Disease 2019) was first identified in Wuhan city of China in December 2019. Till now (10 July 2020) approximately 5,50,000 people have died due to this virus and nearly 1.2 crore people have been affected by it.
- This virus has spread to the entire world.
- On 30 January, the World Health Organisation (WHO) declared COVID-19 as a Public Health Emergency of International concern.
- Coronaviruses (CoV) are a group of viruses that affect animals and humans. The first coronavirus that can affect humans was discovered in the 1960s. Before COVID-19, this family of viruses caused the SARS outbreak in China in 2002, and the MERS outbreak in Saudi Arabia in 2012.
- COVID-19 is not just affecting the health of the people, but also economies of many countries. So the topic – 'Impact of COVID-19 on the Global Economy' is widely discussed.

Impact

- Many people lost jobs, and the informal sector is badly hit. This is a huge setback for economies.

- Due to the consumption slowdown in the world, exports and imports are affected. This affects the economies of almost all countries.
- Movement of people is restricted due to the fear of further spread of COVID-19, and hence the tourism industry is facing huge losses. Tourists spend money in the countries they visit, so the loss of this money is affecting the economies of many countries.
- Due to low demand for fuel, crude oil prices have dropped. Low crude oil prices are beneficial to oil-importing countries like India and detrimental to the economies of OPEC (Organisation of petroleum exporting countries) and countries like Saudi Arabia.
- According to the World Trade Organisation (WTO), China is the biggest exporter and the second-biggest importer of merchandise as of 2019. Many industries in other countries are depending on China for many raw goods such as pharmaceutical ingredients, automobile components, etc. So, the coronavirus has hit global supply chains badly. As many factories in China were closed at the start of the pandemic, production has halted for the dependent companies in other countries. Some companies are going for alternatives, which is the costlier option.
- Pharmaceutical companies, and hygiene products manufacturing companies are benefitting from this situation.

Conclusion

COVID-19 caused severe damage to the global economy. Nations are trying hard to rebuild their economies and to prevent further downfall. Hope the vaccine is developed soon to prevent further loss of lives and also the collapse of economies.

43. HOW COVID-19 DEEPENS THE DIGITAL EDUCATION DIVIDE IN INDIA

- A total of 320 million learners in India have been adversely affected by the COVID-19 pandemic and have transitioned to e-learning;
- With huge regional and household disparities in access to the internet and technology, this transition has not been possible for all students and educators;
- The rapid shift to e-learning prompted by the pandemic has resurfaced long-standing issues of inequality and a digital divide in India that must be addressed by future economic, education, and digitalisation policies.

The education system in India is facing a new crisis thanks to COVID-19. Besides the effect on short-term learning outcomes, extended school closures will result in a loss of human capital and diminished economic opportunities in the long run.

What does This Mean for India and its People?

India has the world's second-largest school system, after China. The pandemic has not only caused the wide rift in educational inequality to balloon but also exacerbated existing disparities.

A total of 320 million learners in India have been adversely affected and transitioned to the e-learning industry, which comprises a network of 1.5 million schools. An NSSO 2014 report highlights that 32 million children were already out of school before the pandemic

E-learning, as the name suggests, relies on the availability and accessibility of technology, but little or no availability of electricity is a significant challenge to taking advantage of education online. In a recent 2017-18 survey, the Ministry of Rural Development found that only 47 per cent of Indian households receive more than 12 hours of electricity and more than 36 per cent of schools in India operate without electricity.

NSSO 2014-2015 data suggests that economic factors are critical to children dropping out of school in India. The pandemic and lockdown have affected 1.4 million migrant workers and others working in the unorganised sector (90 per cent of India's population is engaged in disorganised work).

According to the Key Indicators of Household Social Consumption on Education in India report, based on the 2017-18 NSSO, fewer than 15 per cent of rural Indian households have internet access (as opposed to 42 per cent urban Indian households). Of the mere 13 per cent of people surveyed (aged above five) in rural areas—just 8.5 per cent of females—could use the internet.

The scope of e-learning is enormous and can help realise the potential of each student. There lie both opportunities and challenges for the government and the private sector. The aim should be to ensure equal and adequate access to such platforms as the country continues to globalise and catch up with advanced economies. If the Indian education system aims to transit to online learning in the future, it must emphasise policies that bridge the digital divide and move the country closer to achieving the Sustainable Development Goals.

44. WORK FROM HOME: PROS AND CONS

What is a Work from Home Job?

A work from home job is a job you can perform from home. They often require an internet connection so you can collaborate and network with colleagues and managers. Working from home—or telecommuting—gives employees the flexibility and freedom to perform their work tasks from their home offices.

Pros of Working from Home

More Independence

Working from home can provide autonomy and independence in your job that might be absent in a physical workplace

No Commute to Work

Work from home jobs mean you can eliminate your commute. Even if you work from home one or two days during the week, you travel less.

Save on Expenses

When you eliminate commuting, you can reduce your fuel and transportation expenses. Telecommuting can also help you reduce other expenses like work clothing, meals, and even childcare.

Increased Productivity

When you work independently in a quieter environment, you may be more productive. Increased productivity relates to several factors including the ability to move around your home freely and take breaks.

Improved Technical Skills

Telecommuting often requires using technical applications such as online meeting, communication, and team collaboration platforms. You are able to develop technical skills that you may not typically use in a physical workplace.

Improved Communication Skills

Working from home requires consistent communication between teams and managers, which likely requires more emails, phone calls, video calls, and chats in messaging platforms.

More Work Flexibility

You have a lot of flexibility with most telecommuting jobs. For instance, many work from home positions are unaffected by normal business hours, making it easier to attend to life events like medical appointments. Work from home roles can be a huge benefit for parents who work unconventional schedules to accommodate their families.

No Office Distractions

You have no office distractions when you work from home. Office noise like co-workers talking, office equipment running, or phones ringing can be highly distracting in a work environment. A home office does not have these same distractions.

Collaborate Across Locations

Telecommuting can be an advantage to multi-divisional companies that have office locations around the world. The ability to communicate with professionals in diverse areas can open additional paths for business development.

Reduction in Work Absences

Since working from home offers flexibility, it can also reduce work absences. Whether you are sick or have to schedule an important appointment, working from home can reduce how often you need to take a day off.

Increases Satisfaction

Employee satisfaction in remote positions may be higher because of the flexibility in performing their jobs. Not only are you able to make decisions independently, you are also able to work comfortably.

Cons of Working from Home

Increased Isolation

You can become quite isolated working from home if you spend the majority of your time by yourself, working independently.

Home Office Costs

Some remote positions require specific equipment like headsets, webcams, or software to perform essential tasks and projects. If you want to set up a desk, chair, and other furniture, you can expect to cover some initial costs to get your home office organised.

Risk of Overworking

Telecommuting also comes with a risk of working longer than you should. This can definitely lead to burn-out and increased work-related stress.

Distractions at Home

Distractions like the television, pets, or household chores can affect how you perform your job. Too many distractions can lead to a decrease in your productivity.

Workplace Disconnect

Telecommuting can sometimes lead to a disconnect between you and your co-workers. Working from home means you will not have access to immediate information about important business processes.

Less Face Time

With isolation and workplace disconnect comes less face time. Working remotely, you will not have the same opportunities to speak face-to-face with co-workers and the community unless you get out and about.

PART II
APTITUDE

Quantitative Aptitude and Reasoning

THEORY AND FORMULAE

1. **NUMBERS:** A number is denoted by group of digits called numerals.
   - Write the number in the place value chart.
   - E.g.: Nine crore four lakh six thousand and two.
   - Use the place value chart.

Crores	*Ten Lakhs*	*Lakhs*	*Ten Thousands*	*Thousands*	*Hundreds*	*Tens*	*Units*
9	0	4	0	6	0	0	2

   - 9 – crore
   - 4 – lakh
   - 6 – thousand
   - 2 – unit

2. FACE VALUE, AND PLACE VALUE (LOCAL VALUE)
   - **Face value:** It is its own value at what even place it may be.
   - **E.g.:** For the numeral 87,34,925, write down:
     i. Face value of 7 = 7
     ii. Face value of 9 = 9
     iii. Place value of 4 = (4 × 1,000) = 4,000
     iv. Place value of 8 = (8 × 10,00,000) = 80,00,000
     v. Place value of 5 = (5 × 1) = 5

Ten Lakhs	*Lakhs*	*Ten Thousands*	*Thousands*	*Hundreds*	*Tens*	*Units*
8	7	3	4	9	2	5

3. TYPES OF NUMBERS:
   i. Natural Numbers: counting numbers are known as natural numbers.
   N = 1, 2, 3, 4………
   ii. Whole Numbers: All counting numbers and '0' (zero) form the set of whole numbers.
   W = 0, 1, 2, 3, 4……...
   So, all natural numbers are whole numbers. 0 = whole number.
   iii. Integers: All counting numbers, zero, and negatives of counting numbers are integers.

$Z = -3, -2, -1, 0, 1, 2, 3$

iv. Even and odd numbers: A counting number divisible by 2 is called an even number.
   - 2, 4, 6, 8, 10, 12… = even numbers
   - A counting number not divisible by 2 is called an odd number
   - 1, 3, 5, 7, 9, 11… = odd numbers

v. Prime Numbers: A counting number is called a prime number if it has exactly two factors, itself and one (1).
   - A number divisible by one and itself.
   - 2, 3, 5, 7…
   - P = Given number and n = smallest counting number.
   - n2 > p
   - Test if 'p' is divisible by any prime number <= n;
   - If yes, p is not prime, else, 'p' is prime.
   - E.g.: 137 (Test whether it is prime)
     p = 137
     n = (12)2 ≥ p
     (12)2 = 144 ≥ 137
     Prime number < 12 = 2, 3, 5, 7, 11
     None of them divides 137; so, 137 is a prime number.

vi. Composite numbers: Natural numbers which are not prime numbers.
   - Numbers having factors other than one and themselves.
   - 4, 6, 8, 9, 10…

vii. Co-primes: Two natural numbers, a and b, are co-prime if their HCF is 1.
   - (2, 3); (4, 5); (7, 8) pairs of co-primes.

4. TEST OF DIVISIBILITY

- Divisibility by 2:
  A number is divisible by 2 if the unit digit is 0, 2, 4, 6, or 8
  E.g.: 58694 is divisible by 2.
- Divisibility by 3:
  If the sum of the digits is divisible by 3.
  E.g.: 695421
  Sum of the digits is 27. So, it is divisible by 3.
- Divisibility by 9:
  If the sum of its digits is divisible by 9.
  E.g.: 246591 = sum = 27 is divisible by 9.
- Divisible by 6: if the number is divisible by 2 and 3.
  E.g.: 654
- Divisibility by 7:
  Take the digits of the number in reverse order from right to left and multiply successively with 1, 3, 2, 6, 4, and 5 as long as necessary.

Add the products and check if it is divisible by 7.
Ex: 1603 is divisible by 7.
1603
$(3\times1) + (0\times3) + (6\times2) + (1\times6) = 21$
So, 1603 is divisible by 7.
Remove the last digit, double it, substract it from truncated original number and continue till only one digit remains. If the number is 0 or 7, then it is divisible by 7.
1603
160
$= 3 \times 2 = 6$
$160 - 6 = 154$
154
=15
$= 4 \times 2 = 8$
$= 15 - 8 = 7$
7 is divisible by 7.

- Divisible by 4:
  If the number formed by the last 2 digits is divisible by 4.
  6879376 = 76/4 = 19
- Divisibility by 8:
  If the number formed by H, T, U (last 3 digits) is divisible by 8 and if the last 3 digits are 000.
  16789352 = 352/8 = 44
- Divisibility by 10:
  If the unit digit is '0'.
- Divisibility by 5:
  If the digit is '0' or '5'.
  E.g.: 76895, 68790
- Divisibility by 11:
  Difference between the sum of digits at the odd places and sum of digits at the even places
  = 0 or multiple of 11
  (sum of digits at odd place) – (sum of digits at even place)
  = 0 or multiple of 11.
  E.g.: 29435417
  $(7 + 4 + 3 + 9) - (1 + 5 + 4 + 2) = (23 - 12)$
  = 11 is divisible by 11.
- Divisibility by 13 = Remove the last digit, multiply it by 4, and add the resultant to the remaining digit.

5. **SERIES / SEQUENCE (FORMULAE):**
   - $(1 + 2 + 3 + \ldots + n) = \dfrac{n(n+1)\,(2n+1)}{6}$ sum of n terms.
   - $(12 + 22 + 32 + \ldots + n^2) = \dfrac{n(n+1)\,(2n+1)}{6}$
   - $(13 + 23 + 33 + \ldots + n^3) = \left[\dfrac{n(n+1)}{2}\right]^2$
   - sum of first 'n' odd number = n^2;
   - sum of first 'n' even number = $n\,(n+1)$
6. ARITHMATIC PROGRESSION: (A.P)
   A series where the common difference remains the same.
   - 1, 2, 3, 4, …
   - $a, a + d, a + 2d, a + 3d \ldots$
   - a = first term
   - d = common difference
   - n = number of terms
   - l = last term
   - nth term = $a + (n - 1)\,d$
   - sum of 'n' terms = $n/2\,[\,2a + (n - 1)\,d]$
   - or = $n/2\,(a + l)$
7. GEOMETRIC PROGRESSION: (G.P)
   - A series where the common ratio remains the same a, ar, ar^2, ar^3
   - 1, 2, 4, 8, 16, …
   - a = first term
   - common ratio = r
   - last term = n
   - nth term = ar^{n-1}
   - sum of 'n' terms = $\left[\begin{array}{ll} \dfrac{a(1-r^n)}{(1-r)} & ;r<1 \\ \overline{(r-1)} & a(r^n-1);\, r>1 \end{array}\right.$

PRACTICE QUESTIONS

1. $839478 \times 625 = ?$
   $= 839478 \times (5)^4$
   $= 839478 \times (10/2)^4$
   $= \dfrac{839478 \times 10^4}{2^4}$

$= \frac{8394780000}{16}$

Ans. 524673750

2. $1396 \times 1396 = ?$

$(1396)^2$

$(1400 - 4)^2 = (a - b)^2 = a^2 + b^2 - 2ab$

$(1400)^2 + (4)^2 - 2 \times 1400 \times 4$

$1960000 + 16 - 11200$

Ans: 1948816

3. $(475 \times 475 + 125 \times 125) = ?$

$(a^2 + b^2) = \frac{[(a + b)^2 - (a - b)^2]}{2}$

$(475 + 125)^2 + (475 - 125)^2 \times 1/2$

$\frac{(600)^2 - (350)^2}{2}$

$\frac{360000 - 122500}{2}$

$\frac{241250}{2}$

Ans. 241250

Method 1 : $(a + b)^2 = a^2 + b^2 + 2ab$

$(a - b)^2 = a^2 + b^2 - 2ab$

$(a + b)^2 + (a - b)^2 = 2(a^2 + b^2)$

Method 2 : $(a + b)^2 = a^2 + b^2 + 2ab$

$(a + b)^2 - 2ab = a^2 + b^2$

$(475+125)^2 - 2 * 475 * 125$

$(600)^2 - 118750$

$360000 - 118750$

Ans. 241250

4. $(796 \times 796 - 204 \times 204) = ?$

$(a^2 - b^2) = (a + b)(a - b)$

$= (796 + 204)(796 - 204)$

$= 1000 \times 592$

Ans. 592000

5. Find the last value of 'x' for which 7x5462 is divisible by 9.

Let the required number be x.

Sum of the digits is divisible by 9

$(7 + x + 5 + 4 + 6 + 2) = (24 + x)$

$9 \times 3 = 27$

$24 + 3 = 27$

Ans. $x = 3$

6. Show that 52563744 is divisible by 24.
   $24 = 3 \times 8$
   Sum of the digits = 36 divisible by 3.
   Last three digits = 744/8 = 93 divisible by 8.
   Therefore, 52563744 is divisible by 24.
7. What is the least number that must be added to 2010 to obtain a number which is completely divisible by 19?
   Least number subtracted = Given number – remainder
   Least number added = Given number + divisor – remainder

   ```
   19) 2010(105
       19
        11
         0
        110
         95
         15
   ```

   R = 15 add 4 = 19/19 = divisible by 19.
   2010 + 4 = 2014/19 = 106 Ans
8. On dividing 12401 by a certain number we get 76 as the quotient and 13 as the remainder, what is the divisor?
   [Division × quotient] + Remainder = Dividend

   ```
   x) 12401 (76
        13
   ```

   12401 – 13 / 76 = 163 Ans
   Divisor = Dividend – Remainder / Quotient
9. On dividing a certain number by 342, we get 47 as remainder. If the same number is divided by 18, what will be the remainder?

   ```
   342)  x  (K (let)
        47
   ```

   Case 1: $R > y$, so the remainder of the smaller divisor = (R/y)
   Case 2: $R < y$, so the new remainder = 'R'
   Case 3: $R = (r^1 + r^2)$ – divisor.
   Let the quotient be 'k'.
   Number = $342 \times K + 47$
   $(18 \times 19)K + (18 \times 2) + 11$ (second time the same number is divided by 18)
   $18\,(19K + 2) + 11$ (Ans)
   So, the same number, when divided by 18, gives remainder 11.
10. Simplify: $\dfrac{(893 + 786)^2 - (893 - 786)^2}{2}$

$$\frac{(a+b)^2-(a-b)^2}{ab}=\frac{4ab}{ab} = 4 \text{ (ans)}$$

$$\frac{(a^2+b^2+2ab)-(a^2+b^2-2ab}{ab}=\frac{a^2+b^2+2ab-a^2-b^2+2ab}{ab}$$

$$=\frac{4ab}{ab}=4$$

11. Simplify: $\dfrac{658 \times 658 \times 658 - 328 \times 328 \times 328}{658 \times 658 + 658 \times 328 + 328 \times 328} = ?$

 $a^3 + b^3 = (a + b)(a^2 - ab + b^2)$ ...(1)
 $a^3 - b^3 = (a - b)(a^2 + ab + b^2)$ ...(2)
 $(a + b)^2 = a^2 + b^2 + 2ab$
 $(a - b)^2 = a^2 + b^2 - 2ab$
 $a^2 - b^2 = (a - b)\ (a - b)$

$$\frac{(658)^3 - (328)^3}{(658)^2 + 658 \times 328 + (328)^2}$$

$$\frac{a^3-b^3}{a^2+ab+b^2}=(a-b)$$

 = 658 – 328 = 330 (Ans)

12. What is the unit digit in $(264)^{102} + (264)^{103}$ = ?
 $(264)^{102}(1 + 264)$
 $(264)^{102} \times 265$
 Unit digit = $(4)^{102} \times 5$
 [Ud = $(4^4)^{25} \times (4)^2] \times 5$
 = $(4)^4 \times 4^2 \times 5$
 = 256 × 16 × 5
 = 6 × 6 × 5 = 180
 The unit digit is '0'
 4 odd power unit digit is always 4; 4 even power unit digit is always 6
 6 + 4 = 10 = unit digit = 0 (Ans.)

13. Find the remainder when 2^{31} is divided by 515 ?
 $(2)^{31} = (2^{10} \times 2^{10} \times 2^{10}) \times 2^1$
 $(210)^3 \times 2^1$
 $(1024)^3 \times 2^1$
 Unit digit = 4 × 2 = 8
 8/5 the reminder is 3 (Ans)

14. Find the sum of all even numbers less than 75.
 Required sum = 2 + 4 + 6 + 8 … + 74
 $a = 2$; $l = 74$; $d = (4 - 2) = 2$

$n = 74/2 = 37$
Required sum = Sum of n terms = $n/2\ (a + l)$
$37/2\ (2 + 74)$
$37/2 \times 76$
37×38
$37 \times (40 - 2)$
$(37 \times 40) - (37 \times 2)$
$1480 - 74$
1406 (Ans.)

15. Find the sum of $(2 + 2^2 + 2^3 + 2^4 \ldots + 2^{10})$.
This series is in Geometric Progression.
$a = 2;\ r = 4/2 = 2$
Sum of n terms = $\dfrac{a(r^n - 1)}{(r - 1)}$
$\dfrac{2(2^{10} - 1)}{(2 - 1)}$
$\dfrac{2 \times (1024 - 1)}{1}$
(2×1023)
2046 (Ans.)

H.C.F AND L.C.M OF NUMBERS

Theory and Formulae

1. **Factor and multiples:** If a number '*a*' divides another numbers '*b*' exactly, then '*a*' is a factor of '*b*' and '*b*' is a multiple of '*a*'.
$4 = 2 \times 2$
2 is a factor of 4 and 4 is a multiple of 2.
2. **Highest common factor / greatest common divisor / measure:** HCF of two or more numbers is the greatest number that divides each of them exactly.

Methods of Solving

- FACTORIZATION METHOD:
Express each number as product of its prime factors.
The product of the least powers of the common prime factors gives the HCF.
Ex: 10, 15, 20
$10 = 2^1 \times 5^1;\ 15 = 5^1 \times 3^1;\ 20 = 5 \times (2)^2$
HCF = 5 (Ans.)
- DIVISION METHOD:
Divide the larger number with the smaller one.
Divide the divisor by the remainder.

Repeat the process till the remainder is '0'.

3. **Lowest common multiple (LCM):** The least number which is exactly divisible by each of the given numbers.

Methods of Solving

- FACTORISATION METHOD:
  Express each number as a product of its prime factors.
  Product of the highest power of all the factors is the LCM
  E.g.: 20, 25
  $20 = 2 \times 5 \times 2 = 2^2 \times 5$
  $25 = 5 \times 5 = 5^1 \times 5^1 = (5)^2$
  $22 \times 5^2 = 100$ (Ans.)
- COMMON DIVISION METHOD:
  - Arrange the given numbers in a row.
  - Divided by a number that divides exactly two of the given numbers and carry forward the remaining which are not divisible.
  - Repeat the process till no two numbers are divisible by the same number except 1.

4. **Product of two numbers** = product of HCF and LCM.
5. **Co-primes:**
   - Two numbers are said to be co-primes if HCF = 1.
   - A number *n* is perfect if the sum of the divisor, excluding *n*, is equal to *n*; $6 = 2 \times 3 \times 1 = 6$
6. **HCF and LCM of fractions:**

   $$\text{HCF} = \frac{\text{HCF of Numerators}}{\text{LCM of Denominators}}$$

   $$\text{LCM} = \frac{\text{LCM of Numerators}}{\text{HCF of Denominators}}$$
7. **HCF and LCM of Decimal fractions:**
   - Consider the numbers without decimal point.
   - Find HCF or LCM and then mark off decimal places.

PRACTICE QUESTIONS

1. Find the HCF of 108, 288, and 360 by factorisation.
   $108 = (2)^2 \times (3)^3$
   $288 = (2)^5 \times (3)^5$
   $360 = (2)^3 \times (5)^1 \times (3)^2$
   $\text{HCF} = (2)^2 \times (3)^2$
   Ans. 36
2. Find the HCF of 513, 1134, and 1215. The division method.

- Divide the larger number with the next smaller number and the remainder with the divisor till the remainder is '0'.

```
1134)1215 (1
     1134
   81)1134 (14
       81
       324
       324
         0
```

- HCF of 1215 and 1134 is 81
- Required HCF = HCF of 513 and 81

```
81) 513 (6
    486
27)  81 (3
     81
      0
```

- HCF of 3 numbers = 27(Ans).

3. Reduce $\frac{391}{667}$ to lowest terms.
   - Since HCF is the greatest number that divides the given numbers equally.

```
391) 667 (1
     391
     276) 391 (1
          276
          115) 276 (2
               230
                46 )115 (2
                     92
                     23) 46 (2
                         46
                          0
```

   - HCF = 23

     $\frac{391}{667} = \frac{391 \div 23}{667 \div 23} = \frac{17}{29}$ (Ans)

4. Find the LCM of 72, 108, and 2100 by factorisation.
   - $72 = 2^3 \times 3^2$; $108 = 3^3 \times 2^2$; $2100 = 2^2 \times 5^2 \times 3 \times 7$
   - LCM = choose the highest power.
   - LCM = $2^3 \times 3^3 \times 5^2 \times 7^1$ = 37,800 (Ans)
5. Find the HCF and LCM of 2/3, 8/9, 19/81, and 10/27.
   - HCF = $\frac{\text{HCF of 2, 8, 16, 10}}{\text{LCM of 3, 9, 81, 27}}$ = 2/81

- HCF = 2 = 2^1; 8 = 2^3; 16 = 2^4; 10 = 2 × 5
- HCF = Least power = 2^1 = 2
- LCM = 3; 3^2; 3^4; 3^3
- LCM = highest power = 34 = 81
- LCM = $\frac{\text{LCM of 2, 8, 16, 10}}{\text{HCF of 3, 9, 81, 27}}$
- LCM = 80/3
- LCM of 2, 8, 16, 10 = 2, 2^3, 2^4, 2 ×5
- Highest power = 2^4 × 5 = 80
- HCF = 3 = 3^1; 9 = 3^2; 81 = 3^4; 27 = 3^3
- Least power = 3

6. Find the HCF and LCM of 0.63, 1.05, and 2.1.
   - Convert all numbers into same decimal places 0.63, 1.05, 2.10
   - Without considering decimal places, the numbers are 63, 105, and 210.
   - HCF = 63 = 7^1 × 3^2; 105 = 5 × 3 × 7; 210 = 5 × 3 × 7 × 2
   - Least power = 3 × 7 = 21
   - LCM = highest power
   - LCM = 32 × 7 × 5 × 2 = 630
   - HCF = move decimal point two places left.
   - HCF = 0.21
   - LCM = 6.30
7. Two numbers are in the ratio of 15: 11. If their HCF is 13, find the numbers.
   - If two numbers are in ratio; multiply them with the given HCF to find the numbers.
   - HCF is common number that divides both the numbers.
   - Let the numbers be 15x and 11x.
   - Then 15x / 11x; x = 13
   - 15 × 13
   - 11 × 13
   - 195 and 143 are the two numbers (Ans.)
8. Find the greatest number which, on dividing 1657 and 2037 leaves remainder 6 and 5 respectively.
   - Required number = (1657 – 6) and (2037 – 5)
   - HCF of 1651 and 2032

```
1651) 2032 (1
      1651
       381) 1651 (4
            1524
             127 ) 381 (3
                   381
                     0
```

   - Required number = 127 (Ans.)

9. Find the least number, which when divided by 6, 7, 8, 9, and 12, leaves remainder 1 in each case.
   LCM of 6, 7, 8, 9, 12
   3 6, 7, 8, 9, 12
   2 2, 7, 8, 3, 4
   2 1, 7, 4, 3, 2
   1, 7, 2, 3, 1
   LCM = $3^2 \times 2^3 \times 7 = 504$
   Required number = 504 + 1 = 505
10. Find the largest number of four digits exactly divisible by 12, 15, 18, and 27.
   3 12, 15, 18, 27
   3 4, 5, 6, 9
   2 4, 5, 2, 3
   2, 5, 1, 3
   - LCM = $3^2 \times 2^2 \times 5^1 = 540$
   - Largest four digit number is 9999.
   - But the required number is < 9999.
   - = 9999 – 540
   - R = 279
   - = 9999 – 279 = 9720 (ans)
11. Find the smallest number of five digits exactly divisible by 16, 24, 36 and 54.
   - Smallest five digit number = 10,000
   3 16, 24, 36, 54
   3 16, 8, 12, 18
   2 16, 8, 4, 6
   2 8, 4, 2, 3
   2 4, 2, 1, 3
   2, 1, 1, 3
   - LCM = $3^3 \times 2^4 = 432$
   - On dividing 10,000 by 432 = R = 64
   - Required number = 10,000 + (432 – 64) = 10368.
12. The traffic lights at three different road crossings change after 48, 72, and 108 seconds, respectively. If they all change simultaneously at 8.20 hrs, then at what the time will they again change simultaneously?
   - We have to find the common time that divides all.
   - We have to find the LCM of (48, 72, 108)
   3 48, 72, 108
   3 16, 24, 36
   2 16, 8, 12
   2 8, 4, 6
   2 4, 2, 3
   2, 1, 3

- $3^3 \times 2^4 = 432$ seconds
- 432 minutes = 7 minutes and 12 seconds.
- Next time = 8.27 : 12 hours.

AVERAGE

Theory And Formulae

1. Average = $\dfrac{\text{Sum of all objects}}{\text{Total number objects}}$
2. Average speed = $2xy / x + y$
   - x = certain distance at x kmph.
   - y = same distance at y kmph.
3. When 'n' number of new items are added;
   - Then, average of 'n' new items = $A + (1 + N / n)^x$

PRACTICE QUESTIONS

1. **Find the average of all prime numbers between 30 and 50.**
   Prime numbers = numbers divisible by themselves and 1.
   31, 37, 41, 43, 47 = 5 prime numbers between 30 and 50.
   Average = $\dfrac{31 + 37 + 41 + 43 + 47}{5}$ = 199 = 39.8 (Ans.)
2. **Find the average of the first 40 natural numbers.**
   Sum of n natural numbers = $n (n + 1) / 2$
   $n = 40$
   $40 (40 + 1) / 2 = 40 \times 41 / 2 = 820$
   Required average = 820 / 40 = 20.5 (Ans.)
3. **Find the average of the first 20 multiples of 7.**
   Required average = $7 + 14 + 21 + \ldots + 140 / 20$
   $= 7 (1 + 2 + 3 + \ldots + 20) / 20$
   $\dfrac{7}{20} \times \dfrac{20 \times 21}{20}$
   147 / 2 = 73.5 (Ans.)
4. **The average of 4 consecutive even numbers is 27. Find the largest of these numbers.**
   Let the number be x.
   4 consecutive even numbers
   $\dfrac{X + (x + 2) + (x + 4) + (x + 6)}{4} = 27$
   $\dfrac{4x + 12}{4} = 27$

$\frac{4(x + 3)}{4} = 27$

$x + 3 = 27$

$x = 27 - 3$

$x = 24$

$\frac{4x + 12}{4} = 27$

$4x + 12 = 27 \times 4$

$4x = 96$

$x = 24$

Largest number = $(x + 6) = 24 + 6 = 30$ (Ans.)

5. **There are 2 sections A and B of a class consisting of 36 and 44 students respectively. The average weight of section A is 40 kg. and section B is 35 kg. Find the average weight of the whole class.**

   Total students = 36 + 44 = 80

   Total weight of both of the sections = (36 × 40 + 44 × 35) = 2980 kg.

   Average weight = 2980 / 80 = 37.25 (Ans.)

   Average of '*m*' items in one group is '*a*' and '*n*' items is *b*.

   Average of combined group = $ma + nb / m + n$

6. **Nine persons went to a hotel for taking their meals. Eight of them spent Rs. 12 each and the ninth spent Rs. 8 more than the average expenditure of all nine. What was the total money spent by them?**

   Let the average expenditure = Rs. x

   A.Q. = $12 \times 8 + (x + 8) = 9x$

   $96 + x + 8 = 9x$

   $104 = 8x$

   $x = 13$

   Total money spent = $9x = 9 \times 13$ = Rs. 117 (Ans.)

7. **The average age of a class of 39 students is 15 years. If the age of the teacher is included, then the average age increases by 3 months. Find the age of the teacher.**

   Total students in the class = 39

   Total age of 39 persons = 39 × 15 = 585 years

   Average age of 40 persons (including the teacher) = 15 years 3 months

   = 15 + 3 /12 = 180 + 3 / 12 = 183 / 12 = 61 / 4 years

   Total age of 40 persons = 40 × 61 / 4 = 610 years

   Age of the teacher = 610 – 585 = 25 years (Ans.)

8. **The average weight of 10 oarsmen in a boat is increased by 1.8 kg. when one of the members, who weighs 53 kg., is replaced by a new one. Find the weight of the new one.**

Total weight increased = 10 × 1.8 = 18 kg.
Weight of the new man = (53 + 18) = 71 kg. (Ans.)

9. **A batsman makes a score of 87 runs in the 17th innings and thus increases the average by 3. Find the average after the 17th innings.**
   Let the average after the 17th innings be 'x'.
   Average till the 16th innings = $(x - 3)$.
   $16 (x - 3) + 87 = 17x$
   $16x - 48 + 87 = 17x$
   $x = 39$ (ans.)

10. **Distance between 2 stations A and B is 778 km. A train covers a journey from A to B at 84 kmph. and returns back to A with uniform speed of 56 kmph. Find the average speed of the train during the whole journey.**
    Average speed = $2xy / x + y$ kmph.
    $$= \frac{2 \times 84 \times 56}{84 + 56} = \frac{2 \times 84 \times 56}{140}$$
    = 67.2 kmph (Ans.)

PERCENTAGE

Theory and Formulae

1. Percentage: That may out of the hundredths.
   $x\,\% = x / 100$
   $a / b = a / b\% = a / b \times 100\ \%$
   $1 / 4 = 1 / 4 \times 100 = 25\%$
2. Price of Commodity:
   A. If the price of a commodity increases by R% with no increase in expenditure; then the reduction in consumption.
   $= R / (100 + R) \times 100\%$
   B. If the price of commodity decreases by R% with no decrease in expenditure; then the increase in consumption.
   $= R / (100 - R) \times 100\%$
   C. Rate percent of a number: Rate percent / 100 × number
   Base number = Value / Rate percent × 100
3. Results on population:
   Population = P
   Population increases = $R\%$ p.a.
   Population after n years = $P\,[1 + R / 100]^n$
   Population n years ago = $P / [1 + R / 100]^n$
4. Results on Depreciation:
   Present value of machine = P
   Depreciation rate = $R\%$ p.a

Value of machine after n years = $P / 1 - R / 100]^n$
Value of machine n years ago = $P / [1 - R/100]^n$

5. Comparison:
A is $R\% > B$;
Then b is $< A$ by = $[R / 100 + R \times 100]\%$
A is $R\% < B$;

- Then B is $> A$ by = $[R / 100 - R \times 100]\%$

PRACTICE QUESTIONS

1. **Express each of the following as a fraction:**
   - **0.6%** $= \frac{0.6}{100} = \frac{0.6 \times 10^1}{100 \times 10^1} = \frac{6}{1000}$
     $= 3 / 500$
   - **0.08%** $= \frac{0.08}{100} = \frac{0.08 \times 10^2}{100 \times 10^2} = \frac{8}{10000}$
     $= 1 / 1250$
2. **Express each of the following as a decimal.**
   - $0.2\% = 0.2 / 100 = 0.002 = (0.2 \times 10^{-2})$
   - $0.04\% = 0.04 / 100 = 0.04 \times 10^{-2} = 0.0004$
3. **Evaluate:**
   $16\frac{2}{3}\%$ of 600 gm $- 33\frac{1}{3}\%$ of 180 gm
   $= 50 / 3 \times 1 / 100 \times 600 = 100 / 3 \times 1 / 100 \times 180$ gms
   $= 100 - 60 = 40$ gms (Ans.)
4. **If the sales tax be reduces from $3\frac{1}{2}\%$ to $3\frac{1}{3}\%$, then what difference does it make to a person who purchases an article at a price of Rs. 8400?**

   $R_1 = 3\frac{1}{2} = 7\%$

   $R_2 = 3\frac{1}{3} = \frac{10}{3}\%$

   $R_1 > R_2$
   Required difference

   $= (3\frac{1}{2}\%$ of Rs. 8400$) - (3\frac{1}{3}\%$ of Rs. 8400$)$

   $= \left[\frac{7}{2}\% \times 8400\right] - \left[\frac{10}{3}\% \times 8400\right]$

   $8400 \times \left[\frac{7}{2} - \frac{10}{3}\right]\%$

$$8400 \times \left[\frac{21-20}{6}\right]\%$$

$$8400 \times \left[\frac{1}{6}\right]\%$$

$$8400 \times \frac{1}{6} \times \frac{1}{100}$$

Rs = 14 less for $3\frac{1}{3}$ (Ans.)

5. **In an election between two candidates, 75% of voters cast their votes out of which 2% of the votes were declared invalid. A candidate got 9161 votes which were 75% of total valid votes. Find the total number of votes enrolled in the election.**

   Let the total number of votes = x.

   Votes cast = 75% of x

   2% were invalid votes; valid votes = 100% - 2 % = 98% (75% of x)

   (Total is always 100%)

   Candidate got 75% of valid votes.

   = 75% of (98% of (75% of x)) = 9261

   $$\left[\frac{75}{100} \times \frac{98}{100} \times \frac{75}{100} \times x\right] = 9261$$

   $$X = \left[\frac{9261 \times 100 \times 100 \times 100}{75 \times 98 \times 75}\right]$$

   $$X = \left[\frac{9261 \times (100)^3}{551250}\right]$$

   $$X = \frac{9261000000}{551250} = 16800 \text{ (Ans.)}$$

6. **If 50% of $(x - y)$ = 30% $(x + y)$; then what percentage of x is y?**

   50 / 100 × $(x - y)$ = 30 / 100 $(x + y)$

   $5\ (x - y) = 3\ (x + y)$

   $5x - 5y = 3x + 3y$

   $2x = 8y$

   $x = 4y$

   ? % of $x = y$

   ? 1 / 100 × $x = y$

   Required % = $100y / X$%

   = $y / 4y \times 100\%$

   Required % = 25% (Ans.)

7. **10% of the inhabitants of a village died of cholera, during which 25% of the remaining inhabitants left the village. The population reduced to 4050. Find the number of original inhabitants.**

Let original inhabitants = x

(100% – 25%) of (100% – 10%) of x = 4050 (During cholera: 25% left)

$$\left[\frac{75}{100} \times \frac{98}{100} \times x\right] = 4050$$

$6750x = 4050 \times 100 \times 100$

$$x = \frac{4050 \times 100 \times 100}{6750}$$

x = 6000 (ans)

8. **Raman's salary was decreased by 50% and subsequently increased by 50%. How much percent does he loose?**

Let the original salary = Rs 100/-

Decrease in salary = $\left[\frac{50}{100} \times 100\right]$

Subsequent increase = $\frac{100 + 50}{100} = \frac{150}{100}$

New salary $= \left[\frac{150}{100} \times \frac{50}{100} \times 100\right]$

= Rs. 75

% decreased = 25% (100 – 75) = 25% (Ans.)

9. **When the price of a product was decreased by 10%, the number of pieces sold increased by 30%, what was the effect on the total revenue?**

Let the price of product = Rs. 100

Sold pieces = 100 pieces

Total revenue = 100 × 100 = 10,000

When price decreased by 10% = Rs. 90

Sold pieces increased by 30% = 130 pieces

New revenue = 90 × 130 = Rs. 11,700

Difference Rs. 1,700

Increase in revenue = 1,700 / 10,000 × 100 = 17% (Ans.) (U.L. – L.L.) / L.L.

10. **In a budget, the price of kerosene oil rose by 25% by how much percent must a person reduce his consumption so that the expenditure on it does not increase?**

Reduction in consumption = $\left[\frac{R}{100 + R} \times 100\right]\%$

$\left[\frac{25}{125} \times 100\right]\%$

= 20% (Ans.)

11. **The population of a town is 1,76,400. If it increases at the rate of 5% per annum, what was the population 2 years ago?**

2 years hence $= \left[176400 \times 1 + \frac{25}{100}\right]^2$

$$176400 \times \left[\frac{105}{100}\right]^2$$

$176400 \times 1.10225 = 194481$ (Ans.)

$$2 \text{ years ago} = \frac{p}{1+\left[\frac{R}{100}\right]^n}$$

$$\frac{176400}{1+\left[\frac{5}{100}\right]^2} = \frac{176400}{\left[\frac{105}{100}\right]^2}$$

$$176400 \times \left[\frac{105}{100}\right]^2$$

$$176400 \times \frac{20}{21} \times \frac{20}{21} = 1{,}60000 \text{ (Ans.)}$$

12. **The value of a machine depreciates at the rate of 10% per annum. If its present value is Rs. 1,62,000, what will be its worth after 2 years and what was the value of the machine 2 years ago?**

Value of the machine after 2 years:

$$= p\left[1 - \frac{r}{100}\right]^n$$

$$162000 \times \left[1 - \frac{10}{100}\right]^2$$

$$162000 \times \left[\frac{90}{100}\right]^2$$

$$162000 \times \frac{9}{10} \times \frac{9}{10} = \text{Rs. } 131220$$

$$\text{Value of the machine 2 years ago} = \frac{p}{1-\left[\frac{r}{100}\right]^n}$$

$$\frac{162000}{1-\left[\frac{10}{100}\right]^2} = 162000 \times \frac{10}{9} \times \frac{10}{9}$$

200000 (2 lakhs)

PROFIT AND LOSS

Theory and Formulae

1. Cost price = the price at which the article is purchased. (merchant purchases an article)

2. Selling price = the price at which the article is sold. (price at which the merchant sells to the customer)
3. Profit = gain = if selling price > cost price
4. Loss = if selling price < cost price.

Formulae

1. Gain and loss = calculated on cost price.
2. Loss = cost price – selling price.
3. Gain = selling price – cost price
4. Loss = cost price – selling price.
5. $\text{Gain \%} = \dfrac{\text{Gain} \times 100}{\text{Cost price}}$
6. $\text{Loss \%} = \dfrac{\text{Loss} \times 100}{\text{Cost price}}$
7. $\text{Selling price} = \dfrac{(100 + \text{Gain \%})}{100} \times \text{Cost price}$
8. $\text{Selling price} = \dfrac{(100 - \text{Loss \%})}{100} \times \text{Cost price}$
9. $\text{Cost price} = \dfrac{100}{(100 + \text{Gain \%})} \times \text{Selling price}$
10. $\text{Cost price} = \dfrac{100}{(100 - \text{Loss \%})} \times \text{Selling price}$
11. If an article is sold at a gain of 35%; selling price = 135% of cost price. Loss of 35%; selling price = 65% of cost price.
12. If two similar items are sold at a gain of x% and the other at a loss of x%, then the seller always incurs loss.
    $\text{Loss \%} = \left[\dfrac{\text{Common loss and gain \%}}{10}\right] = \left[\dfrac{x}{10}\right]^2$
13. Trader sells goods at cost price but uses false weights.
    $\text{Gain \%} = \left[\dfrac{\text{Error}}{(\text{True value} - \text{Error})} \times 100\right]\%$
14. Trader incurs loss by selling a product but what should be selling price of product at which he gets profit.
    (100 – loss%) : (1st selling price) = (100 + gain%) : (2nd selling price)
15. Two successive discounts at a% and b%.
    $= \left[a + b - \dfrac{ab}{100}\right]\%$
16. If there are multiple successive discounts.
    $= 100\left[1 - \dfrac{a}{100}\right]\left[1 - \dfrac{b}{100}\right]\left[1 - \dfrac{c}{100}\right]\ldots$

PRACTICE QUESTIONS

1. **If a radio is purchased for Rs. 490 and sold for Rs. 465.50; find the loss percentage.**

Cost price = Rs. 490

Selling price = Rs. 465.50

Loss = (cost price – selling price)

= (490 – 465.50) = Rs. 24.50

$$\text{Loss \%} = \left[\frac{\text{Loss} \times 100}{\text{Cost price}}\right]$$

$$\text{Loss \%} = \left[\frac{24.50 \times 100}{490}\right] = \frac{2450}{490}$$

Loss % = 5% (Ans.)

2. **Find cost price, when selling price = Rs. 51.70 and loss = 12%.**

$$\text{Cost price} = \left[\frac{100}{100 - \text{Loss\%}}\right] \times \text{Selling price}$$

$$= \left[\frac{100}{100 - 12}\right] \times 51.70$$

= 100 / 88 × 51.70 = Rs. 58.75 (Ans.)

3. **Find the selling price when cost price = Rs. 56.25, and gain = 20%.**

$$\text{Selling price} = \left[\frac{100}{(100 + \text{Gain \%})}\right] \times \text{Cost price}$$

$$= \left[\frac{100 + 20}{100}\right] \times 56.25$$

= 120 / 100 × 56.25

= Rs. 67.50 (Ans.)

4. **A person incurs 5% loss by selling a watch for Rs. 1140. At what price should the watch be sold to earn 5% profit?**

Let the new selling price = Rs. x

$$\frac{(100 - \text{Loss \%})}{(\text{First selling price})} = \frac{(100 + \text{gain \%})}{(\text{Second selling price})}$$

$$\frac{100 - 5}{1140} = \frac{100 + 5}{x}$$

$$\frac{95}{1140} = \frac{105}{x}$$

$$x = \frac{105 \times 1140}{95}$$

x = Rs. 1260 (new selling price)

5. **The cost price of 21 articles is equal to the selling price of 18 articles, find gain or loss%.**

When you purchased 21 articles and sold 18 articles; you sold them at Rs. 21.
Let the price of each article = Rs. 1
Cost price of 18 articles = Rs. 18
Selling price of 18 articles = Rs. 21

$$\text{Gain \%} = \left[\frac{21-18}{18}\right] \times 100$$

$$= \frac{3}{18} \times 100 = \frac{100}{6}\ \%$$

$$= 16\frac{2}{3}\ \text{(Ans.)}$$

6. **A vendor bought bananas at 6 for Rs. 10 and sold them at 4 for Rs. 6. Find his gain or loss percentage.**

1 dozen = 12 bananas
LCM of 6, 4 = 12

$$\text{Cost price} = \left[\frac{10}{6} \times 12\right] = \text{Rs. } 20$$

$$\text{Selling price} = \left[\frac{6}{4} \times 12\right] = \text{Rs. } 18$$

$$\text{Loss \%} = \left[\frac{\text{Loss} \times 100}{\text{Cost price}}\right] = \frac{2 \times 100}{20}$$

$$= 10\%\ \text{(Ans.)}$$

Cost price = 6*b* = Rs. 10

$$\text{Cost price} = 1b = \frac{10}{6} = \text{Rs. } 1.66$$

$$\text{Cost price of 4 bananas} = \frac{10}{6} \times 4 = \text{Rs. } 6.66$$

Selling price of 4 bananas = Rs. 6 (given)
Loss 6.66 – 6 = 0.66

$$\text{Loss \%} = \frac{0.66 \times 100}{6.66} = \frac{66}{6.66} = 10\%\ \text{(Ans.)}$$

7. **A grocer purchased 80 kg. of sugar at Rs. 13.50/kg. and mixed it with 120 kg sugar at Rs. 16/kg. at what rate should he sell the mixture to gain 16%?**

Cost price of 200 kg. (80 + 120) of mixture.
(80 × 13.50 + 120 ×16) = Rs. 3,000

$$\text{Selling price} = \frac{(100 + \text{Gain \%})}{100} \times \text{Cost price}$$

$$= \left[\frac{100+16}{100}\right] \times 3{,}000$$

$$= \left[\frac{116}{100} \times 3000\right]$$

Selling price = Rs. 3,480 (for 200 kg.)
Selling price per kg. of mixture = 3,480 / 200
Selling price per kg. = Rs. 17.40 (Ans.)

8. **Pure ghee costs Rs. 100 per kg. After adulterating it with vegetable oil costing Rs. 50 per kg; the shopkeeper sells the mixture at Rs. 96 per kg., thereby making a profit of 20%. In what ratio does he mix the two?**

$$\text{Cost price} = \frac{100}{(100 + \text{Gain }\%)} \times \text{Selling price}$$

Mean cost price (two products are mixed)

$$= \left[\frac{100}{100 + 20} \times 96\right]$$

= Rs. 80 per kilogram

By rule of allegation:

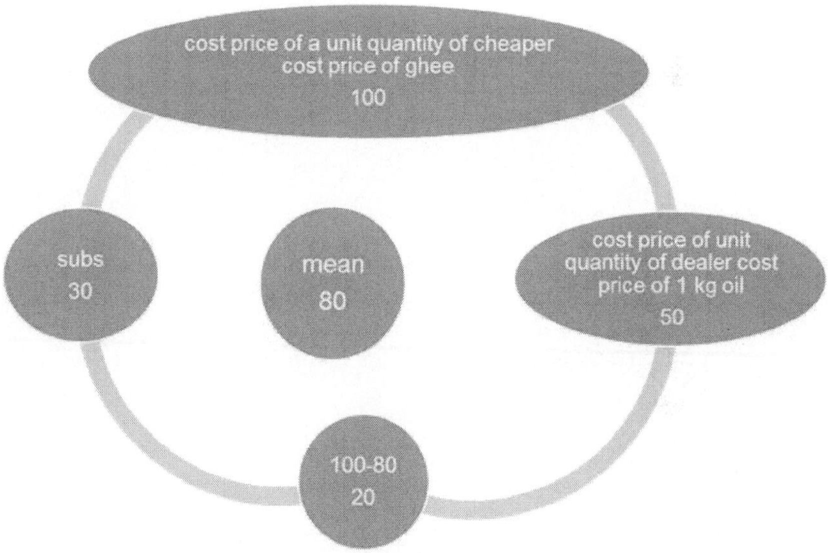

$$\text{Ratio} = \frac{30}{20} = \frac{3}{2} \text{ (Ans.)}$$

9. **A dishonest dealer declares to sell his goods at the cost price but uses weights of 960 gms for a kg. of weight. Find his gain percentage.**

$$\text{Gain }\% = \left[\frac{\text{Error}}{(\text{Total value} - \text{Error})} \times 100\right]\%$$

$$= \left[\frac{1000 - 960}{960} \times 100\right]\%$$

$$= \left[\frac{40}{960} \times 100\right]\%$$

$$= \frac{400}{96}\%$$

$$= 4.166\% = 4\frac{1}{6}\% \text{ (ans)}$$

10. Monika purchased a pressure cooker at 9/10th of its selling price and sold it at 8% more than it selling price find her gain percentage.

Let selling price = 100

$$\text{Cost price} = \frac{9}{10} \times 100 = \text{Rs. } 90$$

Selling price = 8% more = Rs. 108

$$\text{Gain \%} = \frac{108 - 90}{90} \times 100$$

Gain % = 20% (Ans.)

11. A man sells two flats for Rs. 6,75,958 each on one he gains 16% while on the other loses 16%. How much does he gain or lose in the whole transaction?

In such a case, there is always loss. (selling price not counted)

$$\text{Loss \%} = \left[\frac{\text{Common loss and train \%}}{10}\right]^2$$

$$= \left[\frac{16}{10}\right]^2 \% = \frac{64}{25}\%$$

Loss % = 2.56% (Ans.)

12. A man bought a horse and carriage of Rs. 3,000. He sold the horse at a gain of 20% and the carriage at a loss of 10%, thereby gaining 2% of the whole. Find the cost of the horse.

Let cost price of horse = Rs. x

Cost price of carriage = Rs. $(3000 - x)$

$$\text{Profit} = \frac{20}{100} \times x$$

$$\text{Loss} = \frac{10}{100}(3000 - x)$$

$$\frac{20}{100} \times x - \frac{10}{100}(3000 - x) = \frac{2}{100} \times 3000$$

$$\frac{x}{5} - \frac{3000 - x}{10} = 60$$

$$\frac{2x - 3000 + x}{10} = 60$$

$3x = 60 \times 10 + 3000$

$3x = 3600$

$x = 1200$ (Ans.)

13. Find the single discount equivalent to a series of dicounts of 20%, 10% and 5%.

$$100\left[1-\frac{a}{100}\right]\left[1-\frac{b}{100}\right]\left[1-\frac{c}{100}\right]$$

$$100\left[1-\frac{20}{100}\right]\left[1-\frac{10}{100}\right]\left[1-\frac{20}{100}\right]$$

$$100\left[1-\frac{20}{100}\right]\left[1-\frac{10}{100}\right]\left[1-\frac{20}{100}\right]$$

$$100\times\left[\frac{80}{100}\times\frac{90}{100}\times\frac{95}{100}\right]$$

$$100\times\left[\frac{95}{100}\times\frac{90}{100}\times\frac{80}{100}\right]$$

$$\frac{684\times 10^5}{10^6}$$

Rs. 68.40

Required discount = 100 – 68.40 = 31.6% (Ans.)

14. **A retailer buys 40 pens at the market price of 36 pens from a wholesaler. If he sells these pens giving a discount of 1%, what is the profit percentage?**

Let the market price of each pen = Re. 1

Cost price of 40 pens = Rs. 36

Selling price of 40 pens = 99% of Rs. 40 = Rs. 39.60

Cost price = Rs. 39 (40 pens)

Selling price = Rs. 39.60

$$\text{Profit \%} = \left[\frac{\text{Gain}\times 100}{\text{Cost price}}\right]$$

$$= \left[\frac{3.60\times 100}{36}\right] = 10\%$$

= 10% (Ans.)

TIME AND WORK

Theory and Formulae

- 'A' can do a work in '*n*' days; 'A' s one day work = 1/*n* and vice-versa
- 'A' is thrice as good as 'B'; ratio of work done by A and B = 3:1
  Ratio of time taken by A and B to finish the work = 1 : 3.

PRACRICE QUESTIONS

1. **Worker A takes 8 hours to do a job. Worker B takes 10 hours to do the same job. How long should it take both A and B working together but independently, to do the same job?**

'A' s one hour work = 1/8

B's one hour work = 1/10

(A + B)'s one hour work = 1/8 + 1/10 = 9/40

A and B finish the work in = 40/9 = $4\frac{4}{9}$ days (Ans.)

2. **A can do a piece of work in 7 days of 9 hours each and B can do it in 6 days of 7 hours each. How long will they take to do it working together $8\frac{2}{5}$ hours a day?**

   A = 7 days, 9 hours each = 9 hours per day for 7 days.
   B = 6 days of 7 hours each = 7 hours per day for 6 days.
   A can complete the entire work = 7 × 9 = 63 hours.
   B can complete the entire work = 6 × 7 = 42 hours.
   A's one hour work = 1/63
   B's one hour work = 1/42
   (A + B)'s one hour work = [1/63 + 1/42]
   2 + 3 / 126 = 5 / 126
   Both working together = 126/5 hours

   Number of days of $8\frac{2}{5}$ hours each day = 126/5 × 5/42

   = 3 days (Ans.)

3. **A and B do a piece of work in 18 days, B and C can do it in 24 days, C and A in 36 days. In how many days will A, B and C finish it working together and separately?**

   (A + B)'s one day work = 1/18
   (B + C)'s one day work = 1/24
   (A + C)'s one day work = 1/36
   Since two persons are working together
   2(A + B + C)'s one day work = [1/18 + 1/24 + 1/36]
   = 9/72 = 1/8
   (A + B + C)'s one day work = 1/16
   A + B + C can finish work together in 16 days.
   A's one day work = (A + B + C) one day work – (B + C)
   = 1/16 – 1/24
   = 3/48 – 2/48 = 1
   'A' alone can do the entire work in 48 days.
   B's one day work = 1/16 – 1/36 = 5/144

   B can complete the work in 144/5 = $28\frac{4}{5}$

   C's one day work = 1/16 – 1/18 = 1/144
   C can complete it in 144 days.

4. **A can do a certain job in 12 days. B is 60% more efficient than A. How many days does B alone take to finish the same job?**

Ratio of time taken by A and B = 160 : 100
B is more efficient by 60% = 8 : 5
If 'B' take 'x' days to finish the job

$8/5 = 12/x$

$8x = 12 \times 5$

$x = 12 \times 5 / 8 = 15 / 2$

B = 7 ½ days (Ans.)

5. **A and B undertake the piece of work for Rs. 600. A alone can do it in 6 days and B in 8 days. With the help of C, they finish it in 3 days. Find the share of each.**

   (A + B + C)'s one day work = 1/3
   Because (A + B + C) = total work = 3 days.
   C's one day work = 1/3 – [1/6 + 1/8]
   = 1/3 – 4 + 3/24
   = 8 – 7/24 = 1/24
   To find the share of each
   1/6 : 1/8 : 1/24 = 4 : 3 : 1
   A's share = 600 × 4/8 = Rs. 300
   B's share = 600 × 3/8 = Rs. 225
   C's share = (600 – (300 + 225))
   = Rs. 75 (ans.)

6. **45 men can complete a work in 16 days. Six days after work started, 30 more men joined them. How many days will they now take to complete the remaining work?**

   45 men = 16 days.
   45 men in one day would do = 1/16 work
   (45 × 16) = 720 men can complete the work in one day.
   One men's one day's work = 1/720
   45 men's 6 day's work = [1/16 × 6] = 3/8
   Remaining work = [1 – 3/8] = 5/8
   45 + 30 = 75 men's one day's work = 1/720 × 75
   = 5/48
   Remaining 5/8 work is done = 5/8 × 48/5 = 6 days (Ans.)

TIME AND DISTANCE

Theory and Formulae

- Distance = Speed × Time
- x km/hr. = [x × 5/18] m/sec.
- x m/sec. = [x × 18/5] km/hr.
- Ratio of speed of A and B = $a : b$; then ratio of time taken to cover distance. $1/a : 1/b = b : a$

- A man covers certain distance = x kmph. and equal distance at y kmph. Average speed = $2xy$ / $x + y$ kmph.

PRACTICE QUESTIONS

1. **How many minutes does Ankita takes to cover a distance of 400 metres, if she runs at speed of 20 km/hr.?**
   D = 400 meters
   S = 20 km/hr. = 20 × 5/18 = 50/9 m/sec.
   T = D = 400 ÷ 50/9 = [400 × 9/50] sec.
   $T = 72 \text{ sec.} = 1\frac{12}{60} = \left[1\frac{1}{5}\right]$ min. (Ans.)
2. **A dog takes 4 leaps for every 5 leaps of hare, but 3 leaps of dog are equal to 4 leaps of hare. Compare their speeds.**
   Let the distance covered in 1 leap of dog = x, and hare = y.
   $3x = 4y$
   $x = \frac{4}{3}y$
   $4x = 4 \times \frac{4}{3}y = \left[\frac{16}{3}y\right]$
   Ratio of speed dog : hare = Ratio of distance covered by the in the same time.
   $4x : 5y = \frac{16}{3}y : 5y$
   $= \frac{16y}{3} \div 5y = \frac{16y}{3} \times \frac{1}{50}$
   Ratio = 16 : 15 (Ans.)
3. **Peter can cover a certain distance in 1 hour 24 minutes by covering 2/3rd of the distance at 4 kmph. and rest by 5 kmph. Find the total distance.**
   Let D = x km.
   D/S = T
   $\frac{2/3x}{4} + \frac{1/3x}{5} = 1\frac{24}{60} = 7/5$ hrs
   $2x/3 \div 4 = 2x/3 \times 1/4 = x/6$
   $x/3 \div 5 = x/3 \times 1/5 = x/15$
   $x/6 + x/15 = 7/5$ $\quad 5x + 2x / 30 = 7/5$
   $7x/30 = 7/5$
   $x/30 = 1/5$
   $x = 1/5 \times 30 = 6$
   $x = 6$ km (Ans)
4. **A man travelled from the village to the post office at a rate of 25 kmph and walked back at a rate of 4 kmph. If the whole journey took 5 hours 48 min. find the distance of the post office from the village.**
   Average speed $= \left[\frac{2xy}{x + y}\right]$ kmph

$$= \left[\frac{2 \times 25 \times 4}{25 + 4}\right] = \frac{200}{29} \text{ km / hr}$$

T = 5 hours 48 minutes = 5 × 48/60 = 29/5 hrs

Total distance = 200/29 × 29/5 = 40 km

Distance from village to post office = 40/2 = 20 km (Ans.)

5. **An airplane flies along 4 sides of a square at speeds of 200, 400, 600, and 800. Find the average speed of the plane around the field.**

   Let each side of the square = x km and average speed = y km/hr

   $$\frac{x}{200} + \frac{x}{400} + \frac{x}{600} + \frac{x}{800} = \frac{4x}{y}$$

   $$\frac{12x + 6x + 4x + 3x}{2400} = \frac{4x}{y} = \frac{25x}{2400} = \frac{4x}{y}$$

   $$y = \frac{2400 \times 4x}{25x} = 384 \text{ kmph (Ans.)}$$

6. **A thief is spotted by a policeman from a distance of 100 meters. When the policeman starts the chase, the thief also starts running. If the speed of the thief is 8 kmph, and that of the policeman is 10 kmph, how far will the thief have run before he is overtaken?**

   Relative speed of the policeman = (10 – 8) = 2 kmph

   Time taken by the policeman to cover 100 m = 100/1,000 ÷ 2

   $$= \left[\frac{100}{1{,}000} \times \frac{1}{2}\right]$$

   = 1/20 hr.

   So, in 1/20 hr., the thief covers a distance

   $$= \left[8 \times \frac{1}{20}\right] = 2/5 \text{ km}$$

   D = 2/5 × 1,000

   = 400 m. (ans)

7. **A train travels at an average of 50 miles/hr. for 2 ½ hrs and then travels at speed of 70 miles/hr. for 1 ½ hrs. How far did the train travel the entire 4 hrs?**

   Distance = Speed × Time

   = (50 × 2½) + (70 × 1½)

   = (50 × 5/2) + (70 × 3/2)

   = 125 + 105 = 230 miles (Ans)

8. **A man notices that he can count 21 telephone posts in one minute. If they are 50 meters apart, then at what speed is the train travelling?**

   Number of gaps between 21 posts = 21 – 1 = 20

   Total distance of 21 posts in 1 min = (50 × 20) = 1000 m / 1 km.

   Time = 1 min. = 1/60 hr

   S = 1 / 1/60 = Speed = 60 km / hr. (ans.)

REASONING

SERIES: ODD ONE OUT, WRONG NUMBERS, AND MISSING NUMBERS

Find the Odd One Out

1. 3, 5, 7, 12, 17, …
   (a) 19 (b) 17 (c) 13 (d) 12
   - Each of the numbers except 12 are prime numbers.
   - So, 12 is odd man out.
2. 1, 4, 9, 16, 23, 25, 36, …
   (a) 9 (b) 23 (c) 25 (d) 36
   - Every number except 23 is a perfect square of its number.
   - $1^2, 2^2, 3^2, \ldots, 5^2, 6^2$
3. 385, 462, 572, 396, 427, 671, 264
   (a) 385 (b) 427 (c) 671 (d) 264
   - Middle digit is the sum of the other two except in 427.
4. 835, 734, 642, 751, 853, 981, 532.
   (a) 751 (b) 853 (c) 981 (d) 532
   - The difference (1st digit – 3rd digit) is the middle one.
   - $8 - 5 = 3, 7 - 4 = 3$
   - Odd = 751
5. 2, 5, 10, 17, 26, 37, 50, 64…
   (a) 50 (b) 26 (c) 37 (d) 64
   - $X^2 + 1$; $x = 1 \ldots 8$
   - $1^2 + 1 = 2$ (1st number)
   - $2^2 + 1 = 5$ (2nd number)
   - $3^2 + 1 = 10$ (3rd number)
   - $7^2 + 1 = 50$ (7th number)
   - $8^2 + 1 = 65$ but **64** is there so 64 odd one out.

Wrong Number

6. 22, 33, 66, 99, 121, 279, 594
   (a) 33 (b) 121 (c) 279 (d) 594
   - Except **279**, all numbers are multiples of 11.
7. 36, 54, 18, 27, 9, 18.5, 4.5
   (a) 4.5 (b) 18.5 (c) 54 (d) 18
   - The terms 1st, 3rd, 5th alternately multiply by 1.5 and 2nd term, 4th term and 6th term are divided by 3.
   - $36 \times 1.5 = 54 / 3 = 18 \times 1.5 = 27 / 3 = 9 \times 1.5 = 13.5$
   - So **18.5** does not satisfy.
8. 1, 8, 27, 64, 124, 216, 343

(a) 8 (b) 27 (c) 64 (d) 124

- $1^3, 2^3, 3^3, 4^3, 5^3$ (125), $6^3, 7^3$
- **124** is not equal to 53(125) so it is the wrong one.

9. 105, 85, 60, 30, 0, –45, –90

(a) 0 (b) 85 (c) –45 (d) 60

- Sub. 20, 25, 30, 35, 40, 45 this is the series minus from the questioned number series. So **zero (0)** is the wrong one.

Insert Missing Number

10. 4, –8, 16, –32, 64, ?

(a) 128 (b) –128 (c) 192 (d) –192

- Each number = proceeding number × (–2)
- 4 × –2 = –8 ; –8 × –2 = 16
- 16 × –2 = –32 ; –32 × –2 = 64
- 64 × –2 = –128 (Ans.)

11. 8, 24, 12, 36, 16, 54, ?

(a) 27 (b) 108 (c) 68 (d) 72

- Alternatively, multiply by 3 and divide by 2
- 8 × 3 = 24 / 2 = 12 × 3 = 36 / 2 = 18
- 18 × 3 = 54 / 2 = 27 (ans)

12. 2, 4, 12, 48, 240, ?

(a) 960 (b) 1440 (c) 1080 (d) 1920

- Multiply the numbers by 2, 3, 4, 5, and 6
- 2 × 2 = 4 × 3 = 12 × 4 = 48 × 5 = 240 × 6 = 1,440

Ans. (b)

PROBLEMS ON TRAIN

Theory and Formulae

1. Time taken to cross a pole / man / signal post by a train
$$= \frac{\text{Length of train}}{\text{Speed of train}}$$
2. Time taken to cross another train / bridge / platform, etc., by a train
$$\text{By train} = \frac{\text{Length of (train + platform, etc.)}}{\text{Speed of train}}$$
3. If two trains are going in the same direction, then their relative speed = difference of their speed $(u - v)$ m/s and opposite direction = relative speed = $(u + v)$ m/s.
4. If two trains of a and b metres are moving in opposite directions at u m/s; then time taken by the trains to cross each other $= a + b \,/\, u + v$ sec.

5. If two trains of a and b meters are moving in the same direction at u m/s and v m/s; then the time taken by the faster train to cross the slower train $= a + b / u - v$ sec.
6. If a train starts with a speed of u km/hr and after t hours another train starts from same point and direction with speed of v km/hr then time taken by the 2nd train to cross the first train
   $T = u \times t / v - u$
   $D = v\ [ut / v - u]$
7. If two trains (bodies) start at the same time from points A and B towards each other, and they complete their journey in a and b hours respectively in reaching B and A; then
   $\frac{\text{Speed of A}}{\text{Speed of B}} = \frac{\sqrt{b}}{\sqrt{a}}$
8. A train is running with at a speed of a km/hr when going to it's destination and returning back with at a speed of b km/hr ($b < a$). If the total distance is x km and the total time is T hrs; then
   $$\text{Total distance} = \text{Total time}\left[\frac{\text{Product of two speeds}}{\text{Sum of two speeds}}\right]$$

PRACTICE QUESTIONS

1. **A train is moving at a speed of 132 km/hr. if the length of the train is 110 meters, how long it will take to cross a railway platform 165 m. long?**
   - Speed of train $= \left[132 \times \frac{5}{18}\right]$ m/sec.
     $= \left[\frac{110}{3}\right]$ m/sec.
   - Distance = (LT + LP) = (110 + 165) = 275 m.
   - Time $= \left[275 \div \frac{110}{3}\right]$ sec $= 275 \times \frac{3}{110}$
   - 15/2 = 7½ sec (Ans.)
2. **A man is standing in a railway bridge which is 180 m. long. He finds that a train crosses the bridge in 20 sec. but he himself takes 8 sec. find the length of the train and its speed.**
   - Let the length of train LT = x m.
   - Train covers x m. in 8 sec. and (x + 180) m. in 20 sec.
   - S = D / T

     $x/8 = \frac{x + 180}{20}$
     $20x = 8\ (x + 180)$
     $20x = 8x = 1440$
     $12x = 1440$

$x = 120$

- Speed of train = 120/8 = 15 m/sec.
  = [15 × 18/5] km/hr.
  = 54 kmph (Ans.)

3. **A train of 150 m. is running with a speed of 68 kmph. In what time will it pass a man who is running at 8 km/hr in same direction in which the train is going?**
   - Relative speed T : M = $(u - v)$ m/s
     = 68 – 8 = 60 km/hr = [60 × 5/18] = 50/3 m/sec
   - Time taken to cross the man = time taken to cover 150 m. (F1)
   - T = D/S
     = [150 ÷ 50/3] sec = 9 sec (Ans.)
4. **Two trains, 137 m and 163 m in length are running towards each other on parallel lines; one at 42 km/hr and the other at 48 km/hr. In what time will they be clear of each other from the moment they meet?**
   - Relative speed of the trains = 42 + 48 = 90 km / hr.
     [90 × 5/18] = 25 m/sec
   - Time taken to cover = (137 + 163) (total distance)
     T = [300/25] sec = 12 sec (Ans.)
5. **Two trains, 100 m and 120 m. long are running in the same direction with speeds of 72 km/hr. and 54 km/hr. in how much time will the first train cross the second?**
   - Relative speed of the trains = $(u - v)$
     72 – 54 = 18 km/hr = 18 × 5/18 = 5 m/sec.
   - Total distance = (100 + 120) = 220 m
     T = 220/5 = 44 sec (ans)
6. **A 100 m. long train takes 6 sec. to cross a man walking at 5 km/hr. in the direction opposite to that of the train. Find the speed of the train.**
   - Relative speed = St : Sm = $(x + 5)$ 5/18 m/sec.
     T = D/S
     $$\frac{100}{(x + 5)\ 5/18} = 6 \text{ (time)}$$
     $100 = 6\,(x + 5) \times 5/18$
     $$100 = \frac{6\,(5x + 25)}{18}$$
     $1800 = 30x + 150$
     X = 1,800 – 150/30
     = 1,650/30
     X = 55 km/hr (Ans.)

7. **A man sitting in a train which is travelling at 50 km/hr. observes that a goods trains travelling in the opposite direction takes 9 sec to pass him. If the goods train is 280 m. long, find its speed.**
   - Relative speed = D/T = [280/9] m/sec.
   - 280/9 × 18/5 = 112 km/hr.
   - Speed of goods train = (112 – 50) = 62 km/hr. (Ans.)
8. **Two trains approach each other with speeds 50 km / hr. and 60 km / hr from stations A and B. when the two trains meet each other, the second train had covered 120 km more than the first train. What is the distance between A and B?**

   $$D = \frac{x\,(v + u)}{v - u}\ \text{km}$$
   $$= \frac{120\,(50 + 60)}{(60 - 50)}$$
   $$= 120 \times 110/10$$
   $$= 1320\ \text{km (Ans.)}$$
9. **Two trains are approaching each other from two different points at the same time. They complete their journey in 31/3 and 44/5 hours after they meet each other. Speed of A is 8 kmph. What is the speed of B?**
   - $$\frac{\text{Speed of A}}{\text{Speed of B}} = \frac{\sqrt{4\ 4/5}}{\sqrt{3\ 1/3}}$$
     $$8/B = \frac{\sqrt{24/5}}{\sqrt{3\ 1/3}}$$
   - Squaring both sides
     $$\frac{64}{(B)^2} = \frac{24/5}{10/3}$$
     $$(B)^2 = \frac{64 \times 10 \times 5}{3 \times 24} = \frac{400}{9}$$
     $$(B)^2 = \frac{400}{9}$$
     $$B = \frac{20}{3} = 6\frac{2}{3}\ \text{km/hr (Ans.)}$$
10. **A man travels a distance by train with a speed of 25 km/hr. and returns back by foot with a speed of 11 km/hr. The total time taken to complete the journey is 5 hrs 48 min. What is the total distance covered?**
    - $$\text{Total distance} = \text{Total time}\left[\frac{\text{Product of two speeds}}{\text{Sum of two speeds}}\right]$$
    - $$5 \times \frac{48}{60} \times \left[\frac{25 \times 4}{25 + 4}\right]$$
    - $$\frac{248}{60}\left[\frac{100}{29}\right] = \frac{29}{5} \times \frac{100}{29}$$
    - D = 20 km (Ans.)

11. A train with a speed of 25 km/hr starts from Delhi at 10.00 am and another train with a speed of 35 km/hr starts from there on the same day at 3.00 p.m. in same direction. Find out what distance from Delhi will both the trains meet and also find the time of their meeting.

- Meeting point from Delhi

$$= \frac{(\text{Speed of T1} \times \text{Speed of T2} \times \text{Interval of times})}{\text{Difference of two speeds}}$$

$$= \frac{25 \times 35 \times 5}{35 - 25}$$

$$= \frac{25 \times 35 \times 5}{10} = 437.5 \text{ km.}$$

$$\text{Time} = \frac{437.5}{35} \text{ hrs. after 3:00 p.m.}$$

= 12.5 hrs. after 3:00 p.m. (2nd train would meet 1st train)

Time = 3:30 a.m. next day (Ans.)

12. If a train covers a 162 m. long station in 18 sec. and a 120 m. long station in 15 sec., then what is the length of the train?

- Length of train $= \frac{\text{L1 T2} - \text{L2 T1}}{\text{T2} - \text{T1}}$
- Ratio of time $= \frac{18}{15} = \frac{6}{5}$

$$= \frac{162 \times 5 - 120 \times 6}{6 - 5} = 810 - 720$$

- Length of train = 90 m (Ans.)

BOATS AND STREAMS

Theory and Formulae

- The direction along the stream = Down stream
  The direction against the stream = Upstream
- Speed of boat is u km/hr and speed of stream v km/hr in still water
  Speed of downstream = $(u + v)$ km/hr
  Speed of upstream = $(u - v)$ km/hr
- Speed of downstream 'a' km/hr and speed of upstream is 'b' km/hr
  Speed of still water = $\frac{1}{2}(a + b)$ km/hr
  Rate of stream = $\frac{1}{2}(a - b)$ km/hr

PRACTICE QUESTIONS

1. A man can row upstream at 7 km/hr and downstream at 10 km/hr find the man's rate in still water and the rate of current.

- Rate in still water = ½ (10 +7) = $\frac{17}{2}$ = 8.5 km/hr
- Rate of current = ½ (10 – 7) = 1.5 km/hr (Ans.)

2. **A man takes 3 hours 45 minutes to row a boat 15 km downstream of a river and 2 hours 30 minutes to cover a distance of 5 km upstream. Find the speed of the river current in km/hr.**
   - Speed downstream = $\frac{15}{3\frac{45}{60}}$ km/hr

     15 / 3¾ = 15 ÷ 15/4

     15 × 4 / 15 = 4 km/hr
   - Speed upstream = 5 / 2½ km/hr

     5 ÷ 5/2 = 5 × 2/5 = 2 km/hr
   - Speed of current (stream) = ½ (4 – 2) = 1 km/hr (Ans.)
3. **A man can row 18 km / hr. in still water. It takes him thrice as long to row up and as to row down the river. Find the rate of the stream.**
   - Let upstream rate = x km/hr
   - Let downstream rate = $3x$ km/hr
   - Speed in still water = ½ $(3x + x) = 4x / 2$

     = 2x km/hr

     $2x = 18;\ x = 9$
   - Rate upstream = 9 km/hr and rate of distance = 9 × 3 = 27 km/hr
   - Hence, the rate of stream = ½ (27 – 9) = 9 km/hr (Ans.)
4. **There is a road besides the river. Two friends start from place A and move to a temple at place B and return to A again. One of them moves in a cycle at 12 km/hr while the other sails on a boat at a speed of 10 km/hr, if the river flows at a speed of 4 km/hr which of the two friends will return to place A first?**
   - Average speed of cycle = 12 km/hr
   - Downstream speed of boat = $(u + v)$ = 10 + 4 = 14 km/hr
   - Upstream speed = (10 – 4) = 6 km/hr
   - So, average speed of boat= $2xy / x + y$

     $$= \frac{2 \times 14 \times 6}{14 + 6} = \frac{2 \times 14 \times 6}{20} = \frac{42}{5}$$

     = 8.4 km/hr (Ans.)
   - Average speed of cyclist > boat. So, he will return to A first.
5. **A man can row 7½ km/hr in still water. If the river is running at 1.5 km/hr it takes him 50 minutes to row to a place and back. How far off is the place?**
   - Speed of downstream = 7.5 + 1.5 = 9 km/hr
   - Speed of upstream = 7.5 – 1.5 = 6 km/hr

D = x km.

T = D / S

$x / 9 + x / 6 = 50 / 60$

$2x + 3x / 18 = 5 / 6$

$5x / 18 = 5 / 6$

$5x = 5 \times 18 = 5x = 15$

$x = 3$ km (Ans.)

6. **In a stream running at 2 km/hr a motor boat goes 6 km upstream and back again in 33 minutes. Find the speed of boat in still water.**
   - Let the speed of the motor boat = x km/hr
   - Speed downstream = $(x + 2)$ km/hr
   - Speed of upstream = $(x - 2)$ km/hr

   T = D/S

   $$\frac{6}{(x + 2)} + \frac{6}{(x + 2)} = \frac{33}{60}$$

   $$\frac{6 (x - 2) + 6 (x + 2)}{(x + 2) (x - 2)} = \frac{33}{60}$$

   $$\frac{6x - 12 + 6x + 12}{x^2 - 2x + 2x - 4} = \frac{33}{60}$$

   $$\frac{12x}{x^2 - 4} = \frac{33}{60}$$

   $12x \times 60 = 33x^2 - 132$

   $720x = 33x^2 - 132$

   $33x^2 - 720 - 132 = 0$

   $3 (11x^2 - 240x - 44) = 0$

   $11x^2 - 240x - 44 = 0$

   $11x^2 - 242x + 2x - 44 = 0$

   $11x (x - 22) + 2 (x - 22) = 0$

   $(11x + 2) (x - 22) = 0$

   $x = 22$ (Ans.) (Speed can't be negative)

7. **A man can row 40 km upstream and 55 km downstream in 13 hrs. Also, he can row 30 km upstream and 44 km downstream in 10 hrs. Find the speed of the man in still water and the speed of the current.**

   Speed upstream = x km/hr and speed downstream = y km/hr

   T = D/S

   $40/x + 55/y = 13$ ...(1)

   $30/x + 44/y = 10$ ...(2)

   Multiply equation 1 by 3 and equation 2 by 4.

   $3 [40/x + 55/y = 13]$

   $4 [30/x + 44/y = 10]$

$120/x + 165/y = 39$
$120/x + 176/y = 40$
(–) (–) (–)

$-11/y = -1$
$y = 11$
Putting $y = 11$ in Eq. 1
$40/x + 55/11 = 13$
$440 + 55x / 11x = 13$
$440 + 55x = 13 \times 11x$
$440 = 143x - 55x$
$88x = 440$
$x = 5$

- Rate in still water = ½ (11 + 5) = 8 km/hr
- Rate of current = ½ (11 – 5) = 3 km/hr (Ans.)

PIPE AND CISTERN

THEORY AND FORMULAE

1. If a tap fills s tank in 'n' hours, then in 1 hour it fills = $1/n$
2. If a tap can empty a tank in 'm' hours then in 1 hour, the emptied tank = $1/m$
3. If a tap can fill an empty tank in 'x' hours and another tap can empty the full tank in 'y' hours, then work done by both the taps in 1 hour.
   = $[1/x - 1/y]$
   and time taken to fill the tank = $xy / y - x$ hrs.
4. If a tap can fill and empty tank in 'x' hours and another tap fills same tank in 'y' hours then tank filled by both the taps in 1 hour
   = $1/x + 1/y$
   and time taken to the fill tank = $xy / y + x$ hrs
5. Two pipes A and B take x hours and y hours respectively to fill a tank and another pipe C takes Z hours to empty the tank; then the part of the tank filled when the three taps are opened together in 1 hour
   = $[1/x + 1/y - 1/z]$
   Time taken to fill tank = $xyz / xz + yz - xy$ hrs
6. Time taken to fill the tank when all 3 pipes are open = $xyz / xy + yz + zx$ hrs (Three pipes are used to fill tank)

PRACTICE QUESTIONS

1. **Two pipes can fill a tank in 15 hrs and 20 hrs., respectively. How much time will be taken to fill the tank?**
   $xy / x + y$ hrs = Time taken

$$\frac{15 \times 20}{15 + 20} = \frac{300}{35} = \frac{60}{7} = 8\frac{4}{7} \text{ hrs (Ans.)}$$

2. **Three pipes A, B, and C, can fill a tank in 10 hours, 12 hours, and 15 hours. If all the 3 pipes are opened together, how much time will they take to fill it?**

   Time taken to fill the tank when all the pipes are opened.

   $$= \frac{xyz}{xy + yz + zx}$$

   $$= \frac{10 \times 12 \times 15}{10 \times 12 + 12 \times 15 + 15 \times 10}$$

   $$= \frac{1800}{120 + 180 + 150}$$

   1800 / 450 = 4 hours (Ans.)

3. **Two pipes can fill a cistern in 12 minutes and 15 minutes, the third pipe can fill empty the cistern in 20 minutes. How long will it take to fill the cistern if all the three pipes are opened in at the same time?**

   Time taken to fill the cistern by all the three pipes.

   $$= \frac{xyz}{yz + zx + xy} \text{ min}$$

   $$= \frac{12 \times 15 \times 20}{15 \times 20 + 20 \times 12 - 12 \times 15}$$

   $$= \frac{3600}{300 + 240 - 180}$$

   = 3600 / 360 = 10 minutes (Ans.)

4. **Two pipes A and B can fill a tank in 15 minutes and 24 minutes. Both pipes are opened together. After how much time should B be turned off so that it takes 12 minutes to fill the tank?**

   - Let B be closed after x minutes.
   - Part of tank filled by (A + B) in x min + part of tank filled by A in $(12 - x)$ min.
   - A.Q. : $x\,[1/16 + 1/24] + (12 - x)\,1/16 = 1$ (work is 1)

     $x\,[3 + 2 / 48] + (12 - x) / 16 = 1$

     $x \times 5/48 + (12 - x)/16 = 1$

     $5x / 48 + (12 - x)/16 = 1$

     $$\frac{5x + 3\,(12 - x)}{48} = 1$$

     $5x + 36 - 3x = 48$

     $2x = 48 - 36$

     $2x = 12$

     $x = 6$ mins (Ans.)

5. **Three pipes A, B, and C can fill a tank in 6 hours. C is turned off after 2 hours and so, the remaining part of the tank is filled by A and B in 7 hours. How much time will C alone require to fill the tank?**
   - Part of tank filled by (A + B + C) in 1 hour = 1/6
   - (A + B + C) tank filled in 2 hours = 2 × 1/6 = 1/3
   - Remaining part = 1 – 1/3 = 2/3
   - Part of tank filled (A + B) in 7 hours = 2/3
   - (A + B) in 1 hour = 2/3 × 1/7 = 2 / 21
   - C's 1 hour work = (A + B + C) 1 hour work – (A + B)'s 1 hour work
     = 1/6 – 2/21 = 7 – 4/42 = 3/42 = 1/14
   - C alone can complete in 14 the hours (Ans.)
6. **Due to some leakage, a tank is emptied in 8 hours. A tap fills the tank at the rate of six litters per minute. If this tap is opened, the tank will be emptied in 12 hours due to leakage. What is the capacity of the tank?**
   - Tap will fill in $\frac{12 \times 8}{12 - 8} = \frac{96}{4} = 24$ hours
   - Capacity of tank = 6 × 60 × 24 = 8640 litters
   - (1 hour = 6 × 60 = 360 litters.)
7. **Two pipes A and B can fill a tank in 36 minutes and 32 minutes respectively. A third pipe C can empty the tank in 20 minutes. If all the 3 taps are opened together, in what time will half the tank be filled?**

$$\text{Time} = \frac{xyz}{xz + yz + xy}\text{ hrs}$$

$$= \frac{36 \times 32 \times 20}{36 \times 20 + 32 \times 20 - 36 \times 32}$$

$$= \frac{1440}{13}\text{ minutes}$$

$$\text{Half fill time} = \frac{720}{13} = 55\frac{5}{13}\text{ (Ans.)}$$

8. **Pipes A and B can fill a tank in 24 minutes and 32 minutes respectively. If both the pipes are opened together, then after how much time should B be closed so that the complete time to fill the tank is 18 minutes?**

x [1/24 + 1/32] + (18 – x) 1/24 = 1

$$\frac{56x}{24 \times 32} - \frac{5}{24} = 1 - \frac{18}{24} = \frac{1}{4}$$

$24x = 24 \times 32/4$

x = 8 minutes (Ans.)

CLOCKS

Theory and Formulae

1. A clock has a circular dial whose circumference is divided into 60 equal divisions, called minute divisions. It has a minute hand and an hour hand.
2. 1 minute division = 360° / 60 = 6°
3. Each hour is divided into 5 minutes divisions = 5 × 6° = 30° apart.
4. In 1 minute, the minute hand moves 6° and hour hand moves 60/30= ½° so the minute hand gains = 60° – ½° = 5½° more than the hour hand.
5. In 1 hour, the hour hand goes 5 minute divisions and in 1 minute, the minute hand goes 60 minute divisions.
   So in 1 hour, the minute hand gains 60 – 5 = 55 divisions = 55 × 6° = 330° over hour the hand.
6. If both the hands start moving together from the same position (0°), both the hands will coincide after $\frac{720}{11} = 65\frac{2}{11}$ minutes.
7. Angular difference between 2 hands at different timings.

S. No.	*Difference between minute hand and hour hand*	*Initial position of hour hand*	*Required time (T)*	*Similar angle difference occurs in every hour*
I	0°	H = 0 to 11	2/11 (H × 30) Past hour	Once
II	180° > A > 0	H = 0 to 11	2/11 (H × 30 + A) Past hour 2/11 (H × 30 – A) Minutes past hour Or (–v) 2/11 (360° + H + 30 – A)	Once
III	360° > A ≥ 180°	(a) H = 0 to 6	2/11 (H × 30 + A) Minutes past hour	Once
		(b) H = 6 to 11	2/11 (H × 30 – A)	Once

- H = Initial position of the hour hand.
- A = required angle.

8. Incorrect clock:

- If the two hands coincide in less than $65\frac{5}{11}$ = fast clock.

  $> 65\frac{5}{11}$ = slow clock.

  (wrong time – actual time)

  $$\frac{\text{Travel time interval}}{\text{Time interval in incorrect clock}} = \frac{1}{1 \pm \text{hr gained/lost in 1 hr by in the clock}}$$

  (+) = gain time

  (–) = clock loses time.

- If both hands coincides in x min. $65\frac{5}{11}$ of the correct time, then the clock is incorrect and the total time gained/lost = $(T \times 60)\dfrac{\left[65\frac{5}{11} - x\right]}{x}$.

PRACTICE QUESTIONS

1. **At what time between 3 and 4 o' clock do the hands of the clock coincide?**

   Two hands of a clock coincide at 00 only once.

   Required time = T = 2/11(H × 30) min. past hour.

   T = 2/11 (3 × 30)

   T = 2/11 × 90 = 180 / 11

   $T = 16\frac{4}{11}$ min. past 3 (Ans.)

2. **At what time between 4 and 5 am will the hands of clock beat right angle?**

   H = 4 (hour hand) H × 30 = 4 × 30 = 1200

   Required angle A = 900

   $T = \frac{2}{11}(H \times 30 + A)$ min. past hour.

   $T = \frac{2}{11}(4 \times 30 + 90) = \frac{2}{11}(120 + 90)$

   $\frac{2}{11}(210) = \frac{420}{11} = 38\frac{2}{11}$ min. past 4 am.

   $T = \frac{2}{11}(4 \times 30 - 90) = \frac{2}{11}(30) = 5\frac{5}{11}$ min. past 4 am (Ans.)

3. **At what time are the hands of the clock at right angles between 7 a.m. and 8 a.m.?**

   H = 7

- In between 7 and 8, 1 hour duration, the hands of the clock are at right angles twice.
- Required time $T = \frac{2}{11}(H \times 30 \pm A)$ min past hour.

$\frac{2}{11}(7 \times 30 + 900)$ and $\frac{2}{11}(7 \times 30 - 90)$

$\frac{2}{11}(210 + 90)$ and $\frac{2}{11}(210 - 90)$

$\frac{2}{11} \times 300$ and $\frac{2}{11} \times 120$

$\frac{600}{11}$ and $\frac{240}{11}$ min past 7

$54\frac{6}{11}$ min past 7 and $21\frac{9}{11}$ min past 7 (Ans.)

4. **Find out what time between 7 o' clock and 8 o' clock will the hands of the clock be in the same straight line but not together.**
H = 7 and A = 180° 360° > A ≥ 180

Required time $T = \frac{2}{11}(H \times 30 - A)$ min. past 7

$T = \frac{2}{11}(7 \times 30 - 180°) = \frac{2}{11}(210 - 180)$

$T = \frac{2}{11} \times 30 = \frac{60}{11} = 5\frac{5}{11}$ (Ans.)

5. **At what time between 5 and 6 are the hands of the clock 7 min. apart?**
1 minute division = 60
7 min. division = 7 × 60 = 420 = A = 420
H = 5

$T = \frac{2}{11}(H \times 30 \pm A)$ min. past hour.

$\frac{2}{11}(5 \times 30 + 42)$ and $\frac{2}{11}(5 \times 30 - 42)$

$\frac{2}{11}(192)$ and $\frac{2}{11}(108)$

$\frac{384}{11}$ and $\frac{216}{11}$

$T = 34\frac{10}{11}$ min. and $19\frac{7}{11}$ min past 5 (Ans.)

6. **A clock I set right at 1:00 pm. If it gains at one min. an hour, what is the true time when the clock indicates 6 pm the same day?**
   - True time interval = 1

$$\frac{\text{True time interval}}{\text{Time interval in correct clock}} = \frac{1}{1\pm \text{ hr gained in 1 hr by incur.}}$$

- Time interval in incorrect clock = 6 pm – 1 pm = 5 hrs.
- Hours gained by incorrect clock in 1 hour = +1 min. = $\frac{+1}{60}$ hr.

$$\frac{\text{True time interval}}{5} = \frac{1}{1 \pm 1/60}$$

$$\frac{\text{TTI}}{5} = \frac{1}{1 \pm 61/60}$$

$$\text{TTI} = \frac{5 \times 60}{61} \text{ hrs.} = \frac{300}{61} \text{ hrs.} = 4\frac{56}{61} \text{ hrs.}$$

- True time = 1 pm + $4\frac{56}{61}$ hrs. (clock time)
- When clock time is 6:00 pm, true time < 6 pm as the clock is faster per hour by $4\frac{56}{61}$.
- True time = 5 pm and $\frac{56}{61} \times 60$
- True time = $55\frac{5}{61}$ past 5 pm. (ans).

7. **At what time between 2 o'clock and 3 o'clock will the two hands be at right angles to each other?**
   - H × 30 – A (-ve)
   - H = 2; A = 90°
   - $T = \frac{2}{11}(H \times 30 \pm A)$

     $= \frac{2}{11}(2 \times 30 + 90)$ and $\frac{2}{11}(360 + 2 \times 30 - 90)$

     $= \frac{300}{11}$ min. and $\frac{660}{11}$ = 60 min. past 2
   - $T = 27\frac{3}{11}$ min. and 3 o'clock (Ans.)

8. **The minutes hand of the clock overtakes or coincides the hour hand at intervals of 65 minutes of correct time. How much does the clock gain or lose in 12 hours?**

   $65\frac{5}{11} > 65$ so clock is going time.

   $$\text{Gained T} = \text{T} \times 60 \frac{\left[65\frac{5}{11} - x\right]}{x} \text{ min.}$$

Where T = 12 and x = 65.

Total gained time in 12 hrs. $= (12 \times 60) \dfrac{\left[65\dfrac{5}{11} - 65\right]}{65}$ min.

$$= 12 \times 60 \times \dfrac{\left[715\dfrac{5}{11} - 65\right]}{65}$$

$$= 12 \times 60 \times \dfrac{\left[720 - \dfrac{715}{11}\right]}{65}$$

$$= 12 \times 60 \times \dfrac{5}{11} \times \dfrac{1}{65} \text{ min.}$$

Time gained $= \dfrac{36000}{715} = 5.034$ min. or $5\dfrac{5}{143}$ (Ans.)

9. **At what time between 12 and 10 o'clock are both the hands of the clock at right angles?**

   Initial position of the hour hand = 12

   H = 0 and A = 900

   $T = \dfrac{2}{11}(H \times 30 + A)$

   $T = \dfrac{2}{11}(0 \times 30 + 900)$ min. past 12.

   $T = \dfrac{2}{11} \times 90 = \dfrac{180}{11} = 16\dfrac{4}{11}$ min. past 12.

   And $T = \dfrac{540}{11} = 49\dfrac{1}{11}$ min past 12 (Ans.)

CALENDER

THEORY AND FORMULAE

- The day of the week on a given date can be found with use of the concept odd days (excess days).

Leap Year and Ordianry Year

- Every year divisible by 4 is a leap year; if it is not a century.
  Ex: 1984, 2004, 2004, and 1674 are leap years.
- Every 4th century is a leap year.
  Ex: 400, 800, 1200, 1600, 2000
- The year which is not a leap year is an ordinary year.

- An ordinary year has 365 days while a leap year has 366 days.

Counting of Odd Days

- In a given period, the number of days is more than the complete weeks.

Steps:

1. One ordinary year = 365 days = 52 weeks + 1 odd day.
2. One leap year = 366 days = 52 weeks + 2 odd days.
3. 100 years = 76 ordinary years + 24 leap years
   76 = 100/4
   = 76 × 1 (odd day) + 24 × 2 (odd days)
   = 124 days.
   = 124/7 = 17 weeks + 5 odd days.
4. 200 years = 5 × 2 = 10 days = 3 odd days 10 / 7.
5. 300 years = 5 × 3 = 15 days = 1 odd day.
6. 400 years = (5 × 4 × 1) = 0 odd day.
7. 800 years, 1200 yrs., 1600 yrs., 2000 yrs., = 0 odd day.
8. Odd days in 58 years = 58 / 4 = 14 leap years.
   - (58 – 14) ordinary years + 14 leap years.
   - 58 = 44 ordinary years + 14 leap year.
   - (44 × 1 + 14 ×2) = 72
   - 72 / 7 = 2 odd days.
   - 10 weeks + 2 odd days.
9. To find number of odd days in a particular month; divided the number of days of the month by 7; the remainder = number of odd days.
10. Day of the week related to odd days:
    Number of days: 0 (sun.), 1 (mon.), 2 (tue.), 3 (wed.), 4 (thur.), 5 (fri.), 6 (sat.).

PRACTICE SETS

1. **Find the day of the week on 27 June 1974.**
   1973 years + 5 months + 27 days.
   1973 = 1600 + 300 + 73
   1600 years = 0 odd day ...(1)
   300 years = 1 odd day ...(2)
   73 years = 73 / 4 = 18 leap years.
   73 – 18 = 55 ordinary years.
   (55 × 1 + 18 × 2) odd days
   = 91 odd days = 91 / 7 = 0 odd days.
   Number of odd days in 5 months and 27 days.

January (31), February (28), March (31), April (30), May (31)

Odd days = 3 0 3 2 3

= 11 + 27 = 38 odd days.

38/7 = 3 odd days ...(4)

Total odd days = 0 + 1 + 0 + 3 = 4 odd days (Thursday) (Ans.)

2. **On what dates of October 1980 did Monday fall?**

First we have to find the day on 1 October 1980.

1980 = 1600 + 300 + 80

1600 years = 0 odd days

300 years = 1 odd day.

80 years = 80 ÷ 4 = 20

= 60 ordinary years + 20 leap years

= 60 × 1 + 20 × 2

100 odd days

100 ÷ 7 = 2 (remainder) odd days.

Jan. (31), Feb. (28), Mar. (31), Apr. (30), May (31), Jun. (30), July (31)

3 0 3 2 31 2 3

Aug. (31), Sep (30), Oct. (1)

3 2 1

Odd days = 22 = 22 ÷ 7 = 1 odd day (remainder)

Total number of odd days = 0 + 1 + 2 + 1 = 4

1.10.1980 = Thursday

5th October = Monday.

Hence Monday falls on = 5, 12, 19, and 26 October (Ans.)

3. **What was the day of the week on 16 July 1976?**

1976 = 1775 years + 6 months + 16 days

1775 = 1600 + 100 + 75

1600 years = 0 odd days

100 years = 5 odd days

75 year = 75 ÷ 4 = 18 leap years

18 leap years + (75 – 18) = 57 ordinary years.

(18 × 2 + 57 × 1) odd days = 93 odd days.

13 weeks + 2 days = 2 odd days

Jan. (31), Feb. (29), Mar. (31), Apr. (30), May (31), Jun. (30), July (16)

3 1 3 2 3 2

14 + 16 = 30 odd days = 30 ÷ 7 = 2 odd days.

Hence, the required day is Tuesday. (Ans.)

4. **Prove that the calendar for the year 2003 will serve for the year 2014.**
   - 1 January 2003 and 1 January 2014 must have same day.
   - Number of odd days between 31 December 2002 and 31 December 2013 must be 0.

- In the 11 years, we have 2004, 2008, 2012, three leap years and eight ordinary years.
- $(3 \times 2 + 8 \times 1) = 14 = 14 \div 7 = 0$ odd day (remainder)
- The calendar of 2003 will serve as the calendar of 2014 (Ans).

SIMPLE INTEREST

Theory and Formulae

1. SIMPLE INTEREST:
   - If a person 'x' borrows money (P) from another person 'y' for specified period (T); then x has to return = money borrowed + additional money.
   - This additional money the borrower pays is known an INTEREST.
   - R% = R / 100
   - If the interest is calculated uniformly for the borrowed money (p) and period (T), then it is called simple interest (SI).
   - Simple interest (SI) = P. R.T/100
2. AMOUNT:
   - A = P + SI
   - A = P [1 + RT/100] = SI [1 + 100/RT]
3. AMOUNT BECOMES N TIMES OF PRINCIPAL:
   - P = principal R% = rate of interest T = time
   - $A = N \times P$
   - R = [N – 1/T] 100%
4. REPAYMENT OF DEBT IN EQUAL INSTALMENTS:
   - M = Debt borrowed amount.
   - X = amount of equal instalment.
   - n = number of instalments.
   - r% = rate % p.a ;
   - quarterly = r/4%
   - monthly = r/12 %
   - M = nx [1 + r (n – 1) / 200]
5. RATE AND TIME ARE NUMERICALLY EQUAL:
   - Here, R = T, then,
   - $\text{R or T} = \dfrac{\sqrt{100 \times SI}}{P}$
6. If after t years the difference between SI and P at r% = Rs. x
   - SI and P = Rs. x
   - $P = \dfrac{100 \times x}{100 - r \times t}$
7. RATE IS NOT THE SAME THROUGHOUT THE PERIOD:
   - R_1 p.a = for t_1 years.

- R_2 p.a = for t_2 years.
- $T = t_1 + t_2 + t_3 \ldots$
- $P = \dfrac{S_1 \times 100}{R_1 t_1 + r_2 t_2 + r_3 t_3 + \ldots}$

8. DIVISION OF SUM OF MONEY:
   - The interest received on each part is equal.
     M = sum = divided into 'n' parts at r_1% for t_1 years and r_2% for t_2 years and r_3% for t_3 years are equal; then
     $M_1 : M_2 : M_3 = 1/r_1t_1 : 1/r_2t_2 : 1/r_3t_3$
   - Amount (M+SI) received on each part is equal
     $M_1 : M_2 : M_3 = 1/100 + r_1t_1 : 1/100 + r_2t_2 : 1/100 + r_3t_3$

PRACTICE QUESTIONS

1. **Find the following:**
   P = Rs. 100; R = 3% per annum; T = 2 years; A = ?
   A = P [1 + RT/100]
   100 [1 + 3 × 2/100]
   100 × 106/100 = Rs. 106
   A = 106 (ans)
2. **P = Rs. 500; R = 6% per annum; T = 4 months; A = ?**
   $$A = \left[\frac{500\ 1 + 6 \times 4/12}{100}\right]$$
   $$500\left[1 + \frac{6 \times 4}{100 \times 12}\right] = 500\left[1 + \frac{24}{1200}\right]$$
   $$500 \times \frac{1224}{1200}$$
   $$500 \times \frac{1224}{12} = 102 \times 5 = 510$$
   A = Rs. 510 (Ans.)
3. **P = Rs. 400; R = 3.65% p.a., T = 150 days; A = ?**
   T = 150 days = 150 / 365 year
   $$A = 400\left[1 + \frac{3.65 \times 150}{100 \times 365}\right]$$
   $$A = 400\left[1 + \frac{0.01 \times 150}{100}\right]$$
   $$A = 400\ \frac{101.5}{100}$$
   A = 4 × 101.5
   A = Rs. 406 (Ans.)

4. **A = Rs. 540; S1 = Rs. 108, R = 5% p.a. T = ?**

   A = SI [1 + 100/RT]

   $$540 = 108\left[1 + \frac{100}{5 \times T}\right]$$

   $$540 = 108\left[\frac{5T + 100}{5T}\right]$$

   $$540 = \frac{540T + 10800}{5T}$$

   540 × 5T = 540T + 10800

   2700T – 540T = 10800

   $$T = \frac{10800}{2160} = 5 \text{ years (Ans.)}$$

5. **At what rate of interest per annum will a sum double itself in 8 years?**

   R = [N – 1/T] × 100%

   Here T = 8 years and N = 2.

   R = 2 – 1/8 × 100

   R = 1/8 × 100 = 100/8 = 12½%

   R = 12½% (Ans.)

6. **A sum when reckoned at simple interest 2½% per annum amounts to Rs. 630 after 2 years. Find the sum.**

   A = P [1 + RT/100]

   $$630 = P\left[1 + \frac{5 \times 2}{100 \times 2}\right]$$

   630 = P [1 + 10 / 200]

   630 = P [210 / 200]

   630 = P × 105 / 100

   630 × 100 / 105 = P

   P = Rs. 600 (Ans.)

7. **A sum of money lent out on simple interest amounts to Rs. 720 after 2 years and to Rs. 1,020 after a further period of 5 years. Find the sum and rate %.**

   Difference of SI in 5 years = Rs. 1020 – 720 = Rs. 300

   In 2 years = SI = 300/5 × 2 = Rs. 120

   A = P + SI

   P = 720 – 120 = Rs. 600 (in 2 years)

   SI = PRT / 100

   $$120 = \frac{600 \times R \times 2}{100}$$

   $$= \frac{120 \times 100}{600 \times 2} = R$$

R = 10 % (ans)

8. **Simple Interest of a certain sum is 16 over 25 of the sum. Find the rate percentage and time if they are equal.**

   Here R = T; SI = 16; P = 25

   $$R = \frac{\sqrt{100 \times SI}}{P}$$

   $$R = \frac{\sqrt{100 \times 16}}{25}$$

   R = $\sqrt{64}$ = 8%

   T = 8 years (Ans.)

9. **If after 8 years the SI is less than the principal at a rate of 4% p.a. by Rs. 340, then what was the principal?**

   $$P = \frac{100 \times x}{100 - r \times t}$$

   T = number of years.

   Difference between SI and P = r% p.a.

   A = x

   $$P = \frac{100 \times 340}{100 - 4 \times 8} = \frac{34000}{68} = 500$$

   P = Rs. 500 (Ans.)

10. **Out of a certain sum, 1/3rd is invested at 3%, 1/6th at 6%, and the rest at 8%. If SI for 2 years from all the investments amounts to Rs. 600, find the original sum.**

    Rest part = 1 – [1/3 + 1/6]

    = 1 – [2 + 1/6]

    = 1 – [3/6]

    6 – 3/6 = 3/6 = ½

    Average rate % per annum on total sum

    [1/3 × 3] + [1/6 × 6] + [½ × 8] = 6%

    P = 100 × SI / R.T. = 100 × 600 / 6 × 2 = Rs. 5000 (Ans.)

11. **What annual instalment will discharge a debt of Rs. 4200 due in 5 years at 10% simple interest?**

    M = nx [1 + r (n – 1) / 200]

    M = borrowed amount = Rs.4200

    n = 5 (number of instalment)

    x = amount of equal installment = ?

    r = 10%

    4200 = 5x [1 + 10 (5 – 1) / 200]

    4200 = 5x [1 + 40 / 200]

    4200 = 5x × 240 / 200

$$= \frac{4200 \times 200}{240 \times 5} = X$$

X = 4200 / 6 = 700

X = Rs. 700 / year (Ans.)

12. If Rs. 85 amounts to Rs. 95 in 3 years, what Rs. 102 will amount to in 5 years at the same rate %?

$$R = \frac{100 \times SI}{P \times T}$$

95 – 85 = 10

$$\frac{100 \times 10}{85 \times 3} \quad ...(1)$$

$$\frac{100 \times (A - 102)}{102 \times 5} \quad ...(2)$$

$$\frac{100 \times 10}{85 \times 3} = \frac{100 \times (A - 102)}{102 \times 5}$$

$$\frac{10}{85 \times 3} = \frac{A - 102}{102 \times 5}$$

$$\frac{10}{255} = \frac{A - 102}{510}$$

10 × 510 = 255 (A – 102)

5100 = 255A – 26010

31110 = 255A

$$A = \frac{31110}{255}$$

A = Rs. 122 (Ans.)

13. A sum of Rs. 3,800 is lent out in two parts in such a way that the interest on one part at 8% for 5 years equal to another part at ½% for 15 years. Find the sum lent out at 8%.

Let the sum lent out at 8% = P1 and sum lent out at ½% = P2

$(SI_1) = (SI_2)$

$$\frac{P_1 \times 8 \times 5}{100} = \frac{P_2 \times ½ \times 15}{100}$$

$$\frac{P_1}{P_2} = \frac{1 \times 15}{2 \times 8 \times 5}$$

$$\frac{P_1}{P_2} = \frac{3}{16}$$

$$P_1 = \text{Sum lent out at 8\%} = \frac{3}{3 + 16} \times 3{,}800$$

P_1 = Rs. 600 (Ans.)

COMPOUND INTEREST

Theory and Formulae

1. **Compound interest (CI):** Money is said to be lent at compound interest. If the interest is not paid soon, it is added to the principal after a fixed period. So that the amounts at the end of the period becomes principal for the next period.
   Ex: P = Rs. 100; R = 10% on SI.
   $$100 + \frac{10\% \text{ of } 100 \text{ SI}}{+10} 110 + \frac{10\% \text{ SI of } 100}{+10} 120 + \frac{10\% \text{ SI of } 100}{+10} 130$$
   P = Rs. 100%; R = 10% on compound interest.
   $$100 + \frac{10\% \text{ SI of } 100}{+10} 110 + \frac{10\% \text{ SI of } 110}{+11} 121 + \frac{10\% \text{ SI of } 121}{+ \text{Rs. } 12.10}$$
2. **Compound interest:**
   A = P [1 + R / 100] t
   CI = A – P
   CI = p $[1 + R/100]^t - 1$
   Compound interest half yearly
   $$A = P\left[1 + \frac{R/2}{100}\right]^{2t}$$
   Compound interest quarterly
   $$A = p\left[H + \frac{R/4}{100}\right]^{4t}$$
   HALF YEARLY:
   $$A = P\left[1 + \frac{R}{n \times 100}\right]^{nt}$$
   n = number of compounding/year; T = years.
   When interest is compounded :
   Half yearly = n = 2
   Quarterly = n = 4
   Monthly = n = 12
3. **When R% is not equal every year and the interest is compounded yearly.**
   $$A = P\left[1 + \frac{R}{100}\right]\left[1 + \frac{R}{100}\right] \ldots t \text{ times.}$$
   If r% is not the same every year.
   $$A = P\left[1 + \frac{R_1}{100}\right]^{t1}\left[1 + \frac{R_2}{100}\right]^{t2}$$
   R_1 = r% p.a. for t_1 years. R_2 = rate % p.a. for t_2 years.

When interest is compounded yearly but time is in fraction:

$t = 5\frac{3}{4}$ years

$$A = P\left[1 + \frac{R}{100}\right]^5 \times \left[1 + \frac{\frac{3}{4} \times R}{100}\right]$$

4. **Difference between compound interest and simple interest.**

When $t = 2$ years

$CI - SI = P\,[R / 100]^2$

When $t = 3$ years

$CI - SI = P\,[R / 100]^3 + 3\,[R / 100]^2$

5. **Equal annual instalment to pay debt / borrowed amount:**

Let B = Borrowed amount.

R = r% p.a.

a = amount of each instalment

t = Time (years)

$$a\left[\frac{100}{100 + R}\right] + \left[\frac{100}{100 + R}\right]^2 + \ldots + \left[\frac{100}{100 + R}\right]^t$$

Borrowed amount B.

6. **Sum becomes 'a' times in *t* years at compound interest. In *n* years, it becomes 'b' times, then**

$n = t \times \log b / \log a$

7. **If at certain rate of compound interest Rs. 'A' amounts to Rs. B in *n* years.**

If a sum of money amounts to Rs. A in a years at compound interest and in b years it becomes Rs. B then rate:

Rate = $[(B/A)^{1/n} - 1] \times 100$ %

8. POPULATION GROWTH :

Population after 't' years = $P\,[1 + R/100]^t$

Net increase in population during 't' years

$= [P\,(1 + R / 100)^t] - 1$

Rate R_1% in t_1 years and R_2% in t_2 years net.

Population after $(t_1 + t_2)$ years

$= P\,[1 + R_1 / 100]^{t1} \times [1 + R_2 / 100]^{t2}$

If constant rate of decrease = R % p.a.

Population after 't' years = $P\,[1 - R/100]^t$

9. DEPRICIATION:

- If a machine is used for constant time there is wear and tear due to which the price of the article decreases with time.
- This relative decrease in the value of the machine is called depreciation.
- Depreciation per unit time = rate of depreciation.
- The value at any time is depreciated value.
- Constant rate R% p.p. depreciation.
- Value of m/c after 't' years = $v \times [1 - R/100]^t$
- If R_1% in t_1 years and R_2% for next t_2 years…

Value of m/c at the end of $(t_1 + t_2 \ldots)$ years
$= v\,[1 - R_1/100]^{t1} \times [1 - R^2/100]^{t2} \times \ldots$

PRACTICE QUESTIONS

1. **Find the amount on Rs. 4,000 for 2 years at 5% p.a. C.I.**
   $A = P\,[1 + R / 100]^t$
   $A = 4{,}000\,[1 + 5/100]^2$
   $= 400\,[105/100]^2 = 4{,}000 \times 1.05 \times 1.05$
   A = Rs. 4,410 (Ans.)
2. **Vijay obtains a loan of Rs. 64,000 against his fixed deposits. If the rate of interest in 2.5 paisa/rupee/annum. Calculate compound interest after 3 years.**
   P = Rs. 64,000
   t = 3 years
   R = 2.5%
   Note: (x pse / rupee / annum = Rs. x% p.a.)
   $CI = 64{,}000\,[(1 + 2.5/100)^3 - 1]$
   $= 64{,}000\,[(102.5/100)^3 - 1]$
   $= 64{,}000 \times [(1.025)^3 - 1]$
   $= 64{,}000 \times (1.076 - 1)$
   $= 64{,}000 \times 0.076 =$ Rs. 4,921 (ans)
3. **Find the compound interest on Rs. 2,000 for 9 months at 8% p.a. and when interest is reckoned.**
   Quarterly
   Half yearly
   P = Rs. 2000; R = 8% p.a.; t = 9 months = 9 / 12 year
   n = 4 (quarterly compounding)
   $CI = P\,[(1 + R / n \times 100)^{nt} - 1]$
   $= 2{,}000\,[(1 + 8 / 4 \times 100)^{4 \times 9/12} - 1]$
   $= 2{,}000\,[(408/400)^3 - 1]$
   $= 2{,}000\,[(102/100)^3 - 1]$
   $= 2{,}000\,[(1.02)^3 - 1]$
   $= 2{,}000 \times 0.061$
   C.I = Rs. 122 (Ans.)
   Half yearly: $n = 2$
   $CI = 2{,}000\,[(1 + 8/100 \times 2)^{9/12 \times 2} - 1]$
   $= 2{,}000\,[(208 / 200)^{3/2} - 1]$
   $= 2{,}000\,[(104 / 100)^{3/2} - 1]$
   $= 2{,}000\,[(1.04)^{1.5} - 1]$
   $= 2{,}000\,(1.060 - 1)$
   $= 2{,}000 \times 0.060 =$ Rs. 121.60 (Ans.)

4. **The difference between SI and CI on a certain sum of money for 3 years at 10% p.a. is Rs. 15 paisa 50. Find the sum.**
   It is not 16 paisa but 15½ paisa.
   CI – SI = P [(R/100)^3 + 3 (R/100)^2]
   15 ½ = P [(10/100)^3 + 3 (10/100)^2]
   31/2 = P (1/1000 + 3/100)
   31/2 = P (31/1000)
   1,000/31 × 31/2 = P
   P = Rs. 500
5. **A sum of money put out at CI amounts in 2 years to Rs. 672 and in 3 years to Rs. 714. Find the rate of interest.**
   Rate = [(B/A)$^{1/n}$ – 1 × 100%]
   B – A = 3 – 2 = *a*; *n* = 1
   R = [(714/672 – 1) × 100%]
   $$\left[\frac{(714-672)}{672}\times 100\%\right]$$
   $$R = \frac{4{,}200}{672}\%$$
   R = 6.25% or 6¼% (Ans.)
6. **If a sum of money doubles itself in 3 years placed at CI, in how many years will it be 4 times?**
   Required time = *t* log *b* / log *a*
   t = 3 years
   a = 2
   b = 4
   Required time = 3 log 4 / log 2 = 3 log (2)^2 / log 2
   3 × 2 log 2 / log 2 = 6 years (Ans.)
7. **What annual payment will discharge a debt of Rs. 50,440 in 3 years at 5% p.a. compounded annually?**
   Let each instalment annually = Rs. *a*
   a [100/100 + R] + [100 / 100 + R] + … + [100 / 100 + R]^T
   a [100/100 + 5] + [100 / 100 + 5]^2 + … + [100 / 100 + 5]^3 = 50440
   50,440 = *a* × [100/105] [1 + 100/105 + [100/105)^2]
   50,440 = *a* × 20/21 [1 + 20/21 + 400/441]
   $$50{,}440 = a \times \frac{20}{21}\left[\frac{441+420+400}{441}\right]$$
   $$50{,}440 = \frac{20a}{21}\times\left[\frac{1{,}261}{441}\right]$$
   $$\frac{50{,}440 \times 21 \times 441}{20 \times 1{,}261} = a$$
   a = Rs. 18522 (Ans.)

8. **A sum of money invested at compound is payable annually. The interest in the successive years were Rs. 225 and Rs. 238.50. Find *r*% p.a.**
Interest in 2 consecutive years Rs. 225 and Rs. 238.50
So, interest in 1 year on Rs.225 = 238.50 – 225 = Rs.13.50
P = 225
I = 13.50
T = 1 year
$$R = \frac{100 \times T}{PT}$$
$$= \frac{100 \times 13.50}{225 \times 1} = \frac{1350}{225}$$
R = 6 % (Ans.)

9. **The population of a town was 2,50,000, 3 years ago. If it increased by 3%, 4%, and 6% in the last 3 years; find the present population of the town.**
Let x be the present population.
x = 2,50,000 [1 + 3/100] [1 + 4/100] [1 + 6/100]
x = 2,50,000 × 103/100 × 104/100 × 106/100
x = 2,83,868
Present population = 2,83,868 (Ans.)

10. **The population of a city two years ago was 1,25,000, due to migration from other cities it decreased every year at 4% p.a. Find its present population. How many persons have migrated in the last 2 years?**
Population 2 years ago = P = 1,25,000
Rate of decrease = 4% p.a.
$P\,[1 - R/100]^t$ (–ve) for decrease
$1{,}25{,}000\,[1 - 4/100]^2$
$1{,}25{,}000\,[96/100]^2$
1,25,000 × 24/25 × 24/25
Present population = 1,15,200
Number of persons migrated = 1,25,000 – 1,15,200 = 9,800 (Ans.)

11. **A teak tree was planted 3 years ago. The rate of growth is 30% p.a. if at present the height of the tree is 670 cm. What was its height when the tree was planted?**
Height of the tree after 3 years = present height.
Height of the tree after 3 years = $P\,[1 + R/100]^t$
$670 = x\,[1 + 30/100]^3$
$670 = x\,[130/100]^3$
$670 = x\,[13/10]^3$
$$x = \frac{670 \times 1{,}000}{2{,}197}$$
x = 305 cm (Ans.)

12. The value of a TV that was purchased in January 1999 depreciates at 12% p.a. If its value in January 2001 is Rs. 4,840 then what is the cost pay of the TV?

Let V = C.P of TV at 1999

Value of m / c after t years = $v\,[1 - R/100]^t$

Value of TV in January 2001 (after 2 years)

$v\,[1 - R/100]^2$

$4{,}840 = v\,[1 - 12/100]^2$

$$4{,}840 = v\left[\frac{100 - 12}{PT}\right]^2$$

$4{,}840 = v\,[88/100]^2$

$4{,}840 = v\,[22/25]^2$

$$v = \frac{4{,}840 \times 25 \times 25}{22 \times 22}$$

v = Rs. 6250 (Ans.)

PERMUTATIONS AND COMBINATIONS

THEORY AND FORMULAE

A. Definition

- There are 3 digits 2, 6, and 7.
- We have to make number of groups by choosing two out of three digits, 2, 6, and 7 at a time.
- Group (a) = (2, 6) or (6, 2)
- Group (b) = (6, 7) or (7, 6) Selection of groups
- Group (c) = (2, 7) or (7, 2)

Different groups made from a given number of objects / persons by taking some or all at a time irrespective of their order are called **combinations**.

Total combinations = total number of groups = 3

Relative space occupied by the two digits is different in 26 and 62. Such a selection with different order is called an **arrangement**.

Different arrangements that can be made out of a given number of objects/ persons by taking some or all at a time are called **permutations**.

26, 62, 67, 76, 27, 72 = 6 number of arrangements.

B. Fundamental Rules

Sum Rule

- Assume a work 'A' can be done in 'P' number of ways and work 'B' can be done in 'K' number of ways.
- Another work 'C' is done only when either 'A' or 'B' work is done / completed. According to the sum rule work 'C' number of way c = p + k (or is involved).

Product Rule

C = $p \times k$ (and) both events occur together.

C. Theorems on Permutations:

Theorem 1

- Permutation of r out on n different things.
- Number of different permutations of 'n' different things taking 'n 'different things at a time.
- $nPr = n! \,/\, (n - r)!$

  n different things → r different things taken at a time for arrangement →

  Total number of arrangements = *nPr*

- **Ex. 1: How many three digit numbers can be formed by using the digits 7, 3, 5, 6, 2, 1, if reputation is not allowed?**
  Here, the number of digits = 6 = *n*.
  Number of digits taken at a time = 3 (require 3 digit number) = r.
  Number of 3 digit number formed = as per theory 1.
  $nPr = 6_{p3} = 6! \,/\, (6 - 3)! = 6 \times 5 \times 4 = 120$ (Ans.)

Theorem 2

Permutations of n things, some alike and some different:

- Number of different permutations of 'n' things taking all at a time when 'p' are similar of one type, 'q' of them are similar of another type, and remaining $n - (p + q)$ are all different:
  $n! \,/\, p! * q!$

  n things
p = of one type
q = things of another type
rest = $n - (p + q)$ of different type → all 'n' things at a time → $n! \,/\, p! * q!$

- **Ex. 2: Find the number of ways the words can be formed from 'success'**
  SUCCESS = 7 letters therefore n = 7
  Type 1 = 3 's' same type.
  Type 1 = 2 'c' another type
  And the rest are different = $n - (p + q) = 7 - (3 + 2) = 2$
  Using theorem 2 = $n \,/\, p\, q$

$$\frac{7}{3 \times 2} = \frac{7 \times 6 \times 5 \times 4 \times 3}{3 \times 2 \times 1}$$

$$= 420 \text{ (Ans.)}$$

Theorem 3

The number of different permutations of *n* different things, taking all *n* things at a time = *n*!

n different things	→	All *n* things at a time	→	*n*

- **Ex. 3: How many permutations can be made out of the letters of the word 'ADVICE'?**
  The given word 'ADVICE' contains 6 different letters, $n = 6$
  So, the number of permutations = $n! = 6! = 120$

Theorem 4

The number of different permutations of 'n' different things taking 'r' things at a time when each may be repeated any number of times in each arrangement is n^r

n different things	→	*r* things taken at a time	→	each of the 'n' things may get repeated once… *r* times	→

- n = repeating thing
- r = non-repeating thing

Total arrangement = n^r

- **Ex. 4: In a wedding ceremony a person has 7 friends to invite. In how many ways he can send invitation cards to them if he has four servants to carry the cards and to deliver them same.**
  - Invitation cards cannot be sent to a friend by a different servant, i.e. a friend cannot be invited more than once.
  - But invitation cards may be sent to different friends by the same servant, i.e. the same servant may be repeated to invite different friends.
  - Friend number

1	2	3	4	5	6	7
↓	↓	↓	↓	↓	↓	↓
4	4	4	4	4	4	4

  Number of ways the invitation cards can be sent
  - Required number of ways = $(4)^7$

Theorem 5

Sitting arrangements in a row:

- If there are 2 different groups of persons.
- 1st group has 'n' persons and 2nd group of 'm' persons. n ≥ m.
- All the persons are to sit in a row will the condition that no two persons of the group should sit together.

Arrangement:

- Number of arrangement of 'n' persons in 1st group = n
- In between 'n' persons there are $(n + 1)$ blank spaces.
- Number of arrangements of 'm' persons of the second group = $(n + 1)$ blank space.
  = $(n + 1)$ pm
- Total number of arrangements = $\lfloor n$ * $n + 1$ pm

- **Ex. 5: In how many ways can 6 boys and 4 girls be arranged in a row in such a way that no two girls are together.**
  Required number of arrangements
  $\lfloor 6 \times {}^{6+1}p4$
  $\lfloor 6 \times {}^{7}p4$
  $\lfloor 6 \times 7 \times 6 \times 5 \times 4$ (Ans.)

Theorem: 6 (Circular permutation)

- Number of different permutations of 'n' different things arranged around a circle is $\lfloor n-1$
- $\lfloor n-1$ = If clock-wise and anti-clock-wise arrangements have been considered.
- ½ $\lfloor n-1$ = If clock-wise and anti-clock-wise arrangements are not considered.

- **Ex. 6 : In how many ways 6 can delegates be arranged at a circular table?**
  Number of arrangements = $\lfloor n-1 = \lfloor 6-1 = \lfloor 5$ (Ans.)

Theorems and Combinations

Theorem 1: Combination of 'r' out of 'n' things

Number of different combinations of 'n' different things taking 'r' different things at a time = $nCr = n! \,/\, r!\,(n - r)!$

- **Ex. 7: Out of 7 students in how many ways can a committee of 3 be made?**
  - A committee of 3 different students is to be formed, i.e. number of students is repeated.
  - ${}^{7}C_{3}$ $n = 7$; $r = 3$
  - ${}^{7}C_{3} = \lfloor 7 \,/\, \lfloor 7-3 \lfloor 3 = 7 \,/\, \lfloor 4 \lfloor 3$
  - $\dfrac{7 \times 6 \times 5}{\lfloor 3} = 35$ (ans)

Theorem 2 : (Division into Groups)

- Number of ways in which $(m + n + p)$ different things can be divided into 3 groups containing m, n, and p things.
- ${}^{m+n+p}C_{m} \times {}^{n+p}C_{n} \times {}^{p}C_{p} = \lfloor m + n + p$

$(m + n + p)$ different things available	→	Each combination Group 1 = m things Group 2 = n things Group 3 = p things	→	Total combination

$$\frac{(m + n + p)!}{m! * n! * p!}$$

Theorem 3

Total number of selections by taking some or all given 'n' different things = $2^n - 1$

- **Ex. 8: In how many ways can a person select one or more of the 5 songs from a music album?**

  Required number of selections = 25 – 1 = 32 – 1 = 31 (Ans.)

PRACTICE QUESTIONS

1. **How many numbers greater than 5000 can formed with four digits, 3, 4, 5, 6, 7? (No digits is to be repeated).**

   Use only 5, 6, 7 in the starting of the number because only they make the number greater than 5,000.

   Remaining 3 places can be occupied by any of the remaining 4 digits available = ${}^4p_3$.

   By the product rule $= {}^3p_1 \times {}^4p_3$

   $= \frac{31}{21} \times \frac{41}{11}$

   $= \frac{3 \times 2 \times 1}{2 \times 1} \times 4 \times 3 \times 2 \times 1$

   = 72 (Ans.)

2. **How many words with or without meaning can be formed by using all the letters of the word PENCIL; using each letter exactly once.**

   6 letters in PENCIL.

   Permutation theorem 3. Permutation of n different things at a time is n.

   $\lfloor\underline{6} = 6 \times 5 \times 4 \times 3 \times 2 \times 1 = 720$ (Ans.)

3. **In how many ways can 5 books on English, 3 on Science and 6 on Geography be arranged on a shelf so that the books on each subject are always together?**

   All books on the same subject as I unit; we got a total of 3 units.

   Number of total arrangements = $\lfloor\underline{3}$ ways

   5 books in English can be arranged in $\lfloor\underline{5}$ ways.

   3 Science book is $\lfloor\underline{3}$ ways.

   6 Geography books in $\lfloor\underline{6}$ ways.

Using product rule = $\lfloor\underline{3} \times \lfloor\underline{5} \times \lfloor\underline{3} \times \lfloor\underline{6}$

= 31, 10, 400 (Ans.)

4. **Find the number of ways in which 6 different beads can be arranged to form a necklace.**

   This relates to a case of circular permutation.

   Theorem 6:

   - 6 beads can be arranged in $\lfloor\underline{6} - 1$ ways.
   - If clock-wise and anti-clock-wise direction is not given so required arrangements

     $= \frac{1}{2} \times \lfloor\underline{6} - 1$

     $= \dfrac{5 \times 4 \times 3 \times 2 \times 1}{2 \times 1} = 60$ (Ans.)

5. **Out of 5 boys and 2 girls, a group of 3 is to be formed to coordinate a cultural programme. In how many ways can it be formed if at least one girl is to be included?**

	Number of boys (5)	Number of girls (2)
Case 1:	1	2
Case 2:	2	1

- Number of ways = $5C_1 \times 2C_2 = 5 \times 1 = 5$
- Case 2 ways = $5C_2 \times 2C_1 = 10 \times 2 = 20$

  $= 5 + 20 = 25$
- Total number of ways = 25 (Ans.)

References

1. Aggarwal, R.S. & Vikas Aggarwal, 2017 Objective General English, S. Chand and Company (P) Ltd.
2. Aggarwal, R.S,2017 Quantitative Aptitude, S. Chand and Company (P) Ltd.
3. https://www.careerride.com/
4. https://www.groupdiscussionideas.com/
5. https://www.weforum.org/
6. https://www.indeed.com/

Some More Tips

WHAT IS TRAINING AND ITS PURPOSE?

Training is teaching someone a particular skill set or a particular behaviour. In practical words, TRAINING is mentoring, guiding, coaching, facilitating, directing, inculcating, honing, and most importantly, UNDERSTANDING AND OBSERVING.

TRAITS OF AN EFFECTIVE TRAINER AND COACH

- Adaptable
- Away from ego and show off
- Away from blame and excuses
- Away from 3 cancers – Complain, Criticise, and compare
- Knows when to speak and what to speak
- Approachable
- Always a smile on the face

PRE-REQUISITES OF A TRAINER

- Generate open discussion
- Ask open ended questions
- Knowledge of the subject matter
- Being patient
- Move with the pace of the trainees
- Read the mood of the participants
- Maintain eye contact
- Hold the participants
- Articulate clearly
- Courage to face questions
- Use different methods adaptable to different situations
- Use all types of tools
- Being lively and dynamic
- Being spontaneous
- Emotionally intelligent

CROWD MANAGEMENT

- Words
- Stories
- Anecdotes

- Ice breakers
- Energiser
- Role-play
- Purpose based activities
- Mind Engagement Tools (MET)

MIND ENGAGEMENT TOOLS

- WAT
- SRT
- SJT
- Lateral Thinking
- Brain Teasers and riddles
- Humor

TEN COMMANDMENTS FOR A FACILITATOR/TRAINER

1. Share learning with the trainees, rather than imparting knowledge to them.
2. Be creative yourself and also encourage the trainees to be creative.
3. Supplement your talk by suitable illustrations with a view to make your presentations more interesting by using different types of visuals like pictures, drawings, flash cards, models, samples.
4. Start the talk by inculcating in the trainees an interest in the subject matter being covered and end up by creating a curiosity to learn more about the topic in future.
5. Make maximum use of two-way communication by inviting comments and queries from the trainees and sharing your views with them.
6. Remember, the job of a trainer in TTT is not only to build a potential cadre of trainers for preparing functionaries for different development activities, but also to inspire, encourage, and enthuse them to be the facilitators of a self-sustaining growth process through participatory approach.
7. Assess the impact of your role as a committed and competent trainer and do it as objectively as you can. This can be done by constant monitoring of the extent to which the trainees have been receptive, responsive and reinforced by the information input provided to them.
8. Equip yourself with knowledge of recent developments in the materials and methods of training skills. This can be done by keeping yourself in touch with the latest literature and widening your knowledge by frequent interactions with those who have earned a 'status' of a successful professional in the field of training.
9. Inculcate a sense of ideal role performance while facilitating TTT. The success of such efforts can be judged in terms of some of your trainees following your example while himself/herself practicing the same principle as a trainer.

10. Finally, continue to think and act on developing new tools and techniques which may further enrich the exciting area of training. For this one needs not necessarily be highly educated or enormously resourceful, as some of the most valuable inventions have been made by persons and professionals of a very modest background. By doing this you will not only share an experience of excitement and achievement, but also a feeling of pride and privilege.

Purpose of Training is to Produce Change in:

- Attitude (ethics/values and behavior)
- Skills (How to/steps)
- Knowledge (critical thinking and decision making)

Andragogy (Adult Learning)

Andragogy (adult learning) is a theory that holds a set of assumptions about how adults learn. It uses approaches to learning that are problem-based and collaborative rather than didactic (traditional lecturing or teacher 'knows all' model).

Andragogy as a study of adult learning originated in Europe in the 1950s and was then pioneered as a theory and model of adult learning from the 1970s by Malcolm Knowles, an American practitioner and theorist of adult education, who defined andragogy as 'the art and science of helping adults learn'.

CHARACTERISTICS OF AN ADULT LEARNER

- Adult Learners can be Motivated and Self-directed
- Adult Learners Emotionally well-quipped
- Adult Learners are Goal Oriented
- Adult Learners are Practical
- Adult Learners bring Life Experience and Knowledge
- Adult Learners like to be respected

Principles of Adult Learning	
Dialogue	20/40/80 rule
Create a safe space for learning	Relevance to previous experience
Respect	Teamwork
Affirmation	Engagement
Sequence and reinforcement	Accountability
Practice	Motivation
Ideas, feelings, and actions	Clarity
Feedback	

TYPES OF TRAINING

Conventional Training	Participatory Training
It refers to the transfer of Knowledge from trainer to the trainee.	**It is based on the principles of Adult Learning.**
Learning as a product	Learning as a process
Teacher controlled	Student centered
Transfer of knowledge	Discovery of principles
Trainer = expert	Trainer = facilitator, resourceful person
Learner = knows nothing	Learner = full of capacities, knowledge of reality
Learner = passive, receptive	Learner = active, discovering
Encourages conforming, coping	Stimulates Independent
	coping thought, creativity

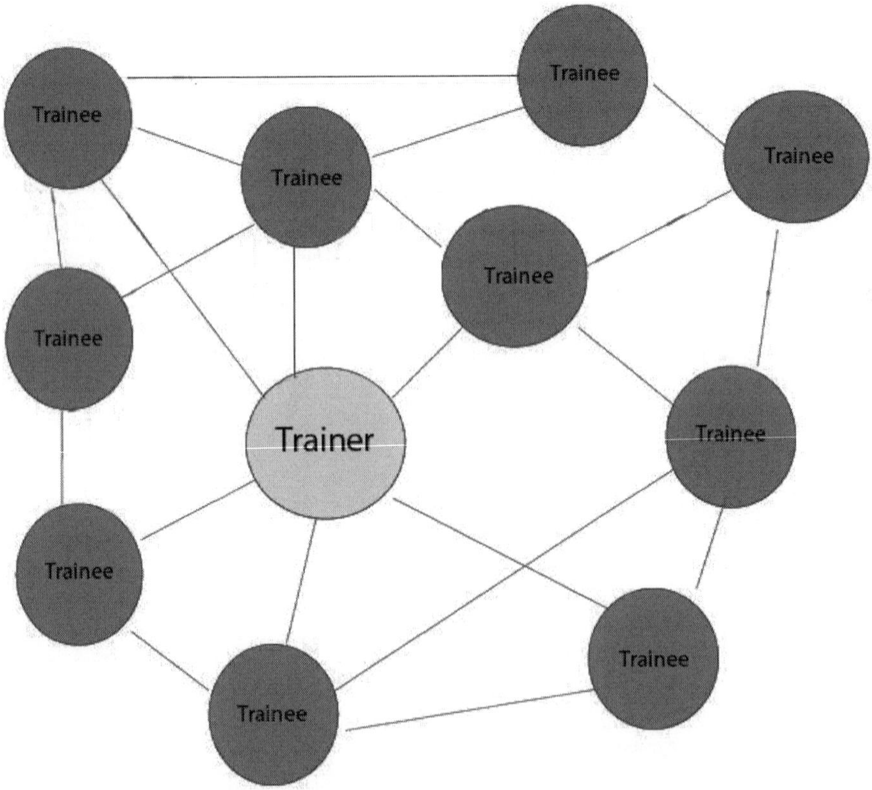

RESUME

SMART RESUME

A resume which can be screened between 10 to 30 seconds. Your resume gets less than 10 seconds to get scanned by human eyes, and a fraction of a second while being processed through 'an automated resume filtering software' that scans for keywords. It should be easy to read and glance through. And a shorter resume is always the better.

TYPES OF SMART RESUME

- Professional/Standard (More than a page)
- Professional/Standard (Single Page)
- Pictorial (Single page)
- Infographic (Single page)
- Digital

PROFESSIONAL RESUME (More than a page)

This format gives priority to content rather than length and presentation. However, it should not be a pile summarising everything in the portfolio. It is recommended for undergraduates who have done a lot of projects and performed various roles and responsibilities in the college and outside. This is crafted as per the latest industry standards, having handpicked keywords, and 'Power Verbs/ Action Words' nicely embedded in the resume. This type of resume is generally made in black and white or gray format. This format was very popular 10 years back and gradually it is losing momentum. However, this is still considered the safest.

PROFESSIONAL RESUME (More than a page)

With 2 academic certifications and few years of college, most students have just enough skills to display. They choose and optimise the single-page resume. Optional categories like objective, hobbies, and personal information can be eliminated from the resume to showcase Technical Skills, Trainings, projects, Certifications, activities and awards. By varying the fonts and order of the contents, even such simplistic CVs can be made to stand out in the crowd of hundreds of similarly formatted documents.

PICTORIAL RESUME

With age, people started making resume more colorful and attractive to stand out from the crowd hence 'Pictorial Resume' came into frame. This type of resume is very colorful and uses 15–25 per cent Pictorial in the form of Pictures, icons,

Graphs, timeline, Info graphics and Vectors. A favourite of the younger HRs, such format employ colourful fonts, candidate's photos, self-appraisal of skills, and geometric shapes containing assorted data. Readily available as templates online, they should be printed on solid paper to retain the classy feel as seen onscreen. While this is an appealing way to exhibit your strengths, you should also match it with your oral performance in the interview. This format is gaining momentum now and 4 out of 10 candidates are going with pictorial resume.

INFOGRAPHIC RESUME

It is an advanced version of pictorial resumes. It is creative and gives a very different look to the resume. This came into the vogue, out of the concept—our brain is wired to answer to visual storytelling where the images grab our attention. It focuses more on timeline, photo, statistics, logos, and vectors.

DIGITAL RESUME

A fairly new trend that seeks to do a micro-interview before the real one, this format is a cakewalk for the Insta-generation. By setting the right angle of camera, lighting, volume, attire, and body language – perfect video resumes can be created by almost everyone. Digital resume is the next generation resume. It starts with PDF resume, and video resume. It is more about visual presentation of your credentials: academic, cocurricular, extracurricular, work experience, and accolades. The Ideal duration of the a Video resume' is 60 to 90 secs. Remember to speak impromptu and not read from a script. A smile and tone management will set your profile a class apart and increase your selection chances What matters in video resumes' / Visume' is : P R E S E N T A T I O N.

CONTENT OF A CV / RESUME

IMPORTANT SECTION (Recommended)

HEADER – Start your resume off with the most important information first: your personal information! Include your full name, phone number, email. Its also appropriate to include your permanent mailing address, but this can be optional. A passport size photograph is meant to be pasted on the top right corner as instructed by the T&P cell or Recruiter.

CAREER OBJECTIVE

Job position
Functional area
Technical expertise related to functional area
Industry

Ex. A final year Mechanical Engineering Graduate with designing skills and a grip over quality control concepts, seeking to apply for the position of a QC Mechanical Inspector the Fabrication Industry.

EDUCATION AND QUALIFICATION

It is recommended to write all your details in reverse chronological order, i.e. Most recent is listed first. We can use either a tabular form or descriptive form. Examples:

BACHELOR OF TECHNOLOGY IN ELECTRICAL | KIIT University |Odisha | 9.2 CGPA	2014 - 2017
12TH SCIENCE | CHSE| ODISHA| 85%	2014
10TH |ST. PAULS | ROURKELA | 92%	2012

Internship Experience / Project Experience/ Industrial Training

Mention title, and brief summary of the project with duration.
E.g. Intern, Investiga, Mumbai

Learning **05/2016 – 08/2016**

- Received insight to the financial industry a sit-in phone team observer.
- Attended in-service training classes for wholesale and investment representatives. Prepared documents needed to implement plans selected by clients.
- Gained functional overview of daily operations of insurance/investment firms.
- Sold the company on advice of an intern in spite of poor global market.

Technical Skills

- LANGUAGE: C, C++. Java
- VLSI/Embedded system
- Machine learning
- IOT

Awards and Achievements

This section is mostly not for school-related awards. Rather, this section is for awards received, commendations, or praise from senior sources. Make sure to mention what the award was for if you can. By writing about your experience in terms of achievements—not boring job descriptions—you convey three things:

- You have the required experience or skills.
- You are good at this work or at using these skills.

- You take pride in and enjoy your work.

E.g.: Use action verb forms like Completed, Won, Achieved, participated, received, etc.

- Awarded as the best dancer in the eastern zone region by the state government.
- Arranged and hosted a team building activities, which resulted in improving communication with classmates of my department.
- Captained my college team in inter university cricket championship

Extra-Curricular Activities

We mostly get confused with what to write under this section. Let us have a clear understanding on this. We can categorise this into two types:

Sports/Athletics

- Football (Soccer)/Volley ball/Basketball/Hand ball/Rugby (American Football) – Have/Has/Was a part of the inter/Intra-School/College/University team.
- Cricket/Soft ball/ Baseball – Have/has actively participated in Inter/Intra-School/College/University Cricket tournaments.
- Track and Field- Have/Has participated/represented my Stream/College in Inter/Intra School/College/University Track and Field sports events with a special interest in 100/200/400 Metre. Race (Dash/Relay/Hurdles), High-Jump, Long-Jump, Triple-Jump, Shot-put thrown, Javelin Throw, Archery, etc.
- Indoor games – Chess, Carom.

Non-Athletic Activities

- Singing/Dancing/Mimicry- Have/Has/Was a part of the inter/Intra- School/College/University Band/Group/Association or Solo-performer.
- Acting/Actor/Drama/Theatre - Have/has actively participated-in/Associated with Inter/Intra-School/College/University Society for performing Arts.
- Debate/Elocution/Quiz/Social Activities (Service)/Volunteer (National Service Scheme)-Under Ministry of Youth Affairs and Sports. General Awareness Programme
- Modelling /Photography.
- Paper Presentation, Any event management, cultural club member, students representative also include Extra-curricular activities

Certifications/Courses/Programmes

These stand for courses which are offered after being customised as per industry requirements. For examples,

C, C++	Big Data Analysis using Hadoop and Spark
Java C Core (Advanced)	Artificial Intelligence and Engineering Applications
Oracle	IOT and Industrial Application
Dot Net	Machine learning and AI
J2EE	VLSI
PHP with My SQL	Embedded System and Robotics
Android	Mobile Computing
AR and VR	ITIL
Drone	Six Sigma
Cloud Computing	VLSI
Ethical Hacking	AutoCAD
Enterprise Network	SCADA
Advance Concept of Networking	CATIA
Web Development with Mongo DB, NodeJS, ExpressJS and ANgularJS	Ansys
3D printing	Staadpro

Seminar and Workshops

- Workshop on 'Ethical Hacking'
- Seminar on 'Robotics'

Industry Visit (If Any)

E.g. Adonis Electronics Pvt. Ltd, Mumbai
We learnt how the electrical and electronic parts of cars are developed and tested before going to production.

Don'ts for a Resume

- Do not title your resume as 'resume'.
- Do not include personal information beyond your name and contact. Interviewers hardly show interest in your age, race, marital status, sexual orientation, or hobbies.
- Do not include a photo of yourself until asked.
- Do not use personal pronouns (I, my, me) in your resume.
- Do not use a funny email address.
- Do not mention declaration at the bottom of your CV.

Note: However, stay flexible to mend your resume as per expectation and instructions of the HR recruiters.

GROUP DISCUSSION

WHAT IS GD AND WHY IS IT CONDUCTED?

A GD is a communication act where the candidates are given a topic to discuss on and they are supposed to discuss both the positive and the negative aspects of the given topic. It is different from a Debate in the sense that nobody is here to exclusively speak for or against a topic. It is just that all the negative and the positive aspects of a topic are being discussed with everyone respecting each other's views. The primary objective is to find out the degree of consensus and a fruitful outcome on a topic at the end of the GD.

CATEGORIES OF GROUP DISCUSSION TOPICS

There are generally two types of GD topics:

(i) Topic Based – Based on specific topics, Could be Factual, Controversial, or Abstract topics. Normally used during recruitment processes in organisations.

(ii) Case studies – Tries to simulate a real-life situation with an objective to get you to think about the situation from various angles. Information about the situation is given and participants are asked as a group to resolve the situation. There are no incorrect answers/perfect solutions. These types of GDs are normally used by Management Institutes. Group tasks are given where participants are asked to present followed by a discussion. Mostly Consulting companies are use case studies as a part of their recruitment process.

Topic Based Group Discussion

- **Factual** – These topics are about practical matters, which people in general have heard of are aware of. Typically these are socio-economic topics which may have been in the news lately, or could be unbound by time. It gives a candidate a chance to prove that he is aware of his environment.
  E.g. The Education Policy of India, Tourism in India, Lokpal Bill
- **Controversial** – Generally argumentative in nature and are meant to generate controversy. Noise level is usually high, there may be tempers flying. Objective is to see how much maturity the candidate displays by keeping his temper in check, by rationally and logically arguing his point of view without getting personal and emotional.
  E.g. Reservations should be removed, Women make better managers
- **Abstract** – These are about intangible things. Usually not given for discussion, but their possibility cannot be ruled out. Objective is to test your lateral thinking and creativity.
  E.g. A is an alphabet, Twinkle Twinkle little star, The number 10

CASE STUDY

It is one of the crucial rounds in the recruitment process, adopted by many companies to assess the following:

- Communicating ability
- problem-solving skills
- analytical Ability
- strategic and logical thinking
- practical judgment
- professional demeanour
- Willingness to participate

Basically, a situation or a problem will be given to your group. You have to work as a team and find out a solution to that. You may have to give a short presentation of the discussed solution or recommendations that problem/situation requires.

Types of Case Study

Mostly case studies are of market scenario and business sector related. It can be of:

- A merger between two related organisations, for example, merging of technologies, merging of leadership teams.
- a well-established company wanting to set up production or distribution in another country.
- A company wanting to launch a new product or service.
- A company facing declining profits due to increasing competition.
- A company wanting to upgrade their existing technologies.
- A company wanting to boost sales, or to grab market share.
- A company wanting to restructure the prices of its products and services.
- A company wanting to invest in a new business.
- A company wanting to reduce its costs.

It can also be from:

- Digital Engineering
- Technology Transformation
- Data Analytics
- Architecture Strategy
- Human Capital
- Strategy and Operations
- Change Management
- E-commerce Platform

PROCESS OF GROUP DISCUSSION

- 10-12 students are generally asked to participate in a group, though in some cases, up to 16 participants may be included in a group. The GD generally lasts for 15-20 minutes.
- For a topic-based GD, 2-3 minutes of thinking time may be given; though the group is often told to start right away. For case studies, however, about 5 to 10 minutes is given.
- Evaluation is done by Moderators or GD experts. Experts observe all details, even if the GD is chaotic.
- Candidates may be seated in a circle or in a rectangular arrangement, without a table. Seating arrangements may be prefixed.
- Discussion may be stopped at the set time/even earlier. Conclusion and summary may be asked for if not made during the stipulated time period given.

EVALUATION CRITERIA OF A GROUP DISCUSSION

- **Content** – Combination of knowledge, relevance and ability to create logical arguments on the basis of that knowledge.
- **Communication Skills** – It includes Inter-personal skills and assertive communication. Besides listening, evaluators observe your ability to express ideas clearly and concisely, build on others' points, and sum up the discussion made by the entire group.
- **Body Language** – The seating posture, gesture, eye contact, and facial expressions are observed here.
- **Group Dynamics** – The evaluators observe participants' willingness to listen and discuss various points, ability to appreciate good points made by others, ability to disagree politely, and summarise.
- **Leadership** – Evaluators evaluate on basis of who initiates the discussion, allows others to express their views and channels discussion to a probable decision.

PREPARING FOR GROUP DISCUSSION

Have you heard yourself saying these while participating in a GD?

'I could not finish'/'I could not start'/'nobody let me speak'/'I didn't understand the topic'/'Someone else dominated the GD'.

Here is how you can better prepare for GD:

I. Content

- Develop subject knowledge on current affairs, general awareness and business trends.

- Structure arguments (for and against) on selected topics, considering both sides of the argument.
- Plan for short and crisp points.

II. Display Behavioral Traits

- Leadership trait by showing direction to the group whenever the group moves away from the topic, coordinate the effort of participants.
- Assertiveness is displayed when you put your point to a group in a very positive and confident manner.
- Listening skills can be displayed by striking a proper balance between expressing your ideas and imbibing suggestions.
- Creativity is reflected when you put across a new idea, such that it is discussed at length by the group.

III. Practice

- GD skills cannot be learned from books. Get into practice groups.
- Get skilled people to observe and give feedback.
- Spend a lot of time analysing each GD performance. Plan specific improvements.

1. Frequently Asked Questions

(a) If the group members are not allowing me to speak, how I can take my chance to speak?
Ans. In a GD chance is not given, its taken. Put your efforts repetitively and you are sure to get a chance.

(b) What should one do when someone is deviating from the subject?
Ans. That is surely your chance to score an extra point, when you put an effort to bring the team back to the discussion without offending the speaker who was deviating.

(c) Is subject knowledge really needed for GD?
Ans. Yes, however, not inevitable, with vague knowledge also you can win the fort.

(d) What is the power position?
Ans. A position in the geometric form of the sitting arrangement from where you can see all the candidates to make a better conversation.

(e) When you do not understand the topic what should you do?
Ans. You simply wait for someone to start, once the GD starts, you get an idea of what to speak and then shoot your point.

(f) When all the members of the group do not understand the topic, what should be next things to do?
Ans. If all members do not understand, then you can request the panel to change the topic.

(g) What does a moderator do once given the topic?

Ans. He could watch you within the room or may be through some camera in some other room. Ensure that you do not look at him till the GD ends.

(h) Can a moderator interfere in the discussion?

Ans. Usually not until it is really needed.

(i) When the discussion goes beyond the time, and the moderator does not say you anything, what should someone do?

Ans. It is better to keep a track of time, so if the time is up and you are not instructed to stop, then kindly pay a heed to the watch and take an initiation to summarise and end.

(j) If the entire group cannot reach in a conclusion, what should you do? Should you ask to the moderator to conclude this?

Ans. Never. No topic is so difficult that no one will be able to reach an end to it. Recollect the main points discussed throughout and then summarise them.

(k) Difference between summarisation and conclusion?

Ans. Summarisation is just a recap of all the important points discussed and conclusion is what you draw from the summary of the GD, ending with a thanking note to the team members for their participation and the moderator for his facilitation.

(l) What shall you carry in a GD?

Ans. A notepad and a pen.

(m) What should be my gesture?

Ans. Correct usage of hands and facial expressions without pointing fingers to anyone and that suit the topic and your own personality.

(n) How will you pass the topic to the next person sitting in a GD?

Ans. After you are done, kindly pass it on by saying phrases like 'This is what I had to say, would request my friends to add something regarding the same.'

(o) When someone is trying to speak but is not able to do, what should you do?

Ans. Your chance to score an extra point. Make a chance to that person but still if he/ she doesn't speak then no going back.

(p) When your opinion /statement is over and you give chance to others but the members of the group are not saying anything then what will you do?

Ans. May be the topic is a little too difficult for others, so help them by putting forward a question relevant to the topic so that they capitalise on the idea to speak to the topic.

(q) Two Minutes left how will you inform the group?

Ans. Phrases like 'This discussion is going really very good, however we are running out of time so would request add points if any so that we can summarise the discussion or keeping the time frame in mind, I would like to summarise the topic by saying...', 'would someone like to add something to this?'

(r) Difference between starting and initiating?
Ans. Starting is easier; it is just wishing everyone present and thanking the panel. But it is always advisable the person who starts should always initiate. Initiation needs a sound knowledge on the subject matter and good communication skills. An initiator not only starts but also shows path to the entire team which way to follow for the entire course of discussion. You must Initiate by wishing the group members, Introducing self and the topic, setting up the agenda, followed by sharing your own opinion and then inviting the other members to speak.

(s) How to speak if I do not get a chance?
Ans. Nobody gets a chance, you will have to snatch it.

(t) What to do if I see someone contradicting my views?
Ans. You just have to remember that you are in a GD and not a debate, so accept and acknowledge his/her point too and add yours.

(u) Is it that I speak more and I earn more points?
Ans. You speak sense and you earn points, but do not overdo that, if you are the only noticeable person there suppressing others, then it is going to get you some negative points! So be careful.

(v) What do I do if I see someone is not speaking at all?
Ans. if you make way for someone to speak once, you score a bonus for that, but the trick is that you cannot do this frquently. It is definitely not that you will keep making ways for others and your score board will go up. Showing the skill that you are a team player is good, but overdoing it can spoil the game.

(w) What do I do if the Topic is alien to me?
Ans. First of all, do not expose yourself by expressing that you are lost. Stay patient, let some members contribute, then listen to them and connect with them with your opinion or questions.

PROBABLE GD TOPICS

General /Factual	*Current/Trending*	*Controversial*	*Abstract*
IIT: Every child's dream	Are digital payments secure enough for the Indian economy to go cashless?	Modi Government Cabinet – right person, right portfolio	Alphabet starts with A and ends with Z
Dark side of the glamour Industry	Automation: a serious concern for the Indian IT industry	Is 'Smart City' just a buzz word or a reality?	How free are We

Smart work or Hard work.	Making Aadhaar mandatory : boon or bane	Demand for special state status: Is it a good sign	If I could, I would, should I?
Gender bias in portraying Women in Advertisements	Who is responsible for Nirav Modi fraud Case?	War, not dialogue; will end Kashmir Crisis	A1
Break the news for Breaking News	Decline in GDP growth rate: good and bad news for the Indian Economy	Do we need smart cities or smart laws in India	Roses are red, crows are black
The road to happiness is always under construction	Is there any way out to catch hold of sophisticated criminals living freely abroad?	Nirbhaya Case – Justice delayed is justice denied.	Geography may remain same, History need not
A coward dies many times before his death	Has Donald Trump really proved himself a successor to Barak Obama	CAA – Pros and Cons.	Man is saved not by faith but by work
Menace of drug addiction	GST : Falling from frying Pan into the Fire	Women Empowerment – A Cause for Increasing Divorce Rate in India	Silence has a voice
Narendra Modi's foreign policies	Netflix, Amazon, hotstar: impediment to youth success.	Merit or Seniority – Better criterion for promotion?	The third eye
Indian culture: a myth or a reality	Impact of Technology on jobs	Make in India : A distant truth	Life is a chair
Tolerance is the new key to national unity	Political separation from Congress by J. Scindia – Was he right in taking this decision?	Military politicisation: unhealthy to India's safety	Last is not the least

Politics, Bureaucracy and Politics: India's own Bermuda Triangle	Is Modi government worth of getting another tenure?	How ethical is Hacking	Patience: A virtue in business and management?
Globalisation versus Nationalism	Indian Cricket performance against New Zealand: 5-0 to 0-3 and 0-2	Do brands rule our lives?	It does not matter
Corona: a human made disaster	Merger of Public Sector Banks: How beneficial is the merger of Banks?	Using animals in medical research helps people	Straight trees are cut first
Cheap labour in India	Triple Talaq – boon or bane for Muslims	DIGITAL WALLETS: Have they made life easy?	Brevity is the soul of wit

PERSONAL INTERVIEW

1. INTERVIEW PREPARATION

Mind (What do Recruiters Look for in a Candidate)

We all know first impression is the lasting impression. In a first meeting an employer can judge how you are as an individual. The following and the qualities that an employer mostly looks for in a candidate.

2. APPEARANCE

Attitude	Communication skills (Verbal, Written, and Listening)
Ethics	Multi-tasking
Pro-activeness	Basic managerial Skills (Team Building Leadership)
Confidence	Industry knowledge
Domain knowledge	Analytical
Industry know-how	Time manager
Honest/Integrity	Computer skills
Emotional Quotient	Event Management skills

Formal Attire (Men)

- **Shirts:** Men can wear a plain light colored formal shirt and tie. White, off-white, pale, and blue shirts are preferred. Try and avoid broad or thick striped and also checkered shirts. Shirt should be tucked-in
- **Trousers:** The trouser should be plain and of dark shade. In the winters, a conservative suit or blazer of solid (e.g. black/navy) color. Trousers could be with or without pleats. Both are acceptable.
- **Ties:** To play it safe, choose a traditional silk tie. No loud colors or patterns. The tie should be simple, conservative, and not too flashy. It should match or be in contrast to the color of your shirt or the suit. It may be wise to avoid ties with images and designer logos. Your tie should coordinate with your attire. The knot should be a perfect triangle.
- **Socks:** Choose a color that coordinates with your trousers (usually black, dark gray, dark brown, or dark blue). Make sure they are long enough to not expose your skin when you. As a thumb rule, do not wear white socks.
- **Shoes:** Wear a good pair of leather shoes- black and brown/tan shoes. Shoes must be neatly polished. Do not wear shoes that look casual. Also, do not wear shoes with worn-out heels.
- **Belts/Girdles:** Wear only formal belts with a sleek buckle. As a thumb rule match your belt to your shoes.

- **Watches:** Preferably wear leather strapped watches. If you wear a metal strapped watch, make sure that it fits the wrist well.
- Avoid casual dressing such as jeans and T-shirts.

Formal Attire (Women)

In India, women are often in a dilemma when it comes to dressing for an interview. The reason is they cannot decide whether to opt for western outfits or the traditional Indian formals. And since most of the companies hiring in India allow both of them, it is suggested to choose that style of dressing in which you feel comfortable.

- **Indian Formals:** If you go for Indian formals, use a plain cotton salwar kameez/chudidaar with a plain dupatta. Avoid low-cut necklines. Preferably light pastel shades. Do not go for very colourful clothes.
- **Western Formals:** When choosing western formals, use a plain light coloured blouse with a formal trouser or skirt of conservative length, up to the knee. Preferably dark shades for the trouser. In winters, a blazer or a conservative suit could be used. Preferably choose small prints. Avoid plunging necklines, sleeveless, and tight fitting clothes
- **Shoes/Sandals:** Shoes with 1½-inch heels are standard. You may wear a pair with smaller heels or a flat pair. Stick to a black/brown pair. Kindly ensure your shoes are polished and that your heels are intact. Do not wear colourful sandals. Avoid heels and sandals with bling. Avoid white colour sandals as they get dirty easily.
- **Bags/Vanity:** Apart from your working bag if you are carrying an additional bag, preferably, carry a black or a brown one.
- **Hair style:** Either a bun or pony tail.
- **Accessories:**
  - **Ear-rings:** Wear stubs or small rings. Do not wear hoops or dangling earrings.
  - **Bracelets/Bangles:** You may wear either a bracelet or a bangle. Avoid chunky bracelets or too many bangles.
  - **Rings:** Keep them simple and not chunky or the ones that do not catch the one's eye easily.
  - **Chains:** You may wear thin chains with small lockets.

PERSONAL HYGIENE

- Use comfortable cotton clothes
- Get your clothes cleaned and ready a day before the interview
- Before going for an interview, ensure that you have all the required clothes.
- Nails and teeth should be neat and clean

- Hair should not be too long; beard should be properly trimmed and kept. (Men)
- Do groom your hair, long hair can be pulled back into a low bun. Ensure it does not fall over the face while interacting. Avoid coloured streaks for hair. (Women)
- Shoes should be polished
- Take care of your body-odour. Use a talcum/deodorant after your bathe but ensure not to overdo it
- Try not to wear sneakers, noisy shoes, or very high heels for an interview
- Never bring chewing gum, coffee, iPod, etc., to the interview.
- Wear a smile on your face.
- Ensure you carry a handkerchief.

3. TONGUE

Probable FAQs in the Interview (Frequently Asked Questions)

I. Tell me something about yourself.

There is no fixed format to respond to 'Tell me something about yourself', however you can highlight the following to create a good first impression. Most importantly, ensure it should be descriptive and in paragraph form. 50 to 60 seconds' preparation is good enough. Neither too much nor too less:

- Place you are from
- Personality Traits
- JRS (Job Related Strength)
- Hobbies or Interests
- Accomplishments if any
- Learning (academic/parent/teacher/friends/life)

II. What are your career goals?

- **The reason of this question:** This question will test your ability and ambition to develop yourself as well as the ability to plan for the future.
- **Levels of career goals:** If you are not sure about your goals, then answer: To be honest, I have not focused much on my long-term personal goals, however, have always wished to excel in what I do.
  - For example, you are applying for a sales manager job, but your career goal is to become the head of marketing department in the next 5 years.
  - Current job oriented career goals: For example, you are working as a sales manager, you goal is to become the area sales manager in the next 2 years and in the next 5 years, you will be the regional sales manager.

How to achieve those goals?

- Identify what you have to do to achieve your goals.
- In the next 6 months, 1 year, 2 years, what will you do?

III. What are your key strengths?

This is another common question in any HR interview. The idea here is to understand how much you know about yourself and how confident you are about your strengths. Just stay positive. Collect some job specific and industry related skills which you can match with the job position. You can also change this as per the requirement of the interview. Knowing a bit about the profile you are being interviewed for helps as well. Explaining your strength with an experience from the past is desirable here.

Example

- 'Sir, my greatest strength is my ability to learn things quickly. For example, I had to represent my college in an inter college science exhibition, and was introduced to the team at the very last minute. I was able to understand our exhibits and artefacts and present them with great success.'
- 'I think my greatest strength is my positive attitude, even during the most hardest of times. During my college project, there have been a couple of occasions, when our idea was not falling in place and the results were negative. I had to believe and think positively and keep my team motivated to persist on our idea, and we finally we got the desired result.'
- 'My best skill would be my verbal ability and articulation skill. I have worked as an editor for our college magazine and have been involved with various literary forums during my school and college days.'

IV. What is the one thing, which you want to improve about yourself? (OR) What are your weaknesses?

This is a tricky question. The expectation here is to answer a negative trait with a positive twist. Something which in general is a weak point of a person, but is alright from an organisation's perspective.

Example

- "I tend to try to take up too many things, leaving little time for myself." I have learnt to prioritise my tasks and being selective to come over it.
- I usually prefer to stay perfect. 'Sometimes I become over-detailed while executing a particular task, leading to too much concentration on one single task to get it to perfection. I have started giving a final touch to all the tasks instead of going in detail all by myself.'

V. Where do you see yourself in 5 years from now?

This is a question intended to know, what your career aspirations are, how long you would be committed to the organisation, if there are any immediate plans for you to move on, etc. If you have an actual plan, explain it with reasons. If you do not have any specific plans as of then, give a generic answer along with some interesting activity you would like to take up.

Example

- 'I would like to see myself in one of the senior positions in the organisation contributing to technology as well as participating in business growth. I hope, I can position myself with relevant experience by then.'
- 'As a fresher, I am assuming by first five years will be a huge learning curve. I want to absorb much of the industry knowledge and also to sharpen my technical abilities. In the next five years I see myself playing various roles in the team from a developer to leading a team.'
- 'I would like to see myself as a technical architect in next five years. My core competency is with technologies, and I would like to work and contribute in the field of the most recent technologies and advancements. I would like to get some of the major technology certifications.'

VI. Have you been in some challenging situation? Explain how you handled it.

This is usually an add-on question to explain your strengths that you mention previously. This is good opportunity to give a suitable example, as to why you mentioned what your strengths are.

Example

- 'Yes, we did have some challenging situation during our final semester project delivery. Usually, the kind of code logic we were trying to implement, works with a 64-bit processor, while we were trying to make it work with a lower configuration, due to budgetary constraints.' Theoretically, it was possible, but result was not coming through and the team wanted to give up and upgrade the hardware. I was positive, that this will work and that we stick to the plan and figure out our actual problem. It took some effort to convince my team, a lot more hard work and a few extra hours of reading, but finally we stayed positive and cracked the issue and delivered the project.
  (The above example, explains your strengths like Positive thinking, hard work, etc.)
- 'I have a huge passion for sports and have been a regular member of the college athletic team. There was an event coming up slightly ahead of one of

our exam schedules. Although our coach said I could skip the competition, I was sure I can win points for the college. So I decided, I will put in extra time in studies late evenings, while also practicing and attending the event. I had to stretch a bit physically and mentally, and also manage my time tightly. But finally, I was able to win the tournament and also come out with good scores in exam.'

(The above showcases you multitasking capability, time management, passion for things, and hard work)

VII. Why should we hire you?

As a fresher, you cannot commit to any expertise in any specific domain. So this question is intended to understand what quality of yours will be the most helpful for the company. Knowledge about the company and what quality of yours suits the organisation is the key to answer this. In case you do not know much about the company, quick learning ability, flexibility, being a team player, etc., are few common qualities that will fit any organisational needs.

Example

- 'I have had some internships and industry exposure. So being a fresher, it will still be easy for me to adapt to the new environment and technology, which will significantly lessen my training cost.' In addition to the job responsibilities, I can also contribute to the company by managing its events, product launches, and in proposing to think-tank team.
- "I have a sharp learning curve, which will help the company ramp me up quickly as a productive resource. An example of my learning curve is my final year project, where I have worked in a short span of time on an entirely new technology"
- 'I am a strong team player and good leader. I have been leading teams for technical and cultural activities during my college days. In your company, I will be a great player within any challenging team and provide leadership when the opportunity arises.'

VIII. What are your hobbies and interests?

You cannot say you do not have any interests, other than academics. Even if you are very studious, your answer should include reading non-textbooks and following cutting edge development in technology. A company looks for a candidate who is more rounded and keeps diverse interests in life. Identify one of your interests other than academics and prepare an answer based on that (do not include eating, watching TV, sleeping, etc.).

Example

- 'I love singing and I also play instruments like the guitar.'
- 'My interest lies in outdoor sports. Specifically cricket.'
- 'I write. I am a blogger too.'

IX. Who is the most inspiring person in your life?

The important part is not who, but why. When you answer this question with a name, you should follow it up with why he/she is the most inspiring person. Try mentioning someone besides your parents to grab the attention of the recruiter, however, parents are not negated.

Example

- 'My greatest inspiration is Sachin Tendulkar. He had such a humble upbringing and his hard work took him to the greatest heights in the world of sports. He still keeps himself rooted and stays humble. I also believe in hard work and humility.'
- 'My greatest inspiration is my dad. He has always guided me to not to worry about my weaknesses and take most advantage of my strengths. This has developed a lot of confidence in me during difficult times.'

X. Are you willing to change your role and profile when required for a project?

As a fresher, your most sought after quality is flexibility. You need to showcase you are flexible and ready to learn. Saying you are flexible does not necessarily mean you will be forced into things, you do not like. It just shows your positive attitude to learn and try new things.

Example

'Yes, most definitely sir. As a fresher, I hope and wish to learn as much as possible. I believe taking up different roles and profiles only helps me learn and grow in this industry.'

XI. Are you ready to relocate?

As long as you do not have any compelling reasons, being a fresher it is better to be ready for relocation. Today's IT industry works on global operation model, where they have offices located at several locations. These are staffed strategically, as per needs and business requirements and there could be a need for your skills at a particular location. Being flexible enough to suit the staffing need of a company is a great advantage for a fresher, and since most of the freshers move around with less baggage (e.g., being single), it is easier for the company to move them at short a notice. Remember, this applies for a foreign country placement also. So denying a relocation means you are also saying 'No' to an onsite opportunity as well.

Example

- 'Yes, most definitely. I believe being at different locations helps me learn about new cultures and people.'
- 'Yes, I do not see a problem in relocation. It is always a better learning experience than being around with the same people in the same environment.'

XII. Do you wish to pursue higher education?

Directly saying yes may cost you the selection; hence your responses could be –

- 'I am interested in higher studies, but not immediately. I want to get started working and then look for higher education based on my experience and career progressions.'
- 'Yes, but not immediately. I plan to take up part time studies, with either an MBA or an VLSI engineering masters, depending on which will be more beneficial for my line of work.' Some companies support and provide various incentives for part time and full time studies. If you already know of any such programmes, it will be good to align your answer according to that.

XIII. Interview Questions About the Company

In today's world, with so much information available online and through various sources, it is a grave mistake to remain unaware about the company you are attending the interview for. A good knowledge about the company during the interview shows your genuine interest in getting placed. A few basic things that you need to look up about a company are

- Domain expertise of the company
- Various industries they cater to
- Few niceties about being employed at that company (Eg: Best employer award by Times magazine)
- Locations they operate from and main business geographies.
- Company history, its current leaders
- General working culture
- Any subsidiaries or affiliated companies

XIV. Why do you want to work for us?

Mention some good word about the company, and at the same time, try to align a strength of yours with the company's vision, goal, or work culture.

Example

- 'Working for an organisation, which has won best employer award multiple times in itself is a motivating factor. But more importantly, I would like to

start off my career at a place which values ethical practices and encourages overall development of a person.'
- 'I have always admired XYZ (company), for the cutting edge products and developments it brings about in the modern world. The impact of our work is directly reflected among the society in general, which is a great feeling. I would like to be a part of this modern day game changer bandwagon.'
- 'I believe life is always a mix of hard work and fun. I find the work culture of your company to carry the same principle. "Work hard... Party harder". What better way to start off my career than at a place where I will feel like home.'

XV. What is the one thing that you like about our company?

Again, always know about the company before choosing your answer. A wrong line of answer could cost you the job itself. A detailed research about the company may give you lots of advantages.

XVI. What are your expectations from your first job?

You can always quote a simple vision or strategy which you like about the company. As a fresher, your most important expectation should be 'To Learn' and this is what most companies expect from you. There could be additional personal expectation like contributing to society, placing yourself within the corporate world, paying off your education loan, etc.

Examples

- 'I have had lot of studies during all these years, but mostly theoretical leanings. My first and foremost expectation from my first job would be to learn how all these are applied in a practical and industrial way. I also want to be a part of the corporate culture and learn how this is run.'
- 'I consider my first job as an extension of my studies. More like a practical class. I want to learn a lot of new technologies, learn how the corporate world works, be part of a big energetic team and contribute to the projects, develop my soft skills, and prepare myself for tougher challenges in future.'

XVII. Do you want to ask us anything?

THE MOST IMPORTANT QUESTION!! Never ever, go into an interview without preparing to ask any question. Always keep a question handy. This is your opportunity to voice any of your concerns regarding the job profile, company profile, location, timing, etc.; if not already covered in pre-placement talks. If you really do not have any questions, ask some general questions like does the company provide any higher education opportunity, etc., does company encourage corporate social activities, etc.

XVIII. Suppose you win a amount of money in a jackpot, would you still work?

Few tricky questions like this might be thrown at you during HR interviews. These are not harmful or make-or-break your chances type of questions, however, it is wise to take such light-hearted questions, in a light-hearted manner (of course, with a smile).

Example

- "Would go for a fixed deposit, will try to gain a lot by serving your company for at least 2 to 3 years, then I will pursue MBA, and start off with a business venture of my own.
- "I always wanted to encourage entrepreneurship and motivate youth in job creation. I guess I might invest the money in some start-ups.

XIX. What is the difference between Hard work and Smart work?

Hard work may give results but it takes much time. Smart work will give optimum results with less work and within less time. Smart work is an intangible asset of genius. Or, In simple words: Hard work means work and then think. Smart work means think and then work.

XX. Can you work under pressure?

Interviewer would like to know how good are you at handling tough and challenging situations.

Example

- 'I believe that if we love what we do, we never feel pressure. We must always be ready to face upcoming challenges. So, I think I can do well.'
- 'I always try to face challenges in my life. So, pressure does not matter. Working under pressure is the opportunity to know about my ability and gaining confidence.'

XXI. Would you lie for the company?

I am afraid I cannoy. Lying is only the tool which helps us to escape the current situation, but one day later, we have to face it, with some more consequences. So, it is better to face it today and find the solution.

XXII. How long do you expect to stay with us if hired?

Potential employers must ask about your expected timeline to determine whether hiring you is a good investment. Some positions are short-term by nature. Alternatively, other jobs deal with long-term projects that rely on a dependable longstanding team. Remember to be truthful about your current timeline. Give a positive answer. This will assure the hiring manager or interview panel that you are ready to contribute to the company either in the long-term or the short-term. You do not need to give a speech, but you do want to give the impression that you are excited for the position.

Example

- I have already heard about the company and the friendly work environment. I know it is going to be a pleasant place to work in. I am looking out for a long-term career here. I want to grow along with the company.
- I would like to work here till my talents are best utilised for the company's growth, if the company still needs me then there is no way of quitting it, but I am not thinking of how long to work here since this would be my first company to work for, I need to give my best performance so the company is proud of me.
- I am a steady sort of person, I do not like changing jobs as far as possible. If the challenges are as great as I feel from this interview and I make good progress in the organisation, it would be a long term commitment.

XXIII. What if you are not selected for this position?

This question will be asked to see whether the incumbent has any alternative plans or how much he is interested in the company. But always show a positive attitude to answer this tricky question.

Example

- First thing to say, I came here to give my best, have not really thought anything about what to do if not selected. So, I take this as a positive learning curve and ensure I come back stronger the next time round.
- Success and failure are both imperative aspects of our life. If I do not make the cut today, I would take it in a positive way, but I would like to know where I lack and what areas I could sharpen up so that I can ensure future success.
- Obviously, I will pinch me a little. The ones who deserved got it. Life has to move on, I shall work harder to better my job-specific skills and shall come out shining.

STRENGTH, PERSONALITY, WEAKNESS, HOBBIES

INTRODUCTION

Students usually find it difficult to rightly articulate at the time of interview on their Strengths, Weakness, and Hobbies/Interests. Some of the reasons may be due to vocabulary deficit, and No self-assessment of abilities and areas of improvement. This chapter will show a direction to the students to find their strengths, weaknesses, personality traits and hobbies or interests.

PERSONALITY TRAITS

Cool/calm	*Interactive*	*Expressive/Extrovert*	*Practical/Realistic*
Kind	Cheerful	Empathetic	Helpful
Outgoing/open	Honest/Transparent	Imaginative/ Experimental	Quiet/ Introvert
Mature	Optimistic/Resilient	Open to criticism	Passionate
Uncomplaining	Easy-going	High-spirited	Out-spoken/ straight forward
Always engaging	Well-behaved/ humble/Cooperative	Simple-natured	Passionate

FREQUENTLY USED STRENGTHS BY STUDENTS DURING INTERVIEW

- Excellent Communication skills
- Confidence
- Punctual
- Hard working
- Leadership skills
- Positive Thinking

FREQUENTLY USED WEAKNESSES BY STUDENTS DURING THE INTERVIEW

- Emotional
- I get angry easily
- Short tempered
- Can not say No to people
- Easily trust others
- Mom/family
- Homesick
- Ice cream

IDEAL STRENGTHS STUDENTS CAN USE DURING INTERVIEW – I

Inter-Personal	*Intra-Personal*	*Adaptability*	*Quick Learning Ability*
Supervising/ directing	Creative/innovative	Accountable/ responsible	Result/Goal oriented
Meeting the deadline	Persuasive/ motivator	Technical skills	Event manager/ organiser
Ethics/ principles/values	Focused/consistent	Planning Execution	Problem solving/ trouble shooter
Emotional balance	Attentive and Active	Good at team	Initiative

IDEAL STRENGTHS STUDENTS CAN USE DURING INTERVIEW – II

Digital Marketing	*Inquisitiveness*	*Customer Service*	*Business and Social Awareness*
Assertiveness	Lateral Thinking	Detail Oriented	Problem solving
Convincing	Negotiation	Client Management Skills	Peoples skills
Exposure to multiple Internships	Subject knowledge	Time Management	Probing skills
Reliable/ dependable	Ability to work with less supervision	Multi-tasking	Presentation skill

STRENGTH

While citing strengths, it recommended to be descriptive with examples, than just naming your strengths. Descriptive strengths not only show your articulation skills, but also reflect your thorough self-assessment.

SAMPLE STRENGTH

I am adaptable by nature as my father has a transferable job. Wherever I go, I can adjust very well with the surroundings, which has developed my inter personal skills. I connect people very quickly – known or unknown. I Love facing challenges as these always teach you something to become better in life. I believe, I believe I am good at organising events as I have been a part of many seminars, symposiums, presentations, and functions at my college.

WEAKNESS

Interviewers mostly ask the candidates about their weaknesses, which should be understood as Areas of Improvement by candidates. The following way can be tried to describe your weakness.

Step 1 – Say something good about yourself
Step 2 – Share the problem
Step 3 – measures

SAMPLE WEAKNESS

I am good at conversing in English with my friends and teachers. Of late, I realised, that I need to improve my fluency, vocabulary, and presentation skills. Hence, I have started attending public speaking classes, watching movies with English subtitles, and making a habit of regularly conversing in English.

FREQUENTLY USED HOBBIES BY CANDIDATES DURING INTERVIEW

- Watching TV
- Playing Cricket
- Listening to music
- Reading books/novels
- Chatting with friends
- Surfing the internet
- Travelling

PRODUCTIVE, USEFUL, AND NOT SO COMMON HOBBIES

Hiking/Skiing/Scuba Diving/Horse Riding/ Ice-skating	*Blogging*	*Writing Poems/ Stories*	*Cartooning/ Caricature*
Astrology/palmistry	Magic	Small internships	Crafts
Social work	Sports/chess/pool	Martial arts	Research work
Photography	Photoshop and video editing	Dance	Music/singing
Painting/sketching	Bikes/cars	Debating	Musical instruments
Travelling	Yoga	Origami	Exercise/aerobics
Crossword	Juggling	Graphology	YouTubing

TELEPHONE ETIQUETTE AND EMAIL BASICS FOR FRESHERS

TELEPHONE ETIQUETTE – CRUCIAL POINTS TO REMEMBER

- Confirm the person whom are you calling to at the first go, e.g. 'Am I speaking to' or 'May I speak to'
- Introduce yourself with a concrete identity with past meeting or individual reference
- Confirm whether he is free to attend your call, e.g. 'Can I have a few minutes of yours please if you are not occupied', or 'Is this a good time to talk?'
- Avoid jumping into the conversation immediately
- During conversation, try to listen attentively and speak slowly and clearly
- At the end of the conversation, say Thank you for your Time
- Prefer a confident 'hello' than a meek or arrogant Hello while receiving the Call.
- Avoid saying 'Who is this', when somebody is looking for you by your name. 'May I know who is calling' is standard.

EMAIL BASICS

- Subject line
- Salutation
  - Dear Mr or Ms
  - Dear Sir/Madam, Dear Sir or Madam
- Body (KISS) – You email should be precise and crisp. Use about 70 to 80 words in your email. It should be to-the-point and simple.
- Use Block format which is typically used for business letters. In block format, the entire text is left aligned and single spaced
- Leave Taking or Subscription
  - Regards
  - Thanks and Regards
- Signature

BECOMING A MOTIVATIONAL SPEAKER

Ingredients of a Motivational Speaker

- Fluency/communication
- Avoid using negative words
- Image (not look)
- High social skills and networking skills
- Good will earner/being helpful always/avoids gossip

- Impactful short story/anecdotes/examples/facts
- Less citation of legends and more of reality
- High energy/humour/knowledge
- One Personal exemplary achievement which can be cited

BEST WISHES FROM IDENTITY